Florence Lathrop Page

A BIOGRAPHY

Florence Lathrop Page

A BIOGRAPHY

Philip J. Funigiello

UNIVERSITY PRESS OF VIRGINIA

Charlottesville and London

For My Daughter, Alicia

THE UNIVERSITY PRESS OF VIRGINIA
Copyright © 1994 by the Rector and Visitors
of the University of Virginia

First published 1994

Frontispiece: Florence Lathrop Page, c. 1908.
(Courtesy of Swem Library, College of William and Mary)

Library of Congress Cataloging-in-Publication Data
Funigiello, Philip J.
    Florence Lathrop Page : a biography / Philip J. Funigiello.
        p.   cm.
    Includes bibliographical references and index.
    ISBN: 0–8139–1489–2
    1. Page, Florence Lathrop, 1858–1921.   2. Ambassadors' spouses—
United States—Biography.   3. Authors' spouses—United States—
Biography.   I. Title.
CT275.P179F86   1994
977.3'11041'092—dc20
    [B]   93-34693
                                                                          CIP

Printed in the United States of America

337924

Contents

Illustrations

Preface

*T*his book could not have been written without the contributions of my wife, Joanne Basso Funigiello, Associate Professor of Italian in the Department of Modern Languages at the College of William and Mary and Director of its Summer Language Program in Florence, Italy. A feminist long before that term became fashionable, she illuminated for me the importance of both gender similarities and differences by making me aware that the masculine/public sphere and the feminine/private sphere are not as clearly demarcated as one may think and by reinforcing the fact that women often use language in a nuanced form whose meaning sometimes escapes men. She also performed yeoman's service in providing translations from Italian of books and articles essential to understanding the Italian perspective on World War I and the diplomacy of peacemaking. Likewise, she was instrumental in locating and photographing the Palazzo del Drago in Rome, which housed the United States Embassy during Thomas Nelson Page's tenure as ambassador to Italy.

By approaching the subject of this study—an affluent but relatively unknown turn-of-the century woman of America's elite upper class—from both a female and male perspective, my intention was to bring the reader to a better comprehension of the significance and importance of gender and class in the American past and of the way that the two have influenced the present and the future.

How I came to utilize the life of Florence Lathrop Page to examine issues of gender and class illustrates a point which feminists long have insisted upon: that despite the strides scholars have made in putting women back into history, we still have a long way to go. I became aware of the letters of Florence Lathrop Page only by happenstance. While I was introducing a class of graduate students in history to the manuscript holdings in the Earl Gregg Swem Library of the College of William and Mary, so that they might uncover thesis and dissertation topics, Margaret Cook, the curator of manuscripts, mentioned the Thomas Nelson Page Papers. She described his literary achievements to the students and, almost in passing, his service to the nation as ambassador to Italy during World War I, but no member of the research seminar could be persuaded to utilize the Page collection to write a thesis.

Having an interest in Italian culture and society, I returned to the Page Papers sometime after completing a book about American-Soviet trade in the cold war era. The inventory listed about three hundred items under the entry of "Thomas Nelson Page" with a brief notation of his ambassadorship. After I informed my wife of the contents, she suggested that I write an article from the papers focusing on Page's diplomatic career in wartime Italy. To my surprise, approximately one-half of the items consisted of letters written by Mrs. Page to her daughters, Minna Field Burnaby and Florence Field Lindsay, to her brother Bryan Lathrop of Chicago, and to her sister-in-law Helen Aldis Lathrop.

As I scanned the correspondence, the more intrigued I became about this woman. I wanted to know more about her life and times, particularly why she had become so thoroughly lost to history that her letters did not merit a discrete entry in the library's manuscript holdings in her own name but were instead subsumed under her husband's This inventory anonymity seemed a commentary upon a male-dominated society's treatment of women. As my curiosity about this woman grew, I tracked down additional correspondence of Florence's chiefly to her mother-in-law, Elizabeth Burwell Page, at the University of Virginia and at Duke University, again under the rubric of the Thomas Nelson Page Papers. It soon became apparent that Florence Page had a story to tell of her own, one which was, in many respects, more interesting than her husband's story. I therefore abandoned by original intention of writing an essay on Mr. Page's diplomatic career in Italy and focused my attention on Mrs. Page.

Virtually all of the correspondence that has survived dates from the 1890s, so that we do not know as much as we would like about the formative years of Florence's childhood, youth, and adolescence or of her first marriage to Henry Field, who died in 1890. The sources do not become fuller until after her marriage to Thomas Nelson Page in 1893, and really not much before 1900. The extant material does provide hints and glimpses into Florence's early life, and while there are enough gaps in the documentation to prevent me from writing the definitive biography, enough has survived for me to use her life to analyze important questions about gender and class.

In the course of researching and writing this book, I have necessarily become indebted to many institutions and people whose resources and encouragement have enabled me to accomplish my task. Their cooperation and thoughtful comments have been most helpful and greatly appreciated. I take this opportunity to acknowledge their assistance and to record my thanks: to Margaret Cook and her capable colleagues in the Manuscripts Division of the Swem Library of the College of William and Mary for leading me to Florence Page's letters and for their continuing interest in this project; to Robin D. Wear, Technical Services Assistant in the Special Collections Department of the University of Virginia Library, who provided me with important guidance to Florence Page's letters in the very extensive collection of Thomas Nelson Page Papers deposited there; and to Linda McCurdy, head of Public Services for the Special Collections Library of Duke University, for calling my attention to materials related to Florence Page's life shortly before and after she had married Thomas Nelson Page.

Other libraries, historical societies, and individuals also have facilitated my task. Virginia Spiller, Librarian of the Old York Historical Society in York, Maine, deserves special thanks for bringing her energy and enthusiasm to bear in locating documents pertaining to the Pages' summer sojourns in York Harbor. Nancy Wilson, Assistant Curator of the Elmhurst Historical Museum in Elmhurst, Illinois, provided important genealogical data, photographs, and local history references that made possible the reconstruction of Florence Page's early life. A copy of Florence Page's will was obtained from Aurelia Pucinski, Clerk of the Circuit Court of Cook County, Illinois. The Chicago Historical Society reproduced letters from the Thomas Barbour Bryan Collection that illuminated Florence Page's early family history.

I wish to record my appreciation to my colleague Professor Helen Cam Walker, who provided me with the fruits of her knowledge of women's history and who permitted me to borrow freely from her extensive library on the subject; to Theresa Cruz, whose wizardry with the word processor saved the manuscript from more than one disaster; and to Professor Vincent P. Carosso, whose interest in my work spans thirty years and is in the finest tradition of scholarship.

Introduction

*I*n 1893 Richard T. Ely noted in his introduction to Helen Campbell's *Women Wage Earners* that "our age may properly be called the Era of Woman, because everything which affects her receives consideration quite unknown in past centuries; . . . [she] is valued as never before . . . and . . . it is perceived that the welfare of the other half of the human race depends more largely upon the position enjoyed by woman than was previously understood." This statement by one of the founding fathers of the profession of economics in the United States was intended as a paean to the progress that women had made in the late nineteenth century. The same year Thomas Nelson Page, the Virginia-born and nationally acclaimed author of local color stories, was asked to describe the attractive young widow whom he was about to marry, Florence Lathrop Field of Chicago. Page responded, "I am not going to undertake to describe her to you, for it would be impossible. I will say that if you will cull out the best that I have ever written about women in all my stories you will get but a faint idea of what Mrs. Field is."[1]

Ely and Page were contemporaries, but they had markedly different views of women and their role in society. Whereas Ely celebrated women's achievements, Page dwelt upon their graciousness, fragility, and deference. Reconstructing the life of Florence Lathrop Field Page enables us to position her in the complex set of images that men held about women during this period of transition from late Victorian society and before the emergence of modern America. Her life story also may contribute to a better understanding of the influence that women had in a social order which celebrated the achievements of men. As one scholar

[*1*]

has observed, "The more we are able to learn about women—with or without teapots—'the more we will understand about the society that has shaped us all.'"[2]

Thomas Nelson Page was a romantic idealist. His generalized, exaggerated characterizations of the southern woman reflected the exalted position that southern men supposed her to occupy in their society. The southern woman took on diverse, mystical traits, as in *Meh Lady: A Story of the War* where he wrote: "What she was only her husband knew, and even he stood before her in dumb, half-amazed admiration, as he might before the inscrutable vision of a superior being. What she really was, was known only to God. Her life was one long act of devotion—devotion to God, devotion to her husband, devotion to her children, devotion to her servants, to her friends, to the poor, to all humanity."[3]

Florence Lathrop Field Page did, in many respects, fit the idealized portrait that Thomas Page had depicted. She was European-educated, a woman of impeccable manners, a patron of art and music; she also was warm, outgoing, and self-effacing. The great-granddaughter of a governor of Virginia, she had a pedigree as impressive as Page's own. But Florence Page was more than the exaggerated, idealistic, and passive young belle who recurs throughout Thomas Page's fiction. To the extent that comparisons are useful, this southern-born woman who lived most of her life in the North was much closer to the capable, independent plantation mistress than she was to Tom Page's southern belle.

Like the mistress who bore the responsibilities of the plantation's household routine and its numerous domestic industries and oversaw the health and well-being of its sizable human population, Florence Page faced unending demands upon her knowledge, skill, time, energy, and resourcefulness.[4] Premature widowhood and economic emancipation had brought out a side of her personality which Page never fully comprehended. She was more decisive, capable, and independent of thought than he wished to admit. She was a woman who, without visible effort, managed the business of her household and her charities to give quiet, sustaining support to those who were part of her world. Indeed, it was only because of the many roles she played all at once—housekeeper, manager, teacher, doctor, nurse, counselor, and seamstress—that he was free to concentrate on his law practice, literary endeavors, political activities, and ambassadorial career.

The story of Florence Lathrop Page, who lived from 1858 to 1921, is one that draws interest because of the color and varied backdrops of her life. She was a woman who ranked among America's urban elite and one for whom travel was a way of life. Coming from wealth, she married into one of the great mercantile-retail empires of the period. Widowed early in life, she enjoyed an independent and substantial income at a time when relatively few women held money and property in their own right. A devotee of tradition, she accepted moderate change. Above all, she defined herself in relation to her gender and her place in society.

Economic independence allowed her to evade many of the expectations of her gender and class without overtly challenging them. Hers was a private agenda focusing upon her own empowerment even as she advanced the interests of her spouse and children. In her mature years she complemented her private pursuits with a public agenda which has gone unnoticed and little appreciated. She established and funded visiting public health nurse programs in the communities where she resided; contributed to numerous charitable, artistic, and educational programs; and organized a major relief program for the victims of Italy's devastating earthquake in 1915. But what she deserves to be remembered for most of all was her leadership in providing succor to Italy's civilian and military casualties during the catastrophic war of 1915–19.

In pursuing her agenda, Florence Page expanded the boundary of the separate sphere that a nineteenth-century male-dominated society had demarcated for women, without directly crossing it. Widowhood proved to be a mixed blessing: it deprived her of a husband whom she truly loved and left her with the burden of rearing two young daughters, but the wealth she inherited from Henry Field empowered her by enhancing the range of economic and other choices that she was free to make by herself. Economic independence allowed her to choose a second husband who was of lesser means but whose family ancestry and own reputation as a national literary figure, published in *Scribner's,* the *Nation, Outlook,* and the *Atlantic Monthly,* complemented her own status. Florence Page's affluence made possible her second husband's appointment as ambassador to a major European nation during a great international crisis.

Despite a varied and cosmopolitan background, Florence Lathrop Page was not especially well known to the general public of her day, nor is she known to recent scholars of women's history. She is not identified with any great cause, movement, or legislation; she is not listed in *Notable American Women;* her letters are not found in any of the women's history archives. Her extant correspondence is not even catalogued under her own name but is incorporated into the papers of her second husband, reflecting a male-dominated society's penchant for writing women out of history.

Florence Page's own self-effacement contributed in part to her disappearance from historical memory. While pursuing her own agenda, she consciously chose not to flaunt her influence as a woman; nor did she engage in such typical cross-gender and class-conscious activities as having her portrait painted. She remained, instead, in the background while deferring in public to her husband and advancing his career. Nor did she seek or receive in her lifetime public recognition for her generosity to Italy's casualties of natural and man-made disasters.

She perceived almost immediately from her unique vantage point in Rome that World War I would be a crossroads in world history and in the social universe wherein she had been reared and whose values and traditions she cherished. The two would never be quite the same again. "When the news came of my husband's appointment as Ambassador to Rome, my heart sank within me at the thought of the separation from my family and home," she wrote in 1918, "although at that time, June 1913, the possibility of returning home every summer for a few weeks seemed probable; and this encouraged me to start out on an entirely unfamiliar career with less reluctance than had I foreseen the future as it was to be."[5] The future assigned both Florence and Thomas Nelson Page a ringside seat to witness the destruction of war and the even more bitter wrangling that occurred at Versailles. Disappointed and disillusioned with the terms of the peace the peacemakers had hammered out, the Pages returned to the United States in the summer of 1919, weary and aged.

A descendant of Puritan stock, Florence long had a sense of history, and after a brief respite she began to retrieve from her daughters as many of her letters as had survived from her sojourn in Italy, with the conscious intention of preserving them so that her grandchildren would come to know, appreciate, and have a record of their grandfather's work in the cause of international peace. It was her husband's contributions— his place in history—that concerned her, not her own. She attributed little value to her own accomplishment in Italy in organizing a workshop that for nearly four years provided work for poor women, clothing for refugees and the needy, and supplies for army hospitals.

Fortunately for posterity, Florence Page wrote a good letter. No less an authority on the written word than Thomas Nelson Page once declared his wife was "the best letter writer in the world, and gives not only the facts but the life and color as well."[6] Despite her avowed purpose in reclaiming the correspondence that she at the time considered her personal diary, Florence's letters reveal more about herself than they do about either her husband or his ambassadorial career. They provide an almost continuous account of her daily life in wartime Rome and the strain of being separated from family and friends. They also disclose from time to time aspects of her early life for which there is no other extant record. The letters therefore constitute a private and heartfelt record of her aspirations, tribulations, personal successes, and disappointments.

Despite the existence of a paper trail, Florence Page for all practical purposes disappeared from history because she did not fit neatly into the traditional category of a "woman worthy." That this happened to a personage of her stature and social status raises the pertinent question of whether a biographer's subject must be a notable person and, in the case of a woman, a female distinguished for her contributions in social reform, political change, or labor movements. I would argue that anonymity is not the proper condition of women, of any woman, and that despite being a rich woman of little public note, Florence Page *does* have her own narrative to tell. Her very lack of distinction, paradoxically, makes her story important because she is an emblematic figure whose life can enhance our understanding of a gender and class which were experiencing profound change as the conventions and behavioral expectations of Victorian society gave way to a new, modern social order.

By collapsing the boundaries between history and biography, it is possible to reinvent the story of a particular individual, such as Florence Lathrop Page, or even an unextraordinary personage, and bring that figure back into history.[7] Biography as social history is a vital art form only if it disturbs our received notions. This is especially true when the subject of the biography is a woman.[8] In this instance Florence Page's story is a vehicle for exploring larger historical questions of class, gender, and social values and for testing whether scholarly generalizations about women in the nineteenth and early twentieth centuries fit this particular woman.

Textual analysis of Florence Page's letters—which deal less with the public and political issues of the day and more with the ordinary relationships of family members to each other, relatives, and friends, with the daily routine of running a large household or embassy, and with concerns about education, illness, war and death—reveals that almost any one of her letters, no matter how seemingly devoid of practical information, can provide valuable insight into the subject and her times.

Florence Page's life is the text, and the world in which she lived becomes the context. From even her most mundane letters, it is possible to enter into the texture of Florence Page's life and society: to discover the processes and decisions, the choices and the unique pain that lay behind her life story; to examine and to comprehend the ideology and rituals of her behavior, her gender, and her class and in this way to give her life a greater significance than she herself would have accorded it.

A lacuna exists in documenting much of Florence Page's early life before her marriage to Thomas Nelson Page. This at first glance renders the task of writing her biography formidable, but not as daunting perhaps as it was in the first instance to write women into the chronicle of America's development. That task has now been accomplished thanks to the writings over the past thirty years of women—especially younger women—scholars who have approached the writing of history imbued with a modern feminist ideology or sensitivity, have explored new ways of locating and reading the evidence, and have tested new methodologies. Their analyses of women's multifaceted role in the making of American society require the biographer to examine his subject's life from a less traditional perspective; to make reasonable speculations where the weight of evidence is suggestive but not conclusive; and where the evidence indicates otherwise, to question even the received scholarly wisdom about women's status in society. I have drawn upon their insights in reconstructing my subject's life and times, but I have allowed Florence Page's words to direct my attention to what was truly important to her.[9]

Much of the writing about the history of American women since its formative years in the late 1960s has been produced by white middle-class women who have focused on the ways in which patriarchy[10] and industrialization affected their sisters a century earlier. Believing that the problems faced by contemporary American women were rooted in the particular forms taken by patriarchy these scholars analyzed the legal status of white women, their place in the new industrial capitalism, and the gender-driven ideologies of "True Womanhood" and the "guardian of the hearth" that had simultaneously elevated and isolated women from the world taking shape around them.[11]

Theirs was, not surprisingly, a class-based perspective, but their study of male dominance and female subordination spread quickly to encompass other time periods and other socioeconomic groups and races. Whether they traveled backward or forward in time, examined the upper or lower rungs of the social ladder, these scholars drew a stark picture of the restraints upon women's lives. Women's subordination, their subject, often dictated their methodology, portraying women as passive agents, acted upon rather than initiating actions. The exception that proved the rule was found in the subcategory that scholars have dubbed "contribution history," or the recovery of "lost women."

The process of writing women into history first by identifying and then writing about these "women worthies" has sometimes been referred to as "compensatory history." It provided a roll call of notable women of the middle and upper classes, who entered the mainstream of historical experience as reformers (Jane Addams), heroines in war or revolution (Deborah Sampson), or wielders of power or intellectual influence (Margaret Fuller, Harriet Beecher Stowe).[12] These were the exceptional—even deviant—women; recounting their lives did not tell us much about the history and experience of the mass of women in America.

These two related methodologies, nonetheless, enabled first-generation feminist scholars of both genders to restore women to the hitherto "dead white male" landscape of history. They forced into a historical record which trumpeted the celebration of American progress the story of the subordination and oppression of women, offering analyses of that oppression's sources and measuring the extent of oppression along class, racial, ethnic, and regional lines.[13]

The constructs of woman-as-victim and woman-as-achiever were a manifestation of late twentieth-century women scholars' own sense of women's limitations and potentialities in contemporary American society. Woman-as-victim was the collective gender image; woman as historical agent and achiever was the portrait of extraordinary women or groups of women. The tension between this dual portrait was broken by a new conceptualization of women's historical experience. By placing women in a social universe composed of two separate gender worlds, the public sphere of men (defined as the world of war and politics) and the private sphere of women (identified with the world of domestic life), women became both actors and agents of historical change.

By the mid-1960s and early 1970s, feminist scholars were invoking the metaphor of separate spheres as a conceptual tool to interpret women's historical experience. The history of American women, they contended, had to be understood not only by way of events but also through the prism of ideology. The reality of women's lives was cloaked in a pervasive descriptive language which imposed a "complex of virtues . . . by which a woman judged herself and was judged by . . . society."[14] Domesticity was among the cardinal virtues associated with the ideal of nineteenth-century women, the others being purity, piety, and submissiveness. But the metaphor of the separate sphere was also a masculine construct, they noted, invoked to justify the exclusion of women from the circles of power, authority, and prestige.

The metaphor of the sphere, in other words, denigrated women, explaining and justifying their subordination and male dominance. Virginia Woolf had made this point nearly fifty years earlier when she wrote critically that the public and private worlds of men and women were inseparably connected. The tyrannies and servilities of the one were the tyrannies and servilities of the other.

Other scholars carried the analysis further, linking the separation of spheres to the Industrial Revolution, which broadened the distinction between men's and women's occupations and viewed the home as a refuge or "haven in a heartless world," the phrase used to describe women's private sphere.[15] One feminist scholar writing from a Marxist perspective linked together the Industrial Revolution and separate spheres with the notion of class. American industrialization, by depending upon the labor of women and children, she argued, had widened and accentuated the differences in lifestyles between women of different classes. As class distinctions sharpened, social attitudes toward women became polarized.[16]

The metaphor of the sphere with its emphasis on separation, subordination, deteriorating status, and woman-as-victim became the most common conceptual framework for explaining women's historical experience for more than two decades. Like other subgenres of history that responded to the challenges of the sixties' counterculture, women's history redefined and refined itself. Scholars accorded increased recognition to the fact that history happens to nonelites as well as to elites. The focus of their attention began to shift toward the life experiences of working-class women, black women, and women who were not achievers or exceptional as defined by the norms of a male-dominated society.

Even as they were attempting to clarify more precisely the metaphor of separate spheres and to identify complexities within it, women's historians began to write about the existence of a distinctive women's "culture" in nineteenth-century America, one in which women assisted each other and shared emotional ties often stronger than those with their husbands. This culture was replete with its own internal dynamics, unique linguistic and ritual forms, and laws suitable for historical study. The thrust of these scholars' analysis was upon the possibilities rather than the limitations of separation. Separate spheres, they contended, could make possible psychologically sustaining and strengthening relationships among women.[17]

It was a male historian, ironically, who most vigorously applied the concept of a distinctive women's culture to the metaphor of separate spheres. Writing in 1980, Carl Degler pointed to the declining birthrate in the nineteenth century as evidence that women exercised a greater degree of control over their bodies than scholars previously had believed.[18] He concluded from this that domesticity had offered women advantages as well as disadvantages. It had, for example, facilitated public acceptance of women's extrafamilial activities, such as settlement house work and other manifestations of social reform.

Degler's work demarcated the end of another phase in applying the metaphor of the sphere to organize scholarly writing and thinking about women's history. Mining new sources and methods to reconstruct the everyday textures of women's lives, scholars such as Degler, Carroll Smith-Rosenberg, and Nancy Cott, compelled the reader to acknowledge that study of the female world required attention to the everyday event and acceptance that continuity, like change, was part of the historical fabric that women and men wove together.[19] Since then, scholarly writing has sought to embed women's experience in the main course of human development and to unpack the metaphor of separate spheres.[20]

Besides gender, class has played an important role in recent American historical writing. The "new urban history" that emerged in the 1960s coincided with a growing interest in nonelite groups: immigrants, blacks, and laborers and their world of work and family. This "history of the inarticulate" was praised as a corrective to the traditional histories of political, business, or intellectual elites, who, it was argued, were by definition atypical and distorted our view of the American past. The historical study of the working class, whether men, women, or minorities, became so bound to personal sympathies and political commitments that it became quite unfashionable for historians to study elite, upper-class men or women, whether they be J. P. Morgan, Abigail Adams, or Florence Page.

The pendulum fortunately began to swing to a midpoint by the end of the 1970s as scholars recognized that understanding how society functions requires a thorough knowledge of the interaction between rich and poor, male and female, powerful and oppressed.[21] Among historians who have written extensively on American urban elites, Frederic C. Jaher ranks among the most influential. In an exhaustively documented monograph, he delineated in bold, broad strokes the urban upper class that had evolved in the United States in the nineteenth century. Its members were not merely an *haute bourgeoisie* of extremely wealthy male professionals, merchants, bankers, manufacturers, and speculators but also an aspiring aristocracy, at least in the metaphoric sense of a self-proclaimed upper class which had succeeded to varying degrees and for varying lengths of time in denying its bourgeois origins.[22]

Other scholars, meanwhile, examined the elites of Puritan Boston and Quaker Philadelphia, the forging of links between Harvard and Boston's upper class, and the way an economic elite utilized intermar-riage to transform itself into a social class. Like Jaher's work, their focus was primarily on successful males.[23] To the extent that women, the other half of the American population, figured in their writings, they did so only indirectly, usually receiving their class identification from their husband.

Only recently has there been sensitivity to the fact that class is gender neutral: that women belong to particular classes for all the same reasons that men do and that women of different classes will have different his-torical experiences in the same way that men do. Women's experiences, in other words, will lead to different levels of feminist consciousness depending on whether their work, their expression, and their activity are male defined or woman oriented. A lesser-known corollary is that the same principle applies to women within the same class, which often makes pontifications about intraclass membership and gender as hazard-ous as sweeping generalizations between classes.[24]

A good illustration of this last point is to juxtapose Florence Page with Lucy Sprague Mitchell. Born into an elite, fabulously wealthy Chi-cago family nearly twenty years after Florence, Lucy Mitchell was both college educated and broadly immersed in Progressive educational ex-periments. She founded the Bank Street College of Education. Although both were members of America's urban elite, Florence Page never attended college, nor did she participate in Progressive reforms. Their only historical commonality seems to have been a lack of any real comprehension of the struggle of ordinary people who did not have the advantages of their wealth.[25]

Mindful of these pitfalls, I have drawn upon the valuable insights and methodological approaches of these and other scholars in this biography. I have, however, redirected the focus of investigation from working- and middle-class women to another, less well understood category of women: the white, Anglo-Saxon, Protestant woman of America's upper-class elite. And since patriarchy and class are the commonly agreed contexts within which women of the late nineteenth century and early decades of the twentieth century defined their experience, the central aspect of this study is its exclusive focus on the female agent, Florence Lathrop Page, the causal role she played in creating her history, and the qualities of her experience that distinguished it from the male experience.

The interpretation and explanation are framed within the context of the female sphere: examining Florence's personal experiences, her familial and domestic structures, her interpretation of the social definition of woman's role, and the networks of friendships that sustained her. The choices she made, the actions she took—and did not take—during the course of her lifetime are analyzed to attain a rounded portrait of Florence Page as a historical figure. Her husbands Henry Field and Thomas Nelson Page are relegated to important but subsidiary roles.

Florence Page's story also leads naturally into an exploration of other questions that scholars of women's history have raised about the economic, legal, and political status of upper-class women. For example, did the gender system in the nineteenth and early twentieth centuries intertwine with the class structure to limit or to enhance women's opportunities? Did upper-class women acquiesce in gender- and class-determined roles? Did they seek to modify, enlarge, and perhaps even break out of the roles that a masculine society had assigned to them? Does Florence Page's life confirm the scholarly categories of separate spheres, the public/private distinction, True Womanhood, and sexual reticence; or does her story require us to rethink our knowledge of women's culture in a manner which emphasizes the paradoxical nature of women's lives, culture, and possibilities in the nineteenth and early twentieth centuries?

Florence Lathrop Page

Florence Lathrop Page was neither a radical nor a revolutionary activist but one who embraced modest changes even as she tolerated many of the norms of a traditional, patriarchal society. In pursuing both her private and public agendas, she demonstrated that women could reach for and attain greater public authority than the metaphor of separate spheres leads us to believe. In her own life she stretched the boundaries of women's sphere long before women attained the franchise.

1

Family and
Community

*C*onventional usage designates as elite as well as upper class all
individuals or groups that wield power or possess high status
and large fortunes. The terms *elite* and *upper class* refer to a
particular group of families (and individuals within them) whose influence is primarily local and regional, whose functions are specialized, and
who occupy demonstrably significant leadership positions within the
dominant hierarchy of their community. The social biography of Florence Lathrop Page, an elite upper-class woman, reveals how female
members of this class exercised authority, accumulated wealth, and commanded respect in a time when both class and gender roles were in transition as the American people moved from the late Victorian era through
the birth of modern society.

Two questions are crucially significant in illuminating our understanding of "the rich, the well born, and the powerful"[1] in the United
States, as contrasted with European societies: what were the ecological
circumstances and the familial origins of Florence Lathrop Page that
qualified her as a member of the elite upper class, and to what extent
did her beliefs, attitudes, fears, aspirations, and calculations reflect those
of other women, especially elite upper-class women, of her day? To answer the second question, it is necessary first to understand the milieu
into which Florence Lathrop Page was born, how her family and kin
achieved positions of leadership within their community, and how they
exercised lateral authority in spheres beyond their initial successes. Once
we comprehend Florence Lathrop Page's social origins, we may then bet-

ter understand the extent to which her modes of thought and behavior mirrored or diverged from the larger society in which she functioned.

In a society devoted to egalitarianism such as the United States, pride of ancestry often became for the elite an aspect of covert culture which found expression in privately printed and manuscript genealogies, in personal and private papers, and in membership in ancestral and patriotic societies.[2] A social analysis of an elite upper-class woman such as Florence Lathrop Page must rely heavily upon these sources but also upon reminiscences, contemporary biographies, inclusion in who's who directories, and the like. Data from these and other valuable sources provide confirmation that the Lathrop, Bryan, Field, and Page family names ranked in the elite upper stratum of American society of the late nineteenth and early twentieth centuries. Florence Lathrop Page, in fact, possessed the credentials to claim membership both in the patrician elite as well as the moneyed elite of the American social hierarchy.

The Lathrop name was virtually coeval with the beginnings of English society in the New World. Florence Lathrop traced her descent from the Reverend John Lathrop, who had attended Queens College, Cambridge, in 1606. We know very little about the Reverend Mr. Lathrop except that he was a clergyman of the Church of England who renounced his orders and became pastor of the First Independent Church of London in 1623. During the period of Archbishop William Laud's persecution of religious nonconformists, Lathrop was among those clerics thrown into prison. On his release, he entered into that stream of Puritan dissenters who migrated to New England's rocky shores. He settled in Massachusetts where he became minister at Scituate in 1634; he later served as minister at Barnstable from 1639 to 1653.[3] Lathrop's activities thereafter are obscure, but the important fact is that Florence Lathrop Page's ancestry was almost as old as those who had sailed to America on the *Mayflower*.

The story picks up again with Jedediah Hyde Lathrop, who was born on July 5, 1806, in Lebanon, New Hampshire, the son of Samuel and Lois Huntington Lathrop. We know almost nothing about Jedediah's parents except that Samuel Lathrop, who probably was a farmer, died about 1819. Sometime thereafter the son left New Hampshire, most likely in search of better economic opportunities, and relocated to Alexandria, Virginia, which was then part of the District of Columbia. There Jedediah Lathrop acquired a considerable fortune through successful stock investments and also in banking, being associated with the Riggs Bank. A friend of the family described Lathrop as "laden with means."[4]

In 1843 Jedediah Lathrop married Mariana Bryan, the daughter of Daniel and Mary Barbour Bryan, of Alexandria. Her parents were descended from people of considerable culture and influence. Mary Barbour Bryan's father served in the Senate of Virginia, and two of her mother's brothers, James and Philip Barbour, held some of the highest official positions in the government of the early Republic, including Speaker of the House of Representatives, associate justice of the United States Supreme Court, ambassador to Great Britain, secretary of war, and governor of Virginia. The Barbour name, both in the Commonwealth of Virginia and in national politics of the 1830s and 1840s, was identified with the Whig party.[5]

Staunch Unionists, Jedediah and Mariana Lathrop left Alexandria with their children on the eve of the secession crisis and settled in Chicago, Illinois, where Thomas Barbour Bryan had been living since 1852. The Lathrops, leaving the urban, business, and commercial Southeast, were among those pioneers who moved westward not to seek fertile farmlands but to exploit urban economic opportunities. Their experience reaffirms a point we often overlook: that the settling of the American frontier was one of the most ambitious city-building efforts in history.[6] Along with the farmers, ranchers, and miners who trekked westward were merchants, lawyers, and speculators, the people who loved the hum of crowded streets and the excitement of trade. For all these settlers Chicago became the gateway city connecting the new farms and towns of the West with the expanding industrial economy of the Northeast.[7]

Chicago's position as the first city of the West rested initially on its geographic location on Lake Michigan, at the mouth of the Chicago River. There it had served as the Indian portage route between the lake and the principal waterways of the midcontinent, where its proximity to the Mississippi River valley afforded it access to one of the richest agricultural regions in the world. Entrepreneurs in Chicago and the Northeast aggressively capitalized on these natural advantages by building a transportation network of canal, railroad, and lake shipping which allowed this business-driven city to tap its surrounding region.[8]

The hinterland that Chicago exploited was in large part the city's own creation. Wherever the railroads went, they changed frontier to productive territory and brought to the city the surplus products of farms and forests. Grain, meat, and lumber became the staples of Chicago's prosperity. As enterprising capitalists built factories, packing plants, and gigantic grain elevators on formerly desolate and windswept prairie, farmers plowed up the sod. Lumberjacks felled the forests of Wisconsin and Michigan and sent their lumber by lake ships to the port of Chicago where it was unloaded and then reshipped by canal and rail to the sodbreakers, providing them the essential building materials for constructing a civilization in the West. Chicago became the busiest lumber center in the world, a circumstance of importance to the Lathrop family fortunes. With the coming of the Civil War, Chicago became transformed, as if in one violent thrust, from a collection of villages and howling wilderness into an urban industrial metropolis which rivaled the older eastern seaboard cities of Boston, New York, and Philadelphia.

The timing of the Lathrop family's migration to Chicago and its resettlement there from the mid-nineteenth century on coincided with the city's rise to a center of power and culture. The fortunes of the Lathrops were intertwined with Chicago's growth, even as they retained their eastern ties. They also were linked to Mariana's brother, Thomas Barbour Bryan, who also was a transplanted easterner. Like his sister, Thomas Barbour Bryan had been born in Alexandria, Virginia, on December 22, 1828. He graduated from the law school of Harvard University at the age of twenty, a signal accomplishment since 90 percent of the male population of the day never finished the eighth grade. After his marriage to Jane Byrd Page, Bryan settled in Cincinnati, where he entered into the practice of law with Judge Samuel M. Hart, constituting the firm of Hart & Bryan. Cincinnati, however, could not satisfy his energy and ambition, and in 1852 he moved to Chicago, established permanent residence, and set up the law firm of Bryan & Hatch. Lawyers, next to businessmen, comprised the largest segment of Chicago's upper order in the 1850s and 1860s. Their skills facilitated commercial, financial, and political activities that in turn elevated members of the bar to positions of urban leadership.[9]

Bryan soon branched out from the law to include business, banking, and real estate operations among his many interests; he became one of the wealthiest and most socially prominent citizens of Chicago, achieving a reputation as a vigorous and persuasive speaker whose public addresses bristled with eloquent phrases and happy allusions. Though a southerner by birth, he was a staunch Unionist and served as a member of the Union Defense Committee, which President Lincoln warmly endorsed. During the Civil War, Bryan organized troops and provided for them in the field and served as president of the Chicago Sanitary Commission, which raised more than $300,000 for the Union army. His distinguished and arduous services on behalf of the Union accorded him the honor of being elected a member of the Loyal Legion.[10]

After the war, Bryan provided the impetus for establishing the Soldiers Home in Chicago by advancing both money and direction to the project. He then built Bryan Hall, a large arena to serve public meetings and entertainments, and founded a bank, the Fidelity Safe Depository. The bank was unscathed by the flames of the Great Fire of 1871, saving the citizens of Chicago many millions of dollars and bringing public acclaim to its builder. Perhaps his most important accomplishment was to spearhead the drive to promote Chicago as the site of the World's Columbian Exposition in 1893. Bryan framed the initial resolutions presented at the citizens' meeting, held in the common council chamber on August 1, 1891, that officially tendered Chicago's nomination as the host city for the fair. He also argued the city's case successfully before a United States Senate committee. A grateful organizing committee elected him first vice president of the exposition and appointed him special commissioner to southern Europe. In this capacity he met with monarchs and Pope Leo XIII and addressed audiences in the chief European cities to awaken general interest in the exposition.

Bryan was clearly an entrepreneur with a keen eye for the main chance. He capitalized on the rapid physical growth of Chicago with its burgeoning population and industries, its developing retail trades, its rising land values, and its active real estate market to advance his and the Lathrop family fortunes. In doing so, he shrewdly involved other prominent and influential figures of Chicago society to ensure the success of his ventures.

One sees evidence of Bryan's entrepreneurship in his decision to buy eighty-six acres of land on the periphery of the city to found Graceland Cemetery. Bryan recognized that Chicago required new burial grounds because the city's lakefront public cemetery had become dangerously overcrowded. What drove his awareness was the death of his son, Daniel Page Bryan, on April 12, 1855. Daniel was buried in the city cemetery only to be disinterred and temporarily removed along with two thousand others in the course of the cholera fright later that year.[11]

Having purchased the land outright, Bryan proceeded to incorporate the cemetery in 1860. The incorporators included, besides himself, William B. Ogden, the first mayor of Chicago, businessmen Sidney Sawyer and Edwin H. Sheldon, and George P. A. Healy. The last became renowned as the "Painter of Presidents" for his famous seated Abraham Lincoln, which he executed at Bryan's behest. Healy also painted landscapes in the style of the Barbizon painter Daubigny, a style which was very popular in the latter nineteenth century especially among America's cultural elite.[12]

After securing a perpetual charter from the state of Illinois in 1861, Bryan engaged the landscape architect Horace W. S. Cleveland to provide an early design for the cemetery. Cleveland's blueprint proved unsuccessful, and the project floundered until Bryan made the key decision that would ultimately guarantee the financial success of Graceland. He involved his nephew Bryan Lathrop, the son of Jedediah and Mariana Lathrop, in the project. After acquiring additional land for construction of a new section of the cemetery in the early 1870s, Bryan turned over the presidency of Graceland to his nephew. Bryan Lathrop served as president of Graceland Cemetery from 1878 until his death in 1916, an association which had profound consequences not only for the cemetery and the family fortune but also for the development of landscape architecture and the park movement in the United States. Bryan Lathrop had studied in Europe in the 1860s, a sojourn which caused him to view America in an unflattering light. "In Europe [the intelligent traveler] sees almost everywhere evidences of a sense of beauty," he observed afterwards. "In America, almost everywhere he is struck by the want of it. . . . In this new country of ours the struggle for existence has been intense, and the practical side of life has been developed while the aesthetic side has lain dormant."[13]

Between 1878 and 1880 Bryan Lathrop initiated a new campaign for the beautification of Graceland which reflected the ideas of landscape design and gardening he had absorbed as a student on the Continent. In the fall of 1878, he asked the young civil engineer Ossian C. Simonds, who later became one of the city's most prominent landscape architects and designer of parks, to create a lasting plan for Graceland. Bryan Lathrop's vision of the new and undeveloped portion of the cemetery— part swamp, part slough, and part celery field—was one that Simonds also shared. Both young men believed that the world of nature could be re-created as a series of pictures for the landscape gardener to elaborate upon and make more succinct. The vision was along the lines of a Barbizon landscape, although the cemetery was to serve a utilitarian as well as an aesthetic function. Graceland was to be a sleeping place for the deceased and a place of quiet retreat and beauty for the living.

The ideal of Graceland as a vast landscape painting, one which merged novel forms ("the landscaped lawn and the long prairie view, with a vocabulary derived from local nature but having a divine, faraway goal"),[14] eventually was partially compromised by Chicago's rich and powerful, who were more interested in leaving behind impressive permanent monuments of stone as testimony to their economic, political, social, and cultural triumphs. To attract buyers of burial plots, the company had to permit the construction of elaborate mausoleums and statuary. Once this concession was made, Graceland quickly became the favored burial place of Chicago's elite—Potter Palmer, Cyrus McCormick, George Pullman, John Altgeld, Henry H. Getty, and Marshall Field—enjoying its golden age from the late 1870s until just before World War I.

Thomas Barbour Bryan also shared his good fortune with the rest of his kin. He introduced his brother-in-law Jedediah to the attractiveness of Graceland's stock, and over the years they profited handsomely from the sale of burial plots to Chicago's elite families. Besides investing in Graceland and maintaining an active lumber business, Jedediah Lathrop, again with his brother-in-law's encouragement, speculated in the Chicago real estate market. Most of the property Jedediah Lathrop purchased and developed in the boom days of the rapid expansion of the city fell within the Loop. It was he who developed the Lathrop Avenue section of Oak Park and River Forest.

Lathrop's successes in lumber, Chicago real estate, and banking allowed his family to live well. Of his four children, three survived to adulthood. Bryan Lathrop was born on August 6, 1844, in Alexandria, where he was educated at the Dinwiddie School in preparation for his entrance into the University of Virginia. With the outbreak of the Civil War, the Unionist family left Alexandria for Washington, D.C., and then joined Thomas Barbour Bryan in Chicago. Meanwhile, Bryan's parents sent him abroad to shelter him from combat and continue his studies with private tutors. His sojourn in Dresden, Paris, and Italy kindled his interest in art, music, and landscape design, prompting him to declare afterwards that his formative years in Europe had been of more benefit to him than any university education.[15]

Upon his return to the United States in 1865, Bryan Lathrop, now

twenty-one years old, also took up residence in Chicago where he engaged in the real estate, life insurance, and other business activities,
both on his own and together with his uncle Thomas Barbour Bryan.
The extension of Lincoln Park and the reclaiming of the land from Lake
Michigan were largely due to his efforts. In 1875 he married Helen
Lynde Aldis, the daughter of a prominent and influential Chicagoan,
Judge Asa O. Aldis. She became widely known for her activities in civic
betterment and was in close sympathy with her husband's musical, literary, and social interests.

As his business ventures prospered, Bryan Lathrop assumed a more
commanding role among Chicago's rich and powerful. Chicago's upper-
class elite, which was composed initially of the older patrician families
who had arrived in the city in the 1830s and 1840s, was more flexible
than its patrician counterpart of the older seaboard cities in accommo-
dating rising men of wealth, ambition, and power. As befitted a personage of his means, stature, and influence, Lathrop manifested his elite
status by constructing a new home in 1892. The residence was the personal design of Charles McKim, of the architectural firm of McKim,
Mead & White, which had the largest and richest clientele in America,
for his good friend Bryan Lathrop. In 1923 it was acquired by the Fort-
nightly Club, one of the city's oldest and most exclusive women's
clubs.[16]

Bellevue Place, this spacious, dignified mansion located along Chicago's Gold Coast at the juncture of Bellevue Place and Lakeshore Drive,
is the most perfect piece of Georgian architecture in Chicago. In keeping
with Lathrop's preference for the uncluttered, he and Helen furnished
the rooms with Biedermeier furniture, which created a simple, dignified
atmosphere; only occasionally were there decorative touches of the Four
Georges era. The Bellevue residence quickly attracted attention as a
gathering place of distinguished persons, and it gained even greater re-
nown for Bryan Lathrop's collection of Whistler etchings, purported to
be the largest in the country.

For more than fifty years, Bryan Lathrop was, in the words of one
writer, "an effectively influential citizen of Chicago."[17] His business activities and successful marriage earned him a prominent rank among
Chicago's business and social elites. He was one of the founders of the
Chicago Real Estate Board, which gave shape and form to the city;
served as trustee and manager of some of the most important estates in
Chicago; presided over Graceland Cemetery until his death; and was

deeply involved in other aspects of the life of the city. A philanthropist, he helped to underwrite and direct the major cultural and humanitarian institutions of Chicago's elite, notably the Chicago Orchestra Association, the Art Institute, the Newberry Library, the Chicago Historical Society, the Relief and Aid Society, and the Illinois Society for the Prevention of Blindness. When he died in May 1916, he left nearly 90 percent of his large property for public purposes, including $700,000 to the Orchestra Association.[18]

Minna Lathrop, Jedediah and Mariana Lathrop's older daughter, died in 1877, and we know almost nothing about her. Their second son, Barbour, named after Thomas Barbour Bryan, developed a wanderlust for travel around the world which he followed industriously until his death in 1927. He was a news correspondent for various magazines and journals and made San Francisco his home base. In conventional terms Barbour Bryan probably would not have been considered successful by the norms of his generation and social class; indeed, he most likely would have been described as bohemian.

Florence Lathrop, the younger daughter, was, like her siblings, born in Alexandria, on October 19, 1858. She was the grandniece of former governor James Barbour, which gave her more than a passing tie to Virginia, a fact reporters noted in 1893 when she married her second husband, Thomas Nelson Page, who was himself the Old Dominion's most famous literary figure of the day. Because so little documentation of her life before she married Page has survived, we know little for certain about Florence's early years, the formative period of her life.

Florence's diplomatic passport, issued in Rome on April 4, 1916 and signed by Page as the United States ambassador to Italy, includes one of the few photographs of her that has survived and the only known physical description. The photograph is of a mature woman of fifty-eight years, seated on a richly carved chair. She stood only 5 feet 4½ inches tall, was of medium complexion, and had blue eyes and iron gray hair. Her face was oval, with a high forehead, round chin, medium mouth, and regular nose.

This is the woman in the twilight of her life; fortunately, another likeness of her has survived, dating from 1877, while she was still a resident of Elmhurst, Illinois. This is a three-quarter view of a serene young woman of nineteen, a personage of considerable beauty, delicacy, and sensitivity. Her hair is light brown and piled high on her head; and she is wearing a dress of rich fabric whose collar, drawn together to the front and held with a decorative brooch, partially covers her neck. Her ears are adorned tastefully with pendant earrings. All in all, the picture is one of a handsome not to say beautiful refined, and intelligent Victorian woman.[19]

Thomas Nelson Page captured best the essence of Florence's beauty shortly after her death. He declared that it had assumed a more spiritual quality and a more ethereal charm as she passed from youth into her mature years. Waxing poetically, he observed: "If it might be said of her that she had in youth the 'beauty of the sun when it arises in the Heaven,' it might also be said of her that, 'as the clear light is upon the Holy Candlestick so is the beauty of the face in ripe age,' for her beauty increased steadily with her years."[20] She was quietly generous in thought, word, and deed and, contrary to the custom common among the affluent of the day, was so self-effacing that she would not allow her portrait to be painted and did not often allow herself to be photographed.

To say that she exuded a spiritual quality or possessed an ethereal charm is to illuminate only one facet of Florence Lathrop Page's life, and that is from the perspective of the patrician southern male who, as one scholar has noted, traditionally tended to represent upper-class, especially southern, women in idealistic language: ethereal, fragile, pious, possessing unique and superior qualities, but essentially passive and on a pedestal, unrelated to daily life.[21] To achieve a fuller understanding of who Florence Page was, we need to probe more deeply into her social origins, especially the urban milieu in which she was reared. For, the world of her youth was less the South of her birth or Chicago of the mid-nineteenth century than it was Elmhurst, Illinois, an affluent suburb located on the periphery of the northern metropolis where she lived until she was married in 1879. Only then did she return to the city center.

In this respect, Florence's life differed little from the lives of the daughters of other affluent families of the day. The development of the commuter railroad in the 1840s and 1850s, the growing accumulation of wealth from industry, banking, real estate, and other business enterprise during the war; and the availability of vacant land for settlement just beyond the city limits had revised Chicago's social and economic fabric in fundamental ways. The forces of urban expansion had created finer distinctions between social and economic groups within the city, had fostered the development of multinucleated business districts, and had accelerated urban sprawl. Mass transit enabled many of Chicago's affluent upper-class residents to escape the central city by night for the outlying suburban regions. They were the first to work in the city but to live in the country.[22]

For many well-to-do Chicagoans who disliked the dirty, noisy, and overcrowded walking city and who could afford the price of mass transit, the phenomenon of urban sprawl and the accompanying movement to the periphery of the city was made possible in 1845 when the Galena and Chicago Union Railroad (forerunner to the Chicago and Northwestern) established a station in Cottage Hill (the original name of Elmhurst), a small, unincorporated village about sixteen miles west of Chicago. The presence of the commuter railroad assured the growth of the fledgling settlement as the Cottage Hill station gradually became the most important stop along the route, providing easy access to and from Chicago for farmers, commuters, and new residents.[23]

Residential development of Cottage Hill received a boost in the mid-1850s when a transplanted Ohioan, Gerry Bates, staked a claim to a treeless tract of land in what would become the center of Elmhurst. Bates divided the southeastern section of his land into large parcels that he sold to wealthy and socially prominent businessmen from Chicago. The first to purchase land from Bates was Thomas Barbour Bryan, who would be known locally as the "Father of Elmhurst" because of the pivotal role he played in its formative years. Bryan acquired 1,000 acres and built a country estate, Byrd's Nest, at the southwest corner of St. Charles Road and York Street. He gradually persuaded other wealthy Chicagoans to purchase land from him and to relocate to the suburb, including Elisha Hagans, a real estate developer, and the painter G. P. A. Healy. The latter occupied the original Cottage Hill, renaming his estate Clover Lawn.[24]

In the early days of Elmhurst, the word *estate* assumed a particular prominence. Reflecting the owner's wealth and social position, it meant a large mansion house and extensive landholdings with stables, horses, carriage houses, tool sheds, flower gardens, and orchards.[25] Owners of estates normally employed a staff of four to ten employees and servants, and chief among these was the gardener who lived on the estate with his family in a cottage built to the rear and some distance away from the main house. The dozen or so Elmhurst estates of the latter nineteenth century were quite distinctive in appearance and bore descriptive names after the fashion of aristocratic English country places and southern plantations.[26]

The estates were tightly enclosed in arborvitae hedges, clipped annually into exact geometrical shapes by a resident gardener. The Bryans' gardener for many years was a Swedish immigrant, Gustav Swenson; the Lathrops' gardener also was of Swedish descent. On the Bryan estate, besides the landscaping around the mansion house, the lawns, drives, and paths, and the flower and vegetable gardens, there was a fruit orchard with apple, pear, and cherry trees. In the formal flower garden west of the mansion house, the plans centered around a white marble fountain which Jane Bryan had shipped from Florence, Italy, in 1850, while on her honeymoon.[27]

The most striking feature of these estate gardens was the extent to which their owners, including the Bryan and Lathrop families, sought to evoke in Elmhurst the class distinctions of European society. This was not accidental: the Elmhurst mansions and gardens with their precise geometrical shapes, their imported European head gardeners, and their Carrara marble ornamentation were deliberately designed to suggest European money, preferably old European money. The reigning owners of these estates and formal gardens—businessmen, merchants, manufacturers, and lawyers—were attempting to reinvent their own personal histories and identities as Americans. These proud owners of large private estates were the winners of the spoils in a still raw land, entrepreneurs yearning toward Europe and the fixed class system in which their newfound entitlement could be preserved and consolidated; they imagined Elmhurst as a series of private parks or feudal fiefs in a sea of attendant serfs. For them, as for many Americans afflicted by doubts about the course of their increasingly multiethnic nation and the loss of values this was believed to imply, the elaborate homes and gardens were their attempt to retreat into an Arcadia of their own creation.[28]

Elmhurst by the end of the 1850s numbered about 200 inhabitants, out of a total of 1,500 in York Township. During the next decade other affluent Chicagoans established estates there. Jedediah Lathrop purchased a parcel of land from his brother-in-law in 1857 and in 1864 built his home, Huntington, on the south side of St. Charles Road, just west of Healy's Cottage Hill estate. Four years later he, along with Thomas Bryan and other residents, planted a large number of elms along Cottage Hill. In 1869, at Bryan's suggestion, Cottage Hill became Elmhurst, taking its name from these plantings. Development proceeded slowly during the Civil War decade, but the institutional foundations for future growth were being established. Thomas Bryan, for example, organized the first Protestant Episcopal congregation in 1862, and the first resident physician arrived in 1866. The coming of the Chicago Great Western Railroad in 1887 and the Illinois Central in 1888 opened up southeastern Elmhurst to rapid commercial and residential development.[29]

After the Great Fire of 1871, Elmhurst became a permanent refuge for a number of affluent Chicago families. They built new homes, opened businesses, and founded the Lutheran seminary that became Elmhurst College. The composition of the village, which was incorporated in 1882, more and more reflected the migration from Chicago. Ethnically Elmhurst was predominantly English and German; its churchgoers were mainly Lutheran and Catholic, with a number of Episcopalians, such as the Bryan and Lathrop families; politically the community was overwhelmingly Republican. By the 1880s and 1890s, private companies were bringing the amenities of urban living to this pastoral suburb. The Elmhurst Spring Water Company, whose treasurer and future president was Bryan Lathrop, provided running water in 1889; the Elmhurst Electric Light Company furnished electric power in 1892; and the Chicago Telephone Company supplied telephone service in 1897.[30]

The earliest days of Elmhurst, then, were intertwined with the fortunes of the nearby metropolis. Although prosperous Chicagoans like the Bryans and the Lathrops eschewed the central business district for a more pastoral life in the nearby suburb, they remained very much a part of Chicago's economic growth and its social scene. The metropolis, where similarly affluent and delightful people lived elegantly and in close touch with the culture and civilization of the Atlantic seaboard from which many of them had come, was like a magnet continually drawing these suburbanites to it. Chicago's cultural life may have lagged behind its counterpart in the older, established seaboard cities of the East, but its wealthy citizens found time to read, buy pictures, and sit for their portraits. Their touch with the world at large was astonishingly wide.[31]

Those Chicagoans who moved to Elmhurst took this lifestyle with them as part of their intellectual and cultural baggage and never abandoned it in the suburbs. Indeed, the 1870s saw the beginning of Elmhurst's Gilded Age, an era of elegant socializing by the owners of the great estates that lasted into the twentieth century. Prominent Elmhurst and Chicago families entertained each other at garden parties, musicales, amateur dramatic productions, and elaborate balls.[32] These were the circumstances in which Florence Lathrop was reared, and this was the style of life to which she was accustomed by the time she was a young adult. It was the life of the socially prominent young woman of her day, with the usual parties and debuts. She received private tutoring at home, and then, after the fashion of other upper-class families, her parents sent her to Paris to complete her education.[33]

For Florence, traveling abroad and residing in Paris, the artistic and cultural capital of Europe, to finish her education in French and art history with private tutors—even if for only a few months a year over a four-year period—must have been a liberating experience. She was free for the first time from the paternal gaze of Jedediah Lathrop as well as the more careful and probably less indulgent supervision of her mother; she was empowered to express her own thoughts and desires, to make her own choices; she was accorded unprecedented freedom to see and to be seen by dashing young Parisian males who no doubt would have been drawn to this handsome, blue-eyed, American. This experience implanted in Florence a fondness for travel and a sophistication of the aesthetic, of haute culture, to match those of her brother and future husbands; it fostered in her a curiosity and sense of discrimination about the larger world beyond her family, Elmhurst, and Chicago, even when she did not like what she saw.

Living in Paris gave Florence control over her own life; in the City of Light, her parents could not dominate every aspect of her environment, despite their efforts to shelter her from the crudities of the outside world by having a cousin chaperone her and insisting that she board in a respectable establishment. Florence went to Paris a young and inexperienced adolescent, but she returned to Elmhurst empowered, a woman confident to make her own decisions.

The circumstances under which Florence met her future husband Henry Field are obscure. Most probably, the two met through their families' mutual business and social interests in Chicago. Henry Field was the brother of the department store magnate Marshall Field, whose profits from mass-market retailing in the 1860s propelled the Fields into Chicago's elite upper class. The two families had a number of things in common. Like the Lathrops, the Fields were of Puritan descent, their ancestors having settled in New England about 1650. John Field, a farmer of Conway, Massachusetts, and his wife Fidelia had three children: Marshall, Joseph, and Henry. Of the three, Marshall Field became the most well known. Reared in the stern, cheerless atmosphere of a frugal farm family, he grew up to regard money as the key that opened all doors. Like Jedediah Lathrop, Marshall Field eschewed the life of a farmer for commercial pursuits; at the age of seventeen, he went to Pitts-field to work as a clerk in a dry goods store. There he mastered the details of trade, and in 1856, soon after attaining his majority, he migrated to Chicago.[34]

Unlike others who went west to conquer the wilderness and plow virgin soil, Marshall Field took refuge behind the familiar store counter, entering the employ of Cooley, Wadsworth & Co., one of the pioneer mercantile houses of the young western metropolis. He immediately displayed a genius for business and rendered such valuable service to his employers that he was admitted to a partnership in the firm in 1860. When the partnership of Cooley, Farwell & Co. was dissolved in 1865, Field, Palmer & Leiter was formed. Two years later, Potter Palmer re-tired, and the business was conducted under the firm name of Field, Leiter & Co. In 1881 Field purchased Joseph Leiter's interest and contin-ued the business as Marshall Field & Co. In a relatively short time but on a more grandiose scale, Marshall Field, like Thomas Bryan and Jedediah Lathrop, had parlayed a thousand dollars in savings into a multi-million dollar department store and real estate empire. His fortune at his death in 1906 was estimated between $100-$200 million.

Henry Field was only a junior partner in his brother's lucrative enter-prise, but because he bore the Field name, he would have been consid-ered a good catch for any young woman of the day. Happily for Florence, he was quite different in temperament from his brother Marshall, who had gained the reputation for being overly ambitious, determined, cold, and calculating. A member of the Fourth Presbyterian Church in Chi-cago, Henry Field was gentle, unassuming, and of a retiring disposition. More so than his famous brother, he fitted the Victorian stereotype of a true Christian gentleman, possessing as he did the virtues of manliness, self-reliance, helpfulness, calm, strength and tenderness, wisdom and modesty, domesticity, and an appreciation of the aesthetic while easily able to cope with the world of affairs. Despite his wealth, he was neither ostentatious nor obsessively acquisitive.[35]

At the age of twenty-one, Florence entered into nuptials with Henry Field, who was thirty-eight. Her dowry most likely had been arranged by her father and her future husband, although no record of it exists. For her afternoon wedding, held in Byrd's Nest Chapel on October 29,

1879, the Elmhurst neighbors, led by Seth Wadhams, strung Chinese lanterns from the elm trees on Cottage Hill Avenue all the way from the North Western Railroad station to the chapel and to the Lathrop home on St. Charles Road. Special trains on the North Western transported the wedding guests from Chicago and took them back to the city in the evening. The guests drove down the gaily lit avenue below the lanterns, which swung in the nighttime breezes.[36]

When Florence accepted Henry Field's proposal of marriage, she made a decision fraught with social and economic significance for her future. Above all, she was solidifying her position within the upper stratum of American society by marrying within her class (the business elite), her religion, and her geographic background. Among Chicago's Protestants, the Episcopal and Presbyterian churches were identified with the well-to-do, and they offered their members a higher social status to correspond with their wealth. Marriage in general would have been considered a demonstrable step up in the hierarchy of society for any woman because it provided her with the social and economic benefits that her male counterpart ordinarily received through education, the professions, business enterprise, and a good marriage. But Florence's marriage to Henry Field, of the enormously affluent Field family, was the ultimate associational tie that bound together Chicago's elite.[37]

Immediately after the wedding, the couple went abroad, living in Paris for two years where Henry Field acted as the foreign buyer on the Continent for Field & Leiter. Rather than being lonely or isolated, Florence considered Paris her second home. She knew it well, spoke the language fluently, and recalled afterward that these years in the most beautiful city in the world with a new husband were among her happiest.

Unencumbered by family obligations, Florence acted as her spouse's interpreter, guide, and partner as they revisited her favorite museums, historical sites, and public attractions. But living abroad also entailed a deliberate social cost which suggests that Florence most likely exercised a sexual parity within the marriage relationship. For the Fields delayed beginning a family until their return to the United States. Florence did not bear her first child, Minna, whom she named after her deceased sister, until March 1882, when she was twenty-four years old; a second daughter, Florence, came along in December 1883; and a third, Gladys, was born in 1888 but died within eight months.

When the Fields returned from Paris in 1881, they took up residence in Chicago. Henry temporarily left Field & Leiter, which by now had become Marshall Field & Co., rejoined the firm the next year, and then retired from active business in 1883, on account of failing health but also because he had made his fortune. As was frequently the practice of men of his financial and social position, he and Florence went to Europe "for the cure" and returned greatly improved in health. He rejoined Marshall Field & Co. briefly in 1885–86 and then permanently withdrew from active engagement in business in order to pursue the finer tastes of culture, the arts, and charity.[38]

Henry Field was known in Chicago as a connoisseur of good books and a devotee of art, owning one of the city's finest collections of paintings and other objets d'art. His purchasing forays reflected a genuine quest for culture, an interest in European paintings and sculpture for their own sake. If one accepts the proposition that there resides within each human being regardless of gender both characteristics of masculinity and femininity, then Henry Field's pursuit of culture and the arts and his involvement in charitable enterprises might logically be considered a manifestation of the feminine aspect of his nature.

Art collecting among affluent nineteenth-century males, however, also expressed superiority of income through the purchase of commodities that were inherently limited in quantity. Field's art collection, therefore, also may be construed as a measure of his wealth and his abilities relative to those of other men in the economic and social competition of the day. At least he brought refinement and discrimination to the selection of what he purchased, unlike many other self-made men who collected art as they had collected companies, indiscriminately, to be displayed like trophies to demonstrate that they were indeed rich. Field's particular taste ran toward the Barbizon school of French painting and included three examples by Corot, whose works were a must for every serious collector, *The Ferryman, Just before Sunrise,* and *Wounded Eurydice.*[39]

Having made his fortune and earned the title "capitalist,"[40] Henry Field willingly shouldered the gentleman's obligation to participate in all activities that concerned the progress, welfare, and higher culture of metropolitan Chicago. His business and financial interests in the city were extensive: besides his limited partnership in Marshall Field & Co., he was a large stockholder in the West Division Street Railway Company and a vice president and stockholder of the Commercial National Bank, the major source of credit for the grain trade. He also held membership in the city's most prestigious clubs, including the Chicago Club, the Commercial and Calumet clubs, the historical society, and the Literary Club.[41]

Field also contributed generously of his time and money to public and private cultural, charitable, humanitarian, and religious enterprises. He served as trustee of the Art Institute, member of the Art Committee of the Inter-State Industrial Exposition (1884–85), director of Chicago's first opera festival (1885), director of the Chicago Relief and Aid Society (1883–84), which was the most notable humanitarian organization in the city, and president of the Home of the Friendless (1884), a body which included wealthy and socially prominent capitalists.[42] From each of these endeavors, Field derived professional and civic distinction and community influence. His philanthropy enabled him to solidify his position as a member of the upper class, maintain social order, express civic pride, and gratify his conscience.

Florence's status appeared to differ in almost every aspect from that of her husband, and certainly from that of a single woman, who in the nineteenth century enjoyed considerable independence, which encouraged a high degree of self-confidence. Marriage, by contrast, has usually been considered a retrograde step for American women by modern scholars, though not necessarily by nineteenth-century observers. When a young American woman married, noted the French observer Alexis de Tocqueville approvingly, "the inexorable opinion of the public carefully circumscribes [her] within the narrow circle of domestic interests and duties, and forbids her to step beyond it."[43] In that sweeping generalization Tocqueville provided the physical image (the circle) and the interpretation (that it was a limiting boundary on choices) that became the metaphor of separate spheres. Separate spheres is the cultural presupposition that both men and women live in separate spaces: the masculine/public world (the competitive world of business, government and politics) and the feminine/private world (or, "the circle of domestic concerns," as Mary Beth Norton aptly put it).[44] In this separate female sphere, married women engaged in nurturant activities focused on children, husbands, family dependents, and the management or service of the household.

Florence's career as a married woman presents an excellent opportunity to test the validity of the metaphor of separate spheres; to determine whether late Victorian couples adhered rigidly to a polarity between the world and the household, or whether the metaphor needs to be softened, its boundaries overlapping, to give a more accurate representation of gender relations. The separate sphere phenomenon as applied to Florence Page is both simpler and more complex than Tocqueville's conclusion that "in America, the independence of woman is irrevocably lost in the bonds of matrimony" suggests.[45] It is simpler because on one level it does denote the physical space in which Florence lived, but it is more complex because even that physical space was complexly structured by an ideology of gender and class.

The feminine sphere that Florence occupied was complementary to but in significant aspects quite distinct from the masculine/public world of her husband. In the public sphere Florence Lathrop Field, for most purposes, did not exist as an individual in her own right, formally empowered to make the fundamental decisions that would affect her. Other people and the larger society perceived her and referenced her in relation to her husband, Henry Field, whom society expected to speak and act on behalf of himself and his dependents. Florence became Mrs. Henry Field, rather than Florence Lathrop Field, a consequence of the perpetuation of the hierarchical and male-dominant family structure that persisted in the United States through the turn of the century. Furthermore, in the eyes of the law, Henry Field alone was empowered to make the decisions regarding the rearing of their children. Although the married woman's property statutes of the mid-nineteenth century protected the inherited and gift property Florence brought into her marriage, she did not have legal claim to any property that she might have built up in the course of her marital career. Politically, of course, she, like all other American women regardless of class or status, was powerless, unenfranchised. These distinctions flowed naturally from Florence's dependent existence both legally and economically upon Henry Field.

At the center of Victorian life was the family, a hierarchical and patriarchal institution wherein the wife and mother provided a secure, spiritual, and virtuous environment nowhere else to be found, least of all in the impersonal, fiercely competitive business world.[46] Within this context, Florence defined her identity in relation to the members of her family, as the wife of her husband and the mother of her children. Henry Field's economic success and social position made it possible for Florence to forgo the workplace, unlike most working-class and unmarried middle-class women, to pursue domestic activities: creation of the home, care of the family, cultivation of ethical children, supervision of the domestic household staff, service to others, and playing a social, entertaining, or decorative role as circumstances dictated.[47]

There is no evidence to indicate that Florence was unhappy at home or felt her autonomy was being repressed, or that she was sacrificing those qualities of personality and character which had made her attractive to Henry Field in the first place. She was simply exercising her options differently from the single young woman of twenty-one she had been, and certainly from the working- and middle-class women of the nineteenth century whose range of choices was even narrower. If recent investigations into working-class women in the labor force are accurate, such women were segregated into low-paying, unskilled jobs and kept there. Middle-class women were more apt to take in boarders or serve as domestics to advance their families' interests.[48]

The home—the physical space—that Florence created for her husband and children was at once a refuge from the anxieties of modern life, a shelter for the moral and spiritual values that the commercial and the critical spirit were threatening to destroy, and a psychologically sustaining opportunity for Florence to form enduring friendships with women such as her sister-in-law Helen Aldis Lathrop, Cornelia Aldis, Anne Carter Dulany, and Errol Brown Train and to participate with them in charitable and religious associations. Within her sphere Florence was the independent, self-confident, and dominant figure. If her domestic space manifested her class and status, her home became the theater in which she, as mistress of the house, claimed her own space and assigned to the servants the space they would occupy.

Florence's daily management and supervision of her home and household staff inculcated in her managerial skills that assumed greater significance later on when, as wife of the United States ambassador to Italy, she abandoned her decorative role and employed those same qualities of personality and practical skills to shepherd to fruition a relief program for the 1915 victims of the Avezzano earthquake, and when, in the period of American neutrality during World War I, she initiated and supervised a workshop to manufacture surgical dressings and other items of relief to wounded Italian soldiers.

Florence's marriage to all outward appearances conformed to the separate spheres phenomenon except in two crucial respects: the health of Henry Field and the decision to begin a family. Henry Field had a delicate constitution with recurring illnesses that required him periodically to withdraw from the business world to recuperate. During those episodes Florence was required to be strong, the person who made the decisions that kept the family going. The three-year delay between marriage and the birth of their first daughter suggests that the Fields were exercising birth control, a practice not uncommon for couples of their class and status, and that family planning was a mutual decision between husband and wife. This also implies something more fundamental about the Fields' relationship: that Florence exercised sexual equality within the marriage, which most likely spilled over into other aspects of the Fields' lives. This knowledge casts doubt on whether the stereotype of the hierarchical, male-dominated family structure was as ironclad as hitherto believed. More likely, the boundaries of the separate spheres were less sharply demarcated than they appeared to outsiders.

How else may we explain Florence's transition from a woman who appears superficially to be a fairly conventional upper-class wife and mother of the Victorian era to the surprisingly strong-willed individual who emerged after the premature death of her husband? Was she all the while subverting many facets of the separate spheres phenomenon to cloak the fact that she was self-confident, assertive, and independent? Geneaologist Frederick Clifton Pierce, who provided most of the information known about Henry Field, may well have intuited the evolving relationship between husband and wife when he enlisted the dual language of masculine/feminine characteristics to describe Henry Field. "His life was centered in his home," Pierce wrote, and he described Field as "strong and tender, wise and modest, deeply loving the beautiful, yet easily able to cope with the world of affairs."[49] Note the emphasis on the hearth rather than the marketplace, which Pierce included almost as an afterthought. Pierce's use of language, especially his choice of adjectives, suggests a softening of patriarchy and male dominance and the entry of Henry Field into the hearth—the family, the feminine sphere—more as an equal, a partner in decision making, than as the dominant figure.

Unhappily for Florence, Henry Field died unexpectedly at the age of forty-nine, just three days before Christmas 1890, after a sudden brief illness. In keeping with her long-standing desire to avoid publicity, Florence instructed that Henry Field's funeral and burial in Graceland Cemetery be kept simple and unadorned but reflective of his status within the community. The honorary pallbearers included representatives from Chicago's business and civic elite: Owen F. Aldis, successful

Chicago realtor and brother-in-law of Bryan Lathrop; Harlow N. Higginbotham, prominent in the city's retail trade; Franklin MacVeagh, the millionaire wholesale grocer and founder of the National Municipal League; A. C. McClurg, publishing magnate; George Armour, a scion of the Armour meatpacking fortune and philanthropist active in the YMCA and orphan asylum movements; Albert A. Sprague, wealthy wholesale grocer and friend of the Field family; and Walter C. Larned, realtor, lawyer, and, like Henry Field, active in the Chicago Literary Club.[50]

The denouement of Henry Field's death affords yet another insight into how Chicago's elite functioned, and how Florence's status as a widow could be empowering. Widowhood conferred upon Florence economic independence, enabling her to make the fundamental decisions that affected her own environment. But money and power also were the avenues by which upper-class Chicagoans exercised a preponderant influence in such secondary spheres of community life as philanthropy and culture. Three years after Henry's death, utilizing a special trust administered by Bryan Lathrop, Marshall Field, Owen T. Aldis, Albert Sprague, and Martin A. Ryerson, Florence loaned, "in his memory and to perpetuate his name," all of her deceased husband's oil paintings (except family portraits) to the Art Institute of Chicago, one of the city's citadels of upper-class culture and patronage. The collection of forty-one oils of the Barbizon School of French painting, including Millet's *Bringing Home the New-born Calf* and Jules Breton's *Song of the Lark,* besides the Carnots, Delacroixs, Cazins, and a Constable, was the most important accession the museum had received in its fourteen-year history.[51]

The important point, though, is that the initial bequest was not an unencumbered transfer of the Field collection to the Art Institute but rather a carefully crafted deed. Florence retained ownership of the collection, even as she named the museum custodian of the paintings. She also set the conditions under which the museum could exhibit the works of art. For example, the trust instrument specifically prohibited disjoining the collection, hanging the paintings anywhere but together in the Field Memorial Room, hanging other works of art in the same room, and selling or alienating any or all of the pictures for any reason whatsoever. The transfer agreement also stipulated that the collection be housed in a fireproof building, insured, and maintained in good condition. As additional proof of ownership, the agreement declared that if the collection was totally destroyed in a fire the insurance money was to revert to the donor's heirs, not to the museum. Only in the event of partial damage would the museum be permitted to use the insurance monies for restoration. Most of these stipulations continued in force even after Florence made an absolute outright deed of gift to the museum on May 26, 1916.[52]

When this superb collection of Barbizon paintings was presented to the Art Institute, Florence also insisted that she be permitted to select and prepare the gallery in which they were to be hung. The gallery she chose was one of the best in the building in size, shape, and situation, opening off the rotunda on the second floor to the north and also through a small anteroom onto the west loggia. Its decor certainly made it one of the handsomest public galleries in the country, with all of the decorative work being done by Tiffany & Co. of New York from a general plan which Florence furnished. The woodwork of the entire room was of highly polished solid ebony. The casings of the doors and panels were delicately ornamented with square half-inch inserts of mother-of-pearl of the shifting green shades that harmonized with the prevailing green and yellow hues in the room. The mother-of-pearl ornamentations were arranged as narrow straight borders in admirable keeping with the simple elegance of the other decorations. The floor was a pleasing but unobtrusive mosaic in green, yellow, red, black, and pale pink. The Tiffany skylight was a canopy of glass thirty-four feet long and fourteen feet wide; above it wholly out of sight were electric lights. The effect of the tinted glass canopy when the room was lighted, either naturally or with electricity, was visually stunning, making it, in the words of one observer, "a worthy object of pilgrimage."[53]

To complete this memorial to her deceased husband, this labor of love and affection, Florence donated the pair of bronze lions still standing guard on Michigan Avenue at the main entrance of the museum. The lions were the work of Edward Kemeys, the self-proclaimed and self-taught sculptor whose oeuvre was dedicated to memorializing the already vanishing wildlife of his native land. Unveiled to the public on May 10, 1894, they were quickly adopted by Chicagoans as a proud symbol of the city and its prestigious art museum.

How the trustees of the Art Institute came to select the Kemeys lions provides a further demonstration of how a member of Chicago's elite, even in widowhood, could exercise influence upon one of the city's premier cultural institutions. The story began in 1891 with the trustees' decision to incorporate guardian lions into the design of a new, permanent building for the museum. Charles L. Hutchinson, president of the board of trustees, was initially leaning toward commissioning any one of a dozen better-known sculptors for the honor, including Augustus Bauer, Daniel Chester French, Frederick William Macmonnies, Philip Martiny, and Augustus St. Gaudens. On September 24, 1892, Hutchinson received a letter from a fellow trustee of the Art Institute who also happened to be a patron of Kemeys: Bryan Lathrop.[54]

Lathrop's letter recommended Kemeys very highly, affirming his "very strong conviction that there is no other animal sculptor in this country at all to be compared with Kemeys, and if there is any who is his equal now living anywhere I do not know about him." For this reason, Lathrop concluded, "I am . . . very anxious to have him execute the bronze lions." He had talked with his sister, who had "entered into the subject very heartily, and she is equally anxious to have Kemeys intrusted with the commission." He noted that Henry Field had "admired Kemeys's work very much and liked Mr. Kemeys personally." Having declared Florence's interest equal to his own, Bryan put forth a proposal for acquiring the lions for the Art Institute's entrance. If the trustees agreed, Florence wished "to present them to the Art Institute, on condition that she can have them designed by Mr. Kemeys and cast under his directions, and that she be allowed to pass upon the designs." The museum, of course, would retain the right to refuse them even after they had been executed.

In closing, Bryan stated that Florence preferred not to have her name mentioned or in any way publicized, because her intention was to give these lions "as a sort of memento of her husband." On January 31, 1893, the minutes of the board of trustees' executive committee recorded that "the president then stated that Mrs. Henry Field had presented to The Art Institute of Chicago two bronze lions to be executed by Mr. Kemeys." The committee voted to accept the gift and to thank the donor.

The circumstances whereby Chicago acquired Henry Field's collection of Barbizon paintings, the Art Institute established the Henry Field Memorial Room devoted exclusively to exhibiting his art treasures, and the museum came to possess the Kemeys lions demonstrated the convergence of commercial and cultural eminence on the part of Chicago's upper-class elite. Florence had established a visible monument to her deceased husband, one which also amply demonstrated the Field family's affluence, social standing, and status as patrons of high culture. She wielded this kind of influence indirectly, but it was nonetheless potent coming as it did through her brother. It thus appears that in the patriarchal society of nineteenth-century America, it was more acceptable, and probably more effective politically, for a woman of means and influence to exercise power indirectly, through the masculine sphere.

If it was true that the world of upper-class women was not the same as that of middle- and working-class women, neither was it the same as the world of upper-class men. But notions of power and patriarchy paled when Florence confronted the reality of her life; that she was a widow at the age of thirty-two and the mother of two young girls. Following her husband's death, she naturally sought refuge for herself and protection for them in familiar surroundings, dividing her time between the Elmhurst of her youth and the Chicago of her adulthood. She, Minna, and Florence returned to Huntington, the Lathrop family home in Elmhurst, in the summers and passed the winters in the city at the mansion Henry Field had built at 293 Ontario Street after their marriage. Even after she remarried, and for many years after she had departed the Windy City for Washington, D.C., Florence retained her Chicago residence.[55]

Because of her class and economic circumstances, the crises of widowhood and bereavement eventually led Florence to a greater degree of freedom and autonomy than might be expected of the typical Victorian woman. Florence's empowerment, which flowed from her economic independence, her ability to make the kinds of decisions that give a person control over one's life and environment, increased incrementally as her children grew to maturity and her second marriage proved to be without issue. Being an heiress from both her father, who had died on May 24, 1889, and now her husband was critically important. The estate Florence inherited provided her and her daughters not only with a substantial income and an imposing residence but also with their sense of identity within the American class structure. Her wealth guaranteed her continuance in the upper stratum of society, which was manifested in her elegant lifestyle and her continued access to both the patrician-political elites (such as the Roosevelts and the Tafts) and to the moneyed elites (the Astors, Armours, and McCormicks) of modern America.[56]

Florence first met Thomas Nelson Page, the man to whom she would remain married for the next twenty-eight years, two years after the death of Henry Field. On both sides of his family, Page's lineage was of the most illustrious in the history of the colony and Commonwealth of Virginia. His father and mother, John and Elizabeth Burwell Nelson Page, were both grandchildren of General Thomas Nelson, a signer of the Declaration of Independence, governor of Virginia, and commander of the Virginia forces at Yorktown. His father was also a grandson of Governor John Page of Rosewell, a lifelong friend of Thomas Jefferson. The descendant of two governors and a distant relation of Jane Byrd Page Bryan, Thomas Nelson Page was born on Oakland plantation in Beaver Dam, located in Hanover County, north of Richmond, on April 23, 1853. The land on which he spent his boyhood was a part of the original grant of the crown of England to the "Colonial magnate, Thomas Nelson," the grandfather of General Thomas Nelson.[57]

Despite the family's straitened circumstances in the aftermath of the Civil War, Page attended Washington College and read law and tutored in Kentucky; in 1873–74 he studied law at the University of Virginia. In after years Page served as director of the university's alumni society, an influential position which brought him into contact with the Commonwealth's leading citizens. After practicing in county courts, he established a successful legal practice in Richmond, specializing in business, invention, and mining. Law was Page's vocation, but the writing of short stories, novels, and poetry was his avocation. Publication in 1887 of *In Ole Virginia, or Marse Chan and Other Stories,* written in Negro dialect and utilizing southern pronunciation, brought him national recognition as a local colorist and spokesman for the Old South. In 1886, aged thirty-three, Page married eighteen-year-old Anne Seddon Bruce, but their happiness was short-lived. She died of a throat hemorrhage four days before Christmas 1888 without children, and Page threw himself into business in Colorado and Europe in an effort to assuage his grief. Worsening business conditions in London and the panic of 1891 forced him to return to Richmond.[58]

To augment his falling income, Page embarked on the lyceum circuit, reading his stories and sharing the platform with his friend and fellow author F. Hopkinson Smith. During one of his readings in Chicago in 1892 in a private home, Page met Florence Lathrop Field, a beautiful young woman still in heavy mourning for her daughter Gladys, her father, and her husband. Page family tradition says that on the day he met her, he told Florence that he was going to marry her.[59] Whatever truth there was to this story, Page encountered Florence a year later, and after a discreet storybook courtship stretching from Washington, D.C., to York Harbor, Maine, they were betrothed. Page gave Florence three engagement rings, the two extra being for Minna and

Florence, saying that they were now all linked together. With the royalties from *Gordon Keith,* he later gave each stepdaughter a tiny string of pearls with the card, "With love, your Dad and *Gordon Keith.*"[60]

The Field-Page wedding took place in Byrd's Nest Chapel on June 6, 1893, with Florence's little daughters as attendants. For her second marriage she wore a gown of yellow corded silk covered with blue chiffon trimmed in yellow cord and white lace. To avoid a public spectacle, only sixty relatives and close friends of the couple were present, but they included Mrs. Charles M. Bruce and her daughter Sallie Archer Bruce, of Virginia, the mother and sister of Page's first wife. Following a wedding trip to Canada and a short visit to Oakland plantation, the Pages took up residence in Washington, D.C.[61]

Victorian courtships and marriages were never as simple as they appeared, and so it was with the Page-Field relationship. While "companionate" marriages, in which emotion, love, and affection were the dominant motives for the union, were becoming more frequent as the nineteenth century progressed, a significant proportion of Victorian marriages did not take place from love primarily or even at all, but from some interested motive, such as wealth, social position, home and family considerations, or other advantage.[62] The marriage of Florence and Thomas Nelson Page was more complex. In Florence's view love, affection, and respect had weighed equally with economic and status considerations to make her first marriage successful. But now she had other considerations to ponder, including the impact of a second marriage on her wealth, social position, and children.[63] As a widow, she already enjoyed considerable independence and autonomy from male dominance; would she continue to do so with a new husband? In matters pertaining to her daughters, she exercised the dominant voice. Would that also continue? Under existing law, both her wealth and control over her daughters could be jeopardized by the choice of a wrong or unscrupulous mate. On the other hand, she also stood to benefit by being the spouse, and therefore under the protection, of a genteel and cultured male, one who might become a surrogate father to her young daughters.

Florence's relationship with her second husband, then, must be viewed in a different light from her first marriage. At the time she wed Thomas Nelson Page, she was thirty-five, widowed, wealthy, and had completed her family; he was forty, also widowed, of impeccable ancestry and repute but of modest financial means and without an heir. Their relationship together never produced a child of their own, although each was well within the age to have done so. Either they consciously chose to forgo creating their own family (which might be considered an odd decision given Page's illustrious lineage but would be further evidence of Florence's empowerment in the sexual arena) and were practicing contraception, or Page was incapable of siring his own offspring—either with Anne Seddon or with Florence. At the same time Page never sought legally to adopt Florence's young daughters, despite his very deep affection for them. For Florence at least, marriage to Thomas Nelson Page appears to have constituted a bargain; she chose companionship over passion. Sexuality was not the ultimate secret of her genuinely happy marriage to him (although each would develop over time considerable affection for the other), but friendship, conversation, and proper attention to each other in public were.

Page, by contrast, craved financial security, social position, and prominence, which Florence's wealth and background would bring into marriage. He and his family had the name, the land, and the social connections in Virginia society, but they did not have very many liquid assets in the aftermath of Reconstruction. Access to Florence's wealth could provide this in abundance.[64] Only a single Page letter survives from this prenuptial period, but the language provides an insight into Victorian courtship practices. Page's self-admitted "sudden attraction" to the young widow suggests that motives besides love and affection might well have been in his thoughts when he proposed marriage to Florence.

Page's letter of April 21, 1893, is addressed to his former mother-in-law, Mrs. Charles M. Bruce, of Staunton Hill, in Charlotte County, Virginia. Page wanted "to confide everything" to her "as your own son," whereupon he told her that he had "found a sweet woman who has been good enough to undertake to make me happy again and to entrust her happiness to me." Having informed Mrs. Bruce of his intention to remarry, he quickly reassured her of his love for her "as a son," stating, "I shall always claim for me and mine my own place in your heart and home." As further proof of his continuing loyalty, he declared: "You can never be anything to me but my dear, dear mother and no time and no change of condition can make any difference with me. I can never forget my beloved whom you gave me and whose memory will always be with me."[65]

Ever the cavalier, Page had told Florence of his love for Anne, "and she has promised never to be jealous of her memory." Indeed, Florence had entrusted him with a letter for Mrs. Bruce which Page thought would "serve to tell you what she is, and what a lovely character she possesses," adding quickly, "but you will have to know her to appreciate her sweetness and goodness." His decision to remarry had been rather sudden, he admitted, "for though I have known her for more than a year, and she is indeed a connection of mine, being a niece of my cousin, Mrs. Thomas Bryan who is Hugh R. Page's sister, yet it is only within the last two or three weeks that I have come to care for her."[66]

Florence's own note to Mrs. Bruce was tender, loving, and sincere, but it also was a masterpiece of diplomacy in that it neutralized a potential adversary. While she was overjoyed at the prospect of marrying Page, she knew that it would cause Mrs. Bruce great anguish, bringing as it did a final reminder of her daughter's premature death. She promised to strive "with all my heart to win some small corner in your affections, and to make you feel that you shall never have any less of Tom's love than you have now." She assured her that her "dear daughter's name shall ever be sacred in my keeping as well as his." If this had not yet won over Page's mother-in-law, Florence's last sentence certainly was designed to. Alluding to her own tragic losses, she closed, "I have had so much sorrow in my life, that this new happiness makes me long to put my arms around you, and tell you I know all that you have suffered, and hope I may be able someday to bring back some of the sunshine into your life." Signed, "Your friend."[67]

Besides wealth, breeding, and social position, one other quality—and this would have been very important to the courtly Virginian—attracted Page to Florence: her unwillingness not to challenge openly the prevailing doctrine of "True Womanhood."[68] In Page's eyes Florence possessed the virtues of piety, purity, submissiveness, and domesticity. He revealed this in an unpublished biographical sketch that he wrote of Florence shortly after her death in 1921, wherein he employed the metaphor of the angel to portray Florence. She had saved him from darkness following the death of his first wife—"She was . . . a ray of light of especial radiance"; "When she entered she was transfigured and the light came with her and appeared to be reflected in the faces of those she approached the instant their eyes fell on her"—she was the perfect housewife—"Everything had its place and everything was kept in its place"; "She rose early and conserved her time allotting with precision the amount of time necessary for each task or matter which had her attention. Her household was conducted on the same principle of precision and promptitude"; "Or if she were alone she read while her busy fingers applied the needles as though mechanically"—she was pure of heart—"She instinctively took sides and, as for the good of the world, as good women do, she took the side of her heart"—and she was pious— "She was not only deeply religious, with a childlike and unquestioning faith . . . but her Religion was one of love and kindness and of a quality too deep to be bared to the light." Florence "possessed an intuitive faculty" and "was a most generous giver," two characteristics which nineteenth-century males attributed to the True Woman. Above all, she accepted the principle of separate masculine and feminine spheres, especially in the area of politics—"Deeply interested in public life and completely versed in its history and principles, she shrank from any relation to it save the old-fashioned one—that her mother or grandmother might have had. In the modern Woman's movement she took no practical part or interest . . . confining herself to her private and personal duties. She shunned all outward show."[69]

Page's remembrance of his wife was a remarkable document as much for what it disclosed about himself and the ideological prism through which he, the courtly southern gentleman, perceived women of her class and status as for its full and complete characterization of Florence Lathrop Page. His description is idiosyncratic and highly selective but virtually identical to the metaphor of women's sphere in its ascription to Florence of the cardinal virtues of domesticity, piety, purity, and submissiveness. Nearly half a century before scholars were using the term *True Womanhood* and noting the tendency of southern males to place their ladies upon a pedestal—viewing them as pure and noble (spared the earthly pleasure of fornication), pious and humble, whose homes were "havens in a heartless world" Thomas Nelson Page had summoned his considerable literary skills to draw such a portrait of his wife.[70]

The portrait he drew was of an ideal type, not necessarily the actual woman. Gone was the strong-willed, assertive, and independent Florence Page, who had shared in decision making with her husbands; who, though widowed, had successfully raised two daughters from youth to adulthood and families of their own; who had nursed Page through bouts of nervous exhaustion; who had managed two separate households, the social functions of the American Embassy in Rome, to advance her husband's literary and political careers and membership in international café society; and who, though a practicing Episcopalian, had been neither maudlin about religion nor above criticizing an American bishop for delivering a poor sermon or the Church of England for maintaining more prebendaries than it could possibly afford, even as it was driving away parishioners.

If Florence assumed "no practical part or interest" in "the modern Woman's movement," as Page delicately referred to the strident fight to achieve women's suffrage and the other Progressive era reforms affecting women, it was not because of disinterest. She was a major beneficiary of the status quo and had no need of the franchise whereas extending the vote to working- and lower-class women would have further unleashed the masses in politics, which contravened her class interest. Like a large number of women of her class and affluence, she did not possess a sense of gender-consciousness, a feeling of solidarity with other females which transcended considerations of class and wealth. Her goals were more private, more personal and family-oriented: the children's welfare, the health and safety of her grandchildren, the family's financial well-being, the Pages' membership in international café society, and the ambassadorial career of Thomas Nelson Page. Florence was not like the aristocratic educational reformer Lucy Sprague Mitchell, but neither did she ever have the problem that Mitchell faced of how to reconcile the sometimes irreconcilable and competing claims of family, marriage, and satisfying work.[71]

Women's suffrage probably would not have affected Florence's political and material interest for the better, whereas social feminism might well have been counterproductive. Hence, she never confronted the phenomenon of separate spheres directly. Instead, she overtly conformed to the dictates of patriarchy but enlisted her economic independence, class, and social status to escape the usual consequences attending arguments about the essential differences between males and females that a patriarchal society used to justify continuing patterns of male dominance and female subordination. In doing so, Florence softened the boundaries between the spheres to enhance her own arena of decision making.

However complex their individual motives for marrying a second time, the union of Florence and Thomas Nelson Page marked the close of one period of their lives and the beginning of another. Page moved his residence from Richmond to Washington, D.C., gave up his law practice entirely, and abandoned a budding career as a Chautauqua lecturer. By 1910 he also had given up a serious literary career for the life of the leisured gentleman that occupied him until 1913 when Florence's wealth made possible his acceptance of an ambassadorship. She in turn left Chicago behind to take up residence with her daughters and new husband in the District of Columbia.

The reasons that dictated their choice of Washington are not altogether clear, but the decision was a mutual one, and to that extent it further demonstrated Florence's enhanced autonomy and status within marriage. Rosewell Page, her new brother-in-law, believed it to be a compromise between Chicago and Richmond; it may have been a shared decision not to begin their life together in a place haunted by memories of earlier marriages. Whatever the reasons, the Federal City afforded Thomas Nelson Page the recognition and social status he had sought. He broadened his interest in Virginia politics to encompass the national political scene and eventually international affairs.[72] Florence, by contrast, remained discreetly in the background, avoiding public attention while advancing her family's welfare and the interests and career of her husband.[73]

2

Family
and Values

*W*ashington society found the Pages a pleasant, sophisticated addition to their circle. Thomas Nelson Page became a member of the city's most prestigious clubs, including the Metropolitan, the Chevy Chase, the Cosmos, and the Alibi. In New York City, where he traveled frequently to visit his publisher, Scribner's, he also held membership in the leading clubs, including the Authors, the Century, and the University.[1] Florence entertained frequently in part because she delighted in doing so and in part to promote her husband's interests. At the Pages' "little dinners," presidents Theodore Roosevelt and William Howard Taft and other prominent men knowledgeable in world events, national affairs, and recent history mingled with artists, writers, and scientists. David Fairchild, the distinguished plant pathologist of the University of Wisconsin and friend of Barbour Lathrop, visited the Pages on one occasion and reported afterward that he had made his "social debut in Washington. . . . His [Barbour Lathrop's] sister, Mrs. Thomas Nelson Page, had perhaps the most brilliant salon in the Capitol."[2]

In an early 1910 letter to her mother-in-law, Elizabeth Burwell Page, Florence described her typical social calendar. Following the usual round of Christmas and New Year's festivities, she had received some old friends for tea. Then her daughter Florence (now Florence Field Lindsay) came down from Southboro, Massachusetts, with the Pages' granddaughter Minna for an extended visit. She and Florence Lindsay attended performances of the visiting Metropolitan Opera Company of New York on four successive nights, which Florence Page confessed was a bit much but excused by noting that "the opera is such a rarity with us in Washington."[3]

After the holidays, the Pages were to entertain English friends, the Herbert Wards, who would be arriving with their two daughters and maid. Ward had once served as a technical assistant with Stanley in Africa.[4] They were expected to visit for at least three weeks, during which Florence would host a large reception in their honor, followed by a number of small dinners and a luncheon or two. She scheduled a dinner party for twenty-two guests for January 18, followed by one equally large on February 1. Between luncheons, teas, and dinners, Florence reserved Wednesdays for her Italian lesson, which was inspired by her love of Italian art, sculpture, and antiquity. In March the Pages would take "their usual trip somewhere," most likely to Jekyll Island off the coast of Georgia, possibly accompanied by the Wards. Later that spring Florence would travel to Southboro to visit her daughter, son-in-law Tom Lindsay, and granddaughter Minna.[5]

Her tightly crowded social calendar was typical of other elite women's. Beneath the peripatetic quality of this lifestyle there was a kind of natural rhythm: one was in residence in the fall and the winter and was expected to entertain relatives and friends and be invited to the right social functions; after the Christmas holiday, one escaped the depths of winter by retreating to a place of milder climate such as Jekyll Island, Santa Barbara or Cuba; in the summer one escaped the congested city by retreating to the mountains or the seashore. At any time of the year, however, the elite upper class might travel abroad, often to Europe but sometimes to Africa or other exotic destinations.[6]

The Pages adhered to this cycle with remarkable fidelity before the outbreak of World War I in 1914. As members of international café society, they regularly visited London, Paris, the Riviera, Rome, and even Egypt, but never in the summer. Florence reserved summer, beginning in May or June and lasting until October, for Rock Ledge, her beloved "cottage" located in exclusive York Harbor, Maine.

This hectic social calendar, centered around family, kin, and friends, obscured a more serious side to Florence which she carefully shielded from public view because of her innate modesty and to protect herself from the pecuniary demands of strangers. Besides being a cordial hostess, she quietly and with little public awareness made financial contributions to social betterment programs, artistic and cultural institutions, educational programs, and religious endeavors. She gave generously to establish public health nursing programs in Washington, Chicago, York Harbor, and Hanover County, Virginia. She also made a handsome contribution to the endowments of the Associated Charities of the District of Columbia; contributed regularly to the Chicago Symphony Orchestra, which was a favorite project of her brother Bryan Lathrop, and to the Art Institute of Chicago; endowed the Page-Barbour Lectures at the University of Virginia; and contributed to St. John's Parish in Washington and other Episcopal churches.[7]

These and similar activities formed a pattern which remained constant throughout Florence's life. Noblesse oblige, which in its American context meant that successful citizens owed a dual obligation of time and money to the communities in which they have prospered, was very commonly upheld by men and women of America's upper class.[8] Florence Lathrop Page, like many upper-class women of the Victorian era who did not seek gainful employment or a career outside of home and family, lived that combination of society, charity, and pursuit of culture which defined the leisured woman's role. The only deviation was that in her case charity consisted of donating money rather than time to a worthy cause.

Florence's freedom to entertain and to engage in community and voluntary activities, to be a patron of culture and the arts, to shop, to engage in self-improvement, and to maintain large winter and summer residences depended on the availability of other women and men to do the ordinary chores of housework. Like other affluent women she enjoyed the privileges of her class and gained relative freedom by exploiting the labor of lower-class, immigrant Irish and French-Canadian sleep-in women and men.[9] Wherever the Pages were in residence or when they were traveling abroad, they usually were accompanied and assisted by servants and retainers, among whom were their faithful valet, chauffeur, and factotum, Alfred, and Florence's French maid.

The problem of maintaining a cadre of servants could be vexatious. By mutual agreement Florence disciplined the household staff and did the hiring and firing. She held strong views about the type of people in her employ. During World War I she considered all German servants to be "disloyal," and writing from Rome, she urged her friends to discharge them, even as she would not employ them. Italian servants were "good and pleasant" in Italy, but they did not "flourish as domestic servants in America." Devoid of any real comprehension of the struggle of ordinary people without her advantages, she nonetheless foresaw that after the war there would be "a great problem getting people at home for all manner of work." But she refused "to cross that bridge of troubles yet."[10]

To her daughter Minna she often complained of the "servant and labor question" that she expected to confront upon returning to the United States at the completion of Page's ambassadorial duties. Such references to the labor question and the servant problem indicate that Florence, perhaps earlier than others of her privileged status, recognized the profoundly disruptive impact that World War I would have upon the advantages her social class had long taken for granted, even as she sought to postpone that day of reckoning.

The crowded social schedule, built as it often was around her husband's ambitions and interests, the cultural and charitable activities and the servant problem fall within the public persona of Florence Lathrop Page. The more significant and ultimately the more illuminating dimension of Florence Page's character was the private persona. What did she value most; what was her relationship to her family; what did she think about her children; how did she respond to such transcendent and transforming experiences as birth, death, education, or religion? Her views on these and related matters provide insights into her character and the attitudes of typically elite upper-class women.

Widowed at thirty-two, Florence was to encounter death many times in her life. Within the space of a relatively short period, she endured successive tragedies: the Fields' youngest daughter, Gladys, who was born in March 1888, survived for only eight months; Florence's father, Jedediah Lathrop, died on May 24, 1890; her husband, Henry Field, died later that year; Mariana Bryan Lathrop, her mother, died in October 1893.[11] After a short hiatus, the litany of the deaths of kin, relatives, friends, and acquaintances—many old, some young—continued to be noted in her correspondence. In 1906 her brother-in-law Marshall Field, with whom she had a cordial but not necessarily close tie, died; Elizabeth Burwell Page, her mother-in-law, was gone in 1912; four years later her beloved brother Bryan succumbed; and, finally, in 1918 Frank Page, her husband's older brother, died.

Each death of a loved one was a reminder to Florence of her own mortality, especially as she became a mature woman herself. When Elizabeth Burwell Page died, she wrote to Rosewell and Ruth Page: "While our recent experience was harrowing, and hard to accept, I would not give up one hour of the glorious example set me, and the privilege of being with the dear family around the hallowed bed. I never thought that Death could be made so beautiful—. . . but in the order of things it had to be." Death was inevitable, but a good death to the Victorians was ennobling to the deceased and a didactic experience for the survivors; it offered the latter a model to emulate. In May 1917, upon the first anniversary of Bryan's death, Florence wrote to Helen Lathrop, "I know all that this day means to you, and I cannot realize that it is one year ago since that perfect life was ended." Bryan's legacy was the noble life he had led, "and how poorer were the living for his not now being with us." She attributed everything good in herself to her brother as role model: "He was my idol; my ideal; my example."[12]

Like other upper-class Victorian women, Florence confronted death, but within a set of religious beliefs which gave it meaning apart from the natural world. A devout Episcopalian and frequent churchgoer, she believed in Jesus's message of the Resurrection. When notified in Rome in 1918 of the peaceful passing of Frank Page, she wrote to her sister-in-law Ruth that the agony of suffering, death, and destruction of the war around her "make peaceful death seem but a gentle transition to the next world, where all loved ones are awaiting us, and where the sorrows of this life are unknown."[13]

Grief was an emotion to be borne stoically and privately and to serve as an ennobling example to the survivors. When Helen Lathrop sent her a pair of cuff link studs as a memento of Bryan, Florence responded that she had "never allowed herself to grieve, because I know that he would not have me" do so. She then added, "You are so brave and noble in keeping your great sorrow to yourself, and in constantly doing for others, that you are reaping a rich reward in countless friends and setting an example for us all to follow." In other correspondence she emphasized that she did not think of the sad departure of loved ones but dwelt only on the happy memories of them. "[E]ver since precious little Florence's remark about its being 'silly to keep looking at photos of people who are dead because they make you sad every time,' I have had something of the same feeling, and strange to say don't look so often as before at those of darling Uncle Bryan," she wrote to her daughter Florence. In this, she was following her husband's advice: "But Tom is right when he says not to keep these anniversaries; to try to skip over the sad dates in life, and to cling to the joyous ones that we had with our loved ones," she told Helen.[14] This was the mature Florence Lathrop Page, a woman in her late fifties conscious of her own mortality, who wrote these words. Given the ever-present threat of illness, disease, and death in the nineteenth and early twentieth centuries, it is reasonable to presume that these thoughts were conditioned by her many experiences with the death of loved ones, including Henry Field, who was snatched from her suddenly in the prime of his life.

Death, whether of a daughter, a husband, parents, or relatives and friends, while profoundly traumatic because of the emotional, psychological, and physical voids it created in her life, also transformed and empowered Florence. She emerged from these experiences a stronger, self-reliant, and independent woman: the new "patriarch" of the Field family. And while she drew support and sustenance from her brother, Florence alone made the fundamental, life-directing decisions for Minna and Florence until they struck out on their own paths, a practice which continued even after she had remarried.

If death was a constant reminder of one's mortality, so too was birth. The late nineteenth century was the era of the child, the time when families became child-centered, emotional bonds between parents and children intensified, and responsibility for giving children a proper start in life was transferred from the father to the mother. Elite upper-class women, above all else, invested large amounts of their time and energies in their children, and many, especially Florence, remained closely involved with them long after the children were grown, married, and had families of their own.[15]

Florence Lathrop Page's personal values, beliefs, and emotions, as they touched upon the dynamics of the parent-child relationship, may illuminate more fully the upper-class family experience. The task of reconstructing this relationship is a bit precarious because Florence's correspondence from the years when she was married to Henry Field and bore his offspring has not survived. What we know about her role as wife, mother, and parent, which encompasses her views on marriage, sex, family, and childrearing, dates primarily from her later years, after Minna and Florence were grown and no longer lived under Florence's roof. Despite this caveat, the evidence suggests that her perspective on these matters did not change in any fundamental way over the span of her life. Indeed, there is a remarkable consistency in her outlook.

Education was a matter of serious concern to Florence. She herself was of the generation wherein upper-class women did not attend school or university but received private tutoring at home. As was typical of elite families, when daughters reached a certain age (unlike sons for whom college was accessible), they were sent abroad to gain the accoutrements of culture. Florence had studied French and art privately in Paris and Nice for a few months each year over a four-year period. She had gained fluency in the language and an appreciation of fine art which contributed to her cosmopolitan view of the world and her future life-style. It also contributed to her interest in education, which in the nineteenth century had become a feminine sphere, but her perception of the function of education for women was classbound; it was less to acquire a useful skill for competing in the market-place than it was to gain the trappings of culture that made a woman a proper wife and mother. In 1919 she sought to impress upon her daughter Florence the necessity of her granddaughters learning a foreign language. "You ought to start the little girls on their French as soon as possible; it is so much harder to acquire the older they grow; and it is a necessity now to be familiar with that language," she wrote.[16] French was the lingua franca of the cosmopolitan, international upper-class elite. As the children grew older, Florence also advised that they learn other languages, even as she had learned Italian.

The implication of Florence's remarks was that her daughter should follow her own parents' practice. She was not recommending that they learn languages to enhance their future career choices or employment opportunities but to give them the proper tools to function in the world of the international elite. Happily, she was not doctrinaire or rigidly bound to a particular pedagogy. Her mind was receptive to any methodology that would benefit children. Her letter to her younger daughter in 1913 recounting her encounter in Rome with Maria Montessori, whose work with feebleminded children had recently become well publicized, was indicative. She had met the famous physician at a dinner party of an American married to an Italian aristocrat shortly before she was to embark upon a speaking tour of the United States. Florence urged her daughter to attend one of her lectures, if possible, adding, "If we can in any way simplify study and yet develop well-educated persons, it will indeed be a boon to humanity."[17]

If Florence's letters to her daughters are indicative, her attitudes toward sexuality, drinking, and marriage were quite typical of the late nineteenth-century Victorian era. Furthermore, with the exception of divorce and remarriage, they changed very little as other Americans were moving into the modern period of the twentieth century. Florence adhered to the code that sexuality must be kept under wraps, many and voluminous, as is evident from her reaction to a play which the children of the British Embassy staff in Rome produced in January 1919. Florence was not a stranger to the theater or the opera, but her tastes ran toward musicals and the classics. On this occasion she was thoroughly chagrined and departed even before the performance had concluded. The next day she wrote to her daughter Florence and complained: "I never saw a greater display of naked arms, shoulders, and backs in my life. The only thing that kept it from being hopeless, was the fronts [which were] were modest." The girls "were shaved like actresses, so that they could be bare, and it made me blush for their mothers!" This tirade against immodesty was out of proportion to the situation, for she went on to declare: "Art nouveau, *vers libre,* all the rest of modern nakedness is accepted by some people, and it may be that any puritanical prudishness is now obsolete. But heaven help the children on their stony paths!"[18]

Florence's assault was directed only in part against nudity. The real object of her scorn was what she perceived to be the loosening of public moral standards in the contemporary world. Women imbibing liquor openly and excessively, like public displays of nakedness, offended her and had no place in her value system. This was clear from her letter of August 15, 1916, to Florence in which she related the gist of a note from Minna, who had been told on good authority that "drinking had become perfectly terrible in America, and that women were getting to be as bad as men." Increased alcohol consumption among women was symptomatic of the social upheaval between the sexes attendant upon the war. Florence was not against drinking per se and she took it for granted that men would drink, but women drinking alcohol in public frontally assaulted the male prerogative, thereby diminishing their opinion of the other sex. Where alcoholic consumption and women were concerned, Florence held a fairly conventional view, one which idealized women. Of course, she was not blind to changing attitudes toward women and alcohol, but she was unhappy nonetheless. "I have been dreading it for some time, ever since the cocktail custom, and free whiskey and soda became a fashion for the lively sets of men and women. I felt it fast creeping on at York and elsewhere; and now here [in Rome] it is being discussed." It was "a sorry state of things, and a disgraceful one," she wrote, adding, "Our women had the enviable position of being high minded, clean minded, and honorable as a whole, not invariably of course; but to have sunk so low as to be spoken of with disgust, is very depressing."[19]

As with female libation, the Victorian mentality insisted on the utmost privacy and thus the utmost sanctity of sexuality (including nudity) within marriage. Florence Page manifested this attitude in her perception of childbearing. Procreation was an obligation of women, a function to be endured but not necessarily enjoyed. She, like other Victorians, likened the birthing process to illness and recovery, wherein a woman went into confinement ("as though she were ill") and then emerged joyful in the knowledge that she had fulfilled her wifely function. In June 1910, while the Pages were in London, they received a cable from Tom Lindsay announcing that Florence had given birth to their second child, a daughter whom they named after her maternal great-grandmother, Mariana Lathrop. Florence informed her mother-in-law, Elizabeth Burwell Page, of the birth, and her choice of language was indicative of how she perceived the birthing process. "You can imagine our joy when a cable came announcing another dear little girl baby, *after only one hour and a half illness*," she wrote. Continuing the analogy, she proclaimed joyfully, "It is a pleasure to be thinking of my dear Florence as *gaining* each day." [20]

Physical separation of parent from child was also a painful process to the Victorians, but it was frequently viewed as part of the life process. When Florence's younger daughter was seventeen years of age, she dispatched her to Europe for the winter to finish her education. In doing so, she was emulating her own parents who had sent her to Paris for four winters. But separation from her daughter was as painful to Florence as it must have been to her own dear mother, Mariana Lathrop, although she did it stoically and for her child's benefit. "Parents have to make sacrifices for their children, and this was the greatest I could make," she declared. "I trust only good will come of this winter's experience. We acted for the best, and we both feel sure we did what was right." [21]

Enforced separation continued to be painful to Florence even after her daughters had married and established their own homes. In May 1910 she wrote, "This having children living so far apart, keeps a mother's heart always more or less anxious; but God is so good and merciful, I am trusting all to Him; and try not to let my mind dwell upon anything but the bright and hopeful side." [22] This naive, childlike optimism was sorely tried with the outbreak of World War I and the worldwide influenza epidemic of 1916–18. Florence's letters then took on an almost desperate, urgent tone as she awaited the latest correspondence from her daughters. She found herself situated in Rome for nearly six years as the wife of the American ambassador; Minna and her son were in England, while Florence Lindsay remained alone in Southboro, Massachusetts, with three young children (including a newborn) after Tom went to war in 1917. Only short visits to and from Minna and her grandson made the separation bearable; her younger daughter she saw briefly only once in this same period.

Despite the enormous advantages of wealth and class, Florence did not have the perfect family life. Her relationships with her daughters were uneven, characterized by excessive outpourings of love, affection, intense anxiety, and occasionally tension. Physically separated from them during the war years, Florence maintained a more relaxed, open, and warmly cordial relationship with her younger daughter, Florence Field Lindsay, than she did with Minna, her older daughter. Although she would have been the first to deny any such qualitative difference, the evidence is clear. The letters she wrote to Florence Lindsay—she referred to them as her "diary"—are much more candid and revealing than the correspondence with Minna, which impresses the reader as more circumspect and guarded. In the letters she poured out the emotional and physical pain of a mother separated from her children and grandchildren, and she freely confessed her inability to rein in her emotions.[23]

The wartime separation from her younger daughter was occasioned by the hazards of crossing the Atlantic in submarine-threatened waters. Florence discouraged her daughter from attempting to cross the seas to visit, even during the period of American neutrality. She did so with great anguish, however. During the first winter of the conflict, she wrote: "The only thing that makes Christmas seem possible this year, is the excitement among the Embassy children over the promised tree I am going to give them on the afternoon of Christmas Eve. As one can't have the joy of our own happy old times, it is best to turn to other people's happiness, and try theirs." She felt keenly not being able to see her grandchildren, to experience the joy of watching them grow into adolescence; she missed the excitement of being present for the birth of grandson John Lindsay in 1916. "I suppose they will seem very old to us, when we next see them," she wrote, "and it will be like knowing them over again; still their precious little faces don't change as much as their height, and to me they will be my babies for many a day to come." John was nearly three years old when she finally did see him, and the girls older still.[24]

No matter how great the distance, the doting grandmother never forgot the important milestones in the lives of her grandchildren. In 1916 she sent Florence a check for a considerable sum to engage a carpenter to build a playhouse as a joint birthday present for granddaughters Minna and Mariana. "Get to work at once and see what can be built and furnished in great simplicity for $500," she wrote. She could barely contain her own enthusiasm for the project and had very definite ideas about how it should proceed. "You must have something colonial, of course, and a place for a tiny garden, both flower and vegetable. For $500, you ought to be able to have a little kitchen beside the main room." "Keep it all very simple, and you will succeed," she declared. "I am quite as excited as my babies will be over it."[25]

If Florence was the warm, caring, and loving mother and grandmother ever solicitous of the family's well-being, she also could assume the matriarchal role: the mother who directed her offspring down the proper paths of life. She offered parental guidance lovingly but inoffensively—to Florence, at least! During the bleak winter of 1916, she gently admonished her younger daughter for not taking proper care of her health. "I can't say much for your sense, to have gone out with one of your rheumatic throats, which from past experience, you ought to know always is the beginning of something serious," she wrote. "You are all a little mad all the time about paying attention to your health, and quite mad when you insist upon going out with a cold already upon you." What prompted Florence's concern (which also made her "tremble about dear Uncle Bryan") were the "lamentable tales" filtering back to Rome from acquaintances in New York about grippe, pneumonia, and influenza in the States.[26]

The same matriarch who admonished her daughter to safeguard her health also was capable of counseling Florence and Tom, as young marrieds, to step out, socialize, and enjoy life. "I have it borne in upon me how important it is not to cut yourself off from so many normal amusements while you are young," she observed. This last may have been an oblique reference to her widowhood at the young age of thirty-two, but it also was a direct reference to Florence's elder daughter, Minna, who was living an isolated existence in England with her son while husband Algernon Burnaby had gone off to the war. "I see how set Minna is upon going nowhere, seeing no one except her few intimates, and doing nothing but play golf, drive a car, or hunt," she wrote.[27]

This relatively innocuous statement masked the loving but frequently difficult dealings that Florence had with her elder daughter.

Even though it does not appear so in Florence's letters to Minna, their relationship often was strained and tense, and it was certainly the leitmotiv of her correspondence with Florence Lindsay. In January 1918, for example, Florence advised her younger daughter to be patient with her eldest child, also named Minna, who was demanding and difficult and possibly even hyperactive. In counseling patience Florence shifted her point of reference abruptly from her granddaughter to her daughter Minna. "You know I had my own trials at one time, and I also recall that I was criticized as having been mistaken in my management, and not having understood her character," she wrote. "I agree that my own bringing up and ideals made it very hard for me to reconcile the strong headed self-willed young lady as my own child." She, nonetheless, had continued in a gentle way to proffer motherly advice to Minna, hoping optimistically that she would accept it: "And while I know that one letter can't turn the tide, still constant dropping of wise words, may help to wear away the obstinacy." Minna was recovering at the time from a bout with the influenza, and her physician had prescribed tender loving care. He even told Algy not to contradict Minna in anything. "This has made us smile," Florence declared, "for I can't help thinking that our dear Minna has pretty generally had her own way in life."[28]

One source of tension between mother and daughter was Minna's first marriage in 1900. She was just seventeen at the time, a petite brunette who attended the usual round of debutante balls, luncheons, and teas. Following the practice of the eastern establishment, Florence had sent her to a select boarding school, the fashionable Masters School in Dobbs Ferry, New York, with the expectation that Minna, as one of the younger generation would be acculturated into an upper-class style of life and would identify with the particular standards of her class. Minna threw a wrench into her mother's plans when she eloped with Preston Gibson, a young football hero, twenty-one years old and a junior at Yale, who had played in the o-o tie of 1899 with Harvard. The elopement was formalized afterward in a very discreet church ceremony in New York City, but it confounded Florence's purpose in sending her to the exclusive private school and wrecked her plan to present Minna to polite society the next winter.[29]

The match under other circumstances might have been an eminently suitable one, for Preston was the son of Senator Randall L. Gibson of Louisiana and the nephew of Chief Justice Edward D. White of the United States Supreme Court. Besides coming from a highly respectable family, he was a matriculant at a prestigious Ivy League college, a member of certain exclusive fraternities and clubs, and a football hero to boot. Preston was also a rake, and no doubt the young, impetuous Minna was infatuated with him. After the marriage Florence persuaded her brother Bryan to employ Gibson in his real estate business in Chicago. Bryan informed Florence on June 7, 1900, that "Preston is at work in the office every day and seems to like it, which is a very good sign, since he has not had much work to do in this life." But the life of an office worker proved too staid and dull for the football hero; Gibson left the real estate business to pursue an unsuccessful career in New York as a playwright.[30]

Even though the marriage produced a grandson, Henry Field Gibson, who was born in December 1902, the match ended badly. On October 11, 1907, Florence wrote to her husband from New York City where she was visiting Minna that Preston had been behaving erratically and that she was afraid to leave her daughter and grandchild alone with him. "Minna," she declared, "is nervous and under a severe strain, and it is pitiful to see her with her child." Not until her younger daughter agreed to come to New York to accompany Minna and Henry back to Southboro did Florence return to Washington. The marriage continued to deteriorate until the two divorced later that year.[31]

The dissolution of Minna's marriage was a relief for all concerned, but it pained Florence because of her own traditional view of marriage and the mutual obligations of spouses. That it left a lasting scar is clear from a letter she wrote to Minna in October 1918. Dispirited about the progress of the war, Florence turned to family matters, writing: "You can never know the joy you are to my soul, and how devoutly I thank God for the blessing of having you to turn to at all times; for you *are* understanding, and you know just the right thing to do. This is not meant to be my last will and testament, but just a tribute to a darling child *who has wiped away all the tears of former days, and brought a grateful mother to her side to, in her turn, help her whenever she is needed.* God bless you my child for all that you are and mean to me."[32]

The tension between Florence and Minna was part of the age-old intergenerational conflict wherein the daughter—the child—needs to break from the parent—the authority figure—in order to establish her own independence. Why one daughter should do so but not the other remains a mystery to psychiatrists even today. The paradox is that whereas Florence either did not or refused to see this process at work in her relationship with Minna, she recognized perfectly clearly the need of her grandson, Minna's child, to go through the same experience with his mother in order for him to become "a man." The difference may have been that Florence, given her own upbringing, viewed it as more natural that a son should separate from his father—even more so in the case of a matriarch—than that a daughter should separate from a mother.

After the break up of her marriage, Minna sailed to Europe to recuperate from the emotional trauma. While she was in England, she met the man who would become her new husband, Algernon ("Algy") Burnaby, of Baggrave Hall, Leicestershire. A member of the court-connected gentry and friend of the Prince of Wales, Burnaby traced his lineage to the sixteenth century and included among his ancestors members of the Privy Council, Parliamentarians, military heroes, and clergymen. The family's coat of arms, which denoted that the Burnabys were of the armorial gentry, consisted of a lion passant-gardant between two bars, upon a green crest with a demi-man holding a bunch of bluebells in his right hand, and inscribed with the motto *Pro rege.* An outdoorsman who loved to hunt, fish, golf, and play tennis, Burnaby received his education at Sandhurst and Oxford Military College. His first wife, whom he married in 1890 and divorced in 1902, was Lady Sybil Cholmondeley, the only daughter of the second Baron Delamere.[33]

In all matters that were important to the Pages—family, wealth, social status, and education—Minna's new fiancé was eminently acceptable. He possessed all the attributes that Florence admired in a gentleman, despite the fact that he was divorced and, at age forty, nearly fifteen years older than Minna. Florence wrote to her mother-in-law in Virginia informing her of the impending nuptials, and assuring her that Burnaby was "a man of character, birth and breeding, is intelligent, well educated, and has cultivated refined tastes." The age difference may actually have been a boon in this instance, because she noted that Algy had "seen more of life than Minna," implying that he might exercise a stablizing influence upon her daughter's impulsive behavior. Best of all, the couple loved each other, a quality which Florence deemed essential to a successful marriage.[34]

Minna's marriage to Burnaby affords us a glimpse into the lifestyle of the elite. More importantly, it provides a further insight into Florence Page's values regarding marriage, divorce, childrearing, and education. Having declared the criteria for a suitable husband to be manliness, intelligence, good manners, and independent means—the qualities of the Christian gentleman of the Victorian era—Florence noted that a mutual acquaintance had recently struck out in her choice of husbands. "He has good manners, if you care for the kind, and is pleasant enough; but not quite a man. Not a fool, only an ass," she wrote in a devastating commentary.[35] More than she realized, Florence adhered to a double standard: a wife had to be younger than her husband, be natural and not affected, and rein in her intelligence or, as she wrote to her daughter Florence, be "a quiet, old fashioned lady like her aunt," Helen Aldis Lathrop.[36] Given her own experience, the last comment suggests that Florence continued to adhere to the belief that a woman should not frontally assault the phenomenon of separate spheres by openly flaunting her intelligence but that she should outflank it by working around its edges to achieve her own purposes.

That both Minna and Algy were divorced and that both ex-spouses still were alive could have been another source of tension between mother and daughter. Even though divorce was a more common phenomenon within the upper class by the turn of the century, and Florence accepted it in principle, she did not believe a divorced person should remarry while the former spouse was still alive. In 1901, when informed that a female acquaintance was about to marry a divorced man, she wrote to her mother-in-law: "How a nice woman can bring herself to marry any man who has a divorced wife living, baffles my comprehension."[37] Yet when Minna was about to take the same step, she kept such reservations to herself. She may have reasoned, and quite probably correctly given her daughter's headstrong nature, that it would do no good to express them.[38]

Nonetheless, Minna's totally unanticipated announcement that she intended to marry Algy caused the Pages apprehension. On May 18, 1908, Thomas Nelson Page, speaking for himself and his wife, wrote to Burnaby, whom they had not yet met, that they would in time "get accustomed to the change which just now seems quite overwhelming." He qualified this, however, by adding: "I have waited with the keenest anxiety her decision. I do not pretend that I am overjoyed at the course that events have taken, nor will you as a man of sense and experience of the world expect that I shall be. But if you possess the solid qualities that will enable you to influence and guide her for her good—on which alone can rest her permanent happiness, I shall feel not only content; but shall rejoice sincerely at the issue of her visit to Leicester. Make her happy and you will have no trouble on the score of her mother or myself." Having dispelled any misconceptions, Page told Algy that he was fully prepared to extend "as hospitable a welcome as any father could extend to a suitor of a daughter whom he tenderly loves and for whose happiness he earnestly hopes and prays."[39]

Burnaby's visit that summer to Rock Ledge, the family's cottage at York Harbor, Maine, was a smashing success. Florence overcame whatever reservations she may have harbored and accepted him as her future son-in-law. He was Minna's choice, and she put her daughter's happiness foremost. Algy's English heritage also helped, for Florence was an Anglophile, though not an uncritical one. Algy reminded her of her own ancestry. "We are fundamentally the same race, only the difference of manners and voice," she wrote to him; "some day we shall all talk alike if we spend so much time together, as is planned for!"[40]

Having welcomed Algy into their close-knit family, Florence arranged a lovely wedding for the couple at Rock Ledge. Her choice of language in proffering motherly advice to them again revealed how traditional were her views on marriage. The day after the nuptials she wrote to Minna of the great joy it gave her to know her daughter was happy and in the safekeeping of a man whom Florence trusted. Minna had been a "modest, lovely bride," and Algy's manly, intelligent, and pleasant nature suited her in every way. Together they had the power to make their own happiness and to be "useful members of society in its broadest sense." Florence then offered unsolicited advice about a wife's duty to her husband. She told Minna to "be a good, unselfish, noble wife to him, and you will be happy the rest of your life, which I trust may be a long one." The implication was that the husband was head of the family and the wife should follow his lead in all that was reasonable. However, she did leave the door ajar for the wife to exercise some independence and shared decision making by employing negative language to effect a positive end. "Try to do some good each day," she wrote, "and don't be too tenacious of what you may call your rights, but learn the only real happiness of 'giving up.'"[41]

Florence did not intend to be the nagging or meddlesome mother-in-law, as she made clear to Minna. "I hope he will find me not a troublesome mother, but one ever ready to love and befriend him," she wrote. Shortly before the newlyweds sailed for England, she wrote Algy a long, touching letter to reassure him of her goodwill. "Let me be a loving mother to you, and always know that you can depend upon me in every way that is right. I am not going to be in the way at any rate, so don't become uneasy," she declared. But she did offer Algy a suggestion about how to handle her daughter which, by its very nature, implied that a woman/wife had an intelligence of her own and could be expected to exercise it. Minna was used to a great deal of love and affection, she observed, adding, "Many a little understanding can be averted, by just a gentle kiss and kind retort; and you have in Minna the most faithful loyal heart that can be found on earth."[42]

In September 1908, following an emotion-laden farewell, the Burnabys and Minna's son returned to England where Minna would lead the life typical of the English upper class. Upon arriving at Baggrave Hall in Leicestershire, an ancient and charming stone country house set in 2,000 acres of glorious English countryside, farmed by twenty-two tenants, the Burnabys in their chauffeur-driven automobile passed through the main portal where tiny British and American flags were flying and a large household retinue stood in waiting.[43]

Until the outbreak of war in August 1914, the Burnabys followed their own ritual: summers in Scotland or with the Pages at York Harbor, returning to Baggrave Hall in the fall. They geared their lives to the hunt in winter, for Leicestershire was the foxhunter's paradise, where the sporting rich came for a few months to gallop at racing pace over the grassy fields. Horses were schooled and exercised there, hounds were bred and trained, and foxes were protected year round in preparation for the hunt. Baggrave became the center of the best parties and the finest people during the season—even the Prince of Wales was a member of the Quorm Hunt—and there was no grander hostess than Minna.

Minna's marriage had not altered in any fundamental way the lifestyle to which she was accustomed, except that she lived it on a grander scale in the interlude before World War I. And rather than geographical distance weakening emotional and familial bonds between mother and daughter, it had quite the opposite effect; Minna and Algy remained close within the Page family circle. The divorce and remarriage did affect a profound change in the life of Minna's son. Henry informally dropped Gibson as his surname and thereafter became Henry Field, after his maternal grandfather.[44]

The dynamics of the mother-daughter-grandson relationship also illuminate our understanding of the interaction between mother and daughter. Florence and Minna never truly saw eye-to-eye on three matters affecting Henry Field: his upbringing, his education, and his national identity. Florence adored her grandson Henry Field and referred to him as "a dear sweet child, with [a] heavenly disposition." Visiting

Baggrave in 1909, she described the seven-year-old as "a dear loving little boy, very affectionate," who read well for his age and, equally important to Florence, knew the entire Episcopal church service.[45]

When Minna instituted divorce proceedings against Preston Gibson, the Pages rallied to her side and were especially gratified when the court awarded custody of Henry to his mother. Perhaps out of fear of losing her child someday, Minna became a domineering, overly protective mother. She smothered her son in affection, which in Florence's judgment unwittingly prolonged infantile traits in the boy. There is a certain irony in her ability to plumb the depths of her grandson's need to sever the tie that bound him too closely to his mother and retarded his developing independence and maturation, when she had earlier been unable to perceive her relationship to Minna in a similar light.

In 1918, for example, when he was sixteen and a student at Eton, Florence criticized Henry's handwriting as evincing a lack of maturity and manliness. She confided to her daughter Florence Lindsay that she wished Henry wrote "a more cultivated hand." Rosewell Page's two sons wrote "infinitely better" and "quite like a man, both in style and writing." Henry could barely write as well as Florence Lindsay's daughters, who were much younger. "No one seems to bother about our dear boy's illiterate looking hand and unformed style," she declared. Yet, Florence refrained from saying anything directly to Minna for fear that Henry might stop corresponding with her.[46]

Besides immaturity, Henry seemed unfocused. In 1919 Florence noted that he had a deep interest in archaeology which Thomas Nelson Page encouraged whenever he visited Rome, but she did not think he had a scholarly nature, intellectual persistence, or facility in expressing his own ideas on the subject. She attributed these deficiencies to Minna's domineering influence on the boy; she wrote tellingly, "Too much mother is not a good thing, although we have our uses, certainly." Worse still, Minna isolated Henry from other boys and playmates of his age. In 1916, while he was visiting the Pages in Rome, Florence wrote not to Minna but to her younger daughter in Massachusetts: "He ought to have boys here to play with, but Minna has never encouraged it, preferring to keep him by her side all the time. He wouldn't have one chance but for his school life, and I am glad he is going back [to England], much as I will miss his dear little face and lovely nature about us all the time."[47]

Algy had gone off to war in 1915, but even during Henry's preadolescent years, he evidently had not been a strong role model for the boy.

Perhaps this was because he had already raised his own children by his former wife; more likely, Minna had staked out her claim to her son, much as Florence had earlier reared her own daughters without external interference from anyone. In any case, Algy abdicated the role of head of household and Minna made the crucial decisions regarding her son's upbringing. The male who might have fulfilled the function of surrogate father and whom Henry greatly admired, Thomas Nelson Page, was never close enough geographically or for long periods of time to influence decisions regarding Henry's development.

This absence of male companions of his own age and what appeared to the Pages after a visit to Baggrave Hall as the adoption of an unsuitable role model precipitated a family crisis in the winter of 1915. Following Algy's call-up, thirteen-year-old Henry seemingly found a surrogate father in one of the grooms who worked in the stables of Baggrave Hall. Patrick became a dominant presence not only in Henry's life but also in Minna's, which disturbed Florence greatly. She viewed the relationship as unhealthy and unwise, and on December 26, 1915, she informed her daughter Florence that she was "somewhat put to it about Patrick." She was aware that he had become a presence in the Burnaby household, "but I never knew anything more absurd or unsuitable than the attitude Minna has about this." In Algy's absence Minna often joined Patrick and Henry before dinner in the boy's bedroom for a game of cards; when Minna played a round of golf, Patrick always accompanied her, "although he has to be paid for as if he were a licensed caddy." He was a constant companion on family outings. Florence's real objection to Patrick may well have been the aura of illicit sexuality that she feared enveloped the relationship between the groom and her grandson. For, she wrote, "he is nurse to Henry Field, putting him to bed, getting him up in the morning, and until Father commented upon it, he came for him to the boudoir always after dinner to get him to go to bed."[48] Henry depended upon Patrick as companion, nurse, and father-figure.

Even the household staff of Baggrave had noticed and commented upon this highly unorthodox relationship, which violated propriety and the traditional boundaries between the social classes. Josephine, "who loves Minna and is so loyal to her," servant that she was, "thought Madame was making a grave mistake to give Monsieur Henri no other companion than a groom of the stables," Florence wrote. All of the servants were "amazed" at the elevated status Minna had conferred upon Patrick. Florence shrank from allowing herself even to contemplate the possibility that Minna and Patrick might have been engaged in a *liaison dangereuse* in Algy's absence, and, of course, there is no evidence that this was the case. Instead, as though she needed to reassure herself, Florence decided that Patrick was simply Minna's companion, adding, "and never was there a more respectful servant, nor one less inclined to presume upon the position he has been given." Nonetheless, she admitted that the relationship between Patrick and Minna and Patrick and Henry Field had aroused Thomas Nelson Page's ire "to a degree that is suggestive sometimes of an explosion."[49]

Once Algy was mustered out of the service, the immediate danger passed, but the long-term parent-child problem persisted. Minna's overbearing attitude toward her son manifested itself over the recurring issue of Henry Field's formal education, an issue made complicated because Preston Gibson, who had never reconciled himself to the loss of his son, demanded that Henry be educated in the United States. As early as July 1911, Thomas Nelson Page, echoing Florence's suspicions that Gibson's interest in the boy's schooling was motivated by a desire to regain control of his son, wrote to Preston to assure him that Minna was equally concerned about young Henry's education. Everyone wanted what was best for the boy, Page asserted, adding, "His mother is very watchful of him and naturally feels that while he is so young he should be near enough to her for her to keep up her careful watch over him."[50]

After that crisis had subsided, Page subsequently extended advice to Minna about Henry's future. The boy would eventually inherit enough money to lead a comfortable life, but not so much as to become vain and spoiled. He therefore strongly suggested to Minna that she provide Henry with a good education but "let him decide his profession or occupation for himself."[51] Sustained by this fatherly advice, Minna enrolled Henry in one of the finest and most exclusive grammar schools in England.

Henry Field recalled afterwards that his introduction to the Sunningdale School, near Ascot, was the low point of his life. He was and always remained an outsider there, a Yank in a school for England's upper-class elite. He endured the same experience upon enrolling at Eton; in 1916 his classmates taunted him for being a Yank who was "too proud to fight"—a sarcastic reference to President Wilson's wartime neutrality policy. As a privileged outsider with a domineering and overly protective mother, Henry Field had a lonely childhood and adolescence, which may have contributed to his bookish nature and love of the past. His interest in archaeology and anthropology no doubt was sparked by the ancient surroundings of Baggrave Hall and his wartime visits to Rome, but it also received sustenance during the boy's long, lonely days at Sunningdale and Eton.[52]

In December 1915, with Algy posted to Gallipoli, Minna pulled Henry from school to accompany her to Rome to await news of her husband. Florence observed that her grandson did not seem happy being away from school and classmates, but this was not her primary concern. She was now worried that Henry, as a citizen of the United States, was seriously devoid of any knowledge of the land of his birth. She declared, "But oh, how I wish he had some instruction in American history; I blush for his ignorance of the very best known people and events; the plain-as-the-nose-on-your-face things, that our infants know." She cautioned Florence not to breathe a word of her concern to Minna, "for I don't want to seem critical." Yet for some time this had been a thorn in the relationship between mother and daughter.[53]

Embedded in the issue of whether Henry Field was knowledgeable in United States history was the more fundamental question of whether he would assume American or British citizenship. Preston Gibson had broached the subject in 1911 in correspondence with both Minna and the Pages. In response to his inquiries about Henry's education, Thomas Nelson Page wrote that the boy would learn the history of his native country, "and Henry will of course be taught this like any other little American boy." The issue at the time was moot, because the court had awarded custody of Henry to his mother and he was only then embarking upon his formal education. But it remained a matter of concern to the entire family, which expected that at some indeterminant time Henry would be taught the rudiments of American history. By the time Henry entered Eton in 1916, Algy was already in uniform as a lieutenant in the Royal Horse Guards and fighting in Gallipoli and Egypt. Given the turmoil of the war and Henry's attachment both to his mother and stepfather, Florence speculated that Henry might one day seek British citizenship. But what of his future if Algy was killed in combat and Minna had to return to the United States?[54]

Henry's graduation from Eton in 1919 and the question of which college to attend—Oxford, Cambridge, or an American university—brought the long-simmering family concerns to the fore. Late in December 1918, Preston Gibson wrote to Minna, with a copy to Florence, insisting that Henry should return to the country of his birth and attend

Yale University as he, his father, and his grandfather had done. The letter infuriated Florence, who continued to suspect Preston's motives. He was "one persistent impudent scoundrel, and has unequalled assurance," she complained to her daughter Florence. "You will be as indignant over it as I am at this very moment. Henry now nearly six feet, to be disposed of as that person demands!"[55]

While her ire was genuine, Florence also was ambivalent. In a fundamental way she agreed that Henry should attend university in America. "Primary schools and public schools are all right in another country, but a man should finish up in his own," she declared. It was a matter of Henry's national identity, and she freely confessed that she approved of his attending Yale. She thought "it entirely unfair to the boy never to let him see anything of his compatriots, and to be proposing to become an Englishman, to enter that Army." That last pejorative reference was to the British military command which had bungled the disastrous Dardanelles campaign that Florence branded "a criminal sacrifice of human lives." It only reinforced her conviction of the superiority of American citizenship. "Of one thing I am increasingly proud, of being an American by birth and inheritance; a blessing I wouldn't exchange for any other on earth," she declared.[56]

Florence pursued the matter with her son-in-law Tom Lindsay, a United States Army officer on temporary duty in Rome, and the two agreed that Minna was being "selfish" and was making "a terrible mistake" in keeping Henry from the land of his birth. "It appalls me when I see how ignorant the boy is of everything American; he hasn't one single atom of knowledge of American history, and could only just answer last year about G. Washington! but just, no more—and this is the extent of his learning in that line," she wrote to her younger daughter. This rekindled fears of the future: Algy gone, Minna back in America, and Henry a grown man without any background other than his childhood at Baggrave and Eton. He would be a marginal man, adrift between two cultures and peoples; a stranger to his relatives and not truly an Englishman; a man without connections or a fortune to support him. Worst of all, she, his grandmother, would not be there to act as his anchor, "much as I wish to."[57]

Florence's closing comments are perhaps more revealing about her true feelings toward Minna and her grandson Henry Field than she had intended. "P[reston]. G[ibson]. may be wiser than we know," she observed. "So far all has gone smoothly, but Henry ought from now on to be more of a real man, and not so completely under his mother's control, despite her devotion to him." Tom Lindsay was correct, she thought; Minna had always been selfish about the boy. "You know she has always ended with having her own way, the dear child, and she is not going to sacrifice her feelings now regarding the ultimate good of the boy, finding it easier to follow the line of least resistance." She knew Minna would not make any public protest but simply would do things her own way as she had always done. Florence did not wish to carp or be a meddlesome mother, "and yet I don't want to be a coward, and not speak what is so sincerely on my mind." That, of course, was precisely the problem, for Florence was communicating her concerns to the wrong daughter. Perhaps because she and Minna were temperamentally too much alike, she implored her younger daughter Florence to use "her own good influence" with Minna to give Henry the opportunity to know his native land and people.

Gibson's letter had also disturbed Algy, who, like the rest of the family, believed that Preston would "never cease trying to influence" Henry; but he also agreed with Florence's evaluation of the boy. Florence reported Algy as saying that "he has never seen anyone more easily influenced than the boy; he feels sure that he would all too easily fall into bad ways, and that what we love in him now would never be the same after an acquaintance with PG." The one point upon which there seemed to be a family consensus (excluding Minna) was that Henry had not yet exhibited the manly virtues. They saw him as a Mamma's boy: weak, suggestible, and easily influenced. Florence declared that he lacked "initiative, and that he finds it easier to resist any effort at self-assertion, than to go against his mother." Minna would not give him any "real freedom, and he is so used to blind obedience, and to never arguing any question, that he stands but little chance of becoming a big character." Exasperated, Florence returned to the original issue: how could Henry become a good citizen of the United States when he knew so little about it![58]

Despite serious reservations, Florence again deferred to Minna's wishes. "I wish I could help, but seeing that only sharp words result, I am not going to press the matter," she wrote. Fortunately, her concern for Henry's future proved unnecessary. Uncle Barbour Lathrop unexpectedly entered the picture and, utilizing his connections, arranged Henry's introduction to the wealthy pharmaceutical magnate Dr. Henry S. Wellcome of Burroughs, Wellcome & Co., who was residing in London. An avid student of archaeology, Wellcome advised Henry to read at Oxford with the renowned scholar Henry Balfour. Henry not only did so, but he became a distinguished anthropologist in his own right, discovering the earliest known wheel, as well as a husband, father, author, and adviser to Presidents Franklin D. Roosevelt and Harry Truman.[59]

A final source of tension in the relationship between Florence and her older daughter centered on the preservation of wealth. Shortly before Minna was to marry Algy, Florence had requested her lawyer to prepare a deed of trust for the engaged couple to sign, which was afterwards registered with the court of Cook County, Illinois. The deed of July 17, 1908, was in fact a prenuptial agreement intended to shield Minna's inheritance from her late father, Henry Field, from any future claim by Burnaby. Furthermore, the deed asserted Minna's right to a claim upon Burnaby's estate in the event that their marriage failed.[60]

The indenture vested three male trustees—Bryan Lathrop, Owen F. Aldis, and Thomas Nelson Page—with virtually absolute power to act for the protection and conservation of Minna's inheritance. Pending death or dissolution of the marriage, the trustees would decide how to invest Minna's portion of the Field estate, collect the income from the principal, and pay all required taxes and fees. Only after they had discharged these fiduciary obligations would they transfer to Minna the net income from the estate, determining whether it was to be paid monthly, quarterly, or semiannually. Minna was not allowed to anticipate or to encumber the amount of income she might expect in any given year before the trustees actually had disbursed the funds to her. She might, however, draw up to $100,000 for her own use, free of any claim by Burnaby.

In the event Minna predeceased her husband and was without heir, the trustees were to adhere to the terms of her last will and testament. Should she predecease her son before he had attained his majority, they were to apply the income of the estate toward Henry's support and education until he came legally of age, whereupon he would receive both principal and income. Algy, by contrast, agreed to surrender to the trustees any claim he might have against Minna's estate if she predeceased him. If she outlived Burnaby, she would receive the traditional "widow's third" of his estate.

Given the marital record of both parties and what Florence perceived as Minna's tendency toward impulsiveness, the trust deed was not an unreasonable precaution. It indicates that Florence was neither weak nor unduly deferential but a woman of shrewd intellect who, in a manner which did not openly defy conventional behavior, knew how to stretch the boundaries demarcating the masculine and feminine spheres to protect her family's well-being. The idea of drawing up this prenuptial agreement originated with Florence. She took the initiative of consulting her lawyer and instructing him to draft the agreement precisely to her satisfaction. She not only shielded Minna's inheritance successfully and made certain that funds would be available for her grandson's education but also secured a claim to a portion of Algy's estate for her daughter if this marriage also failed. Furthermore, she carefully cloaked her demands in a manner which comported with convention, by having three males she was absolutely confident would act in Minna's best interest named cotrustees. She recognized full well that a woman, especially of her generation, was not expected to concern herself with business matters by demanding to be named a trustee, whereas no one would question the legal standing of male trustees to protect Minna's fiduciary interest. A lesser woman than Florence, in similar circumstances, might well have left her daughter's inheritance vulnerable to an unscrupulous husband or her daughter might well have found herself with nothing to show for another disastrous marriage but a broken heart and an empty purse.

Minna's ability to manage money, never inspiring confidence in Florence, grew even worse as she quickly adapted to the aristocratic lifestyle of the country gentry at Baggrave Hall. Indeed, in February 1911, at Florence's behest, Thomas Nelson Page as trustee admonished Minna for running up bills; in his opinion she seemed to be purchasing every item she saw whether or not she needed it. Two months later Minna's financial resources diminished further when she signed a release of her dower rights against Preston Gibson, her ex-husband.[61]

But it was the outbreak of war in 1914 accompanied by the British government's very heavy wartime taxation that put a further severe strain on the Burnabys' finances. A continued high lifestyle, costly expenditures on refurbishing Baggrave Hall, Algy's enlistment in the military and his absence for lengthy periods, and failure to extract greater productivity from the estate's tenants compounded their fiscal woes. In May 1915 Florence retreated somewhat from the hard-nosed fiscal stance she had taken earlier, writing to her brother that "it seems hard that Minna should have to use some of her capital to free these debts, when she has settled for so many already, and has, as you know best of all, spent so large a sum on Baggrave, from which there will never be any return."[62]

Florence's compassion for her daughter's plight was a thinly veiled request for Bryan to reexamine the terms of the indenture to see whether Minna's income might be increased. Rather than apportioning fault equally, she exonerated her daughter and launched into a tirade against Algy. "My experience with Algy (and as a representative of his nation) is that he will always be in debt, except in so far as Minna has the entire control of the income. She has never been in debt for any serious amount, or not at all, as I believe but don't actually know, since you settled everything for her some time back; then I found it was to shield Algy entirely, not for any of her own extravagances." Minna had now taken charge of paying the bills and keeping track of the accounts, Florence wrote, adding: "English people are born with no conscience for trades people, I believe."

What Florence dreaded most was the public shame and humiliation Minna would suffer should Algy's creditors haul him into bankruptcy court, an embarrassment greater "than if she freed some of her capital." "Minna's trust estate cannot be held for his debts, if as I understand it, it is optional with the trustees whether to free some of it to discharge the debts," she wrote. She said she would accept Bryan's advice in the matter, but what she did not know was that Minna had already cabled her uncle requesting 800 pounds sterling from the trust to settle Algy's debts. Placed in an awkward position, Bryan volunteered to pay the debt out of his own pocket. When Florence learned of this, she thanked him for his generosity but asked him to transfer the debt to her own account without informing Minna.[63]

Florence assumed the Burnabys' indebtedness on this occasion, but this was only a temporary reprieve. The longer the war persisted, the more expensive it became to maintain the estate. Moreover, she had to take into account the imposition in 1916 of American income taxes, wartime taxes, and estate taxes.[64] Their debts accumulated until their fiscal crisis peaked in 1919. This time there was no bailout from Florence. The Pages were adamant in advising Minna to rent out Baggrave Hall temporarily, utilizing the rental income to pay the debts. "You know as well as we do, even far better that the only thing to do is to let Baggrave for a certain time," Florence advised Minna in a lengthy but firm letter. "You don't want me to say it sweetheart, and I hate of all things to say it. Consider for a moment what it entails. The upkeep of such a house, aside from the estate, is one of large proportions. You can no more live there and not keep open house than they can do at Oakland, ,you say you live within your income; this is not the case. No one lives within his income when he faces a yearly deficit; no matter whether it is caused by war taxation or depleted revenue. The result is the same."[65]

She admonished Minna not to count on her trust fund. "For a few years to come, perhaps not more than two, there is no possibility of getting any perceptible increase in our incomes. You have lived the life you love above all others since you married our dear Algy," she wrote. "You have put aside from a small fortune, your heart and soul into the beautiful old home, and it is a part of your very being. It is no easy matter to step out, and let others enjoy your belongings, your intimate things, *your own precious atmosphere itself.* But what else can you do sufficiently big to cover the necessities of the situation?" The cost of hunters and grooms mounted up quickly, and Florence warned Minna that both she and Algy had to change their lifestyle drastically until they had settled their debts.

Ever the concerned parent, Florence balanced her stern fiscal advice to her daughter with a socially acceptable rationale for temporarily renting out Baggrave. "There is no shame in being obliged to move away from one's home, when war has done the havoc," she explained. "Isn't it a finer stand to take to make the sacrifice and to live absolutely within your income, including all taxation[?]" The Burnabys might take up temporary residence in Virginia until their financial situation improved. "It is but a feeble suggestion," Florence observed, "but it may be worth considering."

The one solution that Florence did not make was to rescue her daughter and son-in-law financially as she had done in the past. Experience taught her that to do so was to throw good money after bad, although she couched her unwillingness to assist them more diplomatically. "Had I the money, you know how cheerfully I would give it to you in this critical moment," she wrote. But she and Tom were facing "huge expenses" themselves following his retirement as ambassador and their return to the United States, "with the packing and shipping our furniture, the overhauling and expense of running Rock Ledge, and the complete doing over of 1759," their mansion in Washington, D.C. If Minna still had not gotten the message, Florence put it more plainly. Referring to her brother Bryan's death in the spring of 1916, she asserted: "My own income is tremendously reduced from my precious Brother's time; at a conservative estimate $15,000. This is no small reduction. We are facing problems ahead, all of us in America, with the servant and labor question."

Florence then pointed out the necessity of preserving Minna's trust. "Were your fortune, small as it is, free to be used as you find necessary from time to time in a few years even your present reduced income would seem a huge one, for you would have practically nothing." Pennilessness and dependency were the worst possible situation. "To be a dependent is more appalling than just to make a temporary sacrifice," she reiterated. "I am so far from being unsympathetic Sweetheart, that I could cry my heart out on your shoulder. But I am facing a situation with you, and no matter how many days of reflection I gave to it, the answer to your letter would be the same."

Before putting her letter in that day's dispatch, Florence showed it to her husband, who agreed that Minna and Algy were living beyond their income and should rent out Baggrave until they had recouped their finances. Three days later, on February 10, 1919, Page addressed Minna's tax problems directly, couching his advice affectionately as would a father who loved his child but also self-interestedly as Florence's husband. Taxes were a recurring obligation, he noted, and any financial assistance Florence rendered to Minna diminished her own capital, which he strongly opposed. He especially reproached Minna for having asked her mother to "dispose" of her capital for this purpose, "while you have horses and cattle that can be sold." There was but one way to resolve the tax problem, Page declared, "and that is to pay them."[66]

Page further reminded Minna of her fiscal profligacy and recalled that Uncle Bryan had notified her in 1912 that she had withdrawn $80,000 from her trust and the remaining $20,000 to which she was legally entitled shortly thereafter. The only thing she had not been able to draw down was the principal. He also observed that Uncle Bryan had explained to her how the trust functioned, but that she had exhibited at the time "total ignorance of the facts of the situation." To compound a bad situation, Minna had received $20,000 from her uncles on the Field side of the family, as well as money from other sources, "which I mention only to show you that you have not the habit of living within your income." At this rate, Page warned, she would quickly exhaust what was left of the trust fund. He advised "an absolute and radical change of your style of living."

The Burnabys by most criteria had a large income for the day, about $25,000 by Page's estimate, but they lived a lifestyle costing double that. Page repeatedly admonished Minna to scale back her "present manner of life as a *grande dame* in a signorial home," warning that she would never be able to economize while residing at Baggrave. His advice, repeated over and over, was to rent the manor house, using the income to pay the taxes. Like Florence, he sugared the bitter pill with reassurances, shifting fault from the Burnabys to the "times" and the war. "There is no lowering of one's dignity in giving up a grand style of living at such a time as this. Indeed, it is quite the contrary," he wrote, in words reminiscent of Florence's. "It will secure the respect of all those whose respect is worth having—and later on you can return to your beautiful home and strike a more moderate gait."

Despite the admonitions, Page never believed that Minna would accept this advice, and indeed, she did not. Somehow Minna and Algy managed to hold on to Baggrave where they resided until his death in 1937.

3

Acquiring and
Conserving Wealth

*I*n the bubbling last half of the nineteenth century, money was the
stepping-stone to social recognition in the United States. Having
acquired a passport of suitable wealth, the American millionaire
needed no further visa for his entrée into the upper classes. This was true
especially in Chicago, a city whose booming economy thrust forth a
cadre of newly affluent businessmen and entrepreneurs who, unlike in
the older seaport cities of the East Coast, were welcomed by the pre—
Civil War patrician elite. Chicago's elite families established their he-
gemony as a social class through intermarriage, and they exercised
lateral power in cultural, eleemosynary, educational, and political affairs.
Florence Lathrop Field was the product of this milieu. Throughout her
life she was surrounded with a comfort and elegance that bespoke the
truth of the old adage: "To her who hath shall be given."

To assert that she was an affluent woman does not tell us very much
about Florence Lathrop Field or her mode of life unless we also know
something of the magnitude of her wealth, its composition, and its
standing in relation to that of the other social classes within the society.
Did Florence's wealth number her among the superrich of American
society of the last half of the nineteenth century, ranking her alongside
the oil, steel, and financial barons, or was she among the comfortably
rich? How did her wealth compare with that of Americans of middle-
and working-class status? Where did her wealth originate, and how was
it enhanced during the course of her life? How, finally, did she expend
that wealth?

Documents such as probate court records, wills, estate inventories, contracts, ledgers, house plans, personal correspondence, and other sources allow us to reconstruct Florence Lathrop Page as an economic woman: the sources of her wealth, its magnitude relative to the wealth of income groups above and below her, the ways in which she utilized wealth, and the manner in which she transmitted it to the next generation of Fields. This knowledge helps to illuminate differences of lifestyle not only between social classes but also within the ranks of "the rich, the well born, and the powerful." It also enhances our understanding of the urban industrial society that was emerging.

Inherited from both her parents and her first husband, Henry Field, Florence's wealth was inextricably bound to the growth of Chicago as the dominant metropolis of the West. In the decade before the Civil War, Chicago had emerged as the largest primary grain, wheat, and lumber market in the country; it also was the railroad center of the West. From this base there had evolved a multifunctional elite engaged in diverse business ventures: banking, lumber, meatpacking, real estate operations, and the retail and wholesale trades. That businessmen were optimistic about Chicago's economic future is evident from an early letter by Bryan Lathrop commenting upon the completion of the transcontinental railroad. Lathrop wrote in 1869 to his uncle Andrew Wylie of Washington, D.C., who had invested in Chicago real estate, that "the opening of the Pacific railroad will have some influence, I think, in giving an impetus to the affairs of the city. I never felt more thoroughly convinced of the grand future of Chicago than now."[1]

The railroad was the key both to the city's economic future and to the Lathrops who were active in the Chicago real estate market. "The more I see of the development of the states tributary to it—the great North West, besides all the states and territories through which the Pacific roads pass or will pass—the more sure seems the basis upon which the business of Chicago rests," Bryan observed. Chicago had seen its best days as a grain depot, and Bryan regarded this as "a very good thing for her." Western farmers were quickly discarding the shackles of subsistence agriculture and were producing surplus grain for feed to their hogs and cattle, making their livestock more valuable in the market and their owners wealthier. "The result," Lathrop declared, "will be, first, richer farmers, and secondly, more demand for the merchandise furnished by our city, and better pay."

Bryan Lathrop's prediction proved unerringly accurate, and he, his uncles Andrew Wylie and Thomas Barbour Bryan, and his father Jedediah Lathrop, as investors in real estate, profited from the city's economic growth. A booming economy demanded a new physical infrastructure, but that required first the assemblage and development of land. The Lathrop and the Bryan families, like others, were eager to provide that service. By 1892, of 378 Chicagoans reputed to be worth more than one million dollars, 81 may positively be identified as having made all or a substantial part of their fortune in real estate.[2] With economic power increasingly came social power as the new monied elite took its place alongside the older patrician families of the pre–Civil War generation that had long dominated the city's social order.

The Lathrop-Bryan families' fortunes may not quite have approached the million-dollar mark in 1892, but their assets, generated in shrewd real estate deals and from other business activities in Elmhurst and the Chicago metropolitan area, were very substantial. The sale of plots in Graceland Cemetery to service the urban deceased was one source of their wealth and ownership of the Elmhurst Water Company was another; but it was investments in real estate, especially in the central business district of Chicago, that yielded the greatest profit.

Analysis of Chicago land values during the years when the Bryan and Lathrop families were most actively engaged in real estate operations makes this abundantly clear. The aggregate value of land in the corporate limits of the city rose more than twelvefold between 1873 and 1892 and another 50 percent between 1892 and 1915. Commercial growth particularly drove up property values in the central business district. The Loop, where Thomas Barbour Bryan, Jedediah Lathrop and his son Bryan, and Marshall and Henry Field had focused much of their investment, comprised 12.5 percent of the total urban land value in 1873, 23.3 percent in 1892, and 40 percent in 1910. Loop values soared 500 percent between 1878 and 1892; even in the panic of 1893 prices did not decline as precipitously as they had in 1873. In fact, they decreased only slightly within the central business district and then resumed their upward course. By 1910 Loop values had risen more than 80 percent.[3]

To illustrate just how profitable speculation in Chicago real estate was, one needs only to examine Marshall Field's holdings at the time of his death. By 1905 Marshall Field had amassed a fortune estimated at $150–$200 million, of which real estate assets alone totaled $38 million. Of that figure, real estate in the Loop accounted for $31 million. Even this does not tell the whole story, for profits from real estate investment in Chicago, as in other urban centers of the time, were all the more inflated because this form of property was notoriously underassessed for taxation. Such assessments rarely were calculated above 12 percent of their actual worth; generally they were much lower.[4] Despite the swings of the economic pendulum in the late nineteenth century, a knowledgeable and shrewd investor could succeed handsomely in Chicago real estate.

With the deaths of both parents and then her husband in 1890, Florence inherited a considerable fortune in realty as well as in personalty; the latter consisted of jewelry, furniture, stocks, and bonds. Although she was the beneficiary of her parents' estate, Florence also had derived her wealth from marrying within the elite. Marriage in the nineteenth century was as much an economic and social alliance as it was an affair of the heart. Florence was not unaware of this, and it remained a part of her thinking even after her first marriage ended prematurely. In 1907, for example, she wrote to her second husband, who was attending to business in Richmond, that a suitor had shown up on her doorstep at the Pages' summer cottage in Maine to woo her visiting niece. Florence wrote that she and her daughters, Minna and Florence (who were young adults of twenty-five and twenty-four years of age by now), had been spending "our time devising excuses to be anywhere but with the lovers." She expected the young man to propose marriage to her niece, who most likely would accept. Florence then wrote: "Would that he had something beside his salary, for she hasn't a cent, and her parents will make an awful fuss if she marries him. I think he will have something of an experience with his own mother also."[5] Within the upper class substantial economic assets on the part of both partners were clearly the most desirable component for a good match. Failing that, the prospective bridegroom at least should have resources beyond a salary to support a future wife according to her station in life.

By that standard the marriage of Florence and Henry was a good match. Besides his investments in real estate and his position as bank director, Henry Field's wealth was linked inextricably to the fortunes of Marshall Field & Co. With the formation in 1867 of Field, Leiter & Co., Henry Field, who had been active since 1861 in the retail trade with his more famous brother, and two other employees were rewarded with junior partnerships. Each was given a small share of the gross profits by way of salary and an additional percentage of the net profits corresponding to their share in the partnership. At this time Marshall Field furnished $^{400}/_{725}$ of the capital and obtained that fraction of the net profits, while Joseph Leiter supplied $^{295}/_{725}$ of the capital and shared in the profits proportionately.[6]

In January 1869 Field, Leiter & Co. broadened the partnership to include Joseph Field, another brother. This was part of a new contractual agreement that remained the basis of Field, Leiter & Co. for the next eight years, until 1877. Under this arrangement the firm's capital stock was set at $1.2 million. Marshall Field and Joseph Leiter each furnished $400,000 of this amount, and each obtained one-third of the profits. The four junior partners furnished $100,000 respectively, and each received one-twelfth of the profits. Henry Field retired temporarily from the firm in 1878 but returned as purchasing agent in the Paris office in 1880–81 after Marshall Field had forced out Joseph Leiter so that he could run the company his own way. Henry Field remained active in the firm, now Marshall Field & Co., until 1883, by which time he held a 5 percent interest.

This information makes it possible to estimate how much profit Henry Field derived from his junior partnership in the firm during the two periods in which he was most actively engaged in the company's operations, the years from 1872 to 1877 and from 1882 to 1883. Marshall Field & Co.'s net profits in retailing and wholesaling in the first period were: $869,500 (1872); $752,000 (1873); $1,210,400 (1874); $1,091,700 (1875); $799,800 (1876); $873,900 (1877). If Henry Field's share of the net profits was one-twelfth, then his annual income from this one source alone was: $72,458.33; $62,500; $100,866.66; $90,975; $66,650; $72,825, for a total of $466,274.99. These sums are even more startling when one considers that the nation was in the throes of a financial panic and depression which began in 1873 and continued into 1878.

With the return of prosperity, the Field fortunes grew even greater. In 1882–83, the last two years that Henry Field was actively associated with the firm, its net profits were $1,749,600 and $1,732,200. If his share at this time was 5 percent, he would have earned $145,800 and $144,350, respectively. The record is unclear whether, after he retired to pursue his cultural and philanthropic interests, he retained his 5 percent share of the company. If so, he would have continued to draw down annual sums in excess of $100,000 until his death in 1890.

There are no extant records of other sources of income, although one may assume that Henry Field received compensation as vice president and one of the larger stockholders of Chicago's Commercial National Bank, interest income from utility and transportation stocks and bonds, and income from real estate investments. He also had one other form of tangible, if not liquid, wealth: his superb art collection, which was worth several thousands of dollars.

Apart from a one-third interest in her parents' estate, the major source of Florence's wealth came from Henry Field; she shared it during his lifetime and received it from his estate following his demise. The process of transferring his wealth to his survivors provides us with additional information to ascertain Florence's net worth. Henry Field drew up his will on July 30, 1888, and it was filed for probate in the Probate Court of Cook County, Chicago, on January 6, 1891, approximately two weeks after his death. He bequeathed to his wife all of his personal possessions, including household furniture and ornaments, books, paintings, works of art, articles of virtu, personal wearing apparel and jewelry, plate, horses, carriages, and harnesses. The residue of his estate (real, personal, and mixed) was put into a trust, composed of his wife, Marshall Field, and Bryan Lathrop as cotrustees, to be held, managed, and disposed of as he directed.[7]

Henry Field went to great lengths to spell out what his intentions were when he drafted his will. Once the trustees had liquidated his debts and conveyed the specific bequests to his wife, in the event he died without an heir or a descendant of his heir surviving him, they were empowered to distribute two-thirds of his remaining estate as they saw fit and one-third to charitable institutions as prescribed by the laws of Illinois.

However, if Henry Field was survived by a child or children, the trustees would then hold and manage the residuary estate until his youngest child (i.e., Florence Field Lindsay) attained the age of twenty-five. Until that time they were to apply the income from the residuary estate, up to a maximum of $30,000 per year, to support Florence and his children "according to their station in life and the mode of living to which they shall have been accustomed during my life, and to the education of my children." Florence was to receive this sum semiannually (or more often if the trustees agreed) during her lifetime, to be used at her discretion for the purpose he had intended.

The residue of this $30,000 sum, once its purpose had been executed, was to revert to Florence for her own use and benefit, as Henry Field declared, "it being my intention to provide her with ample means to maintain herself and her children and to charge her only with the support and education of the children in such manner as she may deem proper." A child who attained her majority before Henry's last surviving child reached the age of twenty-five could, upon her own or Florence's request (if the last-named was still alive), elect to be paid her portion of this annual sum of $30,000; if she died, however, the money would go to her heir(s). Beyond this, the trustees had no further obligation to Henry's grandchildren.

Once his youngest surviving child attained the age of twenty-five, Henry Field instructed the trustees to divide the entire remaining trust, including accumulations of undistributed income, into three equal shares and to transfer one-third of those shares to each child living or to her descendant(s). The trustees were to hold the remaining one-third of the estate until his youngest child reached the age of thirty-five, at which time the estate was to be distributed equally to that child and to the descendants of any of Henry Field's children who were deceased. In the event Florence was no longer alive when their youngest child reached twenty-five, Henry instructed that the portions be divided equally between his children.

The will also entitled Florence to draw periodically from the trust estate the excess of income above the $30,000 (prior to the first partition of the estate) as she saw fit, and as much as she desired "to apply in aid of charitable or benevolent societies or institutions," but this was not to be construed in any way as imposing an obligation upon her to do so. She did, however, have to notify the trustees of the purpose of each draft.

Finally, Field established the legal basis that allowed Florence's fortune to grow over the course of her lifetime. He vested in the trustees "full power and authority to sell, convey, lease, mortgage, invest and reinvest said trustee estate or the proceeds or income thereof, or any property acquired by them as trustees hereunder." Their actions were final in all business decisions, and they were not to be held liable or be required to give sureties for their performance as trustees. The remainder of the will constituted legal bookkeeping: authorization for one of the trustees to act as "managing trustee"; provision for replacing a trustee, if necessary; trustee fees, etc.

Henry Field's will is important not only as a legal document per se, but for the economic insights it provides into the transfer of wealth in the late nineteenth century. This is especially so when one reads the will in conjunction with another document published in June 1892. The *New York Tribune* in its monthly supplement printed a ninety-three-page listing of American millionaires who exerted great influence in their communities or in the nation but had attracted less attention than the few score whose names had monopolized the headlines and ultimately the history books, such as Rockefeller, Carnegie, Vanderbilt, and Morgan. The *Tribune's* list, in the opinion of one scholar of capitalism of the Gilded Age, may be more significant for comprehending the composition and sources of the American business elite than are the selective biographies of the leading dramatis personae of this era. Among those reputed to be worth a million dollars or more was listed the estate of Henry Field.[8] Florence, then, was a millionairess when she married Thomas Nelson Page, although her wealth was considerably less than Rockefeller's, Carnegie's, or Pullman's, to name only a few of the superrich.

Henry Field's will also is significant for the social insights it provides into the status of upper-class women, family relationships, the disposition of property, and the like.[9] The actual writing of a will required one to acknowledge the inevitability of one's own death, to determine one's relationship to others, and to come to terms with one's financial standing. Field's will always refers to "Florence Lathrop Field," with no endearing adjectives as often was the case in early nineteenth-century wills. Henry Field intended his will to be a businesslike document, written by a businessman. Its objective was clearly to retain property within the family, and not to liberate his wife and daughters from nineteenth-century legal constraints.

Nonetheless, that he named Florence a cotrustee (which implied equality with the two male trustees) in contradiction of the metaphor of the sphere suggests that their married life, most likely, had been one of equality and shared decision making, and that Henry had retained confidence in his wife as a woman of intellect, ability, and prudence. Even had he not, Florence was entitled to dower rights under the law, which meant that she had a legal claim to one-third of her husband's property upon his death.

The will also continued a practice common to an earlier age, making a bequest to relatives and kin besides the immediate family. Henry left bequests of $25,000 each to his sisters, Laura Field Dibbles and Helen Field James, both of whom had married successfully and did not need the money. This indicated that Henry had considerable affection for his sisters, which is consistent with what we know of his personality.

But the will also contained a note of ambiguity which disclosed that

Henry Field, for all of his confidence in Florence, was realistic where matters of property, wealth, and women were at issue. For in nineteenth-century patriarchal society the more wealth that was at stake, the less likely a woman (in this instance Florence Lathrop Field) would receive unencumbered a major gift of property or money; nor was she likely to act alone as executrix of her husband's estate. In lieu of bestowing property upon Florence in fee simple, Henry Field settled property on his wife. He may well have believed that she was intelligent and sufficiently responsible to be named a testator, but he also named two cotestators, both of whom were males, to participate in making the important decisions regarding his estate. Besides Florence, Henry Field named as testators his brother Marshall and brother-in-law Bryan Lathrop. The reasons for doing so were manifold: a fear that property left solely to a woman might pass out of the testator's bloodline, and possibly even fall prey to creditors of the woman's deceased husband; or if Florence remarried, her new husband might claim to be executor "in right of his wife" and use that position to gain control of the estate.

What pervades the will, then, is an ethic of female gentility which is typical of a nineteenth-century male-dominated society such as the United States. In accordance with the concept of two spheres, a masculine one (the competitive world of business) and a feminine one (the home), Henry Field most likely believed it was necessary to associate males whose legal standing would be beyond question in the disposition of his estate, even as he wished to treat Florence as an equal. The net result of establishing a cotrusteeship was that despite Florence's equal status in this arrangement, it quickly devolved upon Bryan Lathrop and then, after his death in 1916, upon John P. Wilson, Jr., the family lawyer, to exercise day-to-day oversight of Field's estate on behalf of Florence and her children. This became inevitable especially when Marshall Field, who was too occupied with his own business affairs, willingly relinquished the burden.

From one perspective the argument could be made that Florence, being neither a militant feminist nor an accountant, acquiesced in this arrangement and withdrew with a deep sigh of relief from active participation as a cotrustee because she viewed the trustee's fiduciary obligation to the client as falling within the male sphere. Another explanation of why Florence surrendered her role as cotrustee and allowed the decision-making process to devolve upon one trustee, Bryan Lathrop, is equally plausible. This argument suggests that Florence's action was not necessarily the sign of a weak female but rather of a woman of shrewd intellect, knowledgeable about the world and the environment in which she lived and functioned. She knew that women, especially of her generation, were customarily excluded from the experiences that made for a successful business career and the correct business decisions. Hence, she was clever enough to vest this authority in one whom she trusted implicitly—her brother (and later her longtime attorney)—a sagacious financial counselor whose standing in the masculine world of business was above question. She empowered Bryan Lathrop to make investment decisions on behalf of herself and her young daughters but never without her knowledge and consent. Through regular reports Florence always knew what kinds of investments Bryan had made, when he was going to sell, transfer, or otherwise dispose of an investment, and what amount of interest income annually she could anticipate from Henry Field's estate. A lesser woman in similar circumstances could just as easily have lost control of her estate, watched it being frittered away through questionable investment decisions, or been embezzled out of it by some unscrupulous trustee.

Instead, over the next eighteen years Bryan Lathrop's management of Henry Field's estate was a happy and amicable experience for Florence from which she and her daughters benefited financially. The arrangement worked because their fiduciary relationship rested on a solid and loving personal relationship. The older brother over the years became as much a loving uncle as a brother to his younger sister and her daughters. That Florence's fortune was enhanced over the years suggests that Bryan administered her wealth adroitly but prudently.

Besides the bequests of her parents and husband, lesser bequests also enhanced the corpus of Florence's wealth. In 1906 an uncle, William A. Bryan, who held mortgages and rental properties in New York, Brooklyn, Kansas City, and Redbank, New Jersey, and also bank stock and the securities of the Union Pacific Railroad, died. He bequeathed to his niece, Florence, and to his nephews, Bryan and Barbour Lathrop, the sum of $2,041.51 each. In 1916, when Bryan Lathrop died, he bequeathed Florence $5,000 annually for life. He also willed her a valuable collection of watercolors, pastels, bronzes, and whatever books he had not already earmarked for the Newberry Library in Chicago.[10]

If marriage represented an economic decision as much as a social one, the question that arises is to what extent did Florence's second marriage also represent a sound economic decision. The evidence, though fragmentary and incomplete, points to only one conclusion: not at all. For Florence, and this may be the case for wealthy widows in general, the second marriage seems to have been entered into for other than economic considerations: companionship; a surrogate father for her two young daughters; the status that accrued to being married to a well-known author; and the like. Indeed, a persuasive argument could be advanced that it was Thomas Nelson Page who, from a strictly economic perspective, benefitted most of all. Marriage gave him access to the income generated from Florence's inheritances and investments so that he could live the style of life to which he aspired but could not attain himself.

Since this was not a subject that one discussed openly or even wrote about, the conclusion has to be drawn from indirect evidence. The Page family, which was highly respected in Virginia going back to the beginnings of settlement, may have been land rich in the eighteenth and early nineteenth centuries, but it was cash poor in the aftermath of the Civil War and Reconstruction. Thomas Nelson Page did not derive any direct monetary benefit from Oakland plantation where his mother resided until her death in 1912. Whatever inheritance he may have received from the plantation would have been shared with other members of the family, notably Rosewell and Frank Page, his brothers. Moreover, because he had gone through a number of unsuccessful business ventures in the early 1890s before meeting Florence Lathrop Field and then abandoned the law as a career following their marriage in 1893, there was little income from these two sources.

Page's writings were the major source of his income. The extant royalty statements from his writings for February 1900, 1904, 1907, 1909, and 1918 and also for August 1904, 1907, 1918, and 1919 disclose that Page earned a total of $22,399.61 for these reporting periods.[11] Even taking into account that the documentation is partial and incomplete, it is evident that Page's income from this source was not sufficient to accommodate his expensive lifestyle, much less that of his new family.

Even assuming that he received additional income from miscellaneous sources, such as acting as a trustee of estates, it still would not have been enough to support himself, his wife, and two stepdaughters in the elegant lifestyle that the Pages led. Certainly his salary as ambassador to Italy from 1912 to 1919 would not have been sufficient, for Congress had authorized only $17,500 annually, from which he was expected to pay personal expenses and to entertain visiting dignitaries. Indeed, one of the considerations that went into his appointment as ambassador—and this was a fairly common practice—was that he would be able to exercise his duties on the scale the position demanded precisely because of his wife's wealth.[12]

The evidence on income, while circumstantial, is persuasive and once again suggests that the metaphor of the sphere needs to be reconsidered. In this instance, it was Florence's income rather than her husband's that underwrote the family's sustenance. On May 2, 1916, for example, Bryan Lathrop's secretary sent Florence a statement of remittances charged to her income as of the first quarter of 1916 and also from the preceding year. The report disclosed that Florence's brother had been transferring from her trust account in Chicago almost monthly sums of $1,000 and $2,500 to her account at the Riggs National Bank in Washington. A New York bank then transmitted drafts from that account to Florence in Rome. The total amounted to nearly $37,000. Even allowing for personal use of those funds for gifts, Christmas presents, travel, war relief, and the like, a goodly portion of that sum was most likely used to underwrite the entertaining that Ambassador Page had to do.[13]

If it was Florence's wealth that financed their mansion in Washington, purchased their Cadillac limousines, paid for their nearly annual trips to Europe and occasionally to North Africa and Cuba, and made feasible Page's ambassadorial appointment, Bryan Lathrop's task was to conserve and enhance his sister's fortune. Once he had allowed for her living expenses, he diversified her investment portfolio to include, besides real estate, both conservative blue-chip and growth-oriented stocks and bonds. Bryan focused mainly on long-term investments that were relatively safe, yielded a steady if unspectacular return, and were neither volatile nor speculative. His strategy was successful because, inter alia, the areas in which he chose to invest her money coincided with the building of the infrastructure of the Chicago metropolitan area.

Florence quickly reaped the benefits of Bryan's investment decisions. In December 1894, shortly after she had remarried and moved to Washington, D.C., he sent her a draft for $4,409.36 as a return upon investment; she then received another $2,000 as principal from her mother's estate; another check for $8,670 as a "special dividend" from the proceeds of the sale of lots in the Sheridan Drive subdivision of Graceland; and an additional $1,530 of interest income. He wrote to Florence that he had "invested for you personally in stock of the Chicago Edison Company $1,954 for 15 shares @130. Also, for your trustees under father's will as follows: 30 shares C.& N,W. R'way [Chicago & Northwestern Railway] common stocks for $3,090 and 65 shares stock of the Chicago Edison Co. @120 7 Comm.-1e, $11,555.50." In all, Florence held 80 shares of Chicago Edison and 30 shares of Chicago & Northwestern common. The railroad had reduced its dividend to 5 percent, but Bryan was confident that it would "pay more some day." Chicago Edison paid 8 percent on par, or nearly 6 percent on its cost @120, which prompted Bryan to write, "I think it has a very good prospect of gain in the future."[14]

He demonstrated similar prudence in handling her real estate investments. On June 7, 1900, Bryan brought her current on the handling of her properties, noting that he had made a plat of a proposed housing subdivision to be built on real estate she owned in La Grange, Illinois. He had submitted the plat to the town authorities for approval; meanwhile, he had engaged Ossian C. Simonds, the landscape architect of Graceland, to design and estimate the cost of developing the subdivision with sewers, water pipes, cement sidewalks, macadam streets, and shrubs and plantings. The concept, which home developers have emulated ever since, was to install these amenities on one model block and then to hire a local realtor to sell building lots. Following the realtor's advice, Bryan suggested constructing five model homes in the $1,500–$2,000 price range, selling them, and reinvesting the proceeds to build additional homes as soon as possible, "in this way developing the property much more rapidly than if he waited for other people to build houses."[15]

His management of Florence's real estate investments marked the start in many respects of modern land use, development, and marketing strategies. The realtor, for example, received a 10 percent commission for selling homesites, the same he would have received for selling plots for the Graceland Cemetery Company. This was rather generous; but as Bryan informed Florence, "I have found this a good arrangement, since it enables him to pay a liberal commission to other agents and thus sell lots much more rapidly then if he depended on his individual effort."

In this, as in other matters, Bryan kept Florence apprised of how he was handling her funds, and she deferred to his good judgment. Over the years she reaped a handsome return on her investments, even after the formal trustee arrangement set up by Henry Field dissolved in 1908.[16] Her gross income from all sources for the year ending December

31, 1911, for example, amounted to $65,651.39, whereas her expenses totaled $3,338.97. This left her with annual income in excess of $62,000, at a time when there was no federal income tax.[17]

While Florence was in Italy in August 1915, Bryan informed her that he had sold off her remaining properties in La Grange and was preparing to sell the Ramona and the Navona apartments, which she had owned as rental income in Chicago for many years. He was doing so in order to free up capital for other investments. Florence's reaction to his recommendations suggested that she still viewed the world of finance as essentially a masculine sphere, even as she insisted on being apprised of Bryan's handling of her finances. "It is an astonishing game, as long as one's income is not at stake," she wrote to her brother, "and this no one on earth has been so wise in providing for as you." His letter arrived shortly after the Germans sank the *Arabic,* and while she had no objection to his action, she also observed with a certain prescience, "We may all have to retrench our way of living very perceptibly," if it led to war.[18]

Ironically, two days before Bryan Lathrop's death in 1916, the family attorney, John P. Wilson, Jr., of the Chicago law firm of Wilson, Moore & McIlvaine, apprised Florence of the state of her investment portfolio preparatory to drawing up her will. Wilson's letter provides one of the clearest insights into her net worth and how her investments were apportioned. The investments fell into two basic categories: (1) those made with the proceeds from the distribution of Henry Field's estate, and (2) those held in trust for her under the will of her father, Jedediah H. Lathrop. From these two sources Wilson calculated that Florence's wealth amounted to $1,078,558.57. But he conceded that this estimate was conservative inasmuch as he could only approximate the market values of some of the properties. The Ramona and the Navona apartment buildings in Chicago, for example, he valued at $75,000 but then declared that this "is merely a guess on my part." He also was unfamiliar with what certain certificates actually represented and therefore calculated them at par value, noting again that they probably were worth a good deal more.[19]

From her husband Henry Field's estate, Florence derived income from five sources: stocks, bonds, real estate trust receipts, bills receivable, and real estate holdings. The stock included 186 shares of AT&T @128 worth $23,808; 115 shares of Chicago Railways Co., series 1, participation certificates @75 for $8,625; 137 shares of Chicago & Northwestern Railway common @216 valued at $17,262; and 50 shares of National Carbon preferred @121 for $6,050, for a total of $55,745 in communications, utilities, and industrials. She also held 1,000 shares of Commonwealth Edison 5 percent bonds valued at $1,000. Her largest holding was in real estate trustee receipts, holding $284,746.57, of which all but $10,000 came from the Harrison Trustees. In addition, Florence received $100,000 in bills receivable from the firm of Kernott & Beck.

Besides stocks, bonds, and trustee receipts, Florence also owned one parcel of real estate in Chicago for which she had paid $184,893.43. Of that amount, $79,863.94 had been for the land and $105,029.49 for the McDuffie Building that stood on it. She also had paid an additional $41,589.80 for two properties adjacent to the McDuffie Building but fronting on Michigan Avenue. While the outlay had been considerable, Florence did derive rental income from these and other properties: $1,380 annually (as of May 1, 1916) from the Ramona and Navona apartments and $12,876 from the McDuffie Building. By contrast, she paid only $785.47 annually in realty taxes.

The Lathrop estate trust, which Bryan had wisely put into stocks, bonds, and real estate trust receipts, also generated investment income that Florence was able to draw upon. From this trust Florence owned 187 shares of Commonwealth Edison @141, worth $26,367; 52 shares of Graceland Cemetery Company @ $1,400, for $72,800; and 25 shares of Chicago Railway no. 2 @16, for $400, for a total of $99,567. In addition, she held $240,500 in real estate trust receipts, divided among the Harrison Trustees ($121,000), Western City Trustees ($23,000), Duluth Real Estate Trustees ($17,000), Chicago Real Estate Trustees ($12,000), Wabash & Monroe Street Trustees ($55,000), and the Caxton Trustees ($12,000). Finally, she held $2,000 in the bonds of the Chicago Gas Light & Coke Co., @5 percent. The only investments that went sour were her 18 shares of stock in the Chicago, Wil. & Vermillion Coal Company and her 50 shares of Western Stone Co., neither of which had any real value.

Bryan Lathrop's death following a brief illness on May 13, 1916 was not only a severe emotional blow to Florence but also a financial one for herself and her daughters, for they had all come to expect yearly bonuses from Bryan's sagacious investments. This was obvious from Florence's letter to her younger daughter, Florence Lindsay, in November 1916. "I know it is a great blow to you as to Minna about no surplus this year," she wrote. "Naturally, and this we have always known, we can't expect any more windfalls, nor any such personal risks as dear Uncle Bryan took for us all."[20]

Besides being a financial setback, Bryan's death occasioned a minor tempest within the family as to who would now manage Florence's and her daughters' portfolio. John P. Wilson, Jr., the Chicago attorney who had handled the legal affairs of both the Lathrop and Page families for many years, had stepped into the breach, and Florence had confidence in his ability and judgment. Her sister-in-law Helen Aldis Lathrop apparently expected that management of Florence's property and investments would be entrusted to a younger cousin, Francis, as a means of promoting his business. But Florence had little regard for Francis's ability and disagreed. "I am very decided that I won't change the management from Mr. Wilson to Francis," she told Helen. "It was never dear Uncle Bryan's intention to do this, and there is no use in discussing the matter." She hoped that Francis would not be upset, "but it can't be helped, for he is not a trustee, and therefore has no claim upon any of our property." It was unfortunate of Helen to have raised the matter, for Florence simply had no confidence in his judgment. "He did not prove invaluable to the Aldis firm before," she noted, observing that Owen Aldis had retained him only because he was family. "What seems strange to me is, that if dear Uncle Bryan had intended turning over any buildings to him, he would have mentioned it."[21]

Florence, of course, prevailed, and Wilson continued to oversee her investment portfolio. In December 1917, nearly eighteen months after Bryan's death, her estate totaled $802,187.96, down somewhat from the previous year. This may have been the result of market fluctuations but more likely was the consequence of the temporary economic dislocations following the entry of the United States into World War I in April 1917. Examination of the portfolio discloses that Wilson adhered to Bryan Lathrop's strategy of relatively safe investments earning a steady return, although there were a few changes that reflected, no doubt, Florence's deep commitment to the Allied and American war effort to defeat Germany. Wilson, acting in her behalf, had purchased $5,000 in bonds of the United Kingdom of Great Britain and Ireland, which, @5 percent, he got at a discount for $4,925 and also $3,000 in Dominion of Canada bonds @5 percent, for which he paid $2,985. Apart from these war-driven investment decisions, Wilson had purchased $15,000 in Washington Water Power bonds @5 percent; $5,000 of General Electric debentures also @5 percent; and a $1,000 6 percent note of the

General Electric Company, which was worth $997.50, as of December 31, 1917.[22]

While she remained by all indicators a very wealthy woman who was not afraid to assert her prerogatives as to who should manage her investments and which investments should be made, there are hints in her correspondence from about 1916 onward that Florence recognized that economic dislocations, such as war-induced inflation and taxation, would alter demonstrably the Pages' lifestyle in the postwar period. Whether her investment income would keep abreast of changing economic circumstances was uncertain. Cryptic remarks appeared in letters to her daughters about the "servant problem" with the return of peace; Florence also talked of selling the mansion at 1759 R Street and New Hampshire Avenue in Washington, which she had rented out during their six-year absence. The home would need to be totally refurbished, a very expensive undertaking. Upon their return to the United States in mid-1919, Florence pondered about the state of her finances even as she purchased a new Cadillac limousine. "Oh! My but the bank book is low down," she informed her husband, although there still remained "something in the general account at Riggs."[23] That she still had funds in her account should not obscure the more significant fact that she was troubled enough to mention money for the first time ever in the context of shrinking financial resources. More than any other utterance this was a telltale sign that Florence had doubts about whether the Pages would be able to return to their affluent lifestyle of the prewar years.

Having established both the sources and the approximate magnitude of Florence Page's wealth, we may now turn to the question of how this affluent upper-class woman expended it. The documentary evidence here is sometimes fragmentary, suggestive, or nonexistent, which means that although we are able to trace certain expenditures and patterns of consumption, the picture must necessarily be incomplete.

An appropriate point to begin the analysis of how Florence disposed of her wealth is to recall that Henry Field's will permitted her periodically to draw from the estate a certain income "to apply in aid of charitable or benevolent societies or institutions." Motivated by the Christian doctrine of stewardship, Florence was generous not only to family members but also to institutions and the poor. In 1912, for example, following the death of her mother-in-law, she wrote a check to Ruth Page, who was living at Oakland plantation, to purchase whatever items the family might need. This might be construed as a normal response to a situation of grieving and mourning, but Florence's explanation made it clear that she viewed her wealth not simply in this light but as an obligation to share her good fortune. "You see the gods have been so generous with me that it is my pleasure to try to share some of my privileges with my dear ones," she wrote.[24]

She was similarly generous to institutions that had played an important role in her own and the life of her family. That Florence was a practicing Episcopalian should not obfuscate the fact that she did not allow religion or a male-dominated church hierarchy to dictate how she used her wealth. Quite the contrary; she valued the role of the church as the keeper of moral values and a bastion of stability in a society in flux, but she exercised her own choices, being selective in her financial contributions and in keeping with the precepts of the Social Gospel, without actually rubbing elbows with the poor. She often donated money to church building funds and to its work among the unfortunate rather than to the maintenance of the clergy per se. She made regular financial contributions to its work among the urban poor in Chicago, Washington, York Harbor, and elsewhere. In February 1902, for example, she signed an indenture with the "Trustees of Funds of the Episcopal Church in the Diocese of Virginia," donating $3,000 to help maintain "The Fork Church" in St. Martin's Parish, Hanover County, and for its eleemosynary work among the rural poor in the Beaver Dam District, where Oakland was situated. In November 1906 she contributed $200 to the Bruton Parish Church Restoration Fund, of Williamsburg, Virginia, historically one of the oldest Episcopal churches in America.[25]

Florence also was a patron of the arts and other cultural institutions. The Orchestra Association of Chicago, of which Bryan Lathrop was a founder and president, became a regular recipient of her benefactions, even after she had left the city for Washington, D.C. In October 1917, following her brother's death, she added a codicil to her will bequeathing $50,000 to the association to endow the "Bryan Lathrop Memorial" scholarships. The scholarships were to be used in conjunction with the School of Music to be established from a $700,000 bequest of her beloved brother. She likewise provided the Art Institute of Chicago with a small endowment to maintain her first husband's collection and, at the suggestion of her husband Thomas Nelson Page, established the Florence Lathrop Page-Barbour Lecture Foundation at the University of Virginia.[26]

Written on the back of an envelope in Florence's hand is a listing of her annual contributions to charity for the years 1891 to 1897, inclusive. They totaled $95,569.30, which suggests that she was a very generous woman, especially when the nation was experiencing a severe depression for at least half of that period. The pattern of giving is also revealing: $4,450 (1891); $9,430 (1892); $22,414.30 (1893); $41,324.99 (1894); $5,303.21 (1895); $5,119.40 (1896); and $7,527.40 (1897).[27] There is no further breakdown of these figures, but the unusually large sums for 1893 and 1894 may include monies given to the Art Institute in connection with the Field gallery.

Assuming this to be the case, it is reasonable to conclude that Florence normally contributed $4,500 to $5,000 annually to charitable causes in the depression decade and may well have continued to do so thereafter. A perusal of receipts indicates that her contributions covered a wide spectrum of causes, although the amount donated varied according to Florence's ranking of its merit: $100 to the Associated Charities of the District of Columbia; $25 to the Needlework Guild; $5 to the National Plant, Flower, and Fruit Guild; $100 to the William Carey Memorial Fund in New York City.[28] She also sponsored visiting nurses programs for the indigent of Chicago, Washington, York Harbor, and Hanover County, Virginia, although no dollar amount can be identified.

In deciding how she would dispose of her wealth, which causes she deemed worthwhile supporting financially and which she did not, Florence was making a political statement. She was empowering herself to take control over her wealth and her environment, to make choices that satisfied herself alone. Besides contributing to charitable and cultural institutions and underwriting the Pages' almost annual trips to Europe, which included expensive staterooms, first-class hotels, and automobile rentals, Florence's largest expenditures were for her two homes: the mansion in Washington, D.C., and the summer "cottage" in Maine.[29]

To design her resplendent home in the District of Columbia at the corner of 1759 R Street and New Hampshire Avenue, which later became a part of the French Embassy, Florence followed her brother's example in choosing the preeminent architects to America's upper-class elite, the firm of McKim, Mead & White, of New York. In 1896 they drafted a plan for a handsome Georgian mansion to be appointed with a distinct and very elegant entry and the most modern urban amenities: gas, electricity, flush plumbing, and the telephone. Standing five stories tall and consisting of thirty-four rooms, it was constructed entirely of brick and was rendered fireproof.

The original blueprint projected a home of 286,000 cubic feet, which made it nearly 100,000 cubic feet larger than Bellevue Place, Bryan Lathrop's mansion in Chicago. At 31.5 cents per cubic foot, the cost of construction would have been nearly $90,000. The building contract, however, placed the cost at $67,500, indicating that the original size was scaled back. A tally of the architect's commission, lawyer's fees, decorator's services, and other expenses puts the actual cost of construction and furnishing closer to $80,000.[30] Whether the decrease was the result of hesitancy on Florence's part about spending such a huge sum or a response to advice from her brother who was concerned that the election of William Jennings Bryan to the presidency might depress the market is unknown. Florence paid the entire sum in cash disbursements from her inheritances. In design, furnishings, and appointments, the mansion was both a manifestation of her affluence and a visual affirmation of her elite upper-class status.

Rock Ledge, the summer cottage in York Harbor, Maine, was her next largest single expenditure. The "cottage" in reality was a compound, for it encompassed a mansion, pump house, stable, butler's residence, and gardens. The records do not indicate its cost of construction but an undated insurance register indicates that the value of the cottage, household furnishings, and ancillary properties was set at $24,000. The cottage alone was valued at $15,250. These figures are conservative and for insurance purposes only; the actual replacement cost undoubtedly would have been considerably higher.[31]

Besides the maintenance of two large households, an extraordinary but sizable expenditure worth noting was Florence's purchase of war bonds. After the United States entered World War I in 1917, Florence subscribed to each of the Liberty Loan drives, utilizing funds from various sources such as the Jedediah H. Lathrop estate, for a total of about $58,000. The purchase of war bonds was both an expenditure and a form of investment in America. Like other Americans, Florence paid federal income taxes for the first time in 1917, and like them, she also paid a wartime surtax on income.[32]

Bank drafts, construction contracts, and insurance receipts allow us to pinpoint special expenditures with a certain degree of preciseness. The same may hardly be said of Florence's patterns of consumption because the only data available consist of a household ledger listing bills for the months of June and December 1899; a receipt for funds paid to A. R. Forbes, a dressmaker in New York City, dated November 1899; a statement marked "Personal Account for 1911," which Bryan Lathrop drafted for his sister; and some miscellaneous items. Documents such as these enable us to identify some of the goods and services the Page household consumed and required at these particular dates. They reinforce the conclusion that Florence Page enjoyed a superfluity of money and that the items and services she purchased were a visible confirmation of both her own and her family's relative standing in the hierarchy of consumption and wealth. Psychologically, the need that such commodities and services filled was the need to express the fact that she was among the wealthiest of Americans.[33]

In urban, industrial America of the turn of the century, those individuals with the most and the newest commodities or those who purchased goods which were inherently limited in quantity or could not be easily reproduced, such as artwork, antique furniture, hand-sewn clothing, and automobiles, were generally the wealthiest in the community. They expressed income superiority through these purchases and enjoyed a relatively higher standard of living than people who could not afford to purchase as many or as new commodities. To the extent that Florence's extant consumption expenditures are an accurate reflection of her lifestyle, they offer insight into the comfortable world of the upper-class elite woman and indirectly illuminate the larger society of which the Pages were a part.[34]

Categorizing the monthly expenditures into necessities, luxuries, and leisure activities indicates that the Page household had more disposable income to spend in each of these areas than did working-class and even most middle-class families, who spent a preponderance of their income on basic necessities such as food, shelter, and machine-made clothing. Florence had these expenditures also, but she spent proportionately less on them and more on nonessential goods and services. In the months of June and December 1899, for example, the household bills totaled nearly $600. She spent in two months more than the average working-class household would have earned in nearly two years.[35]

Florence's expenditures on furniture might be considered a necessity in furnishing a home, but the sheer number of entries for furniture in the 1899 ledgers points to the luxury of decorating a very large house. Similarly, in November 1899 Florence traveled to New York to engage

A. R. Forbes to custom make dresses for herself and her daughters, an expensive but common practice among upper-class women. She paid on this occasion the sum of $182 to have hand-sewn clothing. That figure, even if repeated only once or twice annually, was almost as much as a working-class family might earn in an entire year. The figure would be higher still if one calculated the cost of lodging at the fashionable Holland House hotel (as she did in 1907) while fittings were being taken.

There is other evidence that she spent substantial sums on luxury items and entertainment that would not have been readily available to lesser households. In 1900 Florence shopped at B. Altman & Co., the upscale department store in New York City, and also at Higgins & Seiter, a specialty store, from which she purchased a fine bone china service for twenty-four. Upon her return to Washington, D.C., she purchased various items of silver from Galt & Bros., Jewellers & Silversmiths, including a tea set. The trail of receipts also shows purchases of silk and chiffon material; New Year's Day gifts to the post boy, the trash collector, and the express man; and eight tickets to the theater, bought in December 1899. Ledger entries for car fares suggest that before the Pages acquired a Cadillac limousine in 1907, they traveled in horse-drawn taxicabs, which, if not beyond the means of a working-class family, would still have been expensive.

Equally significant is the Pages' access to the physical toil of others. The list of bills for December 1899 includes payments to waitresses on five different days of the month and also in early January 1900. Since the payments clustered around the Christmas and New Year holidays, a reasonable assumption is that Florence hired these people to supplement the regular household staff because she was entertaining heavily. The salaries of servants and other hired help who did many of the household chores, such as washing, cleaning, sewing, and laundering, were yet another sign of Florence's affluent upper-class status.

Imbedded in these monetary transfers were the telltale signs of an important social transformation over the course of the nineteenth century. The size of the upper-class family, whose immediate members in the past would have routinely performed these tasks themselves, had decreased. As the nuclear family evolved in the transition to an urban industrial society and as more informed knowledge of contraception became available, upper-class households became smaller, less self-sufficient, and more dependent upon the salaried labor of strangers. With servants and other salaried help to perform many of the household

chores, Florence focused on the management of the home and the rearing of the children. Her duties as household manager included but were
not limited to supervision of the staff, planning menus both on a daily
basis and for the many occasions when friends or acquaintances came to
lunch, tea, or dinner, and keeping track of daily and monthly expenditures.

Thomas Nelson Page attested to her abilities in this segment of the
woman's sphere in his short eulogistic, biographical sketch, but interestingly his portrait emphasizes her decisiveness, normally a masculine
trait, rather than her intuitiveness. "She knew what her actual and possible expenses might be and made in advance provision to meet them.
Thus, she was never surprised. She never permitted a bill to be sent in
twice; it was paid as soon as presented." Florence also knew precisely
the household items she required, wasting neither time nor energy in
indecision. "I will take this—and this, thank you; this is just what I
want, I will not look further," he remembered her telling vendors and
clerks.[36]

When Page praised his wife for being a good homemaker, he was
affirming that she had acquired fairly sophisticated managerial skills.
She had mastered and learned to apply the scientific principles of business management, including the principles of time-motion, organization, and the management of capital, to achieve success in the business
of homemaking. Her abilities in this area allowed her to dominate the
distinctively feminine sphere embodied in the cult of domesticity, first
as the wife of Henry Field and then as the spouse of Thomas Nelson
Page. Freed from economic constraints and worries, she successfully established and sustained family life, was a good mother and wife, and
maintained a comfortable home. Florence's authoritative rendering of
decisions, coupled with her organizational and managerial talents,
would serve her in good stead in wartime Italy.

In the course of examining Florence's expenditures, I have alluded to the
quality of her lifestyle as compared to those of individuals of working-
and middle-class status. However, the historian who attempts to track
Florence's wealth and expenditures relative to other economic groupings
within the society needs to be mindful that the period from 1870 to
1919 is "an empirical Dark Age" for making definitive judgments.[37]
Hard data upon which to base firm conclusions regarding the distribution of wealth are exceedingly few. Anecdotal and some statistical evi-

dence, though, points to the conclusion that these were years of great economic inequality. Writing in 1896, Charles B. Spahr, an economist favorable to the Populist cause, observed that one-eighth of the families in America received more than half of the aggregate income, and the richest 1 percent received a larger income than the poorest 50 percent. "This small class of wealthy property owners receives from property alone as large an income as half of our people receive from property and labor," he concluded. Political scientist George K. Holmes, utilizing data from the 1890 census, earlier had estimated that the top 1 percent of American families held 25.76 percent of the nation's wealth and the top 10 percent of families held 72.17 percent.[38] In this same period between 88 percent and 92.5 percent of American families had annual incomes of less than $1,200. The lowest tenth of native white families in 1900 still earned under $285 annually.[39] For anyone who was foreign born or black, the situation was worse still; nearly 40 percent of southern Italian, Russian, and black families fell below the $285 mark.

The conclusion is inescapable that Florence Lathrop Page possessed substantial wealth, quite unlike anything the lower-and middle-class breadwinner could hope to amass. When Henry Field died in 1890, he left behind an estate in excess of one million dollars, of which she was the chief beneficiary. Compared to the middle- and lower-class income groups below them, the Fields were among the affluent against whom Thorstein Veblen railed in *The Theory of the Leisure Class,* his 1904 diatribe against the conspicuous and competitive consumption of Chicago's elite whose liveried servants and lavish palaces contrasted starkly with the shanties of the city's poor. In 1890, when only 13 percent of the total population of the country had indoor commodes and only 3.1 percent had electricity, her homes incorporated both of these amenities as soon as they became available. When most workers in the labor force in 1900 toiled up to sixty-eight hours per week, Florence had never been gainfully employed.[40]

That Florence was able to dominate the physical space of the household, to maintain large homes and organize cadres of domestics and gardeners to maintain them, that she was able to remain outside of the labor market throughout her life and devote herself to her family attested to Henry Field's success in the economic competition of the day. That she was able to maintain this lifestyle and actually enhance it after her husband's death and subsequent remarriage to a man of lesser financial means was eloquent testimony to her ability to manage her wealth. As late as 1910, when only 1 percent of the population owned an automobile, Florence owned a chauffeur-driven Cadillac limousine both of which she had shipped abroad in 1907 to tour Europe.[41] Florence and Thomas Nelson Page visited Europe, including North Africa, nearly annually from 1900 until the outbreak of World War I, and she footed the bill.

Florence's wealth and her economic rituals evidence a world of affluence which was really a different culture altogether from that at the bottom of the economic heap. But wealth is both real and relative. Was she among the superrich? In comparison to the 4,047 millionaires in the United States in 1892, 316 of whom lived in Chicago, Florence was extremely comfortable but by no means possessed of a large fortune, and unlike the overwhelming majority of them, she had inherited rather than earned her wealth. Even as late as 1913, when her wealth still hovered around the one-million-dollar mark, she would have been considered affluent but not among the top wealth holders in the nation, of whom twenty-two ranked in the $25 to $35 million category and twenty-nine above $35 million. These included the Rockefellers, Carnegies, Morgans, Harrimans, Armours, and the estate of Marshall Field. This suggests that inherited wealth tended to grow more slowly than earned wealth.[42]

The acquisition, conservation, and enhancement of wealth affected the entire context within which Florence Lathrop Page and her brother Bryan Lathrop functioned. The Gospel of Wealth and its corollary Social Darwinism comprised many propositions that they and the majority of Americans had accepted. These included the belief that the American economy was controlled for the benefit of all by a natural aristocracy and that these leaders had risen to the top by a competitive struggle which weeded out the weak, incompetent, and unfit and selected the strong, able, and wise; that politicians were not subject to rigorous natural selection and hence could not be trusted to the same degree as businessmen; that the state should protect property, maintain order, and not interfere in economic affairs; that poverty and slums were unfortunate but inevitable negative results of the competitive struggle and state intervention to eliminate them was misguided; and that the stewardship of wealth, or the Social Gospel, obliged the rich to use their bounty to ameliorate social injustice.[43]

Though these ideas may be regarded as a rationalization of the rule of a privileged class, many Americans outside of that group also accepted them. Notions of wealth and class also influenced thinking about politics. This was especially true of Bryan Lathrop and, to the extent that she thought about politics at all, also of Florence Page. Bryan Lathrop was a Republican, while Florence, disfranchised by virtue of her gender, was socially more comfortable with the Republican presidents, Theodore Roosevelt and William Howard Taft, at least until the Democrat Woodrow Wilson became president in 1912. The same may be said of Thomas Nelson Page, although he remained active in the Virginia Democratic party. What really determined their political outlook was economics; the Lathrops and the Pages were above all else fiscally conservative, anti-inflation, hard money people for whom the gold standard and the absence of debt were sacrosanct.

Bryan Lathrop's adherence to the gold standard was unmistakably manifested in his lengthy letter of August 9, 1896, to Thomas Nelson Page after the Democratic party nominated William Jennings Bryan for the presidency. Among hard money men, there was widespread consensus that Bryan's election would plunge the nation into greater economic and fiscal difficulty, and this prospect was already depressing the stock market. This occurred at the time when Florence had to liquidate some of her securities in order to pay the builder as construction proceeded on the Pages' new mansion in the District of Columbia. "Owing to the apprehension of Mr. Bryan's election," Lathrop wrote, "I am afraid that we shall have to sell at a considerable loss, as the market prices have fallen terribly since the Chicago convention." If William Jennings Bryan were "by any ill chance" to be elected, Lathrop predicted that it would cost Florry "many thousand dollars more to build her house than if the spectre of free silver communism had not been raised."[44]

Talk of a silver standard had already torpedoed the market value of Florence's North Western common stock from 106 to 88, causing Bryan Lathrop to exclaim, "The Lord knows what it would sell for if we really were reduced to a silver standard!" He could understand the western silver states having a selfish interest in free silver but was unable to fathom its attraction to southerners. "They may think that they can pay their debts more easily in 'cheap money,'" he observed, "but they tried that once and I remember that a pair of boots cost $500 to $700."

Worse still, the election of the Populist Democrat would throw the country into the severest depression ever, set class against class, and take many years before the nation and the world recovered from the shock. "No man can foresee what would become of values," Lathrop wrote. "No care & no foresight will enable me, for example, to protect Florry's hold-ings from shrinking and the income from dwindling to an extent that might be appalling." He denounced the Democratic candidate for mak-ing communistic speeches and for seeking "to array the ignorant mass against all the industrious, intelligent & thrifty & especially against all who have accumulated anything."

The people who had a stake to lose, whether Republican or Demo-crat, dreaded the consequences of a Bryan victory. They particularly feared that foreign bondholders and stockholders would unload their securities on the market and thereby drive down all values. "It would be under such circumstances that we should have to sell Florries' securi-ties in order to pay for her house." A Bryan victory would cost his sister thousands of dollars more to build her home, and he would not "even guess at the possible loss in her income." The only hope rested upon "the intelligent and patriotic people of the country," who, Lathrop believed, would "make common cause against a common enemy and vote to elect McKinley as the man who represents the preservation of everything ma-terial which we value and of the honor of the nation."

McKinley's election in 1896 was a victory for upper-class hard money people, whether Republican or Democrat. A nearly identical attitude surfaced in the election of 1912, when the Democratic party once again was on the threshold of nominating an inflationary, soft money candi-date. The Pages were visiting Paris that spring but were well aware of the militant reform spirit sweeping the United States and its divisive impact upon the Republican party. They found the public conflict be-tween President Taft and his predecessor, Theodore Roosevelt, de-meaning to the executive office and personally disagreeable because despite Page's close ties to the Virginia Democracy, he and Florence were socially and in their economic thinking more at ease with a Republican hard money president than with any of the Bryanite, soft money candi-dates of the Democratic party.

This time, however, Florence broke her silence on political issues and condemned the likely nominee of the Democratic party, Congressman Champ Clark. In one of her very few surviving letters that make even the slightest reference to politics, she wrote to her mother-in-law, Elizabeth Burwell Page, "I am almost to the point of hoping for a Democratic President now, only *not Champ Clark;* let us be spared this much." Un-like some other upper-class women, Florence had not previously in-truded into the political realm, which she viewed as the masculine arena;

but this remark indicates that she did follow politics and was aware of the issues even though she was disfranchised. Her agenda was personal, the advancement and well-being of her family, and not public, for she believed that having achieved economic independence, a woman of her class had little to gain from politics. Despite this, she was sufficiently disturbed to break her silence and to complain to her mother-in-law, "All politics are dreadful to me, national, Church, and suffragists!"[45]

Her condemnation of the Democratic Speaker of the House indicated deep agitation, but over what precisely? The answer is to be found both in the Speaker's social standing and in his muddled economic ideas. Roosevelt and Taft had the patrician background and breeding that the Pages identified with, and both were staunch advocates of the gold standard, whereas Champ Clark, of Pike County, Missouri, was narrow and provincial in outlook, undistinguished intellectually, and temperamentally unsuited to lead a great nation. Politically and economically he was the heir of William Jennings Bryan. The endorsement of the Bryan Democrats from the West and the South marked Clark as an inflationary, soft money man and a threat to people of means.[46] Even though Woodrow Wilson was not Thomas Nelson Page's first choice for the Democratic nomination, he and Florence were so relieved to have a cultured, genteel southerner, an intellectual, and a proponent of sound money carry the Democratic banner into the presidential campaign that Page worked for Wilson's election and served in 1913 as chairman of his inauguration committee.

When Florence Lathrop Page died on June 6, 1921, she was an affluent but not extravagantly wealthy woman. Her death occurred eleven months to the day after she had signed her last will and testament. As in the case of Henry Field's will, the act of drawing up such a document assumed social significance because it had required Florence to confront her own mortality. In drafting a will, Florence was also making an economic statement about her life. She required a will because she, unlike the large majority of her contemporaries who died intestate, would be leaving behind both real and personal property. Because the disposition of property was at issue, Florence needed to put her economic house in order beforehand. This meant determining which material goods she valued most, which individuals were closest to her, and who should participate in greater or lesser degree in the final division of her property. Florence's will divided naturally into distinct categories: nonmonetary bequests exclusive of realty, monetary bequests, property bequests, miscellaneous bequests, and the establishment of a residuary trust.[47]

Following a common practice, Florence provided that specific items of jewelry be distributed not only to her daughters but also to kin and lifelong friends. To Cornelia Aldis, Anne Carter Dulany, and Errol Brown Train, she bequeathed, respectively, a diamond and platinum wristwatch, a matrix turquoise and gold lorgnette chain, and a heart-shaped diamond brooch with an opal center. To her daughter Florence Lindsay she bequeathed her string of seventy-one graduated pearls with platinum, diamond, and emerald clasp valued at $15,000 and a pearl and diamond dog collar worth $7,500. Upon this daughter's death, Florence specified that the pearls would pass to her granddaughter Florence Lindsay and the diamond collar to her granddaughter Minna Lindsay. Such specificity indicated that Florence intended for the pieces of jewelry that meant the most to her to stay on the female side of the family. No other disposition that would accomplish the same result was feasible because daughter Minna's only heir was Henry Field Gibson, a male. To avoid the impression of inequality of love between her children or grandchildren, Florence went on to explain that "it is for this reason only that I give them both to my daughter Florence during her lifetime, and do not wish my so doing to be construed in any way as making any distinction between my own two beloved daughters."

Florence's remaining jewelry, articles of personal use and ornament, clothing, watercolors, etchings, engravings, and silverware (save that which Thomas Nelson Page had given to her) were to be divided equally between her daughters. In the event one or both of them predeceased her, the surviving grandchildren were to divide the items equitably. Thomas Nelson Page received all the silverware he had given to Florence and her oil paintings, except the Léon Bonnat portrait of her daughters which was to go to Florence Lindsay. He also inherited her books, with the proviso that they be divided between her daughters or their survivors upon his death, and her household effects, which included furniture, fixtures, tools, automobiles, and the like. However, Florence stipulated that upon her husband's death "all of my marbles, such as tables, vases, fragments of statues, sarcophagi, etc.," were to pass to her grandson Henry Field. If any of her possessions remained after the death of her husband, Florence directed that they pass to her daughters.

Florence's monetary bequests suggested a rank order of closeness to herself, beginning with the immediate family and extending to kin, relatives, friends, and even domestics. Thomas Nelson Page inherited the sum of $250,000, plus the mansion at 1759 R Street and New Hampshire Avenue (Rock Ledge, the summer cottage in York Harbor, Maine, was divided equally between Florence and Minna). If he elected to receive his property inheritance in cash, he could do so, but only after the trustees of Florence's estate had determined the property's fair market value. Florence Lindsay received $50,000; sister-in-law Helen Lathrop, $25,000; brother Barbour Lathrop, $25,000; and sons-in-law Algernon Burnaby and Thomas P. Lindsay, $5,000 each, "as a small token of my love." Nannie Barbour Brown of Lake Forest, Illinois, a cousin through marriage, and Ruth Nelson Page, a sister-in-law, received $10,000 each. Others received lesser sums: Anne Carter Dulany, $5,000; $2,000 to each of four cousins; $1,000 to Josephine Biran, Florence's maid. The Pages' servant Alfred George Barrett received $15,000, a munificent reward for his loyal and long-term service.

Florence's miscellaneous bequests also were directed toward people who were or had been dearest to her. For her grandson Henry Field Gibson, she set aside $50,000 in trust with instructions to the trustees (Thomas Nelson Page, Arthur T. Aldis, and John P. Wilson, Jr.) to hold both the principal and the interest until Henry Field attained his majority. At age twenty-one he was to receive the interest that had accrued, and four years later, both the principal and the interest. Florence also bequeathed $50,000 to the Orchestra Association of Chicago to create the "Bryan Lathrop Memorial," to provide scholarships for the music school her brother had endowed. If she died before the school came into being, that money would go to the Orchestra Association.

Once the trustees had made these disbursements, Florence directed that the remainder of her estate be used to establish a residuary trust whose principal and income were to be disposed of as she had indicated: her servant Nora Foy was to receive a lifetime annuity of $150 annually; Thomas Nelson Page was to receive one-half of the net income from the trust during his lifetime; the remaining 50 percent not directed specifically toward other purposes was to be divided equally between Florence and Minna, or their surviving children. Following the deaths of her husband and daughters, the principal was to be divided equally among her grandchildren and their issue, as determined in her daughters' wills.

A close reading of Florence's will discloses that she had learned and would utilize many of the same principles whereby her first husband had ordered his estate. Like Henry Field, she was concerned primarily with the protection of her property within the family. Therefore, she carefully and deliberately delineated how the division of the major bequests of property and money were to occur to ensure that they did remain within the immediate family: her husband, daughters, and grandchildren. Unlike Henry Field, however, Florence relied more heavily upon the principal of personalism, especially where her daughters were concerned. Once she had provided for her husband, she established separate estates of property and money for each of her daughters. This suggested that she ranked each daughter's need for economic security more important than the principle of male dominance in the family. Florence Lindsay and Minna Burnaby received their inheritances in a manner which shielded them from control or tampering by their husbands, who were not excluded from the will but each received a precise sum of money as a sign of her affection. In doing so, Florence also was precluding the possibility (however remote) of their asserting a claim to their wives' inheritance.

The care with which Florence designated particular items of jewelry, paintings, and "ornaments" for specific individuals and then spelled out in detail the terms of her grandson Henry's trust fund indicates that she might well have been dissatisfied with the disposition of her property if she had died intestate. Moreover, unlike Henry Field, Florence rewarded loyalty to herself and to her family, a practice which appears to have been more typical of nineteenth-century ladies' wills rather than those of gentlemen.[48] This explains the monetary sums for the valet, the personal maid, and the servant.

Finally, Florence appointed males whom she had known for many years as trustees of her grandson's fund and of her residuary trust. This was a common practice, necessary in the case of Henry Field Gibson who was a minor. One might argue that given Minna Field Burnaby's track record of handling money, Florence made the prudent decision; but because it applied to both daughters, it suggests that even in the sunset of her life, Florence adhered to the concept of separate spheres, at least where money and property were at issue: a woman ought not to concern herself with the details of commerce and litigation, and male testators would have a better chance in the courts to protect a wife from a husband who might seek control of her estate "in right of his wife."

Shortly after Florence's death the executors of her estate furnished the Probate Court of the District of Columbia "a true and perfect inventory" of her "Goods, Chattels and Personal Estate." With the exception of monies belonging to her and debts that might have been due to her, this document was the most accurate accounting of Florence's wealth accumulated over a lifetime. Her net worth at death was $780,626.21. This figure reflected the value of her household effects ($40,136.65); jewelry ($40,275.00); stocks ($202,592.28); bonds ($74,037.35); automobiles (1919 and 1920 Cadillac limousines together worth $2,700); and trustees' certificates ($420,884.93). The inventory did not take into account the worth of any books, wearing apparel, horses, carriages, and the like that Florence also may have owned.[49]

The sums are impressive but not very personal. Only upon closer examination does one appreciate both the quantity and the uniformly high quality of Florence Lathrop Page's possessions, denoting a woman of discerning judgment and refined taste who over the years had acquired an extensive knowledge of art, literature, objects, and styles. This awareness affords us a truer and more accurate representation of her lifestyle. For example, she owned an extensive collection of jewelry among which her favorite was the string of pearls. Buried within the two-page inventory of jewelry was included a $1,000 platinum ring set with an emerald, a diamond, and a ruby which was a gift to her from the queen of Italy. Her furniture and household effects were so numerous that it was impossible to accommodate them in any one space. Most of the items were in her residences in Maine and in Washington, but some were also warehoused in the Fidelity and the Security Storage companies in the District of Columbia.

The items were outstanding examples of what Veblen had denounced as "conspicuous consumption." Among them were the mahogany sofa with claw feet and the Steinway parlor grand piano at the summer cottage, valued at $175 and $125, respectively. The Washington mansion was stuffed with Oriental and Turkish rugs, European tapestries, antique mahogany sideboards and cabinets, and other expensive items. Her possessions in storage were no less impressive: thousands of dollars in oriental rugs; French tapestries; an Egyptian sarcophagus; trunks of silk and damask table covers; Jesurum lace from one of the oldest factories in Venice; dinner sets, tea sets, and other fine china from Royal Worcester, Limoges, Dresden, Minton, and Copeland; sterling silver pieces; a Chinese lacquer cabinet valued at $500; Whistler and Haden etchings, watercolors, and old prints.

The inventory also listed her assets in bonds, stocks, and certificates. They, too, were impressive, consisting of investments in both blue chips and the newer technologically driven growth industries of the early twentieth century. Florence held shares of Commonwealth Edison, AT&T, the Studebaker Corporation, First National Bank of Chicago, General Electric, Goodyear, and International Harvester. Real estate, by contrast, occupied a less prominent place in her holdings than in former years. Two equally plausible explanations may have accounted for this. The first is that after Bryan Lathrop's death in 1916, none of the trustees knew the Chicago real estate market as intimately and expertly as he had and so shifted funds from real estate to other investments they felt more comfortable with; more likely, following Bryan Lathrop's lead, the trustees may have decided that nonrealty investments were going to be the more dynamic areas of growth and opportunity in post World War I America. Whatever the reason, the second and third generation of Florence's heirs benefited financially from the manner in which she accumulated, conserved, and transmitted her wealth to them.

4

Trending into Maine

*W*hat city people really like best about country villages, is their natural charm, the fitness of things to their place and surroundings, the absence of all straining after effect," wrote Samuel Adams Drake, the nineteenth-century historian of Maine.[1] Drake employed the metaphor of urbanism to delineate two distinct worlds and peoples, the cosmopolitan world of city dwellers and the rustic world of rural folk. He then observed the paradox of city people: "Yet it is they who have set the fashion of unusual renovation." In a manner which roughly corresponded to the metaphor of the sphere that modern scholars have invoked to delineate late Victorian gender relations, Drake's comment was an unerring description of how the upper-class elite physically and socially transformed the picturesque village of York Harbor, Maine, into an idealized country counterpart of their urban environment.

Like the metaphor of urbanism, the metaphor of separate spheres also may be used to describe literally the physical spaces to which women were assigned, those in which they lived, and those they chose for themselves. The masculine spaces were public: the central community, the meeting places, and the fields; the feminine spaces were what was left: the home, the sleeping places, and the gardens. Within this context, physical space implied social subordination. The Pages' annual summer retreat into Maine affords us an opportunity to test the validity of the phenomenon of separate spheres and to determine whether the historical evidence supports the conclusion that Victorian men and women strictly adhered to it.

• • •

In a society of cement, the summer resort movement, which gained in popularity after the Civil War and experienced its most rapid growth between 1880 and World War I, paralleled the upper class's genealogical escape to the past. The rich, the wellborn, and the powerful chose to flee the city despite the efforts of landscape architects like Frederick Law Olmsted to introduce rural beauty into the heart of the nineteenth-century metropolis. A few upper-class patricians like Theodore Roosevelt went out West to renew their bodies and spirits; others, like Charles William Eliot, the president of Harvard University, spent the summers in Maine with his sons camping in tents until they built their summer cottage in Northeast Harbor in 1881. Whether they were intellectuals, artists, writers, gentry, or millionaires, America's upper class sought solace for its soul in the beauty of nature and the simple life among the "natives" of coastal and mountain communities, especially along the eastern seaboard.[2]

In places like Cape May, Lenox, Bar Harbor, and Kennebunkport, affluent, white, Anglo-Saxon Protestants were able to forget the physiological and physical ugliness of the urban melting pot with its offensive odors, noises, and manners. They could dwell for at least a part of the year among solid Yankees, many of whom possessed more homogeneous, colonial-stock roots than their own. If the simple life was often touching and always relaxing, homogeneity was its essence. All one's kind were there together, and the older virtues of communal life prevailed.[3]

Although these urban patricians professed to admire the rustic life, they very quickly began to remold both the natural environment and the social scene of which it was a part to fit their own particular lifestyle and social requirements. Bar Harbor, Maine, was perhaps the classic example of this process. Between 1890 and World War I, this rural coastal community developed into one of America's most stylish resorts. Joseph Pulitzer built the first $100,000 "cottage" there in 1894, and J. P. Morgan and several Standard Oil partners were among the leaders of the community. The pattern was repeated elsewhere as more and more affluent upper-class families sought relief from the city. They built summer homes that were often traditional but elegant, replete with servants and up-to-date plumbing. They also used their wealth to affirm their social and cultural dominance over these rustic communities and peoples. The Pages contributed to this phenomenon when they retreated from the hot, humid summers of Washington, D.C., for the cool, seaborne breezes of York Harbor, Maine.[4]

Less fashionable than Bar Harbor, more casual and understated, but no less genteel, York Harbor was located on the ocean about forty-five miles southwest of Portland, Maine. The village and its immediate environs were "one of the most eligibly situated and altogether desirable of sea-side resorts."[5] The summer visitors came to York Harbor for the specific purpose of enjoying the past that they had traded away in the urban metropolises for horizontal and vertical integration, interlocking directorates, and all the smoke, steam, coal, steel, oil, and wealth that went with them.

Geographically and historically York Harbor was actually one of three small communities within the larger political jurisdiction of York, Maine, an area of land which skirted the York River and ran to the open sea. Physical proximity notwithstanding, it contrasted sharply and distinctively with York Village and York Beach. York Village was the original townsite of Agamenticus founded by Captain John Smith in 1624. It achieved distinction as the first English city on the American continent when Sir Ferdinando Gorges endowed it in 1641 with a city charter under the name of Gorgeana. The ancient community remained small and serene through the latter nineteenth century, retaining much of its primitive charm. York Harbor, by contrast, lay a mile away, suave and distinguished, its roads lined with cottages and flower gardens, its rocky coast covered with spacious homes. Two miles farther was the more plebeian York Beach, cluttered with a medley of shops, booths, amusement halls, eating places, scores of little boxlike houses with arcadian names, and hundreds of holiday seekers disporting themselves on the sands.[6]

The Yorks were a byway through much of the nineteenth century, remote from main-traveled roads and from the painful possibilities of development. Like the rest of the state, the Yorks had experienced an exodus of farmers and woodsmen to the more open, easily tillable agricultural lands of New York, Pennsylvania, the Midwest, and California. Time and the Industrial Revolution bypassed those who remained behind. Even the maritime industry, once the backbone of Maine's and the Yorks' economy, had relocated, gravitating toward the development of new technology elsewhere. In industry and most other fields, the state sat just too far to the northeast, too far out on the edge of the national transportation networks developed during the Gilded Age. If prosperity, population, and national influence were the benchmarks of a state's worth, Maine and the Yorks had to appeal on the basis of their natural beauty and historic past to the larger world for their future.[7]

The Yorks' revival was inextricably bound to the rediscovery of Maine in the "back to the land" movement that swept America in the decades after the Civil War. The first summer visitors to York Harbor were those who could contrive long vacations in an era when extended holidays were luxuries to be enjoyed only by a favored few. Transportation was the initial obstacle these affluent few had to surmount; but as their numbers increased, those entrepreneurs who provided the means for getting from one place to another saw profit in establishing scheduled services. By the 1890s transportation facilities for conveying passengers to the Yorks had improved dramatically, evolving from the buckboard and stagecoach to steam railroad and electric car line. Steamers also made daily scheduled stops at York Harbor and York Beach during a few summers in the latter 1880s. The most important impetus to growth was the opening of the York Harbor and York Beach Railroad Company as a branch of the Boston and Maine Railroad. Train passengers arriving at York Harbor and Long Beach were met by livery teams who conveyed them to the Hotel Abracca, the Harmon House, or private residences. At the height of the 1895 season, the population of the Yorks totaled 12,720, with future growth curving upward.[8]

As more and more newcomers came into the region, a sociological fault line gradually divided the Yorks: there were the summer visitors and the year-round residents. "Two constituents have thus come in contact, so completely antagonistic in their outward and inward aspects, that, like the ancient auguries, they can scarcely confront each other without laughing," observed Samuel Adams Drake. York Harbor, casual and understated, attracted the wealthy and socially prominent summer visitors, in much the manner of Bar Harbor. They hailed from Boston, New York, Philadelphia, Chicago, and Washington, D.C. By contrast, the summer visitors to York Beach came mainly from the nearby New Hampshire towns of Dover, Somersworth, Manchester, and Concord— mill workers and working-class people who could get away for only a week or a few days. Occupying the neutral ground between these two very different resort communities stood York Village, where most of the year-round population lived, finding employment as cooks, domestics, coachmen, tradesmen, delivery boys, porters, and gardeners to the summer residents of York Harbor.[9]

The Henry Fields joined the migration of wealthy upper-class people who, in the late 1880s, saw in York Harbor a respite from the crowds, noise, and crime of Chicago. Florence's brother and sister-in-law, Bryan and Helen Aldis Lathrop, often accompanied them. For the first few seasons, the Fields and the Lathrops most likely resided in a hotel because of the scarcity of more suitable accommodations. Then, on August 28, 1889, not too long before his death, Henry Field joined Bryan Lathrop in purchasing a parcel of land from Samuel S. Allen. Field owned five-eighths of the parcel, and Lathrop the remainder. The deed of purchase described the property as having no structures on it, "beginning at wall at land of Henry D. Norwood, NE 5 rods, SE 25 rods to beach, SW 15 rods by beach, NE 33 rods, NW 8 rods, NE 6 rods, NW 1 rod to beginning." This bland description obscured the fact that the property, which could be reached only by traversing a private footpath, was among the most desirable on the entire coast of New England, situated as it was close to Millbury Cove but high on a point overlooking the Atlantic Ocean.[10] Following Henry Field's death in 1890 and Florence's remarriage three years later, the Pages constructed a cottage on the site, utilizing monies Florence had inherited from Henry Field's estate. She appropriately christened the cottage Rock Ledge.

The term *cottage* is misleading, however. Originally, it was used humbly, to mean "a modest country dwelling." In the context of a summer resort it denoted the small buildings that were built around large hotels to care for overflow guests. Because of the extra space and privacy they provided, the cottages quickly became more socially desirable than rooms in the hotel. Their patrons became known as "cottagers" or the "cottage colony" and emerged as the social leaders of the resorts. When these patrons broke away from the hotels to build their own resort homes, they were loath to lose their social eminence. They retained the word, if not the spirit, when they built their mansions, palaces, and castles in Newport, Rhode Island, Lenox, Massachusetts, Bar Harbor, Maine; or Cape May, New Jersey. These communities became the pacesetters of the rich and socially prominent eastern summer resorts. York Harbor underwent this same transformation except that it prided itself on being less formal, the summer residence of quietly fashionable people and especially a family-oriented community perfect for all age groups.[11]

It was here at York Harbor that Thomas Nelson Page, departing from his more familiar southern locale, drew inspiration for his writing. Page experimented with the Maine community in an attempt to strike a vein which he could mine extensively. Altogether he wrote four short stories of New England: the two Rock Ledge stories, "The New Agent at Lebanon Station" and "Miss Godwin's Inheritance," and "Leander's Light" and "The Bigot." Another, "My Friend the Doctor," was in reality an outline for a novel. "Miss Godwin's Inheritance" extolled the virtues of the countryside as opposed to the stiffling atmosphere of the city and told of a girl's efforts to restore her grandfather's summer home. It could easily have been written by the native New Englander Sarah Orne Jewett. "Leander's Light," the story of an elderly man who refused to sell his summer home to a speculator and left it instead to the town for a hospital or school, was a rebuke to the vulgar materialism of the new generation. It might have been written by another native, Wilbur Daniel Steele.

If Rock Ledge called to mind the more sequestered life by the ocean and mountains of Maine, it was no less substantial or luxurious a summer residence than other fashionable cottages dotting the coastline. Until her death in 1921, it was the focal point of Florence Page's summer life, the physical space that she dominated, where she was surrounded by family and friends. Rock Ledge also served as the secure haven within herself, the figurative place to which she retreated from the turmoil of wartime Rome where Thomas Nelson Page was serving as ambassador to Italy.

Old photographs, a color postcard,[12] and an architectural survey reveal that Rock Ledge was a massive wood-shingled structure of roughly 12,000–15,000 square feet. Built entirely with local materials and by a local contractor, A. C. Moulton of York Village, Rock Ledge was two and one-half stories high. The cottage, constructed of half-timbered stucco, boasted a gambrel roof, gabled dormers, and double-hung sash windows set in molded frames which were arranged rhythmically on the facade. Five interior brick chimneys crowned the structure, while a spacious screened porch ran from back to front along one side of the house. A circular drive was located in the front of the cottage, which one approached from a private way off the Harbor Road. Large shrubbery and plantings, probably the work of Ossian C. Simonds, the Chicago landscape architect who also designed the foot trails that crisscrossed York, were situated strategically to provide a secluded garden setting for the home.[13]

The size of the Page cottage, the number of domestics required to run the household efficiently, and the employment of both an Italian groundskeeper and a handyman were testimonials to the Pages' affluent lifestyle and Florence's managerial ability to run such a home, and also a marker of the class boundary that separated the well-to-do from the rest of the population.

Even the choice of architectural styles was intended to make a social statement. The Shingle Style, an understated architectural form which featured a preponderance of shingles and often exhibited dormers with convex or polygonal roofs, was essentially a suburban and resort style popular in the 1880s. It connoted a sense of nostalgia, an effort to give the appearance of stability and connection to the past in an age in flux. It was a refuge from the urbanism and industrialization that had become the dominant—and disruptive—factors in American life, reminders that economic progress had been purchased at a high cost in human suffering and social turmoil: extremes of squalor and splendor, urban slums, brutalized labor, racial and ethnic violence, wasted resources, and a deterioration in business and public ethics.[14]

The Shingle Style also was appropriate for an upper-class clientele which was seeking to reevaluate the ideals of the founding fathers in escapist terms. These people were seeking a civilized withdrawal from a brutalizing society through interminable summer vacations to the coast of Maine, where the old houses weathered silver and floated like dreams of forever in the cool fogs off the sea. Not surprisingly, the Shingle Style reached its height of popularity in the resort towns along New England's coast, whose men and women formed a remarkably homogeneous society—for America—of predominantly English, Protestant, and Yankee. As befitted York Harbor, where money, proper breeding, and good taste mattered most, the visible effect of Rock Ledge, with its horizontal lines, dark, natural materials, and absence of ornamentation, was one of simplicity and quietude. Its warm, hollow body suggested permanence and maternal peace. No wonder Florence could say to her mother-in-law that she was drawn each summer to Rock Ledge "like a magnet."[15]

A blueprint of Rock Ledge, Florry's moral compass and Tom's source of inspiration, no longer exists, and the cottage burned in 1960 after passing through the hands of several different owners since 1923. Fortunately, however, the number of rooms, many of which had a spectacular view of the ocean, and some of the decor may be reconstructed as of 1921 from the probate record filed in the District of Columbia. This accounting enables us to appreciate Rock Ledge for what it really was: a mansion, rather than a small cottage; one which clearly overshadowed the nearby Lathrop cottage, the summer residence of Florence's brother and sister-in-law.[16]

The cottage, like the very elaborate residence in Washington, D.C., reflected the Victorian obsession with privacy (a separate bedroom for each child and careful separation of family spaces from parlors where one might encounter the public) and the "professionalization" of space, with a different room designated for a specific activity, reflecting both the male and the female spheres. The private quarters of both the family and the household staff were distributed on the first and second levels of Rock Ledge, with the staff using a separate staircase. The first floor was composed of the bedroom and dressing room of Tom and Florence Lindsay; two "young ladies" rooms (most likely the young Minna and Florence); a nursery occupied by the Pages' grandson young Henry Field when he visited Rock Ledge; a sewing room, where Florence did her embroidery while Tom was visiting his mother and family at Oakland plantation or absent on business; Florry's maid's room; a room for Alfred, the Pages' factotum; two laundresses' bedrooms; a storeroom; and three bathrooms. The second floor consisted of separate bedrooms and bathrooms for the Pages, a white guest room and a pink guest room; two smaller guest rooms, five bathrooms. and eight servants' rooms.[17]

The public spaces included a parlor and dining room for family and guests, separate servants' dining room, library, billiard room, telephone room, kitchen, pantry, and laundry rooms, porch and sun parlor, and piazza. The house had both electricity and gas for illumination, cooking, and heating, as well as a Franklin stove in the nursery. The garage, which held a 1919 eight-cylinder Cadillac touring car, also had two bedrooms and a kitchen, presumably for the chauffeur.[18]

The cottage's furnishings, which were valued in 1921 at $5,935.50, adhered to the maxim of the English poet and artist William Morris, who wrote in 1880: "Have nothing in your houses that you do not know to be useful, or believe to be beautiful." The cottage incorporated the latest technologies, for Florence as early as 1907 made reference to its having a telephone, at a time when there were no more than 1.3 million telephones in the entire United States.[19] It also featured other urban amenities to make the rustic life comfortable, including four refrigerators and sophisticated plumbing.

The amount and the type of furniture listed in the inventory for each of the private rooms suggests that Florence perceived a room not necessarily as a single unity but in terms of multiples of space, a common characteristic of Victorian interiors. The furniture itself with a few exceptions was machinemade rather than handcrafted. This, coupled with a fondness of the past, led Florence to borrow, copy, and fuse different decorative styles: Colonial revival, Turkish, Italian Renaissance, and Chinese. She also heaped ornaments everywhere—bronzes, majolica, porcelains—leaving no empty spots. The furnishing of each room significantly denoted rank in the household, from the highest to the lowest. The furniture in the fourth servant's bedroom was adequate but sparse, being valued at $16.75. By contrast, the furnishings in Florence's bedroom were valued at $290.[20]

The probate record, whose valuation was likely to be lower than what Florence actually spent, provides a sketchy description of Rock Ledge's contents except for the more expensive furnishings. The furniture was chiefly, though not exclusively, of the style that was popular at the turn of the century, American Eastlake, a subset of Victorian furniture characterized by its simplicity and functionalism.[21] It utilized natural woods such as oak, mahogany, and willow, with little or no decoration. Horizontal and vertical lines predominated rather than the curves and serpentine shapes of the heavier, more formal Victorian furniture. The occasional ornate or antique piece was the exception, probably a late addition or perhaps a trophy of one of Florence's many trips abroad.

Florence's bedroom reflected both her position within the larger society as well as her dominant status within the family and home. She inhabited a space separate from her husband's, although the two lived under the same roof. Within her private space she exercised control over her environment as she did over the household in general. She decorated it both elaborately and expensively, exhibiting the Victorian tendency to mix styles and fill every nook and cranny. Besides a pair of twin beds with cretonne spreads, the room held four side chairs, a three-panel embroidered linen screen, a snap-top, caribou-foot mahogany table and cover; a cretonne upholstered couch and armchair; a mahogany-framed cheval glass; a cherry dresser; a claw-and-ball-feet, snap-top mahogany table; an inlaid mahogany desk; a mahogany dressing table with bevel-edge mirror; cherry night table; a maple inlay-panel chest of drawers; seven rugs; assorted pictures and cretonne wall hangings; and a rattan piazza lounge.

An Italian chest of drawers and an antique mahogany chest of drawers provided touches of elegance. Even the use of rattan furniture suggested an attempt to dress up the room. Rattan, which became popular in the

United States in the 1850s, was not necessarily porch or summerhouse furniture. It often was used with heavier wood furniture for variety of material and mass.[22]

The guest bedrooms and the family's quarters were slightly less elaborate, containing brass or white enamel beds and white enamel furniture. With slight variation, each bedroom also contained an oak washstand (occasionally golden oak, which was more expensive), an oak or mahogany bureau, and a center table made of oak or mahogany and a cane side chair. Some of the bedrooms contained slat-bottom, cane, or willow rockers; a chiffonier, which was a high narrow chest of drawers often with a mirror attached; and a cheval glass, which was a full-length swinging mirror framed in oak or mahogany. There was an electrolier, or support for electric lamps, in several of the private bedrooms. Two or three rugs covered the floor of each bedroom, and lace curtains covered each of the windows. The Franklin stove in the nursery was connected to a chimney to provide warmth on chilly New England nights.

The quarters of the domestic staff were adequate but spartan by comparison. Besides a white enamel bed, each room contained a simple oak bureau, washstand, center table, and cane-seat side chair. Two scatter rugs graced the floor, and the windows were treated with plain white curtains. The only distinction made between the laundresses' rooms and the Pages' personal maid's and valet's rooms was the presence of a willow- or cane-seat rocker in the latter. The material furnishings of the private rooms, then, connoted hierarchy and order within the household.

The focal point of family life at Rock Ledge was the living room, which illustrated once again the Victorian tendency to visualize a room in multiples of space rather than as a single unit. The Pages' living room served several functions, each of which would have occupied a separate room in their city home: as a music room, a game room, and the traditional parlor. As a space for the enjoyment of music, the centerpiece of the living room was the Steinway parlor grand piano (valued at $125), accented by a mahogany music rack and a piano electrolier with shade. The folding-top mahogany card table and cane-seat side chairs quickly converted the same space into a card room. As a family gathering place on a cool New England evening, the fireplace and oversized furniture suggested that comfort, relaxation, and informality were highly valued. A box couch with deep cushions, two oak Morris chairs with cushions (predecessors of the modern recliner), and an oak armchair with an upholstered back and seat invited the occupants to sit, relax, and be enfolded in the cushions. A line-inlay mahogany secretary, a pair of Dresden candelabra, a banjo clock, and assorted paintings gave the room a slightly elegant touch. The rugs, four-panel painted canvas Japanese screen, and fireplace equipment suggest that greens, golds, and reds were the predominant hues.

The dining room was one of the largest and most elaborate public spaces in the cottage and could be used for formal as well as informal dining. It accommodated a trestle table and twelve leather-cushioned side chairs and two armchairs, one at the head and the other at the foot. Against one wall was a maple-panel mahogany sideboard on which was displayed Florence's modern blue-and-white china serving pieces of English and Japanese origin. A pair of serving tables adorned the other wall. Lace curtains draped the windows, and the bric-a-brac commonly found in homes of this period filled in the spaces. Blue was the dominant motif, in the blue velvet carpet, the cretonne hangings, and the reproduction Della Robbia plaques.

The domestic ideal of late nineteenth-century America was epitomized in the library, a comfortable room inhabited by many familiar and some more ornate objects. Five pairs of portieres hung across the doorways, draperies and curtains adorned the windows, and four rugs, two large and two smaller, graced the floor. Four electroliers were on hand to facilitate reading in the evening. Vases, jardinieres, decorated sapphire glass, and the like were scattered liberally throughout the room. The furniture was more decorative than that found in the private quarters and included a mahogany sofa with carved claw feet, an antique mahogany ball-and-claw-foot side chair with slip seat, a claw-foot mahogany center table, a davenport desk for writing, an upholstered mahogany armchair, two mahogany Morris chairs with cushions, two willow rockers, and a cherry rocker. The fireplace, which was the focal point of the room, was highlighted by shiny brass andirons, fender, shovel, and tongs. On its mantlepiece stood a French-Egyptian bronze and marble clock.

The billiard room, by contrast, supported the popular idea that a house should also be a place of leisure activity, of family amusement and entertainment. The billiard table most likely was located in the center of the room beneath a chandelier, possibly of brass with glass globes. A fireplace, a few side chairs, and some wall hangings are all that the inventory mentions. Other venues for entertainment or relaxation included the sun parlor (which did double duty as Florence's sewing room), the porch, and the piazza (veranda). Furnishings there were eclectic: a blend of commonly used porch furniture, antiques, Arts and Crafts pieces, and esoterica. The sun parlor held eight pieces of hickory porch furniture, an oak table and bench, and two wicker settees with cushions.

Three taborets were conveniently situated, for Florence found embroidery a relaxing and enjoyable pastime on long summer days when her husband was away or when the family was at the beach. Indian baskets, Navajo blankets, and assorted African fleece rugs—mementos of the Pages' travels abroad—adorned the sun parlor. From there, a visitor proceeded out to the large screened porch, which was more simply appointed: seven porch chairs, four tables and a rug. The piazza continued the theme of varying materials and mass, being furnished with grass, cane, willow, and maple porch chairs and tables, lots of cushions and footrests, folding tables, and a Turkish tea table.[23]

The gardens, like the country residence, were quite a remarkable triumph of man over nature, equally suitable for formal or informal entertaining. They bore the telltale signs of the deft hand of a woman who knew precisely what she wanted in a home and who could afford it. Rock Ledge, to use the metaphor of the sphere, was the physical space that Florence defined according to her own criteria and controlled.

The Pages normally used Rock Ledge each summer from June to late September, traveling to York Harbor by train and sometimes by private car. In the early years, they often sent ahead carriages and horses from Washington, just as they did when they passed the winters on Jekyll Island off Brunswick, Georgia. En route to York Harbor they stopped to visit with friends, such as S. Weir Mitchell and Laurence Hutton; or they motored to Maine, as in 1910, stopping in Southoboro, Massachusetts, to visit Florence, and her husband, Tom Lindsay, and their grandchildren. The Holland House, a quietly elegant hotel in New York City, was a convenient resting place along the way; spending a night or two there helped to relieve the monotony of the long journey and gave Florry the occasion to renew her wardrobe and Thomas Page time to visit his publisher or the Century Club.[24]

Whether at York Harbor or Jekyll Island, the Pages' associates were almost without exception either northerners of wealth or affluent expatriate southerners. To better appreciate the class and economic background of the summer visitors with whom the Pages socialized, one need look no further than the 1919 cottage list. Published annually at the start of the summer season, the list described York Harbor as "a high class summer resort comparing favorably with any on the New England coast" and "a village of substantial summer homes." It applauded the fact that "no excursion element or objectionable features have gained a foothold in the community."[25]

Indeed, this was the case. Besides the Pages and the Lathrops, York Harbor listed among the cottage owners: physician Seabury W. Allen, of Charles River Square, Boston; New Yorker John Greenville Bates, treasurer of U.S. Metal & Seal; Boston banker John Perry Bowditch of Beacon Street; Wall Street lawyers John C. Breckenridge and John Hill Morgan; John Cadwalader of Philadelphia, lawyer, president of the Baltimore & Philadelphia Steamboat Co., trustee of the University of Pennsylvania, and president of the Pennsylvania Institute for the Blind; Dr. William Councilman, Shattuck Professor of Pathology at Harvard; Alfred du Pont, head of E. I. du Pont de Nemours & Co. and the Delaware Trust Co.; Charles Noble Gregory of Washington, D.C., lawyer and editor of the *American Journal of International Law;* literary figures William Dean Howells and Robert Herrick; Colonel Frederick L. Huidekoper of Washington, D.C., a lawyer, military writer, and founder of the National Security League; Columbia University philosopher Herbert G. Lord; H. C. Richards, president of the State Bank in New York City, whose wife was a descendant of President Martin Van Buren; and the diplomat J. Herbert Stabler, who served as an adviser to the American delegation at the Paris Peace Conference.[26]

The cottage list reveals that York Harbor attracted a homogeneous clientele: summer residents who were cosmopolitan, influential within their own communities, and predominantly, if not exclusively, white, Anglo-Saxon, and Protestant. Together they formed America's national upper-class elite. Each was affluent by the standards of the time and successful in his chosen profession, whether it be medicine, law, business, finance, diplomacy, or the literary world. Several were highly educated at prestigious colleges or universities in this country and abroad, having attended Harvard, Yale, Oxford, and Göttingen. With few exceptions, they were married or widowers. The women whom the men had married were usually prominent in society in their local communities, whether it be Boston, New York, or Philadelphia.[27]

The evidence on the wives is indirect, for the cottage list often identified the female spouse parenthetically by her maiden name, as in "Mrs. Bates was Anita T. Boulton" or "Mrs. [Theodore] Etting [of Philadel-

phia] was Jeanette Verplanck," or "Mrs. [Gerald] Holsman [whose husband was secretary and treasurer of the Philadelphia & Western
Railway] was Katharine DeW. L. Norton." "Mrs. J. D. Riggs" was the
widow of the founder of the Riggs Bank, of Washington, D.C. Within
the upper class a wife's maiden name was evidently sufficient to establish
her identity. Neither *Notable American Women* nor *Who Was Who* lists an
entry for any one of these wives.[28] Their omission suggests that these
women were not in the vanguard of the various social, economic, and
political reform movements of their day, at least not in the sense of protesting, marching, lobbying, and writing tracts; or, if they did participate, it was within their local communities, quietly and behind the
scenes, or through monetary contributions.

If Florence Lathrop Page was typical of the women who summered at
York Harbor, it was most likely the quiet role that they took. "Deeply
interested in public life and completely versed in its history and principles," Thomas Nelson Page wrote of his wife, "she shrank from any
relation to it save the old-fashioned one—that her mother or grandmother might have had. In the modern Woman's movement she took
no practical part nor interest—leaving it wholly to those who were interested in it and confining herself to her private and personal duties."[29]
Florence Page, Anita Bates, Jeanette Etting, and Katherine Holsman
did not storm the barricades to change society; they protected their interests and pursued their private agenda. They lived that combination
of family, society, charity, and pursuit of culture that defined the leisured
woman's role in the late Victorian and Edwardian ages.

Because none of the York newspapers have survived for this period,
it is difficult to recapture precisely the social life of the elite summer
residents, but certainly a part of Page's characterization rings true. Florence wrote innumerable letters from Rock Ledge but she discussed her
daily activities there only in passing so that one catches a mere glimpse
into what was undoubtedly a full social calendar. In the summer of
1912, for example, there were never less than twenty-six people staying
at Rock Ledge, including the Burnabys, the Cabell Bruces, and friends
Anne Dulany and Belle Hagues. On August 25 "four Southern ladies,"
including the niece of Bishop Polk, motored up for the day from Ips-
wich, "a pretty seashore resort not far from Boston." Florence was always
at home in the afternoons, "when we gather quite a crowd after tennis
on the verandah for tea, which has become an established custom with
us for several years." While she presided over the ritual of tea, the grand-

children played baseball and tennis, swam, and went boating. After so many years the routine of the affluent summer residents was firmly fixed, as Florence noted in a letter of April 15, 1919, to her daughter Florence Lindsay: "You know just what happens at York every summer; golf every day rain or shine; fishing off the rocks; tennis; bathing. Never a glimpse of America outside, and no interest in any part other than York."[30]

In an earlier letter Florence provided a more revealing glimpse into her activities and the society of which she was a part. Her letter of October 2, 1907, was written to her husband who was attending a commemorative ceremony at St. Albans in Vermont and was then to visit his family at Oakland. The note indicates that this was not the first time that Florry was left alone at the cottage. It fell to her to manage the daily household routine, to supervise the domestic staff, and with the assistance of a nanny, to rear the children. A sizable retinue of domestic helpers was always in attendance at Rock Ledge. Often the summer residents hired immigrant workers in Boston en route to York Harbor or employed French-Canadians who had crossed the border. It devolved upon Florence to manage the domestic staff, and this sometimes required her to cope with the "jealousy between upper and lower servants" (the reference to rank order within the household staff was itself symbolic of the Pages' affluence) and to fire a Sicilian worker, James, for "flourishing a knife once" which had frightened two other domestics, Henry and Rose. The latter threatened to quit if James was not dismissed. Florence, interestingly, did not give as her reason for firing James his violent behavior but his inability to speak English clearly on the telephone. That itself provides another perspective on the class and social structure of the period. It also indicates that however uncomfortable she was performing a task which more properly might have been left to her husband, when put to the test, Florence was able to discipline her employees.[31]

When she was not coping with the management of the household, Florence was engaged in the usual feminine rituals: hosting a seemingly endless stream of visitors to Rock Ledge, including her children and their families, and lending assistance to the various clubs and local charities to which the Pages belonged. In 1905 the upper-class summer residents planned a Japanese fete to raise funds for the York Hospital, which they had founded and incorporated the year before. The event was a great success financially and socially. Not only did it raise $6,000 for the hospital, but among those who attended and contributed $500 each were the Japanese diplomats Baron Komura and Count Takahira, who were fresh from the Portsmouth, New Hampshire, peace conference ending the Russo-Japanese War. As her contribution Florence established "The Mariana Bryan Lathrop Memorial District Nurse" trust in memory of her mother. This action not only brought tangible benefits to the community by paying for the services of a visiting nurse to minister to the poor of York Harbor but had symbolic significance as well. Nursing, with its emphasis on nurturing and comforting, fell within woman's domestic sphere. Florence eventually underwrote similar programs in Chicago, Virginia, and the District of Columbia.[32]

Apart from these social and humanitarian obligations, Florence enjoyed her privacy. The solitude of Rock Ledge with its spectacular view of the ocean, taking walks alone, with her husband, and often with her beloved brother Bryan and sister-in-law Helen along the paths overlooking the cliffs, filled her days. She delighted in working in the rose garden, sewing, and doing her embroidery in the sunroom, especially when Thomas Nelson Page was absent. In the early years when her children were young, Minna and Florence routinely went to the beach after lunch; Florence, preferring to avoid the harsh sun, remained at the cottage enjoying the solitude. That she expressed in her letters more than once a reluctance to leave Rock Ledge at the close of the summer season and also spoke with an almost painful intensity of her love for York Harbor suggests a special attachment to this refuge from the turmoil of Washington society. The wealth that had enabled her to build Rock Ledge also allowed her to insulate herself and her beloved ones, for a part of each year, from the turmoil and squalor that was part of the life of the typical urban dweller.

That same wealth also made the Pages a part of the exclusive and inbred group of summer residents who over time created in York Harbor (as they had done earlier in Washington, D.C., Philadelphia, New York, Boston, and Chicago) a series of upper-class institutions from which evolved an associationally insulated national upper class.[33] The specific activities that drew the elite of York Harbor further apart from the other social ranks in the community included the country club, the historical society, the village improvement society, and the reading room. These institutions started out not only as class defined but also gender specific. These were the public spaces that traditionally fell within the masculine sphere, and although it was men who took the initiative in organizing them, men and women together eventually came to form the rank-and-file membership in some but not necessarily all of these associational activities. This is a further indication that the boundaries of the separate spheres were not quite as rigid as the metaphor implies.

Certain that their resort had a history which was "truly interesting," the summer residents of York Harbor formed their societies to identify themselves with the very beginnings of this country.[34] Thomas Nelson Page was one of the twelve prominent male summer residents who formed an association on August 14, 1900, known as the Village Improvement Society, forerunner of the Old York Historic and Improvement Society. The members subsequently elected him fourth vice president of the society and he eventually recruited his wife, Bryan Lathrop, Helen Aldis Lathrop, and her sister Mary Aldis to membership. The society's main function was to inculcate a sense of pride in York's rich Anglo-American heritage by preserving and restoring the most significant cultural monuments from its colonial past: the Old Gaol (c. 1720), the Emerson-Wilcox House (c. 1740), Jefferds Tavern (c. 1750), the Old Schoolhouse (c. 1750), and the John Hancock Wharf and Warehouse (c. 1800).[35]

The country club was another of the main fortresses of exclusiveness in American society. As Max Weber noted on a visit to the United States before World War I, "Affiliation with a distinguished club was essential above all else. He who did not succeed in joining was no gentleman."[36] The surest way of belonging to the right club and hence confirming one's elite status was to found or become a charter member of the organization. The Pages actively participated in the establishment of the country club at York, which originated in Thomas Nelson Page's love of the game of golf, itself an aristocratic sport.[37] Page chaired the committee of gentlemen who were responsible for the planning of the club and transformed the concept into reality. On September 15, 1900, the committee of gentlemen signed articles of incorporation establishing the York Country Club and subsequently purchased a 150-acre tract of land situated on an eminence overlooking the York River near Sewall's Bridge.[38]

Permanent membership in the country club was limited to thirty males, of whom Thomas Nelson Page was one. He served on its first board of governors, was elected vicepresident in 1904, and succeeded to the presidency in 1907 upon the death of Joseph Davis. For the first ten years of the club's life, there seemed to be no desire to fill the quota of thirty permanent members as some died or otherwise terminated their membership. Ownership of the club's property and invitation to annual membership was, in effect, vested in the hands of a few men, a self-perpetuating oligarchy which controlled access and defined the rules by which the club functioned.[39] The extent of the members' wives' involvement in the club, including Florence, Helen Lathrop, Alice Brown Fox of Rittenhouse Square, Philadelphia, and others, was to contribute to the club's decor (a typically female task) and to organize its social and charitable events. Florence donated two handsome lamps valued at $96 to help decorate the clubhouse, a rather considerable gift of money for the time.

With an eighteen-hole (later expanded to a twenty-seven hole) golf course designed by Donald Ross, twelve tennis courts, fine croquet grounds, locker rooms, a caddy house, and a large garage, the York Country Club quickly became one of the social centers of the summer colony. The building of the golf course had other implications as well. When its links opened for the 1902 season, the club joined a select number of country clubs in the United States, such as the Brookline Club, which boasted a golf coourse. Access to the course was restricted to the affluent summer visitors and their guests by imposing a fee structure for membership in the country club both with and without golf privileges. The governors decided initially to limit participation to 150 family and 100 single sponsored memberships and to erect signs warning nonmembers, especially from York Beach, that this was a private club.[40]

The decision to build a golf course not only was an affirmation of the summer residents' elitism but also had cultural and ethnic significance. It enabled the members to identify once again with their British heritage, in this instance with St. Andrews, Scotland, the home of the oldest golf course. Once the links were constructed, the next logical step was for the board of governors to hire a golf professional for the club, a young man named William Wilson who had recently migrated to America from Melrose, Scotland.[41]

The function of the York Country Club, then, was not sport per se but social exclusion. It furthered the social separation that was occurring between the elite and the rest of York's population and also between upper-class men and their spouses. The latter's attendance was restricted to specific times and occasions. By developing a country club where they could play golf, tennis, or croquet, the male members could legitimately think of York Harbor not simply as a refuge from the ills of an urban industrial society but as a fashionable resort to occupy their leisure time.

Religion was yet another activity that, even as it softened gender boundaries, tended to widen the disparity between social classes by accentuating the economic cleavages that existed in the Yorks. The Episcopal church strove to become the sanctuary of the elite in York Harbor as the Pages' identification with the campaign to build a new church, Trinity Church, revealed. The socio-religious dimension of what appeared superficially to be a relatively straightforward decision of whether to erect a new Episcopal edifice is obvious when one realizes that the Yorks had a population of less than 2,000 residents at their peak. There were no Episcopalians there before the development of the summer resort community. The predominant religious denomination of the year-round population was, as to be expected in New England, Congregationalism.

By the late 1890s two Episcopal churches had been founded mainly through the financial efforts of the summer residents. St. Peter's by the Sea was established in 1898 through the largesse of the Conarroe family of Philadelphia; St. George's, which was consecrated in August 1886, could accommodate four hundred people but had so few worshipers that it functioned only as a summer chapel until 1929, when the trustees donated the building to the Women's League.[42]

York clearly did not need a third Episcopal church to service either the upper-class summer residents or the permanent population. There were vacant pews at St. Peter's and St. George's despite the availability of private transportation in the form of a carriage or an automobile that almost certainly rendered them accessible to York Harbor's elite residents. The motivation for constructing yet another edifice thus had to be of a nonreligious nature. Although it was never articulated as such, Trinity Church was built for the convenience of the elite Episcopalian population of York Harbor, enabling it to avoid contact with the lower ranks. Since Florence was not a particularly religious person in a creedal or doctrinal sense, this may well explain why she attached an inordinate importance to the building of this new Episcopal edifice and urged her husband to spearhead the drive for its construction. Her letters to her mother-in-law, Elizabeth Burwell Page, written over several summer vacations at Rock Ledge, frequently commented upon the progress being made toward raising funds to build the church.[43]

Thomas Nelson Page played a central role in founding Trinity

Church as a member of the building committee, though Florence's financial contributions helped it along. In 1904 the committee purchased a lot on the corner of Woodbridge Road and York Street for $7,000. The site was within a short walk of both Rock Ledge and the Lathrop Cottage. A picturesque stone structure with ivy-clad walls, Trinity Episcopal Church had a seating capacity for over six hundred people! The choice of Tudor-style architecture also had symbolic meaning, for it allowed the elite summer parishioners to identify their roots in the English past.[44]

When Trinity Church first opened its doors for services in August 1909, the summer residents had already paid its $25,000 building cost, and the parish continued to thrive thereafter. By 1912 its elite parishioners were contributing as much as $2,400 in two collections for the Episcopal church's missions. The bishop of Maine was invited to consecrate the church and to deliver the inaugural sermon, but Florence's happiness on that occasion was tempered by a sermon which she found disappointing. Instead of preaching on things ethereal, he chose a topic that was too mundane, too much of the grubbiness of this world. Nonetheless, she regularly contributed $1,000 to have the bishop return each summer to preach in the church, a practice that her sister-in-law Helen continued after Florence's death in 1921.[45]

The founding of the reading room at York Harbor was another associational activity that tended to draw the elite into an ever tighter social circle and to distance them from the other strata of York's population. The reading room was so called because it did have a somewhat literary flavor: Thomas Nelson Page, William Dean Howells, Robert Herrick, and Peter Finley Dunne were listed as members. It may be, too, that the title happened to be fashionable at the time since Bar Harbor had its reading room. Whatever its origin, very little reading seems to have occurred in the reading room; it was obviously meant to service some other, chiefly masculine need. Humphrey T. Nichols, one of the charter members upon its founding in 1897, described the reading room as a place where gentlemen could gather to drink and talk in pleasant, convivial surroundings.[46]

Thomas Nelson Page served as a member of the board of governors of the reading room in 1899, 1900, and 1903. In May 1910 the club relocated to a beautiful house and grounds on the oceanfront near the bathing beach. By then, it had begun to admit women, an innovation that some of the more conservative male members thought would spell its doom. There is no doubt that the presence of women ended the informality of earlier days, when the men partook of fish house punch and occasionally discoursed on art, science, politics, and religion. The adoption of a gender-neutral admissions policy, however belated, indicated a further softening of the boundaries of the sphere, as the women entered into the formerly all-male bastion. By contrast, the reading room continued to function as a vehicle whereby the elite summer residents, regardless of gender, maintained the inbred and exclusive nature of their community. Social control was the instrument by which they distanced themselves from exogenous and inharmonious influences.

From the convivial banter of the reading room grew the York Harbor Village Corporation, another associational activity of the elite. The corporation sponsored certain zoning ordinances in response to the threat of expanding tourist accommodations on York's easterly outskirts. The accommodations actually were summer mobile camps, known as "Libby Camps" after the property owner. That there was a class dimension to the controversy is revealed in the writing of Kenneth Roberts, the author of *Northwest Passage*. In *Trending into Maine* Roberts declared that the Libby Camps had "spread with such fungus-like rapidity" that York Harbor "was in danger of being almost completely swamped by young ladies in shorts, young men in soiled undershirts and fat ladies in knickerbockers." In the reading room the decision was made in 1903 to free York Harbor of billboards, tourist camps, dance halls, "and other cheapening manifestations of the herd instinct and Vacationland civilization." Roberts told in some detail how the initial zoning law segregated York Harbor into residential, business, and limited business zones; how it provided for the replacement of combustible roofs with noncombustible shingles; and how it restricted stores, shops, hot dog stands, and public garages to certain localities, required building permits, and forbade billboards.[47]

Even before the ordinance was enacted, the battle went to the Maine Supreme Court. York Harbor won, with a ruling that the zoning statutes and ordinances were constitutional. Roberts hailed the decision as an accomplishment of the reading room: "As a result of the long, long fight of the wise men who founded and maintained the York Harbor Reading Room, York Harbor will always be one of Maine's outstanding resorts and proudest possesssions, a delight to everyone who goes there."

Or as another New Englander put it: "The place has retained its choice quality for so many years, simply because there is no attraction within its limits for the ruder class of pleasure seekers."[48] One of the leaders of the zoning fight was Thomas Nelson Page of Virginia.

The struggle for zoning was one of several that masked more fundamental issues. These included the process of decision making. Who in York would make the important decisions affecting the development of York Harbor, the elite but transient summer cottage owners or the local year-round inabitants? Which class or groups in the community would benefit from such decisions, and which would not? Who would project York Harbor's image to the outside world: a select, affluent, but essentially transient minority of summer residents or the permanent resident population of the larger political entity of York? Fundamentally, these issues involved the distribution of power, and hence the control of the political process, within the community.

These issues were further exacerbated by the natives' resentment of the practice of many summer residents of bringing in their own craftsmen and artisans to erect their cottages and landscape architects, such as Ossian C. Simonds of Chicago, to plan the grounds. Except for the landscaping, the Pages had not engaged in this practice; but other summer residents went to the extreme of acquiring their building materials from outside York or of importing big-city plumbers and craftsmen from Boston to provide them with the amenities of urban living.[49]

A more serious conflict between the locals and the elite broke into the open in 1907, although it had been simmering long before then. The issue of growth was once again the focal point of the controversy. The upper-class summer residents of York Harbor had invested considerable sums of money in their cottages, and despite their professed longing for the rustic life, they wanted to have and enjoy the conveniences of modern life afforded by living in the metropolitan centers. Hence, they began to advocate improved highways, municipal lighting, police protection, and a more extended water supply.

As summer residents of the community, however, this elite segment of the population had no voice in the town's civil affairs, although its members paid a substantial share of the property taxes that went to finance local government. The local, largely farm population had little interest in increasing taxes to pay for amenities that they probably would not be able to afford and enjoy.[50]

In 1901, in an attempt to rectify their disfranchisement, the elite residents of York Harbor went to the Maine legislature and secured a charter for the York Harbor Village Corporation, thereby establishing a municipal corporation within the municipal corporation of the town of York, to conduct its own affairs. But even after the corporation had been founded, York refused to turn back to York Harbor sufficient funds to furnish it with adequate roads, sidewalks, lights, and police protection.

Failure to resolve the issue at the community level eventually led the summer residents, spearheaded by members of the reading room who formed the vanguard of the York Harbor Village Corporation, to institute a secession movement. In 1908 another bill was introduced into the Maine legislature to split off a section of York, corresponding roughly to York Harbor, to establish an independent political entity, Yorktown. The separatist movement failed, but the threat of secession and separatist sentiment did not fade away until the extraordinary procedure was adopted of submitting the question to the electorate of the entire state. The proposal to allow York Harbor to secede from York was soundly defeated in a 1910 statewide referendum.

If York Harbor's elite residents lost the battle, they won the war, thanks in no small part to a similar struggle taking place at Boothbay. There, a corporation of summer residents also went to the Maine legislature and secured a charter giving them the right to receive back a certain percentage of the taxes paid to the town by property holders in the corporation. The town of Boothbay fought this bitterly all the way to the State Supreme Court. The justices ruled that Boothbay could not keep the taxes that rightly belonged to somebody else. The court's decision gave the York Harbor Village Corporation a chance to amend its own charter. The result was that the York Harbor Village Corporation received 65 percent of the taxes paid by its members to the town of York, which enabled it to finance the amenities the summer residents desired.

There were other conflicts between the summer residents and the resident population in which the issues of growth and development figured prominently. In these cases the elite was less successful in molding the community to its wishes. In 1901, for example, the governors of the York Country Club complained that the assessed property valuations of York Harbor were unreasonably high, implying that the local town officials were gouging the affluent summer residents. The club selected James Davidson of the board of governors to negotiate a reduction with the town authorities. Davidson's efforts met with only partial success.[51]

On the other hand, a group of club members, including Thomas Nelson Page, drafted a plan in 1906 to build a road along the edge of the York River from York Harbor to Sewall's Bridge. This would establish a direct route to the country club, one that was a half mile shorter than the existing route, for the convenience of York Harbor residents. A public hearing on the matter was scheduled for July 25, 1906, in advance of a vote at the next town meeting. At the hearing one townsman testified that the proposed route was currently traversed by 10,000 pedestrians at the height of the summer season, from July 15 to September 15, whereas the existing road to the country club was used by 150 teams and 40 to 50 autos. Page was one of a number of summer residents who spoke for the proposal, although his remarks seem to have been both lengthy and irrelevant. When it was submitted to the voters who would have had to bear the cost of constructing the road, the proposal was soundly rejected.

From 1914 to 1919 the Pages were absent from Florence's beloved Rock Ledge, residing in Rome where Thomas Nelson Page served his country as wartime ambassador to Italy. Florence especially missed her summer retreat and the family and friends who gathered there. When she referred to Rock Ledge in her wartime correspondence, it was with a sense of urgency and longing. "I cannot talk about York, and my beloved Rock Ledge, and all the happiness we are losing now," she wrote to her sister-in-law Helen Lathrop in June 1915. "I owe many a grudge to Germany, and this is one not to be forgiven!" She could scarcely bear to mention her cottage, for the pain was "too deep."[52]

During the Pages' absence, their son-in-law Tom Lindsay looked after the cottage. When an opportunity arose, he would rent it for the season, charging $4,000. Of that sum, Florence received $1,000, with the remainder divided equally between her daughters.[53] When no suitable renter appeared, the cottage remained closed. After he enlisted in the military, Lindsay delegated responsibility for paying minor bills as they came due to Bragdon, one of the cottage's permanent staff. Florence did not return to her beloved Rock Ledge until 1920, after an hiatus of nearly six years, but she felt immediately at home there, perhaps for the last time in her life.

Despite their sharp contrasts and differing opinions, change had come slowly to the Yorks before the 1920s. York Beach remained a lively, stirring, and unbeautiful beach resort catering to the middle and working classes; York Village continued to retain much of its primitive charm; and York Harbor persisted as the summer colony for upper-class Victorians, the rustic retreat they desired but with all the amenities of the metropolis they had left behind. The elite of York Harbor remained a well-defined, self-perpetuating, and relatively homogeneous group, isolated from the lower orders. The associational activity and the social and religious lifestyle that the elite families had established in York Harbor in the two decades before the Great War persisted and was confirmation of the growing inequality in American society. Historian Richard Wade's observation on urban elites was fully applicable to the Pages and the other York Harbor cottage owners: they were "bound together by economic interest, fortified by constant social contacts, and set apart by wealth and education."[54]

Wade did not address directly whether the elite summer residents of York Harbor adhered unflinchingly to the phenomenon of separate spheres, but had he done so he might have concluded that the metaphor of the sphere was more complex than a casual reading of it suggests. It was valid as a descriptor. In a literal sense there was a physical space that the upper-class males of York Harbor had carved out for themselves, usually corresponding to the public arena: organization of the reading room and the country club, engaging in sports such as golf, social drinking, and political activities such as the formation of an association to lobby town officials for civic improvement.

Similarly, there was a feminine space that did exist apart from the masculine space. It may have been assigned to the upper-class women of York Harbor, but it may also have been a space, public or private, that they chose themselves in which to pursue their own interests and activities. Florence Page's summer retreat to Rock Ledge is indicative of the private space that she wanted and dominated and in which she achieved fulfillment. The private pleasures of nurturing her children, sewing, and doing embroidery and the daily rituals of entertaining and serving tea were balanced by participation in the public female arena: helping to decorate the country club, organizing its social calendar, and endowing a visiting nurse service program.

But there also was a softening along the perimeter of the sphere, instances where the elite men and women of York Harbor transcended gender-defined roles to interact in, occupy, or share the same space and to defend their class interests. The participation of women with men in the founding of the local historical society, their common interest in historic preservation and material culture, the admission of women to the reading room in 1910, men and women working jointly to raise money for the hospital and to construct Trinity Church, and family membership in the country club were eloquent testimony that the separate sphere phenomenon was both simple and complex.

Florence Lathrop, 1877. (Photography courtesy of Elmhurst Historical Museum, Elmhurst, Illinois)

Huntington, Jedediah Lathrop home, c. 1870s. (Photograph courtesy of Elmhurst Historical Museum, Elmhurst, Illinois)

The Lathrop-Field family and Violet the lamb, c. 1884. First row (left to right): *Helen Aldis Lathrop; Florence Field; Violet the lamb;* second row: *Henry Field; Mariana Lathrop; Jedediah Lathrop; Minna Field; Florence Lathrop;* third row: *Bryan Lathrop. (Courtesy of Swem Library, College of William Mary)*

A seated Florence Lathrop Field, c. 1889. (Courtesy of Swem Library, College of William and Mary)

The Pages' Washington, D.C., residence. (Courtesy of Swem Library, College of William and Mary)

Florence Lathrop Page and grandson Henry Field, 1907. (Courtesy of Swem Library, College of William and Mary)

Rock Ledge, the Pages' summer cottage, York Harbor, Maine. (Courtesy of Swem Library, College of William and Mary)

The Pages and the Lathrops in Taormina, Sicily, c. 1906. Left to right: Florence Lathrop Page; Bryan Lathrop; Thomas Nelson Page (with walking stick); background: *Helen Aldis Bryant. (Courtesy of Swem Library, College of William and Mary)*

Ambassador and Mrs. Page in Rome, n.d. (1913?). (Courtesy of Swem Library, College of William and Mary)

Balcony of the Palazzo del Drago, site of the U.S. Embassy, Rome, Italy, 1913–19. (Photographed by Joanne Basso Funigiello)

Passport diplomatique, Florence Lathrop Page, 1916. (Courtesy of Thomas Nelson Page Collection, acc. no. 8641, Special Collections Department, Clifton Waller Barrett Library, University of Virginia)

Photograph taken in Rome, 1919. Seated: *Florence Lathrop Page and Ambas-sador Thomas Nelson Page;* standing: *Marshall Field III, David K. E. Bruce, Thomas P. Lindsay, Ronald Tree. (Courtesy of Swem Library, College of William and Mary)*

5

The Affluent
Pilgrim

For the social historian travel accounts are windows into the
past, constituting in their perspective and coverage an important and unique source of information on the larger world.
They treat the geographic and physiographic features of the country and
often its people. By making explicit and vivid what the indigenous population took for granted, travelers' accounts provide local color, detail,
and human interest available in few other historical sources.[1]

Florence Lathrop Page's letters to her mother-in-law, Elizabeth Burwell Page, and to her sister-in-law Ruth, the wife of Rosewell Page, fall
into this category. They disclose why the Pages, emulating the English
aristocracy of an earlier day, made the Grand Tour, the values they took
with them when they visited foreign countries in Europe and in Africa,
and what they came away with. Florence's correspondence from her
nearly annual trips abroad, but especially from the winters of 1900,
1905, 1910, and 1912 offers an insight into the social, economic, and
intellectual characteristics of the affluent, upper-class American woman
at the turn of the century. They inform us of the reasons why, as a matter
of routine, she embarked upon frequent pilgrimages to strange lands;
what sights attracted her curiosity, repelled, or astonished her; and how
critically and accurately she evaluated what she was seeing and experiencing.

The years from the latter nineteenth century to the outbreak of World
War I were "the good years," a time when the world was peaceful and
the United States was prosperous. Territorial expansion westward and

imperial adventures abroad in the Carribbean, the Pacific, and the Orient had awakened Americans to a new sense of their position among nations, and they began to "look outward" as never before. One journal editorialized as early as 1856 that, it was "the peculiar privilege of their birth in the New World that the Old World is left them to visit."[2] Across the Atlantic was a Europe where Americans could travel without hindrance and which welcomed them with unabashed hospitality.

The rich and the fashionable remained the most distinctive element among those Americans who traveled abroad. By the turn of the century these elite pilgrims were taking periodic vacations as a matter of routine or to escape Victorian conventions at home. They toured the Continent with their families, passing the season in London, Paris, or Rome. Among the well-to-do was one group with all the advantages of inherited wealth and cultured background who went abroad not in any spirit of ostentation but as the most natural thing in the world. By contrast, the nouveaux riches, the steel barons, coal lords, and dukes of beef and wheat, stormed the citadels of the old aristocracy in America by toadying to foreign nobility through lavish displays of wealth, being presented at Court, or acquiring a foreign title through marriage.[3]

Given the quietly elegant manner and the frequency with which she traveled abroad as a child accompanying her parents, a student, a resident of Paris for two years while Henry Field served as a buyer for Field, Leiter & Co., and then as a tourist during her marriage to Thomas Nelson Page from the late 1890s to the outbreak of World War I Florence Lathrop Page fell into the first group. The duration of her trips (at least three months), her modes of travel (luxury liners such as the *Mauretania* and *Lusitania*, wagons-lit, and private automobiles with chauffeur), and the category of her lodgings (the Claridge in London, the Hôtel de Crillon in Paris, the Grand Hôtel de la Ville in Florence, the Bristol in Rome, and Shepheard's Hotel in Cairo) were visible manifestations of her affluence.

Florence made the pilgrimage to the Old World for many of the same reasons that Americans traveled abroad in the eighteenth century and since: restlessness; a sense of adventure; insatiable curiosity; the special joys of seeing unfamiliar scenery: new cities, strange customs, castles, palaces, cathedrals, and museums; the quest for an antiquity which appealed to the American imagination; the lure of the great storehouses of art for which the United States had no real equivalent; self-culture: to see painting, sculpture, drama, opera in their real setting; rest and recu-

peration from illness.[4] When she returned to Washington, D.C., her objets d'art, her Paris couture, her tales of adventure, and her husband's
assorted African artifacts marked Florence and Thomas Nelson Page as
people worthy of admiration and envy.

Florence also traveled abroad because one, and sometimes both, of
her daughters was residing in Europe. Daughter Florence, for example,
replicating her mother's experience of a generation earlier, went to Paris
to round off her formal education, while Minna and her son Henry Field
moved permanently to England following Minna's marriage to Algernon Burnaby. Visiting her children became a way for Florence to
maintain family cohesion and communication despite the barrier of distance. Or as she wrote to her mother-in-law, commenting upon her
seemingly peripatetic lifestyle, "You see with us life is made up of meetings and partings, with our dear ones scattered as they are; but we take
our joys as they come and accept the sorrows as we must."[5]

Moreover, the Grand Tour was as much an integral aspect of upper-
class culture for the Pages, cosmopolitan members of international café
society, as it had been for the elite of Great Britain. She and Thomas
Nelson Page adhered to a path which was similar to the objectives of
the Grand Tour. The original tour followed a prescribed route: the capi-
tals of Western Europe, mountains of Switzerland, English Lake District, Italian hill towns, spas of Germany, and beaches of France. The
only departure from this itinerary by the late nineteenth century was
the addition of Greece, Egypt, and Africa north of the Sahara. Like the
travelers before them, the Pages satisfied their intellectual and social
curiosity by adhering faithfully to this itinerary.[6] Rome and Florence
were the great centers of art; Rouen, Antwerp, and Cologne were noted
for Gothic architecture; lace could be found in Brussels and silk in Turin. Lovers of music could choose from Leipzig, Vienna, and Rome. Inex-
pensive clothing could be purchased in London, whereas Paris was for
haute couture. The Near East was prized for antiquity and exotica.[7]

By the 1890s Americans were traveling across the Atlantic on the
"greyhounds of the ocean," twin-screw, fast-sailing, 10,000-ton luxury
liners, carrying several hundred first-class passengers. The White Star's
Teutonic and *Majestic,* the Cunard's six-hundred-foot-long *Campania* and
Lucania, "with funnels as high as the Eddystone lighthouse," were the
swiftest ships afloat, averaging in excess of twenty knots and traversing
the Atlantic Ocean in seven days. Steamship fares for first-class travelers
in the 1890s ranged from $100 to $200 per person in gold, while first-

class land expenses for an extensive ten-week tour on the Continent averaged about $6 a day, without wine. Total expenditures for the usual first-class three-month trip averaged $750 in 1900, little changed from the mid-nineteenth century.[8]

The Pages' expenses averaged higher than these figures but less than those of the wealthiest pilgrims who chose to sail to Europe in high season. Because Florence always spent the summer season in York Harbor, Maine, she and Thomas Nelson Page traveled abroad in the off-peak season, from November to March, when the rates were about one-half of the high-season fare. Their expenses nonetheless were not inconsiderable, for the cost of booking a parlor suite for two on the promenade deck of the elegant four-stacker *Mauretania* in 1913 totaled $800.[9]

Luxury was the great boon of all first-class passengers. The liners, which were truly the "floating cities" described by the travel posters of the day, offered gourmet meals, electric illumination in lieu of smoking lanterns, marbled seawater baths, ornate public lounges (such as the François I dining salon on the *Mauretania*), gilded chandeliers and reflecting mirrors, Italian Renaissance smoking rooms, music rooms, libraries, and gymnasiums. The *Mauretania,* which the Pages booked in 1912, was perhaps the best-known ship of its day. Paneling was used lavishly throughout the first-class quarters: mahogany in the lounge, stairs, and passages; maple in the drawing room, walnut in the smoking room; weathered oak in the triple-decked dining room; and teakwood on the promenade deck. The carving was meticulous and extensive, a quality of craftsmanship which would be difficult to replicate. Indeed, every gentleman's urinal throughout the vessel boasted a marble divider, of a quality which improved "according to class."[10]

Although the *Mauretania* was the fastest vessel, accommodations on other ships surpassed hers in novelty and elegance: the *Olympic*'s gymnasium; the *Amerika*'s upper-deck restaurant, staffed by the Ritz-Carlton; the *Titanic*'s Café Parisien, and the *Imperator*'s Pompeian pool. Together they set an unsurpassed standard of luxury which the Pages accepted as a matter of course. For the traveler prone to seasickness one could take a teaspoonful or more of Brush's Remedy, a nostrum containing an opium base which Florence drank whenever sailing the treacherous Atlantic. True, she was unable to keep awake for nearly three days, as she informed Mrs. Cabell Bruce in 1897, but "the journey remained in my memory as among the pleasant experiences of life." When the Pages disembarked in Liverpool or Southampton, there was an army of porters to transport their sixty-odd pieces of luggage and trunks to their first-class hotel. Thomas Cook or a privately engaged chauffeur escorted them on the Grand Tour.[11]

During the winter of 1900–1901, the Pages sailed to Europe along with the Lathrops. After disembarking in Liverpool, they made their way to London for a few days as was their usual habit. Bryan and Helen Lathrop then struck out on a separate itinerary; they would rendezvous in Egypt before returning home. Florence later wrote to her mother-in-law that "Tom and I are having our honeymoon over again and we are enjoying it too." He was "the most delightful companion in the world, and I know he is the dearest husband."[12]

After a few days of sightseeing, the Pages crossed the Channel to begin their tour in Paris. The City of Light was the metropolis Florence loved above all others. "Paris is always most attractive to me," she wrote in 1909. "I feel quite at home here, and then the place is so full of life and animation, and the streets of such noble avenues in size, the buildings of so much one general style that it is the most imposing place in the world, I think."[13]

In Paris the Pages could visit their seventeen-year-old daughter, Florence, who was studying with a private tutor. Leaving her was more difficult for the mother than for the child, but Florence accepted it as part of the natural order of things. "Parents have to make sacrifices for their children, and this was the greatest I could make. I trust only good will come of this winter's experience. We acted for the best, and we both feel sure we did what was right," she wrote to her mother-in-law on December 30, 1900. Happily, the separation was eased by the knowledge that her daughter, though "among uncongenial strangers," had several good American friends in the city with whom she could while away the lonely moments.[14]

From Paris where the weather had been cold and wet, the Pages drove to Monte Carlo, "where are the most famous gambling tables of the world." Then they made their way to Nice, a city which also held "tender memories" for Florence because of the four winters she spent there studying with her deceased sister Minna, and "where my father and mother did so much for our happiness." As winter neared, they boarded a train southward to Rome and the Italian sunshine.

The brilliance of the Eternal City on this occasion, as compared to the Pages' previous sojourns, was a bit dimmed because of the recent political turmoil. "The changes are sad here," Florence noted, "for since we were last in Rome the poor king has been murdered, the beautiful Margherita lives near Turin, and the young King and Queen have ascended to the glory?" She recalled so well "the day we were at the Races, and the King's life had just been attempted and the sweet Queen was so pale, but so affectionate and lovely in her tenderness to him—but what lasts in Rome is Time; the relics are the same, and centuries are as years only."

Despite the uncertain political situation, a large and cosmopolitan colony of artists, intellectuals, and other American residents had flourished in Rome since the early nineteenth century. Margaret Fuller, the high priestess of Transcendentalism and early feminism, had spent considerable time in Italy, where she married an Italian nobleman by whom she had a child and in 1848 had participated in the creation of the ill-fated Italian republic.[15] By the end of the century the fashion was for visitors to make the rounds of the studios, examining and perhaps purchasing works of art. The Pages followed form. Although there is no record of their having purchased any chefs d'oeuvre, they wandered around the city attempting to absorb everything from the splendors of the Renaissance to the sophistication of the ancient Roman Empire. Florence noted that it was "impossible to walk these roads without coming upon some relic of the ancients"; she clearly was versed in antiquity, for she mentioned specifically the Coliseum, the Forum, the Palace of the Caesars, Trajan's Column, and the Arch of Constantine. She and Tom also visited St. Peter's, which she told her mother-in-law was several times the size of Oakland plantation. The devoutness of the Catholic pilgrims impressed her, but as a staunch Protestant she was unable to fathom their adoration of idols. "To see the people kissing the toe of the bronze statue of St. Peter is always a cause of wonder to me," she exclaimed.[16]

The Pages remained in Rome long enough to participate in the social life of the international colony before heading south to Naples to catch a steamer to Port Said. Egypt was then the Florida of the well-to-do who were attracted to it because of the climate; but its antiquity, ancient ruins, and biblical sites also fascinated Americans and Europeans. After the British reconquest of Khartoum and the avenging of Gordon's death, tourists once again flocked there. With a certain panache Florence wrote that she was able to sputter away in several languages, notably French and Italian, "but Arabic is not among my accomplishments."[17] Undaunted, the Pages wended their way from Port Said to Cairo, where

Florence eagerly anticipated the arrival of Bryan and Helen for their planned excursion up the Nile.

On December 9, 1900, Florence wrote from Shepheards' Hotel in Cairo that it was a "strange sensation" actually to be "in the land of Moses." Tom, likewise, was so excited that he felt as though he were living "somewhere between Genesis and the Arabian Nights." Egypt was the first Near Eastern country they had ever visited, "and that alone gives it charm," Florence wrote. She especially admired the natives' industriousness, which she had not expected to find, and also their dress; Arabs, Nubians, Sudanese, "all wear robes of different colors, wonderful shades of blue mostly, but yellows and reds are very abundant."

The people were so different from any whom Florence previously had encountered that she was at once intrigued and repulsed. The harem women "drove about often in carts, with as many babies as women sometimes; their eyes only are not covered; they wear a brass ornament between the eyes over the bridge of the nose, from which hangs a long thin black veil, then over the head a large full cape of black with skirt of same—nearly all are barefooted." As a whole Egyptians revolted her because they did not conform to Western standards of hygiene. "They are the dirtiest creatures I have ever seen, and their eyes are apt to be sore and diseased from neglect, sand, and flies; the babies and little children have swarms of flies on their faces, which make them squint, but it never occurs to them to brush them off," she wrote.

This was an attitude she was unable to transcend, for she reiterated it continually in her letters in her efforts to describe Egypt to her mother-in-law. Cairo, she wrote at the end of the month, "is the dirtiest place I ever saw, and Old Cairo is infinitely worse. You can't imagine the poor wretched little babies, and unwashed children, and the filth in which they seem to live so constantly." The mortality rate from disease was highest among the children, she noted, adding, "It is purely the survival of the fittest from their standpoint." Even Tom, who grew up on a farm, had to reconsider his belief that dirt was healthy, she asserted; he now declared that the unsanitary conditions were "deadly."[18]

Florence also was ambivalent toward the peoples' religious practices. She thought the Muslims were very devout and sincere—indeed, she wondered whether Christians were as fervent—but their rituals were so different from any with which Florence was familiar that she was alternately curious and repelled by them. As it happened, the Pages were visiting in Cairo during Ramidan, the Moslem holy days that corresponded to the Christian Lenten season. Upon entering a mosque they had to put large slippers over their shoes in order "not to defile their sacred temples." This was reasonable, Florence thought, and she could not help admiring the worshipers' devotion, declaring, "But not our most ritualistic pretend to keep Lent as these people do." The peoples' practice of fasting during this period was indicative of their fervor, but she found it mystifying that they had any strength at all for work, and she noted the complaints of housekeepers that during this holy season the servants either failed to come to work altogether or they performed their chores in a slipshod manner. Forgetting her own difficulties with household servants, she was "very thankful" that "her times" had not fallen in this land.

But these were relatively traditional Moslems. The ones whom Florence thought most bizarre were the dervishes, those Arabs, often mendicants, who belonged to one of the mystical religious orders of Islam. She described the ritual of the whirling dervishes to her mother-in-law, explaining that "they have a ring, like a circus ring, into which they go one by one, all bowing to a little piece of carpet opposite them, then the Chief comes in, and he squats down on the rug, and soon up in a gallery above you hear some voice chanting the Koran, then some weird music begins, and after fifteen minutes of this wailing sound, the Dervishes rise from their lowly seats and all march around the circle, stopping to bow to the carpet everyone; this they repeat three times, and the music strikes up a little faster, the dervishes drop their outer capes off, unfurl their flowing white robes, and begin whirling with arms extended, and this they continue to do without stopping for a half hour." Although the ritual was not one that she would have been comfortable with as an Episcopalian and the music of the reed pipe was "weird" to her ears, they at least seemed sincere and devout, unlike the howling dervishes.[19]

Applying Western criteria of hygiene, fastidiousness, and decorum, Florence condemned the latter as "very repulsive in their dirt, and they seem emotional and fanatical, and they can work themselves up into a state of wild frenzy." She considered the howling dervishes barely human and wrote that she was "disgusted with these creatures." Coming from a religious tradition which emphasized a dignified ritual without unseemly manifestations of religious fervor, Florence did not believe "these creatures" were "one particle sincere." Nor did she know enough about Islam to understand that the dervishes were simply a subgroup within the Moslem faith or that many Muslims considered dervishes holy men capable of performing miracles or predicting the future.

Florence did not particularly enjoy the crowds of beggars that roamed the streets of Cairo and was anxious to press on, but the Pages' departure was delayed because of Bryan Lathrop's illness, which Florence thought at first might be typhoid contracted in Athens. As soon as he was well enough to travel, she proposed that they sail the Nile, both the fashionable thing to do and possibly a way to speed her brother's recovery. She specifically had in mind visiting Luxor, "where the air is very clear and dry, and fevers soon disappear," stopping along the way for side excursions. On Christmas Day, 1900, they embarked on their journey, stopping en route to drive to Heliopolis, six miles below Cairo in the Nile Delta, to stand on the spot where, according to tradition, the sun god Ra rested. From there they continued to the temple of Karnak and the pyramid of Cheops to "wander about unmolested," free from the ubiquitous beggars of Cairo. Florence even attempted to mount a camel for a short ride among the pyramids, but finding it "fearfully uncomfortable," she transferred to a donkey.

By the end of January 1901, they were proceeding up the Nile to the falls at Aswan, site of the First Cataract, which Florence thought was "beautifully located", and quite different from the surroundings of Luxor. Here the river narrowed and was filled with rocks "bold and rugged" in contrast to the otherwise sandy shores, giving it the appearance of a small lake. As they continued upriver, Florence spied many small boats flying the British flag at half-mast, the crews wearing black armbands in mourning for Queen Victoria, who had died on January 22, 1901. Florence admired Victoria not because of her longevity, might, or power but because of her femininity; she saw no inherent contradiction in a woman ruling the greatest empire in the world, the masculine sphere of politics, but was pleased that she could do so and still embody the feminine virtues that Florence held in high esteem. Victoria was "unquestionably the most notable woman in the world," whose purity and goodness "elevated the once degraded throne of her ancestors," the early Hanoverians. Life went on, however, and she thought it would be just as natural to have a king as a queen as sovereign. "Albert Edward, no longer Prince of Wales, but Edward the VII, has now a chance to show what he can do for his people," she observed, noting that his initial proclamation gave cause for optimism.[20]

From Aswan the Pages and the Lathrops transferred to a Cook's tourist steamer near the island of Philoe to go up to Wadi Halfa and the Second Cataract. There they visited the temples of Abu Simbel carved in a rocky mountainside beside the Nile River, "the last wonderful achievement of the ancients, excepting always the Sphinx." Pharaoh Ramses II had built the temples c.1250 B.C. for himself and his wife, Queen Nefertari. Four seated figures of Ramses II guarded the entrance to the Great Temple while four of the pharaoh and two of his wife stood at the entrance to the other temple. Florence found the temples a "marvel of majestic dignity, grandeur, and withal the statues had a sweetness of expression very unusual with the Egyptians." The likenesses of Ramses and Nefertari were "the most human and natural looking group of figures we have seen."

While the sight of the ancient monuments overawed Florence, she also thought it "very remarkable" that there were so few reminders of biblical times in Egypt, except for where Moses was believed to have been found and where the Virgin and Child rested, "but nothing else of any kind." Recognizing her own ethnocentrism and religious bias, she observed rhetorically, "Indeed there is certainly but little mention of Egyptian monuments in other histories, and none in the Bible is there?"

By February the Page-Lathrop party abandoned a close itinerary and chose to sail down the Nile on a *dahaobeack,* peacefully drifting on the current and stopping wherever their fancy dictated. Their initial port of call was Wadi Halfa, the British military capital for the entire Sudan, where they disembarked and rode a donkey into the desert. Along the way they passed three very different villages: one Sudanese, the second Nubian, and the third dervish. Florence's reaction to the dervish settlement was not appreciably different from what it had been in Cairo. "It is beyond my power to give you any conception of the utter poverty and squalor of the Dervishes," she wrote to her mother-in-law; "their huts are made of old oil cans, every imaginable kind of rag and other rubbish, and just high enough for someone about the size of Tillie to walk in; the whole country is a wild desert, and on what they exist, one's imagination fails to picture." The Nubians' situation was only marginally better. They lived in a townlike setting, built of mud walls and huts, and when the Pages and the Lathrops passed by, they were having a festival, replete with "wild barbaric music." The people, Florence declared, were "as black as the ace of spades, and they look dull."[21]

The Sudanese, by contrast, were "a good many degrees more comfortable looking." They also lived in mud huts, but they seemed to have some idea of the decorative arts; the fine palm trees all through the village gave it an "attractive air." This was relative, of course, as Florence was quick to note: "Everything is by comparison, and I am afraid I should not be able to see much charm in such a village at home." Nonetheless, Tom and Helen, who were quite taken by the people, collected various Sudanese trophies to bring back home. Their artifacts made their *dahaobeack* look like "an Egyptian armory," with "spears, swords, daggers, coats of mail, helmets, huge shields, drums, clubs, elephant tusks, barbaric chains of beads, etc."

As spring 1901 approached, Florence was beginning to weary of travel, exciting though it had been. She was looking forward to returning home, especially to see her daughters whom she missed frightfully and other members of the family and friends. Ancient Egypt had been interesting, but she, unlike Tom, had no interest in returning to the country or to Africa itself. She had disclosed her true feelings earlier, while still in Cairo, when she stated, "I am glad to have seen Egypt, but hereafter the Continent will be quite sufficient for me."[22] Circumstances dictated, however, that she would visit the Near East more than once in the future.

When the time came for their trip to Europe in the winter of 1905, the Pages traveled in the company of Helen Lathrop's brother, Owen Aldis, and his wife, Leila. Owen was born in New England, at St. Albans, Vermont, and educated at Yale and then Columbia Law School. The son of a judge, he became a highly successful member of the Chicago bar, retiring in 1890 to become, like Bryan Lathrop, a trustee of estates. The Aldises maintained residences in Chicago and Washington, D.C.[23]

Following their customary itinerary, the Pages began their trip in Paris where the weather was wet and cold, and so they made their way southward to the Riviera and sunshine. In a letter of November 26, Florence commented on the beauty of Nice and how the city made her husband feel "young and full of life and enthusiasm," with only an "occasional return of his old enemy," a reference to Thomas Nelson Page's bouts with depression and nervous fatigue.[24]

During a two-week stay at the Hôtel des Anglais, the Pages and Aldises rented a large chauffeur-driven touring car, a relatively new form of technology whose benefits for travel Florence immediately recognized. The automobile made possible the technological destruction of distance, putting even the most remote villages within reach as it traversed mountains more easily and quickly than the fastest carriage or train. It was "a wonderful way of seeing inaccessible places, for no horses, not even a four-in-hand could take one over so much distance in such short time," she wrote to her mother-in-law. By 1909 Florence so enjoyed touring Europe by automobile instead of train that she arranged to have the American Automobile Association and the American Express Company ship both her Packard and her chauffeur to Liverpool in advance of her arrival.[25]

With their chauffeur in tow, the Page-Aldis party made forays into the mountainous region surrounding Nice, returning to their hotel before dark. They drove "through one of the wildest and most interesting mountain regions I ever saw," Florence declared. The Maritime Alps, extending from the Riviera into Italy, were not as heavily traveled as other Alpine ranges, "and I wonder at it after what we have seen these last three days," she wrote. Witnessing the beauty of Nature was like a mystical experience to Florence, for she wrote to her mother-in-law, "But it should make Christians of even the disbelievers, to see God's handwork everywhere, in all the majesty of His greatness." The sight of villages perched atop isolated and inaccessible peaks especially astonished her, as she wondered how their inhabitants lived. From the mountain-tops the Page-Aldis party then descended into deep rocky gorges from which they could see the snow-covered mountains off in the distance.[26]

The "most extraordinary sight" was the terraced farms that crept up the mountainsides, where grapevines and olive trees grew in abundance. This simple pastoral scene caused Florence to reflect upon her own overly civilized lifestyle, which was so hurried that there was hardly any time to take in and appreciate life's simpler pleasures. "Despite apparent lack of soil and any kind of crops other than the most primitive, the people all seem happy and good natured, and free from care and nerves," she wrote to Elizabeth Burwell Page.[27]

From Nice the Pages and the Aldises motored along the Riviera as far as La Spezia, in Italy, where, because of the poor roads, they continued by train to Florence, Rome, Naples, Amalfi, Reggio, and because Mrs. Aldis had never been there, to Taormina, in Sicily. By mid-December they were ensconced in the Grand Hôtel de la Ville in Florence, where Thomas Nelson Page wrote a long letter to his mother describing their visits to the great museums, art galleries, and churches of this "jewel of the Renaissance." Florence resumed her correspondence with Elizabeth Burwell Page from Rome, where they all spent the holidays.[28]

On Christmas Eve the Pages and the Aldises attended midnight mass at the church of San Luigi de' Francesi, St. Peter's Basilica having ceased since 1870 "to be the centre [of the Catholic church] as in former times." The pope now said mass only in his private chapel and in the Sistine Chapel, Florence informed her mother-in-law. Although not a Catholic herself, Florence found midnight mass to be a moving spectacle. San Luigi de' Francesi sheltered Caravaggio's masterwork; the three immense paintings—the *Calling of St. Matthew,* which is set in a tavern, *St. Matthew and the Angel,* and the *Martyrdom of St. Matthew*—represented Caravaggio at his summit. They smite the observer with the artist's powerful use of perspective, the psychological insights of his portraits, and his dramatic focus of light, which rivets attention on the significant action.

The high altar was brilliant with candles, and as the clock struck midnight, Florence heard a voice singing a cappella accompanied immediately thereafter by the full choir. A rich baritone voice then intoned Gabriel Urbain Fauré's *Noel,* which Florence thought was "so beautiful." Finally came a high clear soprano voice, which was so unexpectedly sublime it took Florence by surprise, for she was unaccustomed to hearing women sing in Italian churches. She turned to look, "and behold! it was a big fat man with black moustache, since, I have heard that these men sopranos are not so unusual here." Because the practice of using castrati had died out in the mid-nineteenth century, what Florence actually heard was the voice of the countertenor who regularly sang the high-pitched roles.

The next morning, Christmas Day, the Pages and the Aldises attended services in Rome at the American Episcopal Church of St. Paul on Via Nazionale; following the service they strolled through the center of the city as was the Roman custom and had lunch with the St. George Tuckers, prominent Virginia acquaintances who were passing the holiday in Rome, and with two youthful American tourists who were homesick. After the afternoon siesta, they drove up Monte Mario "to get the beautiful view of Rome and all the surrounding country."

The highlight of their visit was the Pages' meeting with Pope Pius X. They had also hoped for an audience with Queen Elena and the Royal Mother, Queen Margherita, but as Florence observed, the pope was more accessible "than these royalties." The papal audience came about in the most offhanded manner when Page mentioned to the proprietor of their hotel his desire for an audience. In typically Roman fashion the proprietor spoke to a monsignor who mentioned it to yet another; two days later the Pages went to the Vatican to meet the pope's majordomo who, after exchanging courtesies in French, promised a formal invitation would be forthcoming in a few days.

Before they departed, the young monsignor who had accompanied them to the Vatican (whom Florence noted came from a "good old family here" and predicted would soon be wearing a cardinal's hat) gave them a tour of the private gardens where they encountered seminarians from the American College in Rome. One of the students introduced himself to the Pages and announced that he had been a classmate at Harvard with their son-in-law Tom Lindsay. No record of the papal audience has survived, but Florence reported that "Tom and Mr. Aldis will have to wear evening dress complete, while I will have to wear black from head to foot, with veil over my hair, and no gloves."

Florence admitted that the Pages "could easily become attached to the social side of Rome," but they were seeking the warm sunshine to be found farther south. And so, shortly after the new year, they continued southward by train to Naples where they remained through the end of January 1906. There they stayed at the elegant Bertolini's Palace, which, because of its location on a high pinnacle, could be reached only by taking first one elevator and then walking through an attractively decorated tunnel to a second elevator which conveyed guests to a glass-enclosed promenade room. The hotel had a commanding view of the city, the Bay of Naples, and Mount Vesuvius, which was in a mild state of eruption "with at night two fiery streams of lava showing."[29]

During their sojourn in Naples, the Pages and the Aldises took the opportunity to visit the Acquarium, whose marine life was of unrivaled wealth and beauty, and the Museo Nazionale, which the Pages thought was the most interesting in the world because of its holdings of bronzes, frescoes, and Grecian vases from Pompeii and Herculaneum. "We can't brag of our modern instruments after seeing what the ancients made," wrote Florence on January 26, 1906. So impressed were they that they immediately decided to go to the sites themselves, which Florence had visited many years ago with her parents, but which neither Tom nor Mrs. Aldis had ever seen.

The visit to the ancient ruins was one of the more memorable moments of the trip, but the Pages were determined to continue with their ambitious itinerary. After returning to Naples, they pushed on southward to Taormina, in Sicily, for the sun. It was on this trip that the Pages and the Aldises together bought a villa to which they repaired on future trips, a desirable piece of property with a panoramic view of the Mediterranean and Mount Etna, which they kept until 1919. Using Taormina as their base during the month of February, the party relaxed in the sun, explored ancient ruins such as those at Piazza Armerina, drove to Messina to take the eight-hour ferry ride to Malta, and from Malta booked a steamer to Tunis. Somewhere along the way, they rendezvoused with Bryan and Helen Lathrop, who had been touring the Mediterranean, and together the three couples made their way back to Taormina. After a brief respite they would journey together back to the mainland, up the spine of Italy, crossing through France and Spain, until they reached their ultimate destination, Lisbon, where Tom's cousin was a consular official.[30]

By March 1906 the extended family had wended its way back to Naples from which they visited Amalfi and Ravello, an ancient town located 1,227 feet above the sea. Beautifully situated in the folds of Monte Lattari, Ravello was one of the most picturesque towns along the Gulf of Salerno, its bright luxuriant gardens flowered with almost tropical vegetation, making it one of the glories of Italy for the traveler. It had once been an important town of 36,000 inhabitants, prospering during Amalfi's days of glory, but now it contained only 1,800. Ravello was noted for its eleventh-century Duomo di San Pantaleone, whose pulpit, resting on mosaic columns and sculptured wild beasts, was one of the finest examples of the Cosmatesque style common in southern Italy. Within the walls of the nearby Palazzo Rufolo the visitor entered a magical arena of Norman- and Arab-inspired gardens dazzling in the color and variety of their flora and fauna.[31]

So overwhelmed was Florence by the site, beauty, and artistic heritage of Ravello that she began to question some of her stereotypes about the Italian people, especially southern Italians—"these attractive, black soft-eyed people"—who were even then migrating to the United States in great numbers. "I am kept in a perpetual state of wonder at the skill with which these people build their towns on the tops of almost inaccessible heights, and when one takes into consideration the few years that the drive way has been built, it seems a mystery how 36,000 people managed to make an active town in such a locality," she declared. "It is ridiculous to call these cheerful Italians a lazy people, for the results of their labors are on every side, and it keeps them busy every hour of the long day, keeping the hungry mouths of the myriads of little children fed." Still, she was not altogether able to shed her belief in the southern Italian as the equivalent of the American Sambo. She wrote to her mother-in-law that the children "are natural born beggars, and they can annoy you if you let them, but if you are prepared to scatter a few coins in their direction, and to smile at them, they shower blessings on your head, and go on their way rejoicing."[32]

From Ravello, the Page party drove nearly five hours to Sorrento and then to Castellammare where they boarded the train for Naples and Rome. In early April they retraced their steps up the Italian peninsula and along the French Riviera until, after an exhaustive train trip of twenty-seven hours from Biarritz, they arrived in Lisbon. Charley and Jennie Page met them at the station and escorted them to the Avenida Palace Hotel, located two minutes from the American Embassy. After a much-needed evening's rest, they left for Cintra, a "fascinating" resort sixteen miles from the capital, to visit the Moorish palace that was the summer residence of the Queen Mother. What interested Florence was its kitchen, which had two enormous chimneys "running up high above, like cathedral domes." She had never seen their likes before, but her "practical mind" questioned their usefulness since they had no apparent connection to the huge bread ovens. How the royal family managed with such a kitchen was a mystery to Florence, who concluded,: "They don't have good old cornbread and hot rolls I know, and perhaps bread is not of as much importance to them as to us."[33]

After a pleasant lunch at the same ancient inn where Lord Byron had resided while writing much of *Childe Harold,* the Page party drove with cousin Charley Page to the palace of the reigning monarchs, a grand castle close to a thousand years old, "with a superb battlement, and deep and mysterious arched approaches, portcallis and moat." The palace commanded a magnificent view of the sea, the mountains, and the valley whose semitropical foliage was in full bloom. After a quick tour, they drove on to Montserat, the estate of an Englishman who was a friend of Charley Page's; it was reputed to be the most beautiful residence of any private citizen in Portugal.

Because the Pages' visit to Lisbon coincided with Holy Week, they attended the Good Friday service at the English Church, situated in a parklike setting in the midst of an old cemetary where the English author Henry Fielding was buried. Then, following a rail tour of the countryside, they slowly made their way back to Paris, stopping en route in Madrid and Toledo. From Paris they left for England, spending a few days in London before returning to the United States, "and all our loved ones!"

The trip, while pleasant and in many respects fascinating, also had been lengthy and arduous, and by now Florence was longing to return to her home and family. "The return is infinitely better than the coming away," she observed, "and the first glimpse of the dear native shore is one of the most thrilling sensations in the world." Had not Charley Page purposefully rearranged his schedule in order to meet them on their tour, Florence declared, they would have gone home a month earlier.

In the spring of 1910, the Pages once again embarked for Europe, sailing for Liverpool aboard the *Mauretania* on May 12. The voyage was a bit unusual on this occasion because although they had booked a first-class cabin, they found their accommodations disappointing. "We haven't very fine quarters, and are rather badly placed," Florence wrote to Elizabeth Burwell Page shortly before their departure from New York. "The ship is so full that first class people are in the second cabin." The Cunard line had overbooked first class in order to accommodate a large number of "morbidly curious" passengers hoping to witness the state funeral of the British monarch King Edward VII. Reflecting upon the generational differences, Florence told her mother-in-law that "Old Sweet Charlotte would sympathize with this," but she and Ruth, Rosewell Page's wife, "have only the wedding mania so far."[34]

Despite the inconvenience of cramped quarters, Florence determined that she would enjoy the transAtlantic crossing. The *Mauretania* was, in fact, a floating luxury hotel which carried the best sort of people, and as Florence observed, "I fancy we shall find a shipload of friends and acquaintances." The Pages did indeed, for the ship's manifest listed several of their acquaintances, including another Virginian, "Nannie" Langhorne Astor, the wife of William Waldorf Astor, whose multimillionaire father had become first Baron Astor of Hever; the William Randolph Hearsts; and Alice Longsworth, the daughter of President Theodore Roosevelt. But Florence also reassured her elderly mother-in-law that she and Tom were really not very distant from her. The *Mauretania* had set speed records crossing the Atlantic, and so the Pages were only a week away from their home.[35]

After they landed in Liverpool, the Pages made their way to London to witness the royal funeral and also to join with their children Minna and Algy Burnaby and their grandson Henry Field for the journey to Baggrave Hall. En route to Leicestershire, they stopped at Brighton for two days and then at Cliveden to spend the day with the Astors. Florence found Nannie Astor to be "as attractive and amusing as ever", and recounted for her mother-in-law a conversation between Nannie and Thomas Nelson Page. The two were discussing war, when suddenly Nannie looked up and declared impishly, "You and I married beneath us when we married Yankees." Florence wrote that Nannie was "the most impudent and kindly" person she had ever met, with "a heart as big as all outdoors." [36]

On Whitsunday, May 24, 1910, Florence reported their intention to go shortly to the Continent. They would travel to Paris, to Oberammergau in Bavaria, on to Mannheim, where they would visit with their friends the Wards (of Africa and Stanley fame), then back to Paris via Brussels to join brother Bryan and Helen, and finally back to London, paying a brief stop at Baggrave Hall before sailing home on the *Lusitania* on July 9.

This was a very ambitious itinerary, but what occupied most of Florence's thoughts was the world-famous Passion play which the citizens of Oberammergau staged once every ten years. She was ambivalent about it, telling her mother-in-law that she had "a combined feeling of desire to see it, and a shrinking from the handling of such a subject." Given the somber theme of the play, Florence knew she was "not going to like it, and yet I believe it is a good thing once in so often to bring this great event into such prominence, that many who do not think enough about it, begin to appreciate what Christianity really is." People had such different opinions of this Passion play, she noted, that "no one can decide for another." Despite her ambivalence Florence's need to witness the reenactment of Christ's suffering on the Cross, death and resurrection may well have been an attempt to define her own religious beliefs, to affirm her own Christianity rather than to accept the tenets of a male-dominated hierarchy.

On June 25, 1910, writing from the American legation in Brussels, Florence reported to her mother-in-law that the performance had been "all absorbing, and done in great reverence, and showed marvelous skill in those country bred natives." It had been "a strange sensation to spend an entire day in the apparent life of Christ; to come to feel personally associated with the people of that time." The music was solemn and the sets were a perfect reproduction of biblical days, but "it was too realistic at the close, and it was too sad to wish to ever see again; but I cannot tell you how glad I am to have been there this once." Whether Florence comprehended or appreciated the anti-Semitic overtones of the play she did not say. She seemed to accept its theme uncritically.

The last extensive trip abroad that the Pages took before the outbreak of World War I occurred during the winter and early spring of 1912. On February 4, 1912, Florence informed her mother-in-law that Bryan, much to her astonishment, had booked passage on a fast steamer to Europe for both the Pages and the Lathrops. Together, they would tour England, the Continent and North Africa, despite Florence's decision in 1900 that she had seen quite enough of the Near East and had no desire ever to return. The Pages had already been talking about visiting their daughter Minna in England, so Bryan's surprise announcement meshed nicely with their own plans. Their itinerary was ambitious indeed: sailing first to England, then crossing the Channel to Paris, motoring southward to the Riviera and then into Italy, catching the ferry in Sicily for Tunis for nearly eight weeks of sightseeing, crossing back to Palermo to retrace their steps via Taormina, Naples, Rome, Florence, and the Riviera, and ending in a rendezvous with Minna, Algy, and Henry Field in Paris. The Pages, the Lathrops, and the Burnabys together would return to Baggrave Hall before sailing back to the United States.[37]

Transatlantic crossings by this date were quite routine to the Pages, as Florence noted. "An ocean voyage is now as simple an undertaking as one on land, so there is but little effort attached to this one," she wrote to Elizabeth Burwell Page. Such trips had therapeutic value, freeing her from the pressures of managing a large household and frequent entertaining and her husband from the onerous routine of his writing, delivering speeches, meeting with publishers, and attending to Page family business. "The absence of care and numerous responsibilities act as a tonic on me, and I feel these trips are of great benefit to both Tom and me," she declared. "No one knows how tired out Tom was before we left home; he never rested one moment, having manifold irons in the fire; but now he goes along happily and light-hearted, enjoying everything to the full."

After a brief but very pleasant stopover in England, the Pages and the Lathrops arrived in Paris where they engaged "a finished gentleman for our chauffeur and carrier." This Parisian owned a comfortable red touring car, made all hotel arrangements for them in advance, "ordered delicious meals when we pass through villages on our trips to places where we spend the night," and drove them from Paris to Palermo, in Sicily, where the entire party, chauffeur, and touring car boarded the ferry to begin their venture into North Africa. They disembarked in Algiers on February 24 and shortly thereafter visited Constantine, an ancient trading and mining center destroyed in A.D. 311 and rebuilt by the first Christian emperor of Rome; the ruggedly mountainous countryside; El Kantara, a French town with large modern hotels and shops; and Biskra, the great oasis of the Sahara. Some of the inns in the Algerian countryside were the most primitive Florence had ever been in, but they were "spotlessly clean with comfortable beds."[38]

But it was the land above all else that captured Florence's imagination. "It is all so much more beautiful and interesting then we had imagined," she wrote on March 14. "The sudden contrasts from rich fertility to aridity of the desert is surprising, and each has its own particular charm." She was unable to decide which impressed her more: the Atlas Mountains, with the endless Kabylia villages perched on the peaks, the "glorious sea views like the famous French Cornice," or the sterile, endless expanses of the Sahara Desert, "absolutely bewildering you with their beauty or vastness."

The sights and sounds of the region made a profound and lasting impression upon Florence, for she wrote to her mother-in-law, "Our trip has been as full of wonder and beauty as if the result of rubbing Aladin's lamp." Taormina, in Sicily, still remained the "most sublimely beautiful place" she had ever seen, and Egypt was still "the most interesting place in the world" for antiquity, but Algeria astonished and had given Florence "many wonderful sensations" with its blend of beauty and interest. "It is all so surprising, did you ever dream of infinite beauty in Africa?" she asked rhetorically. In a statement that was more revelatory than she intended, she attributed the beauty of Algeria not to Nature or to the indigenous population but to the imperialistic Europeans. "I have always been a friend of the French Nation," she declared, "and now to come here and see what the people have done for this land, how they have fertilized and cultivated it, made thousands of miles of splendid park roads such as only a few states of ours have ever been able to accomplish, started comfortable hotels, etc.; they have risen even higher in my esteem and admiration."

The native population, on the other hand, left much to be desired, for they were sunk in heretical darkness and needed material uplift and moral salvation. Her own ethnocentrism caused Florence to distort her perception of non-European culture by emphasizing the differences rather than the commonalities between herself and the indigenous population and by condemning deviation from the norm of white, Anglo-Saxon Protestantism. Commenting, for example, upon a market scene, she wrote to her mother-in-law: "It is all just like Biblical pictures, and vastly interesting and impressive. But oh! such indescribably dirty people as these Arabs and Kabylies are!" Arab women, especially of the upper class, were veiled, ugly creatures leading dull, uninteresting lives. "They know nothing beyond their own roof tops, where they spend all their waking unoccupied lives, and I must confess that I never in all my life have seen so many ugly ones before and quite understand when they veil themselves in the presence of men."

It never occurred to Florence that assigning American women to a separate sphere in her culture might, in some respects, parallel the Arab males' requiring women to wear the veil. Both connoted separation, social inferiority, and male dominance. Nowhere did her ethnocentrism manifest itself more starkly than in Florence's narration of Helen Lathrop's encounter with an Arab tour guide at a mosque. Helen had tried to enlighten the guide about "the virtues of our way of treating women, and the Christian side of our lives," but he merely shrugged his shoulders, gave her a severe look, and replied: "Our Arab women never, never, never must be seen by men." The American women made no attempt to understand that the veiling of women was rooted in certain gender-based differences, religious and moral precepts associated with the Koran, and ancient historical traditions deriving from the early Persians.

As a practicing Christian of the Episcopalian persuasion, Florence found herself in an intellectual quandry when confronted by Islam. Muslims were the errant children of Christianity, believers who had taken a wrong turn in following the prophet Mohammed and who needed to be brought back to the true faith. The heresy of Islam was for Florence both the counterimage of her own religion and a summons to eradicate an important distinction between the civilized West and the rest of the world. Yet the interaction of these two facets presented a dilemma: on the one hand, to act on the felt necessity of converting Muslims to Christianity would be to eradicate the distinction between herself as the highest product of Western society and peoples of color; to do nothing, on the other hand, would be an unwelcome reminder that she, as a Christian, was not meeting her obligation to her own faith.

Florence resolved this implicit paradox by setting aside momentarily her antipapal, anti-Romish predilections and praising the work of the Catholic church in Algeria. Catholic missionaries, she conceded reluctantly, had done "a great amount of good" among the indigenous population, "although it will take many centuries to Christianize these Arabs."

Nonetheless, she stood in awe of the religiosity of the Muslim population she encountered, and this caused her to question whether Christians (herself included) were equally as committed in their devotion. "I am not sure that they in their devout faith in Allah, aren't quite as consistent as the Christians sent to convert them," she wrote to her mother-in-law. Then, quickly jettisoning such doubts, she sought reassurance in stereotypes, adding: "But as a whole the Mohammedan is a repulsive person, both in appearance and in his manners, and honesty is an unknown virtue, except as to their wives, who are quite safe from the attentions of other men."

By the time the Pages and the Lathrops arrived in Tunis, Florence had moderated her opinion of the Arab population, but only in comparison to another ethnic group. She still neither understood nor accepted Arab customs and practices. Writing from the Tunisia Palace Hotel on March 28, 1912, she told her mother-in-law: "We have found the Arabs a gentle kind of people; not rough or rude as the Italians of the country districts for instance. They beg, of course, but never disagreeably, and the little children have a sweet smiling way that is hard to resist." Arab women were still unattractive physically, but Florence sympathized with them, especially the upper-class women, because of the constricted lives they led. "But oh! The life of the better class Arabian woman!" she wrote. "She has nothing outside of her four walls and roof, which latter is the only outdoor life they ever know, except an occasional walk out at night closely veiled, and carefully guarded."[39]

The following day the Pages and the Lathrops sailed from Tunis to Palermo, Sicily, and made their way to Taormina where they would rendezvous with Florence's brother Barbour Lathrop, who was traveling from Egypt to Naples before boarding a steamer for New York City on April 12. After a family reunion at the estate that the Pages and the Aldises had purchased in 1906, the Pages motored to Rome while Bryan and Helen continued on to Florence and the lake country. Florence's itinerary would put her and Tom in Paris on May 6 where Minna, Algy, and Henry Field would join them for ten days of touring and shopping.[40]

While in Paris, the Pages and the Burnabys motored to Versailles, a place Florence had visited in earlier years with her own parents. The grounds and the flowers were charming and lovely, Florence thought, "but the sad memories of poor weak Marie Antoinette haunt the place." The visit to this site so filled with history and drama prompted Florence to reflect for a moment upon all that she had seen and done. She had thoroughly enjoyed touring the Continent and their foray into Africa north of the Sahara, but now she was weary and nostalgic for her own home. Writing from the Hôtel de Crillon on May 12, she noted that "this year we have seen many places and peoples, and strange customs, and we look back upon our experiences as well worth while. But home looks very enticing after an absence, and I know our dear Rock Ledge is going to be heartily appreciated after our return there."[41]

Tourism emerged in America in the latter eighteenth century, but the intent of travelers then was eminently serious. Much the same was true with Florence Lathrop Page. In touring about Europe and the Near East, she did not have in mind anything like the frivolous leisure pastime that phrase might now suggest; travel was a leading instrument of the spirit of inquiry that valued empirical knowledge over abstract speculation or book learning derived merely from tradition. She learned by being venturesome, by going out and seeing for herself, by becoming a traveler. Travel, in turn, regulated Florence's imagination by reality, and instead of thinking how things might be, she saw them as they were, even when she did not always comprehend what she was viewing.

Florence's correspondence with her mother-in-law, Elizabeth Burwell Page, helps to illuminate the personality, thoughts, and insights of one—but very likely typical—representative of America's female aristocracy of inherited wealth at the turn of the century. Whatever her motives for travel, Florence took along certain ingrained values: her Protestant individualism, awareness of herself as a member of the international upper class, a belief in progress, the benefits of technology, and the superiority of Western culture, and confidence in the democratic process as it had evolved in the United States.

These values conditioned her reaction to the indigenous population she encountered, the sites she visited, and what she did. The correspondence shows that Florence, a staunch Episcopalian, was antipathetic to Roman Catholicism as manifested in papal authority and also to Islam, to the identification of church and state, to a hereditary aristocracy which did not temper its privilege with noblesse oblige, and to the widespread poverty, filth, and lack of ambition that in her opinion flowed from these conditions. More positively, travel imbued her with a sense of history, tradition, and cultural stability which was important to one of her social class in the unsettled conditions that accompanied rapid urbanization and industrialization. Travel also refined her appreciation of natural and man-made beauty and sharpened her awareness of the joie de vivre as practiced especially in France and Italy.

Florence's annual pilgrimages abroad should not be viewed in isolation as the meanderings of one individual, but rather they should be perceived in the broader framework of Westerners who traveled beyond Europe for a purpose. Since Napoleon's foray into Egypt in the early nineteenth century, the Near East was within reach of the European and American traveler who wanted to visit the biblical lands in the hope of encountering personally some portion of the Judaeo-Christian/Greco-Roman experience. The Pages were simply emulating those aristocratic Europeans who were searching for antiquity, the biblical past, and the legacy of the Crusaders.

The problem, however, is that Florence's letters to Elizabeth Burwell Page lack any appreciable sense that Egypt, Algeria, and Tunisia had had a recent past before the imperialism of the European powers. She portrayed North Africa almost as a European invention, a place of romantic exotic beings, haunting memories and landscapes, and remarkable experiences. Florence's correspondence, especially as it pertains to her African ventures, is organized around recorded observations and evaluations of the natural, built, symbolic, and cultural environments. As a transitory observer, she never truly understood or concerned herself with the changes occurring in the politics or general framework of the societies she visited in North Africa but simply accepted Western dominance as a given.[42] In doing so, she extended her carefully cultivated disinterest in domestic politics, which she considered the arena of men, to her travels abroad.

Florence's failure to mention or evince interest in, or comprehension of, political events in the countries she visited is, then, not surprising. Nor is the reader of the letters surprised that the people she encountered come across as part of the geography of the land. Her perspective, as the often lengthy, descriptive references to the landscape demonstrate, was rooted in a search for "a visionary alternative." She was seeking, and was most impressed by, gorgeous colors and spectacular views that contrasted with the grayish tonality of the American city or the provincial landscape of the Chicago prairies. The subjects she chose to write about focused on exciting spectacles, the fabulously antique and the perennially mysterious and exotic, not the all too familiar. It was, perhaps, less the content of what she was seeing but how she was seeing it—the manner in which the primitive but always attractive North Africa presented itself to her—that was foremost in her thoughts.

Florence perceived the Muslim Arab world of the East through a Western prism: the static, backward Africa of the indigenous people and the European Africa of progress, growth, and expansion. She never truly understood that the people who were Islamic, Arabic, and non-European had a unitary system of information, behavior, and belief. This was obvious from the content and the tone of her letters and is easily comprehensible. Florence could not have understood this society because that would have required a knowledge of the Arab world and its people, language, and customs that could be acquired only by living there for an extended period of time, and experiencing their life from the viewpoint of the indigenous population.

An observer and not a participant, Florence nonetheless never felt constrained by ignorance from making sweeping generalizations about the culture, mentality, and society of North Africa and the Near East; nor, in her ethnocentrism, to judge them deficient according to the norms of Western society such as hygienic cleanliness and efficiency. She was aware intellectually that differences existed both between and among the Nubians, the dervishes, and the Arab Muslims, but emotionally she reacted to them as an undifferentiated type, essentially a primitive people by Western standards. Contact with the Arab population, while fascinating, also was repulsive. Arab women did not conform to Western standards of physical beauty, were given to such backward customs as the veil, and lacked freedom. Florence did not make the connection between the physical and psychological separation of men and women in Muslim culture that the veil implied and the same separation, with its connotation of social inferiority, that the metaphor of the sphere implied for women in American society. Instead, the only conclusion she drew from the experience of crossing the Mediterranean into North Africa was the cultural superiority of America, the West, and Christianity.

Florence's antipathy toward the Muslim Arab also must be viewed differently from her disdain of certain Europeans. The former was rooted in the nineteenth-century feeling of racial and cultural superiority of the West toward other parts of the world, whereas the latter was the product of social and economic class differences even more than racial, ethnic, or religious disparities. As members of international café society and later in his career, when Thomas Nelson Page served as ambassador to Italy during World War I, the Pages moved with ease among the European aristocracy of birth and wealth. But Florence's use of language in describing the "lower orders" of European society is very revealing: southern Italians were "lazy," their children were "natural born beggars," Italians of the country districts were "rough" and "rude"; the Germans of Oberammergau were "country bred natives"; English servants did only "a limited amount of work", which implied they were lazy, and thus the Burnabys required a much larger staff to run Baggrave Hall than did their American counterparts.[43]

Florence's correspondence revealed that she was a woman of privilege who shared subconsciously the web of racism, cultural stereotypes, political imperialism, and dehumanizing ideology of the West toward the Muslim Arab and the disdain of the upper class toward the lower orders. She was never mean-spirited to social or cultural "inferiors," but neither did she ever question the validity of class differences or whether the British and the French had a legitimate purpose in occupying Egypt, Algeria, or Tunisia. In Social Darwinian parlance, she not only accepted their dominance as natural but viewed Western imperialists as the agents of progress, technology, reason, enlightenment, and, most importantly, civilized behavior.

In her comments about Arab women to Elizabeth Burwell Page, Florence seems never to have realized that the vast majority of American women also did not possess the broad freedom that she enjoyed largely because of her economic independence. On one of the rare occasions that she did express an opinion on political matters—writing from Paris toward the end of her 1912 pilgrimage—she was highly critical of the "suffragists" for agitating for the vote.[44] And yet American women still were disfranchised, played at best a subordinate role in political decision making, found themselves circumscribed in the ownership of property, and were paid substantially lower wages then men doing the same tasks. Her financial independence, by contrast, had enabled her to rise above the common constraints placed on women.

Despite her many travels abroad in the years before World War I, Florence Lathrop Page in some critically important respects, both emotionally and intellectually, never left home. While her letters echoed the refrain that she was glad to have visited northern Africa and to have made the Grand Tour of Europe, she was overjoyed to slip back into the safe, familiar, comfortable atmosphere of her world back home, the world of 1759 R Street and New Hampshire Avenue and of her beloved Rock Ledge.

6

"A Wildly Interesting Period"

On June 17, 1913, President Woodrow Wilson sent to the United States Senate the nomination of Thomas Nelson Page, "one of the most popular of living American writers," to be "ambassador extraordinary and plenipotentiary of the United States to Italy." The *New York Times* described Page as an intellectual who would have great appeal to the Italians. Four days later the Senate confirmed the nomination.[1] The appointment was neither unusual nor as unlikely as it may seem to the modern observer. Perhaps even more so than today, the dominant criteria for ambassadorial appointments at that time were political loyalty, wealth, and influence rather than familiarity with the politics, economics, or language of the country to which a nominee was posted. Page eminently satisfied the former criteria.

The appointment was even less remarkable when one considered that both Wilson and Page were southerners—Virginians and Democrats—and that they had ties through the University of Virginia. Wilson, a scholar in his own right, was well acquainted with Page's literary works. Although Page had been a social acquaintance of Wilson's Republican predecessors in the White House, Theodore Roosevelt and William Howard Taft, he nonetheless had remained a Democrat. In 1911–12 he was repelled both by what he considered the bankruptcy of Republican policies and the unseemly internecine struggle between a former and a sitting president and by the outmoded soft money views of Champ Clark of Missouri, who represented the Bryan wing of the Democratic party. When the Democrats convened in Baltimore, Page attended as an unofficial observer. His preferred choice for the presidential nomination was Senator Oscar Underwood of Alabama. As it became clear that Underwood had little chance of winning the nomination, Page turned an increasingly sympathetic ear to Woodrow Wilson's New Freedom. He subsequently contributed financially to Wilson's victory and chaired the President-elect's inaugural committee.[2]

Despite Page's assertion that he had not sought after the ambassadorial appointment, neither had he discouraged powerful Virginia politicians and friends from lobbying on his behalf. He had preferred an appointment to the Court of St. James, but when that post went to another Page—Walter Hines Page, no relation—he accepted the Rome appointment willingly and proudly, as the obligation of a member of America's elite upper class. Florence, who often reflected her husband's views, best expressed this sentiment in a letter to Ruth Nelson Page on September 6, 1913. After asserting coyly that "hosts of friend and hundreds of mere acquaintances" had pressed the administration to make this unsolicited appointment, she told her sister-in-law, "But it could not be put aside but had to be accepted, and we must both work our best to be worthy of the honor." What she discreetly did not mention was that her wealth would enable her husband to assume the financial burden of this major diplomatic post without worry, for Page's annual salary of $17,500 was insufficient to cover the expense of maintaining a pretentious residence and entertaining in a manner befitting a great power.[3]

On September 3, 1913, the Pages sailed aboard the *Lusitania* to Europe. Following diplomatic protocol, they traveled to Italy via Great Britain. Florence viewed their departure with mixed emotions: she was proud of the honor accorded her husband, but she also was sad because it meant "quite a new life, amidst new surroundings, and far from those who are so precious and so necessary to our happiness." Their circuitous route to Rome, however, enabled the Pages to visit Minna, Algy, and their grandson, Henry Field. It also foreshortened the interval between Ambassador Page's arrival in Italy and the earliest moment he could present his credentials to King Vittorio Emanuele III, whose presence in Rome was not expected until the Italian Parliament convened in November.[4]

Although Page did not trouble himself about the exact nature of his assignment, he did have some general goals, the most important of which was his desire for a stronger, friendlier relationship between the United States and Italy. Apart from working to persuade the Italian government to ratify an arbitration treaty advocated by Secretary of State William Jennings Bryan, Page devoted the first six months of his ambassadorship largely to routine duties: scouring Rome for suitable quarters for the embassy, upgrading its staff, and learning Italian. Finding satisfactory lodging in Rome for the embassy was a particularly frustrating task, as Florence noted ruefully. "It is a sad commentary upon our diplomatic arrangements," she declared. "I trust Congress will wake to the situation soon, and provide an Embassy or Legation for every country in Europe."[5] Page eventually rented the Palazzo del Drago, located close to the Quirinal palace, from the contessa del Drago, whose fortunes had ebbed. Shortly thereafter, Page's desire for formal recognition was satisfied when the king received the Pages with great ceremony at Via Rossore, his summer estate. "I wish you could have been there," he wrote to Minna on November 30; "we reached the highest point of social eminence."[6]

The Pages, like most Americans in the optimistic spirit so characteristic of the Progressive Era, had accepted uncritically President Wilson's view expressed in his inaugural message of March 1913 that the growing cordiality among all nations foreshadowed "an age of settled peace and goodwill."[7] Within sixteen months, however, World War I broke out, as it consumed the flower of an entire generation of young men. The war also disrupted what both Page and the administration had expected to be a largely ceremonial appointment lasting a year or so. Instead, the exigencies of war allowed the Pages to return to the United States only once in the next five years, and that for only a few weeks in 1916.

As the wife of an ambassador to a country which would slide from neutrality into active belligerency, Florence Page found that the war also required her to be more sensitive to the larger world beyond her family and social class, to redefine her largely ceremonial and leisurely role as ambassador's spouse for one that entailed responsibilities she scarcely imagined she would incur. In both the man-made disaster of war and the natural disaster that struck the remote Italian countryside in 1915, Florence Page was to find her cause; her cause did not find her. When the challenges arose, she was not passive; she responded vigorously and creatively to each of these crises and in the process carved out for herself a new model of individualism to legitimate her role as her husband's equal.

• • •

War commenced while the Pages were in Great Britain on summer holiday in June 1914. Departing from the usual practice of gathering at York Harbor, Maine, the entire Page family had assembled at Banchory Lodge in Scotland, located within driving distance of Balmoral Castle. The lodge was a charming house with beautiful lawns and a delightful garden. About 200 yards away and flanked by large trees, the river Dee flowed rapidly, its water almost black because of the peat through which the burns flowed into the main stream. There were some deep pools to fish for salmon, but the water was very· low that year and the salmon were few. It had been an idyllic summer until the last week of July when people began to talk of war following the assassination of Archduke Franz Ferdinand at Sarajevo.

Florence's first reaction to the war was not so much one of shock and horror but rather the realization that this far-off event might change the ordinary routine of upper-class life of both herself and her family. Twelve-year-old Henry Field had a similar reaction; he could hardly believe that this violent act "in an improbable place called the Balkans could disrupt our summer plans and indeed our lives."[8] But so it did.

Ambassador Page was shaving on the beautiful Deeside morning of August 1, 1914, when a young boy on a creaking bicycle delivered the cable from Washington that ordered him to return to his post in Rome by the fastest transport. A telephone call to the stationmaster requested him to stop the Scotch Express at the little village of Banchory so that Page could proceed at once to London. Traveling alone, Page caught the boat train to Dover where a British destroyer whisked him across the Channel to Calais. A special train sped him to Paris to catch the Paris-Rome Express. Thirty-six hours after leaving Banchory, Ambassador Page was in the Palazzo del Drago to begin the long, frustrating ordeal of unraveling the complex problems of war and peace.[9]

Florence joined him in Rome two weeks later. Page wrote with a sense of relief to their younger daughter, Florence Lindsay, who had returned to Southboro, Massachussetts, that she had finally arrived in Rome. Shock and horror had given way to anger. "I find your Mamma decidedly anti-German," Page wrote to their daughter. "To hear her talk you *would* think her the most bloodthirsty of mortals." Given her English antecedents, Minna's marriage into the English landed gentry, and the pervasive Anglophilia of Americans of her class, Florence Page's hostility toward Germany is not surprising. It is even less surprising that she accepted uncritically Germany's responsibility for the conflict or that she viewed German militarism and its insane desire for territory as a threat to civilization. "The violation of Belgium will ever remain the same, and the sorrows of Europe are on the increase, all attributable to those barbarous Prussians headed by an imperial decree the like of which has not been known," she wrote to her brother Bryan Lathrop. She did not believe all the stories about German atrocities, she wrote on February 20, 1915, "but enough are [true] to make the case a strong one when the final settlement comes." The Germans "have gone mad; all innocent acts of generosity they could safely allow, they rudely refuse." She meanwhile had "thrown prudence to the winds" and was "firmly pro-Ally."[10]

In expressing anger at Germany and blaming it for the war and consequent separation from her children and grandchildren, Florence actually was seeking to exercise control and power over her life and environment. Privately she sympathized with Great Britain and France from the start of the conflict and hoped for an early Allied victory. Like most Americans, however, she also hoped that the United States could avoid direct entanglement in the conflict and was critical of the prowar faction at home. On August 25, 1915, she wrote to her daughter Florence, "I wish someone would strangle [Theodore] Roosevelt's opinions; he says breaking off diplomatic relations wouldn't be enough now, that we must go to war." Judging from the letters and newspapers that the embassy received, she was persuaded that American sentiment remained strongly opposed to war unless the German government flatly refused to reconsider its submarine warfare policy. "Our poor President," she wrote.[11]

Florence's sympathy for the Allies' plight was not without limits, as her endorsement of the president's stance on freedom of the seas and the rights of a neutral nation attested. She hoped for an Allied victory but also shared the traditional American suspicion of Great Britain and wrote to her daughter Florence not to be blinded by British guile. "Don't lose sight of the fact that England only wants us to go to war in order to use us as she may seem fit, and then be able to dictate her marine power to us and all others. America, on the whole, I should say is for the Allies, but she wont stand any nonsense from anyone, least of all the English cousin, who in his heart, has always had a deep-rooted dislike for our Country and people."[12]

When the British Government declared the whole North Sea a war zone in November 1914, sowed its waters with mines, and restricted the entry of neutral ships to the Straits of Dover where they could easily be searched, Florence protested. Such violations of American neutrality would foolishly "breed ill will and dissent" and turn public opinion against England, she told Lady Rodd, the wife of the British ambassador to Italy and a friend. "We cannot show any more friendliness than we have, and preserve an honorable neutrality," she wrote to Bryan on February 20, 1915. "Germany, on the other hand, is still more displeased with us, feeling keenly the neutrality we show towards the Allies." The German press was not likely to sway American sentiment against the Allies, she told her sister-in-law Helen, "but the sarcastic tone of the English might very easily."[13]

Besides criticizing the British for manipulating American neutrality, Florence was equally critical of them for not committing more to the war effort than they had to date. She was referring especially to the commitment of more ground troops in France, whose absence she blamed upon the English lower classes. From her class-bound perspective, they had not rallied to the war effort. "The stolid indifference of the masses is surprising," she wrote to Bryan on August 23, 1915, in contrast to "the flower of the country," the young men from the upper class, who had been "superb." She also criticized the British government for not deploying in any strategic way those forces which were on the Continent. Following the disastrous Dardanelles campaign, she wrote to her daughter Florence, "I have never known such stupid bungling as the British Government's in my life; they don't do anything to encourage their army, and only breed discontent, and crush patriotism among the many."[14]

If Britain was to triumph, it would require the active assistance of its overseas possessions; but Florence wondered what kind of aid they would give when the government at Westminster kept referring to them as "the Colonials," and to the Australians in even more derogatory terms. The defeatist attitudes of certain Englishmen about whom Minna had written also enraged her, for these doomsayers were traversing the Channel to sow their defeatism among the French, who were bearing the brunt of the fighting with "a quiet dignity, entirely unexpected."

If Florence's not uncritical empathy for England was rooted in familial, linguistic, and cultural affinities, her admiration of France and the bravery of its people, which grew exponentially during the war years, was more emotional, more a response to her familiarity with the French language and culture both as a student and frequent visitor to that nation. She counterpoised French bravery with English defeatism, consistently praising the French as "the finest of the Allies" and "courageous and patriotic to the last man." "The Germans are *not* going to win; and it behooves *all* the Allies to keep a stiff upper lip" and to pull together, she wrote to her daughter Florence on July 9, repeatedly reproaching Britain for not providing more assistance. "If the English were as patriotic as the French, they would now have a powerful army in France doing work that would count," she wrote, instead of frittering away the few troops they did have on the Continent. "They may wake up some day, but the victory wont be theirs unless they start in with fresh vigor and determination."[15]

Following their victory over the "Hun" in the First Battle of the Marne in the summer of 1915, Florence waxed "more than ever enthusiastic over my beloved French and her fine people." But like many Americans of her class who admired French culture, she also thought Frenchmen too worldly and slightly decadent. "This war is the best thing that could have happened to them, hard as it now seems to realize," she informed Helen on October 2, 1915. Frenchmen had "too much love of gaiety, and were not sufficiently aware of the existence of the rest of the world." The war was forcing them to face reality, "and all they are learning in endurance and patient waiting, will serve them for all time."[16]

Florence's wartime letters subconsciously disclosed the class and racial prejudices of America's elite toward ethnic Germans at home and the British and French abroad. The former she viewed suspiciously, Americans whose loyalty was in doubt and whose civil rights might have to be curtailed for the good of the country. The latter she criticized for their complacency, arrogance, defeatism and unwillingness to make sacrifices, even as she hoped for an English victory. As she wrote to her daughter Florence on August 25, 1915, "One hears more complaints of the discomfort and horrors from the English than from any other nation. Of course it is much harder to be enthusiastic fighting on foreign soil, than upon one's own; and especially for an Anglo-Saxon to be thrown entirely with Latin races; but as England's fate hangs upon the outcome of this war, it does not become her to stand as much aloof."[17] The French were too worldly. Suffering and hardship were a bitter tonic, but in the end she believed the Gallic race would benefit.

Florence did not view Italy in quite the same critical light as she did England and France and for a time actually sympathized with Italian sentiment to remain apart from the conflict. The Italian government was in a precarious position when war broke out in 1914. Technically it was bound to Germany and the Triple Alliance, but Italy was not prepared for and did not want war. Its foreign minister, the Marquis Antonio di San Giuliano, a realist, recognized the traditional Italian hatred of Austria and the popular belief that Austria was responsible for the war. But he also knew that to fight on either side would be disastrous for Italy, whose army was woefully unprepared and had 50,000 men overseas, in Libya. Neutrality was the only feasible course for Italy, and San Giuliano found an escape for his country in article seven of the Triple Alliance, which specifically required consultation prior to military action.[18] The Austrian government had not notified Italy about its ultimatum to Serbia on July 23, 1914. San Giuliano, consequently, was on sound legal ground when he announced that the Austrian ultimatum did not constitute a *casus foederis* in the terms of the treaty and declared Italian neutrality on August 3, 1914.

Although San Giuliano died in late October 1914, both his successor, Baron Sidney Sonnino, and Premier Antonio Salandra shared his views. Legally, Italy had behaved correctly. Yet it chose neutrality not on the basis of legality but because its own interests demanded it. It was unprepared for war, and the populace disliked Austria and would not willingly fight on its side. Influenced by socialists, Catholics, the majority in Parliament, and Giovanni Giolitti, the highly respected anti-imperialist leader of Italian politics from 1901 to 1909, the Italian people were opposed to the war.[19] Nonetheless, the neutrality declaration did not appreciably diminish the precariousness of Italy's diplomatic position. If its former allies won a decisive victory, Italy could not expect much generosity at the peace table, and Austria most likely would regard Italian neutrality as a pretext to ensure its dominance in areas to which Italy aspired.

The First Battle of the Marne shattered the myth of German invincibility and convinced Italy that it had nothing to gain by honoring the Triple Alliance. By October 1915 Sonnino and Salandra were sure that the Entente would win and reckoned that Italy would gain nothing by remaining neutral whereas if it entered the war on the side of the Entente, it might achieve its goals of national unity and expanded boundaries.[20]

Throughout this period of indecisiveness, Ambassador Page surmised correctly, and had so informed Washington, that Italy was craftily bargaining with both sides to obtain maximum territorial concessions, though he predicted as early as August 1914 that Italy would declare war against Austria to gain territory. Nine months would elapse before Page's prediction came true; in the interim he, like other members of the diplomatic corps in Rome, speculated over Italy's course of action. "We are all in a state of waiting now to see what Italy is going to do," he wrote to Minna on September 27, 1914. "One day the report's that she will declare at once, another day they say she will stick to neutrality come what may. The real trouble is she has no ground on which she can declare war except the good old ground of wanting to grab her share of the loot and naturally she does not want to do this. But should she have a *casus* to go on I think she would jump into the fray quickly enough. She is all ready now or reasonably so."[21]

Florence, too, was caught up in the speculation over whether Italy would renounce the Triple Alliance in favor of the Entente. "No one can tell what Italy's future course will be, but I always believe she will join the Allies by spring anyway, probably the winter," she wrote to Florence on December 3, 1914. Four days later she noted that Italians were pondering the consequences of not quickly entering the conflict on the side of the Allies, observing "that when the war ends and the destruction is made, she will find her share microscopic; and this is far from acceptable to the people as a mass." Italy's prospects of obtaining the spoils of war initially concerned Florence less than the cost to Italians in human lives lost and damaged. "There is no adequate excuse for joining the Allies— no more now than at first, not as much really, and as time goes on and the horrors become more terrible, and the countries involved are so full of mourning and sorrow, it naturally makes another country stop and think before plunging her people into a like condition." As late as January 1915, she told Bryan that "matters in Italy remain the same."[22]

In this atmosphere of suspense and second-guessing, the appointment of Sir Henry Howard as Great Britain's minister to the Vatican was widely interpreted as a sign of the Entente's determination to gain its support. The church had remained neutral and was promoting mediation of the issues that had led to the war. If Howard could persuade church leaders to abandon neutrality, it would put pressure on Italy to side with the Entente. Florence, displaying the traditional aristocratic WASP prejudice toward the papacy, "doubted if he is an able enough diplomat to fathom the Vatican's policies, and to influence anyone there, or connected with it." To her daughter Florence she confessed: "I don't ever want to see this dreadful Pope [Benedict XV], who is the most reactionary one in over one hundred years. He is doing his best to get back the temporal power, but he is more likely to lose his head." Appeals for papal mediation of the conflict simply confused matters, she asserted, for the "Blacks" (i.e., the pope and clergy) were all "pro-German, as against the Quirinal," whereas the people and the army were "hotly anti-Austrian, while indifferent to the Allies on the whole." German ambassador Bernhard Heinrich von Bülow's efforts to neutralize Italy, perhaps by offering it Valona, would also fail, Florence thought; and she concluded that Italy would continue to mobilize but remain out of the conflict to the very last minute.[23]

Although not a deep thinker politically, Florence perceived early in the conflict that the war was a major milestone in the history of Western civilization. Her analysis of the causes of the conflict, however, were unsophisticated, largely derived from her husband's own biased perspective. Ambassador Page attributed the cause of the war to a conspiracy of international munitions manufacturers. These "merchants of death" had encouraged militarism, an arms race, and German imperialism, which in its insane desire for territory was a threat to civilization. Great Britain and the Entente by contrast were fighting to save civilization from a new dark age. Despite their belief that the future of Western society hinged on the outcome of the conflict, both Pages were relieved that the United States was not involved militarily or politically. Florence especially would have preferred to return to the quiet life of the prewar period. "We are living in a wildly interesting period of history," she wrote to her brother on March 15, 1915, "but I should be glad to be back in my own land, among my own kind, and out of politics forever."[24]

But this was not to be, for on April 26, 1915, unknown to the Parliament, Italy, represented by Foreign Minister Sonnino, signed the secret Treaty of London with the Entente powers, promising to enter the war within one month. To woo the Italians into the Entente, Britain and France agreed that Italy would acquire territory inhabited by Italians that still remained under Austrian rule, mainly Trentino and Trieste. It also would receive enough land along the southern Tyrol to give it a strategic frontier against Austria, territory in Dalmatia on the eastern shore of the Adriatic, "a just share" of Turkish lands in the Mediterranean, and either a claim to German colonies in Africa, other colonial spoils, or compensation.[25]

Had the Entente honored the treaty, Italy would have emerged from the conflict with defensible frontiers and dominance of the Adriatic Sea. Promises made in desperation were easily forgotten once the threat disappeared, but the consequences of Sonnino's action rendered it impossible for the Pages to return to the United States and to a normal life far longer than they or anyone else had anticipated.

Meanwhile, a few months before Sonnino signed the London pact, Florence's largely ornamental role as the wife of the American ambassador changed forever. On the morning of January 13, 1915, the Palazzo del Drago began to shake and shiver, its pictures and chandeliers swinging wildly back and forth. In the city the arch of the Porta del Popolo cracked; the statue of one of the apostles that towered above the imposing facade of St. John Lateran—at first thought to be that of St. Paul and later said to be of Judas—crashed to the ground, splintering into fragments and crushing a huge hole in the marble steps. Elsewhere, the bronze statue of St. Paul that crowned the column of Antoninus Pius was rumored to have twisted around and turned its back on the Austrian Embassy.[26]

Soon after the noon hour rumors flew around Rome. In the Abruzzi a town had been severely damaged, with many persons injured and killed; then the name Avezzano was heard. Avezzano was isolated, the railway was interrupted, and the telegraph wires were down. The news became even more detailed: 250 persons were killed, no trains were coming from the Abruzzi, the king had gone to see for himself what had happened. By evening the Pages learned that both the valley of the Liri and the whole region of the basin of Fucino had been stricken by an earthquake. More than 8,000 persons were reported to be trapped under the ruins.

It was twenty-four hours before the full magnitude of the catastrophe was known. The region devastated by the quake covered thirty by forty miles, taking in the valleys of the Fucino and Liri running through the Abruzzi, a beautiful and wonderfully fertile valley, surrounded by snow-clad mountains with more than forty villages perched like birds' nests on the spurs that jutted out above the plains. The hardest-hit town was Avezzano, located forty miles southwest of Rome. Of the 11,279 inhabitants, only 800 survived. When a refugee arrived in Rome on the evening of January 14 and was asked about Avezzano, his reply was simply: "Non c'e niente" (There is nothing left).

Avezzano was the epicenter of the catastrophe and became symbolic of the entire desolated region. Tremors and aftershocks lasting for a week were felt as far north as Florence. As the death toll mounted to more than 30,000, scores of thousands were left homeless. Damages were estimated at $60 million. Twenty-four hours after the quake, rescue workers, the Red Cross, religious and charitable organizations such as Gioventu Cattolica, and soldiers were on the spot. The tortuous mountain road over Monte Bove pass was filled with automobiles and trucks heavily laden with supplies, swaying perilously as they wheeled around sharp curves. The single-track railway did its best to convey food and supplies in and the wounded and stricken refugees out. The entire region was ravaged and dependent on outside assistance.

Once he learned the full magnitude of the disaster, Ambassador Page reacted quickly with a tender of sympathy on behalf of the American people and an inquiry about any aid that the United States might offer. The gesture was accepted, but for political reasons the offer of material assistance was not. On January 14 Page wrote to his older daughter, Minna, that Italy would not accept aid from any foreign government, not even from the American Red Cross, for fear of compromising its neutrality. "The political situation is so delicate they cannot allow themselves to be in debt to any nation now," wrote Florence to her sister-in-law Helen in Chicago. The tragedy, she observed, had not precluded Italy's entry into the European conflict but merely postponed it.[27]

On the day following the catastrophe, Ambassador Page dispatched two automobiles from the embassy to survey the stricken region: one proceeding directly to Avezzano, the other to those towns of the Liri, including Sora, Pescina, and Gioia dei Marsi, that could be reached by road from Frosinone. The next evening the embassy officials returned and reported to the ambassador the extent of the damage. They noted that shortly after rescue teams had entered the region, a blizzard dumped six feet of snow on the mountain passes and three feet on the plains, hampering their efforts. So bitter was the weather, Page later wrote, that "wolves are reported to be prowling around the towns, drawn possibly by the scent of that which is ever in the air."[28]

Since official intergovernmental assistance was not an option, the Ambassador and Mrs. Page made a personal visit to Prince Colonna, one of the syndics of Rome, to offer aid privately. Colonna's response, that the government would not object to private humanitarian aid conducted discreetly, paved the way for American assistance. Ambassador Page appointed his wife Florence to coordinate private American relief efforts. In doing so, he believed that he was giving Florence and the other women of the American community in Rome the opportunity to engage in the eleemosynary functions that defined the leisured woman's role in the society of the late Edwardian era: feminine benevolence and practical usefulness. For he wrote that the chief value of the American assistance was that it gave "to our people the infinite satisfaction of relieving some misery."[29]

What Page did not grasp in making this gesture was that he also had set in motion the process whereby Florence would abandon the passive, decorative existence she had been living to create a separate public female sphere for herself and fellow women workers. For despite the absence of official recognition, she brought to the task boundless energy, a sense of optimism, unquestioned faith in the moral purposefulness of the American people, and sophisticated managerial talents. She demonstrated superb organizational skills and a recognizably female style of professional behavior which relied heavily on cooperation. Under her direction people transcended individual, social, and even religious differences on behalf of the victims of disaster. Americans of various persuasions living in Rome transformed a Methodist school on the Janiculum into a hospital to care for the injured; they sent a trainload of supplies to the devastated area, as far as Scurcola, and followed it by automobile in order to transship the supplies to Avezzano. Florence deliberately channeled the American aid toward the more remote villages that had not yet received help from the Italians, such as Torano, Capelle (90 percent of whose inhabitants were killed), Alba Fucense, Magliano dei Marsi, and Santa Anatolia, whose people had fled to the fields in terror and were exposed to the harsh winter.[30]

Florence's efforts were rendered more effective still by the network of relatives and prominent friends in the United States upon whom she could call for funds and suppplies. She wrote to them describing the plight of the victims of the earthquake, asked for donations to construct shelters and provide clothing for the survivors, and shrewdly persuaded her husband to write an article for *Scribner's* describing the devastation of Avezzano. The last gave her a national forum to advertise and raise additional contributions for the American relief effort.

Rome, meanwhile, was becoming a vast asylum because so many of the homeless and the destitute had fled there for refuge. "It is pathetic to see the number of people, practically all who live only to return to their desolate country; they say they can't breathe in towns; they must live in the open air," Florence wrote. What troubled her most were the orphaned children whose plight tugged at her maternal instincts. "No one seems to be able to answer this question and I see no move on the part of the municipality [of Rome] to provide for them so far," she confided to her brother Bryan.[31]

As the wife of the American ambassador, Florence had to be discreet and mindful of Italian sensibilities. "Our position is a delicate one, we must not appear to be doing anything, and yet it is known openly that we are, and gratefully accepted silently." Italy was walking a fine line between neutrality and belligerency and could not give official cognizance to the American relief effort. "We are certainly living in troubled times," Florence declared, "and no rift in the clouds is apparent." Nonetheless, she persisted in her efforts to provide relief to the victims of this natural disaster.

Privately, she exhibited a decidedly paternalistic and patronizing attitude toward non-Anglo-Saxon governments and institutions, which translated into an attitude of moral superiority toward the people whom she was helping. "Surely there are no people on earth to compare with ours for spontaneous kindness and generosity," she wrote to Helen. Italy "has never been able to cope with calamity, but somehow her people don't seem to expect or wish any better treatment; and they are loyal and devoted citizens." For the first time she drew a parallel between the disaster caused by natural forces and the catastrophe of war induced by man-made forces, and she shuddered to think "what it would be [like] in the case of war," wondering whether the wounded soldier could be cared for. In a letter of March 15, 1915, to Bryan, she was even less understanding of the Italians. "It wouldn't do to come from me, but it is hopeless to see the utter inefficiency of the Italians; their inability to cope with the situation." The survivors of Avezzano, she declared, were "almost in revolt over the inadequate succor they have received."

Despite her intelligence and sensitivity, Florence's criticism of the Italians' relief efforts was unfair and showed a fundamental lack of understanding of Italian society and tradition. She attributed what she took to be indifference to the fact that there were "very few wealthy people in Italy and for so many years they have had as a rule, to struggle with poverty, that they can't grasp a sudden terrible calamity, as we do for instance, and don't quite know where to begin."

This simply was not the case. Italians were quite able to grasp the enormity of the tragedy, but the country was poor in comparison with the United States, the Abruzzi was wild and remote, and the tradition of private charitable relief (apart from the church) was not strongly ingrained as in the United States. The family traditionally cared for its own in times of distress. A cumbersome, inefficient, and highly centralized bureaucracy made matters worse. The devastated area was located southwest of Rome, the region known as the Mezzogiorno, to whose needs the government was notoriously indifferent.

Two thousand years of civilization, war, invasion, and malaria had taken their toll on the region, bringing misery to an already marginal existence. Political unification in 1870 had unleashed northern politicians on a prostrate people. Instead of extending a brotherly hand to restore the ancient equality of the North and South, northerners adopted trade practices that were detrimental to the South. Instead of showing the beleaguered southerners the path to reunification, northerners showed them the exit: mass emigration. Millions had left the harsh South to relieve Italy of its burden—namely, them. Differing political, economic, and cultural traditions between the North and South of Italy, rather than between the United States and Italy, had elicited the different responses to the tragedy of Avezzano of which Florence was so critical, and not the moral superiority of one nation over the other.

The outpouring of American generosity rankled the Italians, causing them to reconsider whether they should accept assistance from outsiders. Florence noted that she had to be "exceedingly careful" to maintain a low profile, even as she pushed forward her relief activities. "As our only wish is to do real good, and not to exploit our own people (although I have spread broadcast their generosity!), we are quite willing to give under cover of the Italians."[32]

Despite an ethnocentrism which curtailed her understanding of the true situation, Florence's compassion for human suffering enabled her to overcome her prejudices. With what she was able to cull in donations from the embassy staff and the American colony in Rome, she equipped a railway van with blankets, warm clothing, hospital supplies, and three tons of bread, cheese, and sausage that were dispatched to the affected area. She also purchased all of the tar paper available in Turin.because the people of the hill towns desperately needed it, "especially for roofs to cover their poor heads." Tent cloth would have been better, she noted, but it was not to be found. The Italian government had purchased all available stocks for the army for field tents in the event of war and was unwilling to redirect its use to disaster relief.[33]

Florence's networking among her American relatives, friends, and acquaintances also bore positive results. Bryan Lathrop, whose contacts with Chicago's elite families were extensive, organized fund-raising efforts in the Windy City and elsewhere. The Italian-American Benevolent Society and the citizens of Savannah, Georgia, contributed 1,955 lire, which Florence used "to shelter the mountain people in small frame houses with tin roofs." She prevailed upon Prince Scalea, who had played the key role in the reconstruction of Messina and Calabria following the disastrous 1900 earthquake, to supervise the construction of the new homes. She personally contributed nearly 7,000 lire to meet "the most pitiful demands," while Ambassador Page donated $750 from the proceeds he had received from the *Scribner's* article.[34]

By the end of February 1915, Florence had raised more than 43,000 lire. Even though the devastation still persisted more than a year and a half after the quake, the Italian people greatly appreciated the actions of the Americans, which fostered Italo-American friendship while preserving Italy's neutral status.[35] The Italian government afterwards conferred upon Ambassador Page a medal for his contribution in alleviating the suffering of the quake victims. Italy was a patriarchal society, and no one thought it odd that the recognition should be accorded to the man who was the accredited representative to the state even though Florence Page had been the dynamic force behind the relief effort.

More important than medals, Florence's efforts among the quake victims revealed more clearly than any other experience of her life, save widowhood, a depth of character which she rarely revealed. Her work among the quake victims tested her ability to cope with unforeseen natural disasters, honed her managerial skills, and provided her with a useful model for confronting a greater, man-made challenge: how to provide succor to Italian casualties of war, military and civilian. For an upper-class woman who overtly subscribed to True Womanhood, charity work among the quake victims was socially approved and self-fulfilling, and it conformed to the traditional role of woman as benevolent, nurturing, and Christian.

A fully accurate portrait of Florence's accomplishments, however, suggests that the metaphor of the spheres needs to be softened at its perimeters, for she also had exhibited traits more commonly attributed to the public masculine sphere. She was a shrewd businesswoman and organizer and an expert fund-raiser and publicist, talents that derived most likely from years of managing a large household and family and meeting the expectations of an elite lifestyle. Her ability to obtain substantial gifts of money and supplies from the social elite of Chicago, York Harbor, and other American cities stemmed in part because she was one of them and knew how to network among the affluent. Without those attributes and connections of class, neither her earthquake relief nor her later war relief activities would have been as successful as they were.

On May 23, 1915, after a carefully orchestrated campaign to arouse Italian public opinion and parliamentary legislators to a war pitch, Italy declared war on Austria.[36] The decision for war had emanated not only from foreign policy and imperialistic considerations but also from domestic political factors. Within conservative ruling circles and the monarchy, the conviction existed that a short victorious war, by imposing stricter discipline on the country, would make it easier for the government to move toward a more authoritarian position, reinvigorate conservatism and the established order, and remove the threat of subversion from the socialists and the labor and peasant parties. Neither Florence nor Ambassador Page really comprehended the extent to which domestic politics played a role in Italy's decision for war. Instead, greatly excited, she wrote to Bryan that Giolitti, the former premier who had been trying to preserve Italy's neutral status, had "made the great miracle of coming to Rome to try to work his own game" but had failed. Sonnino and Salandra, the leaders of the War party or Interventionists, prevailed over him by appealing to Italians' ancient hatred of Austria.[37]

To Florence's relief Austria did not ask the American Embassy to take over its interests, while Germany and Italy, technically still at peace with one another, agreed to respect each other's private property and nationals. "There is no hatred in Italy against Germany," Florence reported; "it is all against Austria; but it is said that Germany has a bitter feeling now against Italy."[38]

The declaration of war drove Romans wild with patriotism. Florence described the scene for her brother, noting on "Sunday the 16th we saw a memorable demonstration first in the Piazza del Popolo, which we saw leaning on the parapet of the Puccio for an hour and a half; later . . . the immense procession moved down to the Via Venti Settembre from the Porta Pia to the Quirinal carrying the flags of the different Allies." The next day the royal family appeared at the balcony of the Quirinal palace where an impromptu demonstration was in progress. They re-

ceived a spontaneous ovation from the crowd below, which then pro-
cessed down the avenue and passed the Palazzo del Drago, the American
Embassy. Carrying the Stars and Stripes, the crowd saluted Florence,
who was watching from the balcony with the Belgian ambassadors to
Italy and the Vatican.

The emotionally charged scene caused Florence to lose her self-
composure, and she summoned the embassy servants to bring out the
flags of the United States and Italy. The applause from below was deaf-
ening. "A feeble old Garribaldian waved his cap up, and I threw him a
rose," she wrote, confessing that she "was overstepping my rights as *still*
a neutral, but I could not help saluting my own beloved flag, even if it
was being borne in a war demonstration." After the excitement, an eerie
quiet descended upon the city, which Florence knew was simply the
calm before the storm.

Despite prodding from England and France, Italy did not declare war
on Germany until August 28, 1916, fifteen months after the start of
hostilities with Austria. A more favorable military situation had
emerged by then: the Austrians had been repulsed in Trentino, Gorizia
was recaptured, and Russia, recovering from earlier defeats, was pushing
forward again, driving before it the Austrian army, capturing Austrian
territory and thousands of prisoners. Italian leaders recognized that the
new military situation might well have a bearing on the political map of
Europe. If, as the Salandra government expected, the war ended quickly
before Italy had the opportunity to stand beside the Allies against Germany, it might find itself at a disadvantage at the peace table.

And so it was on the grounds of *sacro egoismo* (the sacred right of self-
interest) that Italy had declared war against Germany. Writing from
Fiuggi in the south to Minna in Leicestershire, Ambassador Page reported, "At last Italy has declared war on Germany which means, I suppose, that her allies have pushed her into it; for she has no special reason
to wish to take more on her hands then she had already, and a state of
war has really long existed between them." Page's assumption was incor-
rect but indicative of the ambassador's lack of reliable contacts within
the Italian government for accurately assessing the political situation.
This problem would become more serious during the peace negotiations
following the armistice, often putting Page at odds with Wilson's peace
policy. Self-interest rather than pressure from Britain and France had
dictated the timing of Italy's war against Germany.[39]

• • •

Soon after Italy entered the war, fighting along the border with Austria degenerated into a stalemate. The mood in Rome changed from exhilaration at the politicians' promise of a swift victory to one of grim determination to stay the course. Ten months into the conflict, Florence had reported that the capital appeared more normal than at any time since the debate over neutrality. Prices had advanced, but not by much; people were uncomplaining and cheerful; pacifist talk was nowhere to be heard. Italian patriotism was at its peak; "those not called to arms, and not in line to being called, are volunteering and are impatient to enter the service," she wrote to Helen in June 1915. The Italians were doing "very well indeed," she informed her daughter Florence, pressing on "slowly but surely" to Trieste and even talking about going to Vienna. That was unlikely, Florence thought, "but it is good for one to have big aims, and I rejoice in the Italian optimism."[40]

Barely two months later, as the war dragged on with no end in sight, Florence detected a marked change among the population and the members of the diplomatic corps posted in Rome. "Some people I find are discouraged. Some think the Germans are relatively stronger than at the beginning; some that the Allies are at a standstill." She remained optimistic and indomitable. "I feel sure of final victory, even if it is off in the distance," she wrote in August 1915.[41]

Fighting spilled over into the new year, and the mood in Rome became even more subdued. The war was taking its toll on everyone, including the Pages. Henry Field recalled afterwards a visit to Rome in late 1917, twenty-eight months since he had last seen his grandparents. "There had been a distinct change in Grandpa," he wrote. "Now he was an Ambassador in time of war, his mind filled with problems. His normal genial expression rarely appeared." A tension had replaced the twinkle in his eyes, his easy smile, and his charming chuckles. The transformation disappointed the youngster, who remembered Page so differently at York Harbor and beside the Dee. Then he realized everyone else was far more serious. "Anxiety was on every adult face," he wrote. "Even Grandma, whose serenity and radiance still dominated every group, was very quiet."[42]

Shortages of every kind had developed in and around Rome, and inflation was advancing steadily. The normal round of embassy parties, receptions, and balls had been severely curtailed as one European nation after another got sucked into the maelstrom. What entertaining did occur fell largely on the shoulders of the American embassy and Ambassador Page because his Spanish counterpart, the representative of the only other major neutral country, had no wife. The Pages took up the slack as best they could, trying to maintain a facade of normality amid the carnage of war. Florence's letters during this period are replete with references to luncheons, dinner parties, and the like. She ran the social side of the embassy with great efficiency and ease, overseeing the arrangements and making a point of always inviting the Latin American, Mexican, and Cuban ambassadors to these receptions for "political reasons." Her quiet charm and radiant manner made all who came there feel welcome, as she did her best to make the embassy an oasis in a turbulent sea of sand.

The formal and informal dinner parties also enabled Florence to keep in touch vicariously with what was happening on the different battlefields in Belgium, France, and Italy as diplomatic personnel exchanged the latest news, rumors, and predictions. Diplomatic chitchat and the informal talks with her husband, who was privy to official State Department and other governmental reports, gave Florence an overview of the war's progress, while her fluency in speaking Italian gave her access to some of the leading officials in Italy. For security reasons Florence was unable to communicate what she had heard to her children and so confined her remarks to her family about the personalities whom she had met rather than about substantive discussions of the war. Soon-to-be prime minister Vittorio Emanuele Orlando "is always very full of fun and jokes, and never at a loss what to say," she wrote. Sonnino, "an aristocratic Jew, with his far seeing deep set eyes," was reticent but always cordial. The Italian whom she admired most was General Vittorio Italo Zupelli, the minister of war, whose unobtrusive, efficient, and successful organization of the Italian army would make possible the later victories at Vittorio Veneto.[43]

The social life of the embassy both during the period of neutrality and after the United States formally entered the war also brought Florence into contact with traveling American dignitaries, such as legislators, Red Cross officials, and labor leaders who toured the battlefields to get a better sense of the conflict. Florence's encounter with one such figure, the American labor leader Samuel Gompers, was highly revealing of the class attitudes of her day. Gompers was a Jew, a term which to America's WASP elite was synonymous with the adjectives *dark, greedy, avaricious,* and *materialistic,* especially when applied to the Eastern European Jews who had flocked to America's shores in the thousands since the 1880s. Florence herself said, "We have no conscience in Jewing down the men," in referring to Italian manufacturers from whom she purchased heavy, unbleached cotton cloth for her *ouvroir*.[44]

On one occasion in 1918, Ambassador Page disclosed that Gompers and other leaders of the American Federation of Labor—about sixty in all—would be attending a luncheon and then a dinner hosted by the embassy. Florence, who probably had had very little direct personal contact with Jews, was startled, and all of the stereotypes came rushing to her mind. During the small dinner party at which she was the only woman present, she found herself seated with Gompers to her right and the philanthropist David Lubin to her left. Her physical description of Gompers conformed to the stereotype. She wrote to her daughter Florence on October 8: "Gompers has the most moth eaten head I ever saw, he is half a head shorter than I, and is fat and . . . well, not manicured like Marion Smith's husband! He has a forbidding appearance at the first glance." Of Lubin, she wrote, "The latter a Jew the most pronounced in type."[45]

To her surprise Florence discovered that she was at ease in their company, and she ended her letter to her daughter by describing Gompers as having a "pleasant" smile and greeting; "his eye is like an eagle's." She had never heard "a more interesting talker, nor one use more beautiful English." Lubin was a "remarkable" man. What had caused Florence to revise her preconceived stereotypes was, in Gompers' case, not simply his facile use of the language but his staunch support of the war. Fortuitously the German peace proposal was made during the period when Gompers was in Rome, and he immediately cabled the AFL headquarters to instruct the staff not to be misled by the message. He told them, Florence wrote, "to remain firm to our declared principles of fighting this war out to the end of Germany's endurance." She was ready to overlook his stereotypical deficiencies and her own prejudices because his patriotism was as strong as her own. As to Lubin, despite his antecedents, Florence noted approvingly that he was "a member of our Church, and one of the most philanthropic and remarkable men here."[46]

When war broke out in Europe in August 1914, the Wilson administration's initial statements of policy gave official sanction to attitudes that prevailed throughout the nation. The president expressed his faith that the United States could play the role of impartial mediator, urging Americans to be "neutral in fact as well as in name." Florence strongly endorsed this position despite her antipathy toward Germany. While

Wilson adhered to a policy of neutrality, he also adopted a definite diplomatic position in relation to the belligerents: upholding the rights of a neutral nation to trade and to the use of the ocean and defining neutral rights as "the existing rules of international law and the treaties of the United States." But these rules, dating from the early nineteenth century, were vague, especially under the unprecedented conditions created by the tactics of the submarine, the novel weapon on which Germany counted heavily.[47]

Not surprisingly, difficulties soon ensued over Wilson's interpretation of American neutral rights. The German government early announced its intention to adhere to the Declaration of London in its maritime warfare, a pledge it kept until February 1915. German naval restraint meant that the Wilson administration's early troubles were primarily with Great Britain. Determined to use British naval supremacy to the fullest advantage, the cabinet on August 20, 1914, began to tighten the economic noose around the Central Powers, gradually intensifying its economic warfare to deny Germany access to neutral sources of vital materials. The important question was whether the United States would acquiesce in this action or challenge it; whether it would insist, to the point of war, upon freedom of trade with Germany in so-called noncontraband commodities. The two nations also clashed over the contraband list, the status of American-owned ships formerly of German registry, and the search and detention of American merchant ships by British naval craft.[48]

The Wilson administration ultimately decided not to take Britain to task over the important aspects of its economic warfare, a decision which greatly annoyed the German government. That decision also worried Florence, who feared the president's wavering from his neutral posture would undermine his potential role as mediator among the warring nations. "I am very sorry he has stepped down from his high pedestal of what bid fair to be a wise and sane position," she wrote to her brother on February 20, 1915. "It is hard for me to accept his point of view now-a-days, and Tom's loyalty wont permit him to express an adverse opinion." Until then, Florence had believed that "the President acts only on the highest principles, has only the country's good at heart, and that his courage and fearless acts are solely because of his clear conscience." She had applauded the temperate and dignified but firm tone of Wilson's notes to Germany and Great Britain and had even criticized the latter for seeking to sow domestic dissension with the president's policy, even when sentiment preponderantly favored Britain. "We cannot show any more friendliness than we have and preserve an honorable neutrality," she had written.[49]

At the same time Florence recognized the dilemma Wilson faced and displayed a more sophisticated grasp of politics, a subject in which she professed to have no interest, than she normally exhibited publicly. "We have a most difficult path to tread; being the most important neutral Country, all eyes are upon us, and we are being watched for every word we say, or act we commit." The longer the war persisted, the more likely the United States would alienate both belligerents: "We cannot hope to please all, and probably will end by displeasing nearly everyone," she predicted. Her fondest hope was to remain neutral, but Florence eventually concluded that German intransigence over the submarine would drag the United States into the conflict. British violations of American neutrality had injured property, whereas German violations destroyed property and lives.

In February 1915 the submarine issue came to the forefront when Germany proclaimed a war zone around the British Isles and stated that enemy ships would be sunk on sight. The danger of misidentification of neutral ships was obvious to the Wilson administration, which in a sharp reply declared that the destruction of an American ship or the loss of American lives on belligerent ships would be regarded as "a flagrant violation of neutral rights" and an offensive act for which the president would hold Germany to "strict accountability."[50]

German naval policy was bound to bring the United States into the war, a prospect which Florence paradoxically dreaded and welcomed, if it resulted in the swift destruction of German militarism. "Germany's submarine raid and reckless mine sowing will probably bring about a universal war; all of us to be involved," she wrote to Bryan. "Well, if we can help end it by coming in, and by openly encouraging England, for it is She who is the one target really for Germany, then let us do so, much as it means sorrow and suffering." The United States would not enter the fray without just provocation, but Germany had "no intention of sparing our ships or lives, simply because of the President's warning." Only then would America "come forward and give her [England] a friendly hand of encouragement."[51]

Florence's prediction materialized with deadly accuracy. On May 7, 1915, a German submarine sank the British Cunard liner *Lusitania*, with a loss of 128 American lives, the same vessel on which she and her husband had sailed across the Atlantic to embark on Tom's ambassadorial career. A week later and again on June 9, Wilson sent notes to Berlin demanding that Germany abandon unrestricted submarine warfare, disavow the sinking of the *Lusitania,* and pay reparations. A third note of July 21, signed by Secretary of State Robert Lansing, who had succeeded Bryan when the latter quit in protest against what he saw as Wilson's failure to treat the belligerents even-handedly, warned that the United States would regard a repetition of such sinkings as "deliberately unfriendly."[52]

Throughout the latest crisis Florence applauded the president for his firmness. "It looks as though the President's note has brought Germany to terms; but it is still too early to tell," she wrote to her sister-in-law Helen Bryan on June 15. She thoroughly endorsed the president's action and was mystified by the furor that William Jennings Bryan's resignation had touched off at home. "What a mercy that Bryan is off somewhere petting his dove," she wrote to her brother on August 23 in reference to the former secretary of state's pacifism, "and we don't have to see his name anymore in official papers." "With Bryan out the way, and that sensible man Robert Lansing in his place, the President is in far better hands than at any time since his occupancy of the Presidency," she told her daughter Florence.[53]

Florence's greatest fear was that domestic criticism of the president would mislead Germany into believing that the American people were divided. The president's critics were in the minority, but as German violations of American neutrality became more frequent, she evinced less and less sympathy for the civil rights of Americans of German ancestry. Ironically, she was drawing closer to former president Theodore Roosevelt's belief that German-Americans must decide which country to claim. "It is fast coming the time when we must make this so plain, that there can be no more deeds of violence," she wrote to her daughter Florence in reference to an attempted assassination of J. P. Morgan, who was a strong financial supporter of Britain's war effort. "I wonder that a canvass of names isn't begun, and the naturalized citizens made to take a fresh oath if need be. It would be as difficult as the census, but well worth the labor and expense." War-induced stress was beginning to take its toll of Florence, who had succumbed to the anti-German hysteria that was sweeping the United States. A week later she wrote that she was "dreadfully afraid of the pro-German element, and their treachery." Could Americans afford to act toward them as they did toward other citizens? "I say absolutely no, we cannot. We can intern them all, if they refuse to abide by our laws, and we can shoot the traitors at once," she declared. "A few well directed shots, would soon make good Americans of the remainder."[54]

After reason had returned, Florence decided that the most prudent policy for the United States was to sever diplomatic relations with Germany without actually declaring war, much as Italy had done. If the Imperial German government made a satisfactory reply to the president's note, the conditions might exist for talks leading to a general peace. But this was not likely to happen, she wrote to Minna. "I am not sanguine. I see no rift in the clouds." Quite the contrary; Florence expected Greece and Bulgaria to be sucked into the maelstrom. "It looks like a long, long affair and general wearing down of one or the other side or both."[55]

Despite her pessimistic assessment of the situation, Florence anxiously awaited Germany's response to the president's note protesting the *Lusitania* incident. "I am so glad the last Presidential note was despatched so quickly, hope it will end these notes," she wrote to Florence on July 10. She expected "a polite refusal to grant our demands." Then what, she asked rhetorically. The war was unlikely to end soon for the Germans had seemingly limitless resources and "had much still up their sleeves." "Germany," she wrote, "must do one thing or the other, and I don't believe she will ever consent to giving in on the submarine warfare."[56]

As tension between the two nations escalated, Florence reluctantly concluded that American entry into the war was the only solution to ending Prussian militarism. On August 4, 1915, she wrote to Bryan that "the last note of the President seems to have given satisfaction to all the countries, barring the Germans, and I can but pray it *is* the last." America still had to wait patiently for the German reply but, she added, "we know what it will be; this leaves the choice of weapons to us."[57]

In 1915 the United States was not prepared militarily to wage war against the Triple Alliance. Florence recognized this, and she assumed America's initial contribution to the Allies' victory would take the form of loans and material. "I fear our going to war might be a hindrance to the Allies, but not if we can send more ammunition and money to help them," she wrote to Helen. The fleet could be spared if need be, but she was counting upon the ingenuity of the American people to tip the balance. Rather naively, she wrote, "We are so resourceful that we could soon develop some new method of warfare, and perhaps do a little new kind of destruction of our own!"[58]

The more she despaired of Germany making a satisfactory reply to President Wilson's note, the more inevitable it seemed to Florence that the United States would have no choice but to enter the conflict. "The whole war is frightful, and the end a long way off," she observed. While she abhorred war and recoiled in horror at the prospect of the United States being sucked into the carnage, she also recognized that "the future must be considered, and no time can be as advantageous to us as the present."[59]

Two weeks later a German submarine torpedoed the *Arabic* with the loss of American lives. Florence denounced this "act of wanton cruelty and idiotic folly" which might well leave the United States no choice but to declare war. "Can we hold out much longer if the Germans continue to sink passenger ships?" she asked. She did not see "why breaking off diplomatic relations would necessarily mean war," again the example of Italy and Germany came to mind. "I should certainly like to have no more dealings with Germany, and am always hoping we can break off diplomatic relations."[60]

President Wilson, meanwhile, reacted to the *Arabic* incident by demanding full satisfaction from Germany. If it did not render a satisfactory response, he warned that the United States would break diplomatic relations. Again, Wilson stopped short of threatening war, and when Germany promised on September 1, 1915, not to sink passenger vessels without warning and to provide for the safety of noncombatants, the immediate crisis passed.[61]

The Pages, who had not been home in nearly two years, took advantage of the nation's continued neutrality to return home briefly in the spring of 1916. They visited with family, but primarily they attended to business affairs, including rental of their homes in Washington and York Harbor. In August, shortly after they had returned to Rome, Florence received word that her dear brother Bryan had died. The news came as a shock to her since he had not been ill when they saw each other in Chicago. She refused to dwell on his death, however, preferring only to remember his kindness to her and to others.

Perhaps as a means of coping with her loss and because she had invested so much emotional and psychic energy in an Allied victory, Florence became very interested in news of the forthcoming presidential campaign. The trip home had helped to clarify issues for her and to put the election in perspective, even though she as a woman was disfranchised and had never cultivated an overt interest in politics. The irregular mail service between the United States and Italy made it difficult to follow the progress of the presidential campaign from the Palazzo del Drago, especially since the diplomatic pouch was reserved solely for official business. Nonetheless, Florence corresponded almost daily with her younger daughter, Florence Lindsay, about the election. She still clung to the hope that the United States could keep out of the conflict and voiced the fear that if the Republican candidate Charles Evans Hughes was elected, former president Theodore Roosevelt might exert a bellicose influence on his administration.[62]

Although she admired President Wilson's idealism and staunchly endorsed his neutrality policy, Florence did not envy either presidential candidate. Whoever won the election—Wilson or Hughes—would be leading a badly divided people. The victor, she observed, would be faced with the same awesome difficulties, be subjected to the same criticism, and "have only the harsh opinions of the nation, and world entire to reward him." Eschewing sentimentality and emotion, she wrote to her sister-in-law Helen on October 15, 1916, that there was not a man alive who could satisfy "so divided a people as we are." "Only the election can prove whether Mr. Wilson has pleased the majority or not," she declared, adding, "Heaven help his successor or himself whichever it may be."[63]

As the wife of the ambassador, Florence had to follow tradition and remain publicly neutral, but she hoped privately that Wilson would emerge the victor. As much as she wanted an Anglo-French victory, she wanted even more fervently for the United States to remain apart from the conflict. Wilson's neutrality seemed the better guarantee of this. Therefore, when news of the president's reelection reached the American Embassy in Rome, an elated Florence immediately informed her daughter Minna, noting that "all of his villifiers and detractors, whether rascals or fools, or simply well-meaning jackasses, [were] confounded." In a letter of May 2, 1917, to Helen Lathrop, she likened Wilson to President Abraham Lincoln. Both men had been vilified, but both had guided their nation through turmoil with "wisdom, dignity and a firm hand."[64]

Her elation at the president's triumph was tempered by an intuitive feeling that the United States was rapidly approaching a milestone on the road to war. "Personally, I don't see how war can be averted," she had written to Helen in February 1917, "but the submarines will determine this step." The administration in the long run would be unable to protect American merchant vessels from German torpedoes, while each step toward rearmament brought the United States closer to the brink of the abyss, "and this makes one believe that Germany will feel that war is inevitable."[65] This was the ultimate paradox that Florence dreaded: the fear that American intervention would provoke Germany into an act of aggression, thus bringing about the very action it most desired to avoid.

On February 28, 1917, as German submarines wantonly ravaged shipping in the Atlantic with the loss of many lives, Florence reported to Helen that "events are crowding fast these days, and we all of us, at home and abroad, are living in a state of suppressed excitement and expectancy." The tension was both exhausting and exhilarating. "It is a very bad state of mind for everyone, but how thrilling every hour is now," she wrote, a reference to President Wilson's recent address to Congress in which he announced the formal rupture of diplomatic relations with Germany. That speech shifted public opinion at home in support of the president, and also in Europe where neutrality had been roundly condemned on all sides. "All I can say is that whereas the criticism of the President up to the breaking off of diplomatic relations was apt to be severe, and such a sheet as the Paris *Herald* shockingly abusive, now the trend is quite the other way, and the London *Times* has nearly every day a leader on American politics, and invariably something entirely in sympathy with the President and his policies."[66]

Florence had defended the president's policies because she believed in them, but also because she had felt it was necessary to counter anti-Wilson sentiment among Americans living in Europe. "Perhaps were I at home, I might be less violent than now; but over here, where our compatriots are such poor cowardly specimens and find it so 'chic' to denounce America broadly, and to heap on abuse, I am obliged to take the stand I do, and can't be blamed for patriotic sentiments as wrong ones." While she believed that Wilson wanted to avert war, his message to Congress "has shown plainly where he is ready and prepared to act in any eventuality."

Ambassador Page, like Wilson, had hoped that a neutral United States could bring its moral authority to bear on the belligerents to save the world from self-destruction. This was the thrust of his thinking in his early dispatches to President Wilson and the State Department in November 1914; but in subsequent correspondence with public officials, friends, and relatives, he modified his initial beliefs. After Italy entered the war, he abandoned the idea of a concert of neutral powers acting together to end the conflict and pressed for mediation by the United States alone. By mid-1915 Page had decided that German militarism and interference in Latin American affairs constituted a grave menace to American security, a conclusion reinforced by the sinkings of the *Lusitania* and the *Sussex* as well as by publication of the Zimmerman Note.[67] By 1916, while continuing to lean on the slender reed of neutrality, he and Florence concluded that the best guarantee of American security would be an Anglo-French victory, if mediation could not be achieved.

Following Wilson's reelection in 1916, the Pages' hope for a mediated peace was momentarily rekindled. They believed that the European governments would now have to recognize Wilson's power and cooperate with the United States to effect a durable peace. What they failed to comprehend was that each belligerent government by this date had pledged itself to nothing less than victory. The collapse of the Wilson peace initiative in the winter of 1916–17 quickly dashed their optimism, and both Pages reluctantly concluded that American involvement in the war was unavoidable to protect the national security of the United States, to bring the conflict to a swift end, and to create the conditions for making future wars impossible. Confident that these conditions existed in April 1917, Ambassador Page vigorously endorsed Wilson's declaration of war. By defeating Germany quickly and decisively, he believed the United States would be able to establish a just and lasting peace and democratic government throughout the world.[68] A shared state of belligerency also would foster closer Italo-American friendship, and because Italy felt isolated from its allies, he assumed it would be more "liberal" in its relationship to the United States.

These assumptions proved wrong. For most Americans, Italy's role in the war had been and would continue to remain distant and minor. Italians, similarly, were either indifferent to or ignorant of American policy. So poorly informed were they that many Italians in 1915–16 had regarded American opinion as leaning toward Germany. Page recognized that the ignorance was mutual, for he observed, "Ships go back and forth between Italy and America, but there is no bridge over the waters upon which two peoples may walk and meet."[69]

In this atmosphere of misunderstanding the American declaration of war against Germany not surprisingly drew a mixed reaction in Italy.

Italian politicians and the public were superficially enthusiastic, even to the point of marching to the American Embassy in a rigged demonstration of sympathy. Privately they were skeptical. Since the United States had not gone to war against Austria, their major enemy, Italians saw in the intervention little of importance to them. The Wilson administration contributed to this skepticism by rebuffing Ambassador Page's repeated requests to send 50,000 troops to Italy both to make a show of unity and to bolster weak defenses in the Alps, whose collapse might cause all of northern Italy and southern France to fall to the Germans and Austrians. Instead, throughout the American phase of the war, Italy remained engaged in a separate struggle alongside but on the margin of the main conflict, a status expressed in the phrase *la nostra guerra.*[70]

Further complicating relations between the two allies was Foreign Minister Sonnino himself. He was so preoccupied with obtaining a secure Italy through a dogged adherence to the provisions of the Treaty of London that he made no effort to understand President Wilson or his diplomacy, except to recognize that the United States posed the biggest threat to Italy's Adriatic claims. America had not been party to the treaty, nor had it spoken on Italian war claims, leaving Italy uncertain about the part the United States would play in the war and subsequent peace settlement. Thus the seeds were sown from the outset for the policy differences that would develop between the two nations at the peace conference.[71]

Page, meanwhile, continued unsuccessfully to urge the Wilson administration to declare war on Austria. But Italy remained on the periphery of American and Allied concerns at least until the military disaster of Caporetto in October 1917. Until then, Italy and Austria had fought to a stalemate. Despite efforts at an offensive by both sides, by the Italians on the Isonzo and by the Austrians along the valley of the Adige and the Asiago tableland, the front line hardly changed in three years of fighting. The impasse was broken when Austrian and German troops, in a well-planned surprise attack, broke through the Italian lines at this small town in the Alps and swarmed into the plains of Friuli. More than 300,000 soldiers were killed, wounded, or missing in action.[72]

Repercussions from Caporetto affected American policy, because from that moment on the Italian government needed American financial help in order to survive. By the end of the year, Italy was almost wholly dependent upon American loans to purchase grain, coal, food, and military supplies. Caporetto also forced Washington to confront Austria's military alliance with Germany and to reexamine its basic assumptions. President Wilson previously had shown little concern over Austria, the administration believing that it had not committed any "overt acts" against the United States and that a "soft" policy might even induce the Austrians to pursue a separate peace. On December 4, 1917, fearing that Italy would sue for a separate peace, Wilson asked Congress for a declaration of war against Austria.[73]

The request and the token help that followed were symbolic, chiefly intended to build morale in Italy. The Wilson administration did not want Italy to drop out of the war, but neither did it wish to advertise the fact that point 9 of Wilson's Fourteen Points speech delivered in January 1918 was incompatible with Italy's territorial ambitions under the Treaty of London. Ambassador Page, unfortunately, completely misread Washington's motives as he applauded the president's request. "It will I think have a great effect, for a time at least, on Italy and will increase the morale here—though I must say—the Italians have done wonderfully since that frightful crash of five weeks ago," he wrote to Minna. Page was referring to Italy's own efforts to seal the gap opened at Caporetto. "The way in which they have pulled themselves together and held the Austrians and the Germans on the Piave has been worthy of any people in any war in history."[74]

The bravery of the Italian soldiers on the Piave was a beacon of light in an otherwise gloomy year. "I don't see any end anywhere near in sight, not even faintly," wrote Florence on February 16, 1918, to her daughter Florence. "We read of great preparations. The Germans are making for fresh offensives on the French and Italian fronts; of bigger and more powerful submarines under construction, etc." Germany was "so resourceful in crime and in military energy that it makes one shudder at the game she may have up her sleeve." To the east the revolution in Russia and ensuing turmoil had caused the front there to collapse. Florence was especially angry at Russia's "treachery" in pulling out of the war and for "all the vast harm they may have done to us all."[75]

With Russia on the sidelines, the major belligerents except Italy concentrated their strength on the western front, in France. Italian requests for American troops to reinforce its front were cast aside, causing bitter disappointment and leaving Italy alone to confront Austria. On March 21, 1918, the Germans began their great offensive on the Somme in a bold but desparate attempt to end the war before American soldiers and supplies arrived in force. The war was at a critical juncture, and Florence, reflecting a general feeling that events were rapidly spinning out of control, wrote to her younger daughter on March 31: "We are holding our breath in suppressed anxiety over the situation, and for days now I haven't been able to write one letter; not even to my blessed children. It is the most awful moment and not a certain victory, although everyone we meet feels encouraged and full of confidence."[76]

The turning point of the bloody engagement did not occur until July 15, in the Second Battle of the Marne. Within three days the Germans had shot their bolt, and the Allies went on the offensive, breaking the back of the German resistance by August 6. Florence, having regained her confidence, was elated at the turn of events, and especially at the splendid account of themselves that the American troops had given in clearing the south side of the Marne of the enemy. "The news grows more encouraging, and our hearts are going up as high as our hopes," she wrote on July 20 to her younger daughter, Florence. "The Americans . . . behaved like veterans." Two weeks later, she wrote with pride, "We may as well acknowledge now as later that the coming in large numbers of our men has made all the difference." The heroic American soldiers had begun "to weigh heavily on the balance of the conflict." For the first time in nearly four years she allowed herself to think that the end of the war might be at hand. "It is soul stirring," she wrote, "and I too begin to feel the end may be sooner than we have feared for so long."[77]

Toward the close of October, the Germans were in retreat all along the front from Sedan to Flanders. This sudden reversal in the fortunes of war permitted the Pages to hope that the Allies finally would provide military assistance to the Italians. "Italy is keeping up a splendid, but necessarily slow advance on this front," Florence wrote to her younger daughter in America on July 21, 1918, "and if only she had outside assistance, very great things could be done." In August, while on holiday at Aix-les-Bains in France, both Ambassador Page and his wife, the latter unofficially overstepping the bounds of propriety, lobbied American military authorities to send reinforcements to the Italian front, but without success. Writing on August 25 from the Hôtel de Crillon in Paris to her daughter in Southboro, Massachusetts, Florence was astonished at the stubborn refusal of the American military command to do anything to assist the Italians. "But you have no idea of how quite decided officers at G.H.Q. are about the situation in Italy, and people generally here in Paris. Poor side-tracked Italy! Whether she starve, and is beaten, is all the same here. I speak of our own people only. It is the most amazing blindness, and ignorance one can conceive." In October she again noted that "we [had] tried very hard to inspire people of influence with the desirability of sending several divisions to Italy, . . . but to no purpose."[78]

Florence's lobbying on behalf of the Italian war effort was a remarkable action for a woman who was by nature discreet and and extremely private, a woman not normally given to breaking the conventional expectations for womanly conduct. She, of course, had viewed the war from a narrowly Roman perspective—much like her husband—and did not think in terms of the larger military picture as policy makers and generals must. But given the depth of her sentiment for Italy and its heroic struggle against vastly superior foes and her belief that the Allies had neglected the Italo-Austrian front, she was willing to abandon the safety and closure embodied in the ideal of female destiny: that an ambassador's wife should asume a decorative function only and not interfere in the masculine/public realm of politics and policy making. Her criticisms of America's abandonment of Italy, no matter that they were privately articulated, like her later outspoken support of Ambassador Page's diplomatic efforts on behalf of Italian territorial ambitions at the Paris Peace Conference, were a risk she was prepared to take.

Although neither Florence nor Ambassador Page could know it at the time, their lobbying efforts ultimately were unnecessary. With the Germans in general retreat, rumors of an armistice circulating, and the Italians counterattacking against their ancient enemy in the Vittorio Veneto, Allied assistance assumed less importance. Even Florence had second thoughts about whether American reinforcements were needed. Instead, she predicted that the recent Italian victories over the staggering and demoralized Austrian army would, by rekindling Italian nationalism, have dire portents for the postwar settlement.[79]

7

The Travails of
War and Peace

War became a reality for the Pages with the Austrian bombardment of Venice in the spring of 1915. "It is certainly in a critical position, and I fear will meet with a sad fate, our beautiful, incomparable Venice," Florence wrote upon hearing the news.[1] With Italy under seige and the United States adhering to neutrality, she followed closely the shifting military fortunes of the warring nations from her securely distant vantage point in Rome. Intensely hostile to Germany, whom she blamed for starting a war which caused her to be physically separated from her family and beloved grandchildren, Florence decided not to remain simply a passive witness to the conflagration and turned her humanitarian endeavors from the unfortunate victims of the Avezzano earthquake toward assisting Italy's military casualties and civilian victims of the war. This decision allowed her, however modestly, to make a positive contribution to the defeat of the Triple Alliance and to establish a modicum of control over her life and environment.

There was historical precedent for Florence's decision in the personage of Margaret Fuller, one of the leading nineteenth-century figures in American Transcendentalism and early feminism. Fuller had written extensively about the subtle oppression of America's underclass, most notably blacks, immigrants, Indians, and above all women. When she visited Italy from 1847 to 1849, a period of revolutionary turmoil during which Italians attempted to free themselves from the Bourbon and Austrian yoke, she quickly became involved in the destiny of the short-lived Italian republic whose struggle for independence she saw as the counterpart of the American Revolution. While living in Rome, she formed a liaison with a younger, handsome, and politically active Italian nobleman, Angelo Ossoli, and gave birth to a son. Fuller's marriage to the Italian became inseparable from the revolutionary activities of Giuseppe Mazzini, the "Great Man" who had spearheaded the movement for Italian unification.[2]

Florence Page's benevolent and organizational activities in Italy were perhaps not quite so dramatic, but in their own limited way they testified to her own commitment to preserving Italy's independence and freedom from foreign oppression. Like Fuller, Florence was taking a risk of a sort. Within the context of total war, where the demarcation between the military and the civilian had become increasingly blurred, Florence's eleemosynary work among Italy's military casualties in 1915–16 might have been construed as technically unneutral and might have resulted in public embarrassment for the Wilson administration and the recall of Ambassador Page.

Fortunately, there were no repercussions from her activities. Perhaps the scale of Florence's work was too small for the German ambassador to make an issue of it; perhaps, too, Germany was unwilling to antagonize the Italian and American governments while it was courting the one and trying to keep the other neutral; more likely, the male-dominated governments of Italy, Germany, and the United States simply took for granted that women would engage in charitable works of this sort and considered it not worth making a fuss. Whatever the reason, the organization of an *ouvroir*, as Florence referred to it, to produce surgical dressings, bandages, and other items needed by Italy's war wounded enabled her to put to good use one of the most characteristic traits of True Womanhood: domesticity.[3] The same skills that a woman of her class and social position would have developed in supervising a large household, instructing the servants, overseeing the care of the children, organizing formal and informal dinner parties, and participating in a variety of charitable endeavors—which the metaphor of the sphere had consigned to the private realm of women—presumably were transferable to the public realm of charitable work. Florence's assistance to Italian military casualties, like her aid to the victims of the Avezzano earthquake, extended women's traditional role as head of household, nurturer, and comforter.

Florence's *ouvroir* may also be perceived in a different but equally plausible perspective, which does not fit so neatly into the received category of True Womanhood but which attributes greater public authority to women. Her work on behalf of Italy's military casualties may illustrate how a woman's control over her physical space could enable her to acquire practical experience, to bridge the male/public-female/private hierarchy, and to create a public female sphere. The decision to establish first one and then a second *ouvroir* also exemplified female voluntarism in the public sphere that built on a tradition going back at least to the Civil War.[4] The *ouvroir* was an alternative career to the formal and more regimented life of an ambassador's wife; it was the physical space in which Florence learned to be and to act as a professional. There she controlled her own agenda, raised and allocated her own funds, kept her own records, and developed a managerial style that relied heavily on cooperation.

In the wake of the bombardment of Venice and similar attacks along other points of the Italo-Austrian border, Florence anticipated that large numbers of wounded Italian soldiers and displaced civilians soon would be shifted from frontline hospitals to medical facilities in Rome. She immediately offered her services to Queen Elena, who was already transforming a wing of the Quirinal palace, the royal residence, into a modern, completely equipped hospital. The offer, which the queen promptly accepted, was tendered quietly and without fanfare because of the need to maintain the facade of neutrality and avoid intrusion into Italy's domestic politics. "It requires some careful steering to keep off conflicting reefs, but, all the same, I am sure we can work in some capacity," Florence wrote on May 27, 1915, to her brother Bryan Lathrop.[5]

With the queen's approval Florence threw her energies into organizing women volunteers from the American colony in Rome—"and all are more than anxious to help me with it"—and hiring a handful of salaried Italian women employees, mainly as seamstresses. She set aside a room in the Palazzo del Drago as a workroom where this small band of women of differing nationalities, religious beliefs, and social classes occupied their days making hospital gowns and surgical dressings, sewing shirts for the army, and even producing gas masks. Under Florence's disciplinary control, the women volunteers purchased supplies, kept accounts, and collected and dispatched the finished work to the hospitals or supply depots where it was needed. Not surprisingly, Florence believed that her work, modest as it was, was hastening the defeat of Germany.

"Considering I have never engineered anything of the kind before, I think we have an orderly shop, and I hope will be able to help many people," she wrote to her sister-in-law Helen on June 15, 1915.[6] This was a modest evaluation of her abilities; in fact, the *ouvroir* highlighted her managerial skills as well as her fund-raising talents. Not only did she solicit enough funds to pay her Italian seamstresses more than their government would have compensated them for comparable work, but she made certain that the differential was not so great as to cause strife between her employees and seamstresses in the employ of the Italian government.

The most immediate problem for the *ouvroir* was to secure access to a steady supply of scarce materials, especially cotton. "Cotton cloth is getting very limited with the unusual demands," Florence wrote to Helen, "and I fear we wont be able to keep up with the shirtmaking." To cope with the shortage, she again resorted to networking, pressing into service her family and social connections. Besides contributing her own money to purchase cotton, she cabled her daughter Florence in Southboro, Massachusetts, "to ask if she couldn't interest friends with cotton mills, to send us some cloth as a donation." She also cabled William A. Slater, a millowner who was a family acquaintance, for a donation of cotton cloth.

As Italy reeled before the first hammerblows of war, casualties were very heavy, and Florence declared that "we must work harder than ever." Indeed, the Italian army in the first two years of the war was one of the least prepared and worst armed that fought on the various fronts of Europe, lacking in artillery, machine guns, trucks, and even officers. The officer corps had to be hastily improvised, with results that may easily be imagined. Italy suffered a half million dead and a million and a half wounded before peace finally was concluded.

From the first attacks on Venice, Florence's goal was to replicate in Italy the work of Marie Van Vorst, an American woman living in London, who had raised $30,000 for war relief from the American colony there in the first twenty-four hours of the war. "What extraordinary people ours are," she said in reference to Americans' generosity, fully anticipating that they would open their hearts and pocketbooks to the Italian victims of war. By and large they did so, though on a considerably more modest scale than they had contributed aid to the British or French. An early inventory of cotton items that Florence's workshop made for Italian war relief was impressive indeed, especially when one considers that the *ouvroir* had started with almost nothing. It included

1,300 shirts, 250 pairs of felt slippers, 16 dozen towels, 1,500 washcloth gloves, dozens of flannel bed jackets, 543 dozen pairs of socks, 36 sheets, and thousands of bandages and surgical dressings. In June and July 1915 the *ouvroir* produced more than 6,000 items for the wounded, enough to supply two or three hospitals. In June 1915, when Queen Elena asked whether Florence's women volunteers would make 200 hospital sheets, she was able to comply with the request.[7]

Word of Florence's activities quickly reached the United States. In 1916 two groups of volunteer women, one in Philadelphia and the other in Hartford, Connecticut, began to send her surgical supplies on a regular basis. In July 1915, for example, she thanked Bryan and Helen for their generous financial contribution which enabled her to purchase 5,000 yards of cotton cloth. "The poor Italian soldiers will be made infinitely more comfortable, and you will get your happiness out of this, and out of my loving gratitude," she wrote. "Auntie Helen," meanwhile, had raised $3,000 from Chicago's most prominent women for her work, and on February 23, 1916, Florence received a cable from Bryan requesting instruction on how the funds should be expended. She cabled back asking that the sum be divided equally to purchase cotton, outing flannel, eider flannel, chloroform, ether, rubber gloves, and clinical thermometers.[8]

Ironically, just about the only quarter that did not contribute funds or other assistance to Florence's *ouvroir* were her summer friends from York Harbor. Helen Lathrop had informed her of the wonderful work that the women had done that past summer for the Allies, all under the direction of Helen Cadwalader, and added that "it would rejoice your heart." The letter had just the opposite effect, as Florence confessed to her younger daughter, Florence Lindsay. The York Harbor Women's Committee had not forwarded a single aid package to Italy. "I feel the neglect on their part of my work here," she wrote on November 1, 1916. "Not one box has ever come to Italy, as far as I know, from that Committee; considering Father's position here and my being one of the oldest of the York summer colony, and having probably done as much for the place as anyone else, it seems to me it might have occurred to Helen C. to send me one of their boxes for use here in Italy, a country the Cadwaladers profess to love." Other people might beg, she observed, "but I never can, so I don't get as much as some do." Three weeks later the committee's negligence still rankled Florence, for she wrote, "I think this neglect has hurt me more than anything since I left home."[9]

As enthusiasm for her project grew, Florence even contemplated affiliating her small operation with the larger clearing house in Paris for all European war relief, but nothing ever came of that idea, and her *ouvroir* continued to function independently. No matter, for she decided that some day, perhaps when the hostilities ceased, she would draft a report to be mailed to those who had so generously helped her *ouvroir,* adding, "and I think it will rather astonish our friends in its scope and the amount done with so few Americans in Rome to help."[10]

Meanwhile, the bloody fighting on the northern front had bogged down in trench warfare. Optimism gave way to gloom, and a pallor cast itself on the Eternal City as the politicians' promise of a swift victory proved more than ever to be a chimera. "Rome is filling up with the wounded now, and sad little processions of hand ambulances are to be seen from time to time going to the different hospitals," Florence wrote to Bryan on August 4, 1915. The duke d'Ascoli, one of the gentleman in waiting to the queen, had even disrupted an embassy dinner party with a request from Her Majesty "for some of the shirts we are making, for the wounded in the Quirinal Hospital." This was the second emissary Queen Elena had sent recently; and as in response to the first request, Florence dispatched the entire production of the *ouvroir* to the hospital for distribution under the queen's personal supervision. "It is the only way of reaching the right hospitals in Italy," she wrote, alluding to Italy's notoriously cumbersome bureaucracy. Queen Elena later invited the Pages to visit the hospital, which Florence thought was "a doubtful pleasure," but which Ambassador Page found "very interesting."[11]

By 1917 Florence's *ouvroir* had become something of a cottage industry to which she was devoting all of her spare time. Her fund-raising efforts for the purchase of cotton cloth achieved new successes. On May 2, 1917, she thanked Helen Lathrop, now widowed, for sending her the equivalent of 3,070 lire from a bazaar held in Chicago to raise money for wartime charitable work. This sum would keep Florence's workers productively occupied turning out surgical dressings for yet another year, a necessity because the end of the conflict was nowhere in sight. "All our hopes to see the war end during the coming summer are fading away," she wrote; "on all sides one hears of two to three years more!" It did not seem humanly possible to her, but Germany was far from exhaustion.[12]

Florence's contribution to Italy during the period of American neutrality had not been inconsiderable. In December 1917 she wrote to Helen that she had sent 2,000 pairs of socks, which her Italian seamstresses had sewn during the past summer, to the wife of the commander of the Italian Fourth Army for his soldiers. Her relationship with her employees relied heavily on cooperation, and after three years she was beginning to assume a proprietary interest in their welfare as well. She was determined to keep them knitting as long as supplies of cotton and wool held out; but even if the supplies became exhausted, she would "keep up their 10 lire each a week, as a tiny bit toward warding off starvation."[13]

Florence literally was working herself to the bone on behalf of Italian war relief, seeking no recognition for herself and receiving little for her efforts. Ambassador Page conceded as much in a letter of February 17, 1917, to H. Rozier Dulany, a longtime acquaintance. "My wife is working herself nearly to death over her *ouvroir,*" he wrote. "She gets a lot of pleasure out of it, though she gets very little recognition yet from anybody around in these parts, though I know well that the poor wounded fellows that she sends anything to appreciate it although they do not know where they come from, and she gets some warm letters of gratitude from those in the hospitals." He noted that Florence's *ouvroir* recently had assumed the additional burden of making 500 sheets "for some hospital," but Page never stopped to ask why his wife's humanitarian contributions went unheralded and unrecognized. Had he done so, he might have had to confront more critically the validity of separate spheres and the proper role of women. He was not prepared by birth, training, or inclination to raise these questions; instead, he admonished Dulany: "Tell some of your rich friends to send some money to her *ouvroir.*"[14] Whether they did so is unrecorded, but Florence continued to secure funds from various sources that enabled her to expand the scale of relief activities, so much so that she soon ran out of space in her existing quarters.

Shortly before American entry into the war, Florence secured a rent free-apartment in a palazzo next to the Quirinal where she was able to expand her war relief activities. Consisting of eleven rooms, the additional space made possible a second *ouvroir,* which enabled Florence to employ as many as sixty Italian women to make surgical dressings for the military and to sew clothing for displaced women and children.

With the permission of King Vittorio Emanuele, she even agreed to make red shirts for a regiment organized by General Pepperino Garibaldi![15]

After the United States formally entered the conflict in April 1917, the American Red Cross assumed responsibility for the relief program in Italy, discreetly dispensing large sums of money to existing welfare and charitable agencies, taking care not to injure peoples' sensibilities. "Our Red Cross is trying to be tactful and to go carefully into all sorts of charities, so as not to offend, but to assist those already organized, and only starting new ones when especially requested to do so," she wrote in January 1918.[16]

As the large, male-dominated, bureaucratic organization assumed more of the functions of her *ouvroir,* Florence began to experience less personal satisfaction that she was making a direct contribution to the war effort, as she had previously. Her workshops seemed redundant, and she decided finally to close them. The decision was painful because the workshops had been the focal point of her emotional and psychic energies for the past two years. Creating a public female sphere had given direction and purpose to her life in a world gone mad with killing and senseless slaughter. "It seems useless for my *ouvroir* to continue," she wrote to her daughter Florence Lindsay on July 20. "I have sent only this past week the result of several months labor to them [the American Red Cross], and all individuality is gone, and incentive to do the work."[17]

Instead of remaining idle or reverting to the merely decorative role of overseeing dinner parties and attending official functions as the wife of the ambassador, Florence shifted her time and energy to other public war-related activities. "I am going to be honorary chairman of the Y.M.C.A. in Rome, and the Embassy ladies will be the active committee," she wrote to Helen on August 14, "but I am going to do active work myself; loafing doesn't appeal to me." With the same zeal that had inspired the founding of the *ouvroir,* she transformed the workshop into a recreational center for American servicemen on leave, a relaxing place where they could read, write, dine, and play billiards. She also continued to raise money for the poor and war-orphaned children of Italy. When Helen sent her a check for $500, Florence informed her that she had closed the workshop but would use the money for the orphans and the poor. "God knows there are vastly more than we can ever care for; but at least we can help, and we can bring good cheer to many a drooping heart."[18]

Besides running a canteen for American servicemen and raising funds for war orphans, Florence became a publicist throughout Italy of her fellow countrymen's contributions to the war effort. She felt very strongly the need to do this because Italy's allies, including the United States, had been reluctant to divert troops and matériel to the Italian front, leaving it to face the Austrians alone. To counteract the widespread sentiment that Italy was the forgotten ally, she asked her relatives and friends in the United States to send her pictures and postcards of American workers producing war matériel and in other ways contributing to the war effort, whereupon she mounted an exhibition of the photographs in Rome, Milan, and other cities to show Italians that the people of the United States supported their heroic efforts. On March 19, 1918, she wrote to Helen thanking her for sending this visual evidence. It was *"exactly* what we wanted, and even much more expressive of all that is being done, than I had dreamed possible to obtain," she declared. "It was dear of you to take the infinite pains that you did for this propaganda, but I know it will please you to realize how much you have helped."[19]

Besides cementing Italo-American friendship, Florence hoped that the photographs would demonstrate that American idealism and humanitarianism—the values that President Wilson so proudly articulated—had motivated the United States to come to Italy's aid. She certainly believed that America's motive for intervening in the conflict was disinterested and altruistic. "It is not possible to make people understand the magnitude of America's intervention, nor the extraordinary sacrifices without something like these pictures to impress them," she observed. Italians understood why the Red Cross and the YMCA sponsored the programs they did, but they did not truly appreciate President Wilson's grander, more noble purpose in coming to Italy's assistance. "All this can only be made clear by just what these pictures accomplish," she wrote.

Whether this propaganda ploy succeeded is doubtful, but one of the most poignant indications that Florence's eleemosynary activities was appreciated occurred during Christmas 1918. In a rare and very intimate gesture, Queen Elena invited the Pages to the Qurinal to view the Presepio, a hand-carved wood crèche from Caserta, displayed especially for the wounded soldiers in the palace hospital. The king, the young prince, "a tall, handsome erect boy of only 14, and looking 16 or 17," and the princesses Yoland and Mafalda were present. Together, the entourage entered the chapel to view the Presepio. "It was the most beautifully and artistically got up thing I ever saw," Florence wrote to Minna, "really a perfect scene, with the best effect of distance I ever saw. The camels, goats, cows, etc., were true to life." From above, a boys' choir sang "charmingly," although no religious service was conducted because the pope had not rescinded the ban of excommunication from the saying of mass in the chapel following the separation of church and state. Indeed, the queen informed Florence that this was the first time since 1870 that any music whatsoever had been allowed within its walls. The ceremony was nonetheless as sweet, simple and devout as Florence had ever witnessed. Afterwards the Pages and the royal family visited the hospital wing, "where many permanently injured soldiers lay."[20] The sight of their broken bodies was a gruesome reminder of the awful reality of the war whose course remained the focal point of Florence's correspondence, more so after the arrival of American soldiers in Europe.

With the failure of Germany's spring 1918 offensive, the German high command saw the handwriting on the wall and urged the chancellor to end the war. In October the German and Austrian governments appealed to President Wilson for an armistice, accepting the Fourteen Points he had laid out to Congress that January as a basis for peace. "This moment most startling news has come!" Florence wrote to her younger daughter on October 6. "Can it really be true that Germany is asking for peace?" The embassy had heard rumors, but if Germany accepted the president's terms, there was little to be gained from delaying peace talks. If it did not, Florence observed, then there would be "no use in any discussion without this." In either event the peace negotiations would be arduous because of German atrocities. "What can be done about the innumerable crimes," she asked, as she enumerated them: "the *Lusitania;* the torpedoing of hospital ships; the wanton destruction of towns; world's art treasures forever gone; not to mention air raids and Berthas!! how can this be settled except by force of arms; and utter subjugation?" Neither she nor anyone else could reconcile those criminal actions without great difficulty, she told her daughter.[21]

Over the next several weeks there followed an exchange of notes between Berlin and Washington concerning the exact terms of the armistice. The key provisions of Wilson's address, besides demanding the evacuation of occupied territories and democratic government in Germany, had called for nothing less than a new world order with an end to selfish nationalism, unilateral action, and war. This idealistic platform, which failed initially to impress Allied leaders, also had been designed to save them deeper embarrassment. For, with the coming to power of the Bolsheviks in Russia, the new Soviet regime disclosed the contents of the secret treaties that the czarist government had entered into with France and Great Britain. The treaties revealed that the Entente had gone to war for the same selfish ends as Germany, and not for the high principles they claimed. Wilson's Fourteen Points speech may have given their cause a nobler purpose, but it was his threat to make a separate peace that brought the Allies into line.[22]

Florence, too, despite her staunch support for Britain and France, noted that the Allies had delayed accepting the Fourteen Points as the basis for armistice negotiations. Nonetheless, she applied a double standard when judging them, insisting that Germany had to meet every condition imposed by the Allies because of its "barbarity." Even though Britain and France had hedged their acceptance of the president's terms, she wrote to her sister-in-law Helen, "It is so magnificent, so unexpected really, this acceptance of the conditions for a general armistice, agreed upon by the Allies after their recent conference at Versailles." Her heart bounded "with joy at the overwhelming thought of the end of the massacre."[23]

During this prearmistice maneuvering, the Allied armies maintained their pressure against the enemy until Austria's Hapsburg Empire finally disintegrated. On October 27, 1918, following the disaster of Vittorio Veneto, the Austrian foreign minister notified President Wilson that his country would recognize the rights of the subject nationalities and was ready to conclude a separate peace. Rumors of the impending capitulation swept Rome, and Florence repeated them in a letter to her daughter Florence Lindsay. The Austrians had called for quarter and were laying down their arms, she wrote. "This was premature, we know; but it is only deferred, that is all." Desperately anxious to stop the fighting and unable to wait for Wilson's peacemaking, Austria-Hungary negotiated directly with Italy. Representing the Allied powers, Italy signed the armistice with its ancient foe on November 3, 1918, at Villa Giusti, near Padua. The Austrian surrender, which was based not on the president's Fourteen Points but on a military triumph, was a turn of events which would complicate Italo-United States relations at the peace conference.[24]

The triumph of Vittorio Veneto and the subsequent armistice deeply affected the Pages, who viewed them as a vindication of Italian bravery and, more importantly, the legitimation of Italy's irredentist ambitions. Florence praised the Italians for their recent victories in capturing Trieste, Trentino, Udine, and Istria. "Isn't the Italian news thrilling, and isn't it time to help them get all that they have been after these more than three long years?" she wrote to Florence.

That last statement was indicative of the Pages' empathy for Italy's hardships and sacrifices during the period of American neutrality. Ambassador Page had even compared Italy's experience to the suffering of the Confederacy during the Civil War; and once the United States entered the conflict, he believed that a shared state of belligerency would foster closer Italo-American friendship and help Italy to realize its wartime aims. Page shared his sentiments with his wife, just as he kept her abreast of the progress of the military conflict. Because Florence shared the ambassador's views, her statement to Florence Lindsay may be taken as a reliable indicator of the extent to which both Pages had lost their objectivity in assessing Italian versus American interests. Thomas Nelson Page was fast becoming the client of the nation to which he had been posted. It was not surprising, then, that he would go to the Ministry of War to congratulate the Italian nation on its military victories. As he emerged from the ministry, a joyous crowd of Italians, "pelting him with flowers, [and] crying 'Viva L'America,' followed him back to the Palazzo del Drago, where he delivered an impromptu speech from a balcony overlooking the Via XX Settembre to a delegation from Trieste standing below. The Ambassador's address was greeted with shouts of 'Viva L'America,'" a reaction that prompted Florence to wave the American and Italian flags from the embassy balcony. A festive air hung over the nation, Florence reported. "All shops are closed over Italy, and the rejoicing passes description."

The feeling of exhilaration occasioned by the sudden collapse of Italy's archenemy was tempered by the knowledge that Germany, the more treacherous adversary, still had not capitulated. Until it did, Florence rode an emotional roller coaster, exulting one moment because the end of the war was imminent and growing despondent the next for fear that the duplicitous Hun might wiggle out of the terms of the armistice.

Her only concrete information was "a very strong rumor" that Germany was prepared to accept in full President Wilson's "14 Conditions of peace." On October 8 she passed on still another rumor to Minna, her older daughter, living in England, that Germany had signed the armistice agreement. The information was premature, but as Florence correctly perceived, Germany was isolated and "the end of hostilities is in sight."[25]

Armistice was not the same as peace, but "it means pretty nearly complete and permanent capitulation in this case," Florenced observed, referring to Wilson's second note to Germany, which shattered the illusion that the armistice would permit it to resume the war if the peace terms were found to be intolerable. The president's conditions, she wrote, demanded the evacuation of occupied territories, disarmament, abdication of the kaiser, "and ending forever the Hohenzollern inheritance of the Throne." Florence was guardedly optimistic that a general armistice could be achieved before Christmas so that American soldiers could return home in time for the holiday. Her last comment to Minna was especially ironic in light of the events in Europe of the next twenty-five years, for she wrote: "We must pray that a *just* one can be concluded, one to preserve the world from future similar wars, and one that will prove to Germany what she has lost, not gained by her 40 years of war preparations."[26]

On one point Florence was correct. Germany's response to the president's Fourteen Points had not constituted acceptance of them, only an acknowledgment that it was in a greatly weakened state and desperately needed peace. "We all know that this is what is called a peace offensive, and with only Germany's own good in view," she observed. "Still it shows her weakness, and that we are getting nearer day by day to our own terms." The Germans had to be forced back across the Rhine and the Hohenzollern dynasty abolished as absolute conditions of peace. "What use is talk of peace unless this is accomplished?" she wrote. Still, the rumors were so exciting that she found it "very hard to settle down to ordinary life."

The president's response to the German armistice request was a masterpiece of diplomacy because it exploited the divisions within that country. "We have but to read the reports from every section of Germany to see that our hopes are not far from realization," Florence wrote to Minna on October 22. German sentiment pointed to the abdication of the kaiser and the deposal of the Hohenzollerns; even the press was turning against the government. The imperial military party might stubbornly hold out to continue the fight, "but their big funeral pile awaits them in the near future." Florence longed for a looking glass to peer into the German leaders' minds to learn whether they would accept the peace terms; until they did, the Allies could not ease the pressure. "None of us can afford to give them an inch of line in the water," she declared; "we must keep the hook tight in their gills!" She did not trust the Germans; their sense of honor was so corrupt that "we shall [have] to have extraordinary guaranties, and absolute pledges, before we can stop."

Even though the Imperial German government would finally accede to President Wilson's conditions, effectively making it impossible for Germany to take up arms again if the armistice broke down, Florence never forsook her fear of German treachery. Germany had accepted the president's conditions for an armistice, she wrote on October 12, but had not pledged itself to anything beyond withdrawing from occupied territory. "We can't be too wary of that people, and I am sure the Allies, including ourselves, will never fall into a trap, and be caught in any German intrigue with all our knowledge of her sly tricks." She reiterated her distrust to her daughter Florence on October 26, stating that the president's note to the German people, as distinct from the kaiser and the government, "places Germany in a bottomless hole. Whatever she does now will meet with disfavor in some sections of the country." The whole world, she declared, was "breathless with suspense awaiting Germany's decision, although we know that it will be an equivocal answer, in keeping with all their methods." Of one thing Florence was certain: not only would the kaiser have to abdicate and the Hohenzollerns renounce all claims to the throne, but Germany would have to be "split up as before the Empire." This last condition went far beyond President Wilson's expectations for, fulfilling it would have meant the dismemberment of Germany as a nation-state.[27]

Peace continued to elude the peacemakers until November 8, 1918, when Matthias Erzberger, the head of the German armistice commission, met with Marshal Foch. In his railway coach near Compiègne, Foch presented the delegation with the terms of the armistice. When the news reached Rome, Florence was again cautiously optimistic. "Naturally they would not have sent a delegation to confer with Foch, unless they had been prepared to accede," she wrote to her daughter Florence that very evening. "They will try a 'rake off' and will oppose certain points but to no avail." The noose "is tight around their necks and they will have to capitulate or suffer fearful strangulation." The next day she dashed off yet another note, saying: "So far no word of Germany's acceptance of our conditions; so I suppose we must wait another 24 hours; probably no longer, for with only yes or no to reply, it can't be a long discussion. It is like a person bargaining in a shop where prices are fixed; all to no avail."[28] The moment Florence and the rest of the world had been waiting for finally arrived. Germany signed the armistice agreement, and on November 11, 1918, at 11 A.M., hostilities ceased on the Western front.

Florence was euphoric as word of the signing reached Rome. "Oh what a wonderful day!!" she wrote that evening to her younger daughter in America. "We are intoxicated over the news, and it is like a marvelous dream." Germany was "crushed to earth, and she can never again take up the sword as before." She could hardly wait to read with her own eyes the exact wording of the armistice. "The conditions of the armistice will be great reading, and it is hard to wait till they appear," she wrote to Minna on November 12.[29]

The embassy in Rome received a copy of the armistice text only a few hours in advance of the general public, but the excitement had made any semblance of normal routine impossible. "People can't settle down to ordinary life, and I find myself more restless than ever before," Florence declared. "Yesterday was one of great emotion, and Rome, like other cities, was seething with restlessness, joyous half-crazed people, who were like children in their expressions of joy." Huge demonstrations had been mounted in front of the Quirinal palace to celebrate both the armistice and the king's birthday. Pride in the nation and the monarchy was manifested everywhere, as Florence described the scene so that her daughter might envision it in her mind's eye: "Thousands and thousands and thousands of men, women and children; flags of every town that Italy now occupies of her new possessions; women dressed up like circus riders on tame, oh! such tame horses, for whom the crowds parted to make way for their entrance into the courtyard of the Quirinal."

Florence's moment of joy was tempered by the memory of the terrible waste of lives and destruction of property occasioned by the war, by her younger daughter's criticism of the president for not imposing even harsher terms upon Germany, and by the knowledge that the worldwide influenza epidemic was now ravaging Italy. The flu troubled her greatly because her grandchildren in America and England had contracted it. In America alone more than one-half million people died from the influenza. It would be several weeks before Florence received word that her "babies" had recovered with no adverse aftereffects; until then she worried. The epidemic was subsiding in Rome, but it was just now reaching into the provinces. "I suppose we had to have something to counteract the exuberance of joy created by the war bulletins," she declared laconically. Reports that Austria had appealed to the Allies for food to ward off civilian starvation tugged at her humanitarian and maternal instincts, although only a few weeks earlier she had fervently wished for Austria's defeat. "She must be helped now as fast as we can send provisions," she wrote, but so, too, must the hungry and malnourished of Italy, especially those of Trentino and Trieste where the Austrians had left devastation and desolation behind them. "But Italy is very badly off herself, and hasn't enough food to feed her own population; milk for babies and children is almost to be discounted." Eggs and milk were not to be had at all, or only at the most exorbitant prices.[30]

Florence was able to view the sickness and deprivation with a certain fatalism, but she smarted at her daughter's criticism of the president. How could Florence have called the note "weak," when it ended the fighting? Even Romans considered the terms so drastic that they believed the Germans could not possibly accept them. Yet they had. On November 12 Florence wrote to Minna that President Wilson "was the most looked up to man in the world." True, he had erred in asking the voters to return a Democratic majority in both houses in the recent congressional elections, and Florence could foresee the day when "a wave of opposition" might engulf him, but "let us give him credit at all events for his share in the big victory today."[31]

More impressive than the president's note to Germany was his address to Congress. His declaration that the victorious nations could not allow the vanquished to starve without fomenting revolution or interfere with their efforts to rebuild was absolutely correct, but Florence still wished she never had to see or speak to a German again. She still harbored doubts that Germany would abide by the terms of the armistice. "Germany is *not going* to live up to the armistice one sees plainly, and if not this, how are we going to trust any permanent peace?" she wrote to Minna on November 23. Its naval fleet, fortunately, was in the safe custody of the Allies so that it could not go "to bed with an ace this time," but the kaiser was still alive, having fled to Holland. At the very mention of his name, Florence became paranoid, suspecting him of sending secret ciphers from Doorn to his followers in an attempt to create mischief. "I must say 'peace' looks rather stormy to me, and unless we strictly and relentlessly enforce our *severe* conditions, we are going to be back where we were in 1914, or practically so."[32]

Shortly after the armistice the European newspapers began to speculate that President Wilson personally would head the American delegation at the peace conference to advance his liberal program. He thus would become the first president to go overseas on a diplomatic mission, a prospect which disturbed Florence initially, for it violated tradition, always important to her. No sitting president had hitherto left the country, and she feared that his moral stature would be diminished in the maneuvering for advantage that was certain to occur in Paris. On November 15, 1918 she wrote to her daughter Florence, "It seems to me such a grave mistake if he should be allowed to leave America; against our oldest traditions it would be."[33]

To Minna she protested even more vehemently, saying she expected Congress to object to his leading the American delegation. "I am personally greatly distressed and disturbed over the unofficial announcement of the President's arrival in time for the Peace Conference," she wrote on November 17. "Aside from the long tried traditions of our country for a President never to leave American soil during his incumbency of office, it seems to me such a mistake for this one in particular to become common property, as it were, rather than to remain an ideal so long as he can!" Besides expending his moral capital, the president was putting his enormous personal popularity at risk. "Heaven knows it can't last always and it is a pity to risk his popularity at this critical time."[34]

The reservations were valid because Wilson had a great deal of prestige and moral authority to lose if the peace conference failed. But the president evidently had made up his mind, and Florence ultimately resigned herself to his pilgrimage to Paris. "I suppose he has a good reason for breaking the precedent, and probably feels sure that he can best understand all the many problems to be discussed by being at the council," she told Minna. Wilson was a proud man, and she recognized that this was a momentous occasion in history, "ancient or modern"; no man given a similar opportunity would refuse to become a part of it. Momentarily descending from the high ground, she also speculated that the president's wife had goaded him into making the trip, saying Edith Bolling Wilson "may not be loathe to come over and get in the game."

Whatever the motive, Florence concluded that "the President will himself sign the peace document, and it will be the most memorable day of his life, and that of the others who take part in this overwhelmingly momentous event."

But the road to peace was strewn with obstacles, and the peacemakers were not masters of Europe but subject to many influences that they could not escape or control. Even before the delegates convened, Florence predicted that the negotiations would be difficult. The future of the kaiser weighed heavily in her thoughts, as was manifested in a stream of letters to her daughters. She repeated stories about the kaiser that were making the diplomatic rounds: "The Arch Devil of the World" had fled to a beautiful chateau in Holland; he was accompanied by a retinue of aides and retainers and a trainload of provisions, scarcely a difficult exile; he was transmitting secret ciphers to his followers in the fatherland. Her paranoia of everything German once again surfaced. "Every fresh word I read of the determination to bring the ex-Kaiser and all associated with him in criminal acts to justice for trial, comes as a balm to my soul," she wrote. "Let his death be what it may, only let it be death." As long as Wilhelm and the crown prince were alive, they were "a menace to peace and prosperity in the world."[35]

As for Germany, Florence hoped that the delegates would "recapitulate all the crimes in chronological order, and then punish the offenders as they themselves have the innocent and defenseless." This was not the moment "to talk of doing as we would be done by, but as we have been done by," she declared. Her anti-German tirades were tempered only by the knowledge that the Allies' war aims had not been as high-minded and noble as those of the president. "There are several knotty matters that are preoccupying the Statesmen, some rather serious, and which it will require calm judicious handling to settle," she wrote to Florence on November 15. "Jealousies are inevitable after so many strange alliances, some logical, others not."

The euphoria of victory soon faded, especially where Italo-American relations were concerned. America's token support in the war against Austria had disillusioned Italians; even now, after the signing of the armistice, the two nations remained woefully ignorant of each other. The Italian government had no comprehension of Wilsonian diplomacy and his position toward its claims, but it did have some clues from the Fourteen Points that he would not be entirely sympathetic. Wilson had failed to make an explicit endorsement of Italy's war aims as embodied in the Pact of London. Points nine and ten of the Fourteen Points, which embraced the principle of national self-determination, clearly conflicted with the nationalistic aspirations of the Italian population, which was now clamoring for the territories of Fiume, Cattaro, and Trieste, as well as for domination of the Adriatic.[36]

The Paris Peace Conference revealed the divergence between the two countries' attitudes and policies, and Page's unsuccessful attempts to bridge this gap ultimately led to the collapse of his ambassadorial career. When Wilson decided in October 1918 to send his right-hand man, Colonel Edward M. House, to Europe to represent the United States on the Supreme War Council and to gain Allied approval of his peace program, Florence thought it was imperative for House to visit Italy as well as France and Great Britain to reassure the Italians of America's friendship. "But it is of moment that some special representative from our Government should come to Italy, and it is painful trying to keep up an appearance of goodwill with one's country," she wrote to her daughter Florence. Acknowledging that she had overstepped the boundaries of her position as the wife of the American ambassador, Florence told her daughter that this was an "indiscreet statement" and not for repetition.[37]

But the truth was that she, like Ambassador Page, had been embarrassed by America's neglect of its wartime ally. Both Pages had thoroughly embraced Italy's nationalistic claims during the course of the war and saw no contradiction between them and President Wilson's internationalistic vision. Thus, when House agreed initially to consult with Italian leaders in Rome, Florence was delighted, "for no one has ever done so officially since the war began, and poor beautiful Italy has been completely overshadowed."[38]

Her letter to Minna of November 3, 1918, was not only a prescient assessment of Italy's military position upon the politics of peacemaking but a revelation of exactly how much of the Italian viewpoint Florence had incorporated into her own thinking. "The Italians are making their history faster than even the 'extras' are able to print," she wrote, a reference to the unofficial news that Italian cavalry had entered Udine and would take the city in "a matter of hours." Trieste was occupied, and Trentino was "fast coming nearer." Italy would be able to bargain from a position of strength at the peace table, she observed. "It will make all the difference imaginable for the Italians to have taken this offensive; instead of asking for concessions from Austria hereafter. They will be in possession of the very places they have long wanted, and—this by conquest." The victories had "not been child's play," she wrote, "not a quiet walk over in the least, and we can congratulate them upon their courage and endurance."

Colonel House's heavy schedule in Paris eventually caused him to cancel his visit to Rome, a decision which greatly disappointed the Pages. Italian leaders had to travel to Paris to present their position. By now fully aware of the inconsistency between the Fourteen Points and the Pact of London, the delegation that met with House tried to protect Italy's interests by introducing a reservation to point nine that would have safeguarded its territorial aspirations in the north and in the Adriatic. The meeting did not go well; Colonel House focused exclusively upon Germany as the enemy and brushed aside the Italian reservation, saying that point nine did not bear on the conditions of the German armistice. Italy's new prime minister, Vittorio Emanuele Orlando, then committed a tactical error which came back to haunt the Italian delegates to the peace conference. To preserve the facade of amity, he consented to House's request not to insist that the United States acknowledge publicly Italy's reservation to point nine. When House returned to America, he never informed Wilson of the reservation, an omission which set the groundwork for future United States–Italian misunderstandings at the peace conference.[39]

Like most Europeans and Americans, the Pages assumed that after the peace signing the president would embark upon a triumphal tour of France, Belgium, Italy, and finally Great Britain before returning to the United States. Florence wrote to her younger daughter on November 14 that Ambassador Page hoped to speak with President Wilson "but equally hopes that the necessity for urging the Italian trip may be a foregone plan, and he spare his breath." Preparations for the president's anticipated visit to Italy were "hectic," she observed, "and if he should fail to go, it would break the hearts *of America's most unselfishly devoted nation of all.*" She made this observation "advisedly and not lightly," for America had done little to aid the Italian war effort. "America has done almost nothing for Italy," she wrote, "one small regiment is all that has been sent there, and the Government has given but little assistance beyond the big moneyed loan, in proportion to her population." The Red Cross with its relief programs had saved the day. "And yet Italy feels a stronger bond of friendship for us than for any other people on earth. The Italians deify the President and find no wrong in him."[40]

Reservations and apprehensions notwithstanding, Florence determined to witness the president's triumphant arrival on European shores. Ambassador Page had already left for Paris to greet him, and she followed soon thereafter. "All Italy looks to the Ambassador to make certain that Wilson will visit Italy," wrote Gino Speranza, Page's political analyst in the Rome embassy. Page's visit was more than ceremonial; he was going to Paris to underscore the arguments of Orlando and Sonnino. Without making any direct reference to the Treaty of London, Page hoped to persuade Wilson of the necessity for Italian security.[41]

Florence arrived in Paris on December 12, 1918, having motored by car from Rome with members of the embassy staff and the head of the American Red Cross in Italy. She stayed first at the Crillon, the base of the American delegation, and then at the Hotel Ritz, located on the Place de la Vendôme. The City of Light captivated her as always, and she tried to capture the moment for her daughter who was far away in Southboro, Massachusetts. The streets were brilliantly lighted, and this was Florence's first awareness that the war had truly ended. "Excitement reigns supreme, and now not a single thing seems to count but the President's arrival in Paris tomorrow," she wrote on December 13; "every window on every house is hung with American flags; even the shops display practically only American things."[42]

She was fortunate to have an excellent vantage point from which to view the procession of notables the following day. "Our room for the parade proved the most wonderful in all Paris, getting the full benefit of the procession as it filed across the bridge, and looking as we did over to the Invalides, and up the Champs Elysees," she wrote afterwards. "We were directly to one side of the President's carriage, with its six black horses, and Mrs. Wilson behind in another drawn by four, and almost buried under flowers." The spectacle lacked the military bands of American parades, "but in no other spot on earth could we have a piazza to compare with the Place de la Concorde." Perhaps a million people had assembled in the square, and not a single disturbance marred the event. In recalling the emotion of the moment, Florence's thoughts turned southward, to the Italy she also knew and loved. Rome might not equal the splendor of the triumphal procession through the City of Light, but Romans would surely surpass the Parisians in enthusiasm.

The days and evenings following the grand procession were so exciting and hectic, with the continuous round of luncheons, meetings, and receptions, that Florence thought no one had time to reflect upon the problems that lay ahead, "unless it be Mr. Wilson who appears to present the results of mature thought—but I think he must have stored them up in the past." On December 16 Ambassador and Mrs. Page were invited to lunch with the President, Mrs. Wilson and her daughter Margaret Bolling, and Admiral Cary Travers Grayson. The conversation was lighthearted, and the president made a very favorable impression. That evening Florence wrote to Minna, "He certainly is a very magnetic, charming man, with a great sense of humor, and a very sympathetic manner, unusually quiet and dignified, but very gracious and his intellect shines out like a search light."[43]

Because preparations for the peace conference had not been completed at the time of the president's arrival, the formal opening was postponed to January 18, 1919. "Everything appears to be in a state of flux and uncertainty," Florence wrote to Minna on December 20. "No plans are made which are not subject to sudden and unexpected change. No work except preliminary work is being done. Scores of commissions and committees are buzzing about with Headquarters and American soldiers crushing each other, but what the devil this practical application to the grand purpose is, I cannot for the life of me find out. They are as separate as so many stakes stuck in the ground." But there were at least a few clearheaded delegates, and Florence trusted "that things apparently unrelated will be found to be worked in harmoniously."

While waiting for the conference to begin, President Wilson decided to embark upon a whirlwind tour of Italy, prompting the Pages to return to Rome on December 24 to prepare for the visit. As Wilson crossed the border into Italy, Ambassador Page met him at Turin and accompanied the presidential entourage en route to Rome. Wherever he went—to Turin, Milan, Genoa, and Rome—large crowds greeted President Wilson with affection and enthusiasm. Newspapers in Milan reported that "the balconies, roofs, and every vantage point were black with people," and his route through the city "was plastered" with pictures and posters of him and "quotations from his speeches which could be applied to Italy's position." Italians cheered as though he were the American Savior who would bring lasting peace to the world; they showered him with flowers. The people's enthusiasm gave Wilson the impression that he represented the aspirations of the masses more than did their own government. He responded emotionally to their cheers, throwing kisses with both hands to the crowds in Milan. "I have rejoiced personally in the partnership of the Italian and American peoples in an enterprise dedicated to liberty," he said in Rome.[44]

While in the Eternal City, Ambassador Page hosted an official dinner in Wilson's honor, at which King Vittorio Emanuele and Queen Elena were present. The dinner was an immense success, even though it and the weekend visit cost Page his entire ambassadorial salary, with no reimbursement by the State Department. Following the dinner, an incident occurred which demonstrated Florence's sensitivity and generosity in what otherwise might have been an embarrassing situation. While the ladies awaited the arrival of the gentlemen from their port and brandy and cigars, Queen Elena whispered to Florence that she had to confess to having stolen something from the dinner table. Opening her diamond-studded gold lamé purse, the queen revealed a small dinner roll. "Mafalda has not tasted white bread for three years," she explained. Florence's quiet charm and radiant manner immediately put the queen at ease; the next morning she asked Alfred, the Pages' valet and embassy factotum, to take a twenty-pound sack of white flour to the Quirinal.[45]

President Wilson left Rome for Paris on January 6, 1919, mistakenly taking Italian goodwill toward the United States as representing staunch support for his ideas on peacemaking. In fact, he had not reached any understanding with Prime Minister Orlando and Foreign Minister Sonnino over their peace objectives, especially those which were in conflict with his own. Their goal, which had earlier been communicated to the State Department, was to bring all Italy behind secure frontiers and to expand into territories permitted in the Treaty of London. Wilson barely made time to discuss the European settlement with them, although he did meet privately with Leonidi Bissolati, the Italian socialist leader who was not a member of the government but was known to be strongly sympathetic with the Wilsonian outlook in matters such as the League of Nations.

Wilson's visit to Italy not only was barren of political results. By refraining from explicit support of Italy's territorial aspirations, by meeting with Bissolati, and by insisting on addressing the public in defiance of the wish of Italian authorities, Wilson sowed seeds of distrust. Orlando's and Sonnino's only recourse was to go back to Paris to persuade the leaders of Britain and France to recognize Italy's wartime sacrifices by honoring the commitments made in the Treaty of London. Instead, the Council of Four relegated Italy's claims to secondary importance and did not even consider them in any detail until April 19–23. Italy found itself as isolated at the peace conference as it had been during the war, its delegates operating on the periphery of the chief topics of discussion.[46]

Despite Italy's inferior position at the conference, Wilson had conceded its claim to Trentino and the territory up to the Brenner Pass even before the delegates assembled. He justified this decision on the grounds that Italy should have a defensible northern frontier even if it violated the principle of self-determination. He also agreed that it should have three of the keys to the Adriatic: the ports of Pola, Valona, and Lissa. The chief difference between the United States and Italy arose from the disintegration of the Austro-Hungarian Empire. Italian nationalists pressed for more territory than originally contemplated under the terms of the Treaty of London, particularly the port city of Fiume, which would give Italy unchallengeable economic domination of the Adriatic. The president's advisers had studied these claims and on January 21, 1919, submitted a majority report which denied Italy's right to Dalmatia, a number of offshore islands, and, most importantly, Fiume. Taking into account nationality and strategic, economic, and political factors, they instead traced a frontier for Italy running from Switzerland eastward down to its farthest point on the eastern shore of the Adriatic and urged the president not to yield territory beyond it. Wilson accepted his experts' advice.[47]

On February 15, having reported the finished draft of the peace treaty, including the League of Nations, to the plenary session of the conference, the president departed for a monthlong visit home to attend to routine business and to promote the league. Already there were rumblings of opposition in the United States, and on March 4, shortly before the president's return to Paris, Republican senator Henry Cabot Lodge brought forward a statement bearing the signatures of thirty-nine Republican senators and senators-elect, more than enough to block ratification, that the league covenant was unacceptable in the form proposed. Lodge insisted that consideration of the league be deferred until after a treaty had been completed. In a speech that night Wilson condemned the "careful selfishness" of his critics and "their ignorance of the state of the world" and declared that the covenant would be intimately tied to the treaty itself.[48]

When word of Lodge's action reached Rome, Florence angrily accused him of engaging in partisan politics. "The Senate's action will embarrass the President, but not stop the League of Nations, which apparently America stands for in the main," she wrote to Florence on March 10. Lodge was as much of an obstructionist as Robert La Follette, the leading antiwar Progressive, ever had been, she declared. The Wisconsin reformer had been defeated for reelection for opposing the war, and she suggested that Lodge should "beware lest a similar fate befall him."[49]

Though Wilson would not separate the league from the treaty, he realized that the covenant would have to be modified to meet the suggestions of former president Taft and other moderate Republicans. Moreover, virtually the entire Italo-American community, a segment of the press, and Republican and isolationist enemies of the League of Nations were seeking to capitalize on a growing disenchantment with Wilsonian policies at home by supporting Italy's demand for Fiume.

When Wilson returned to Versailles, he reopened the question of the covenant, thereby rendering himself vulnerable to the bargaining of his associates who pressed their own demands for Europe and Asia. Orlando, for example, met with him on March 19, 1919, the very day Wilson arrived back in Paris, to press Italy's claim to Fiume. Wilson again referred the problem to his experts, the majority of whom reiterated that Fiume and all Dalmatia should go to the new state of Yugoslavia. Florence reported to her younger daughter on March 26 that "There is a great discontent on all sides, and a constant uneasy feeling as to the outcome." Her only consolation was that everyone was tired of war, and Germany was in no position to resume the conflict should the peace negotiations falter.[50]

The president's differences with the Italian delegation were particularly ominous and symbolized the widening gulf between Wilson's universalism and the nationalism of the other participants. When, on April 19, 1919, the Big Four got around to considering Italy's claims, Fiume Italiana had become an explosive issue. Orlando once more argued the case for Fiume as a matter of self-determination and a necessity of domestic politics. Wilson again turned aside Italy's claim to Dalmatia, predicting that annexation of Fiume would turn Italy's neighbors on the east into enemies. To placate Italy he offered to make Fiume an international free port, a proposal which Orlando and Sonnino roundly rejected. Shortly thereafter, Italian soldiers occupied the city, a move which cost Italy what little support France and Great Britain had been willing to give it in accord with the Treaty of London.

The exchanges between Wilson and the Italian delegates became so heated at times that they were forced to communicate through Lloyd George and Clemenceau. Growing impatient, Wilson decided to cut through the tangle of controversy by altering his tactics from secret to public diplomacy. He appealed directly to the Italian people in the name of justice, telling them on the evening of April 23 that the Pact of London lacked validity whereas his proposal allowed Italy to increase its borders and to be secure. He reiterated his opposition to Fiume Italiana but closed with an appeal to Italo-American friendship.

This idealistic but miscalculated intrusion into Italian domestic politics was deeply resented by both the people and their leaders. The president's action created a sensation but settled nothing. Orlando stormed out of the peace conference and with Foreign Minister Sonnino returned to Rome to seek a vote of confidence from Parliament. They did not return to Paris until May 6. Italy's position at the peace table by then had become even more precarious. Neither Britain nor France was willing to challenge Wilson's assertion that the Treaty of London was null and void.[51]

The president's appeal also sent shock waves through the Palazzo del Drago. Unwarned by any prior notice, Ambassador Page learned of it several hours after the official news had been broadcast throughout Rome. He surmised correctly that Italian reaction would be virulently anti-Wilson. The sense of disappointment that had for some time been insinuating itself through the country spread rapidly. Page, meanwhile, refused a Foreign Ministry offer to protect the American Embassy from the hostile crowds milling about to protest the president's policy.

As the wife of the ambassador, Florence also found herself in a quandary. Her nationalistic instincts bristled when Italians heaped scorn upon the president whom she had idealized as a messianic figure during the war years. In her correspondence she intimated that Italy should be grateful to the United States, especially to Ambassador Page who had labored five difficult years to promote Italo-American friendship. "I feel as if some one had given me a blow in the back," she wrote to her daughter Florence regarding the Italian press's virulent criticism of the President. "Our five years of sacrifice in being absent from home and dear ones; our true friendship for Italy; our work for the Army and the poor; all, all, so soon forgot; and our friendship put aside as easily as one does a passing acquaintance."[52]

From this time forth, Italians harassed the embassy and ostracized the American ambassador and his wife. Their isolation was such that it reminded Florence of the treatment accorded to her mother, a staunch Unionist, at the start of the Civil War. "Our present position and the attitude of our friends? reminds me of my own dear mother's experience in Alexandria during the civil war, when the family was ordered out of the city, and on their way to the station one friend alone stuck her fingers through the slats of the blind in recognition of the past!" she wrote to Florence. On April 28 she declared, "It is very tense here, and we can go nowhere, other than golf, and one must feel the iciness of the relations." The Foreign Ministry—whether to protect or to intimidate, Florence was never quite certain—had posted a small military detachment in the courtyard outside the Palazzo del Drago. Along the Via XX Settembre in front of the embassy, infantry and cavalry marched to and fro into the late hours of the night. "The feelings of the people are absolutely as mercurial as the thermometer," Florence reported.[53]

Driven by nationalist emotion, the Italian press and government had launched a campaign to drive a wedge between the American people and their president. They also sought to persuade their own citizens that Americans did not support Wilson's position on Fiume. The first was a mistake, Florence thought; Italy would gain little from attempting to divide the American people and their president. "But what I do fear and apprehend is that Italy is going to suffer in the long run, as she is making no friends, and greatly weakening her links with her old ones." Greatly disheartened, she wrote, "It is such a disastrous state of affairs after the glorious work of the Italian Army, the great sacrifices of the people, and the patriotism of the masses."

Florence professed not to comprehend the cause of the furor nor to "have any fixed ideas on the subject under such violent discussion," attributing it to the machination of politicians. "There is some deep layed scheme in all this affair, which none of us yet understand; which will be cleared some day to whose satisfaction remains to be proven," she wrote to her daughter Florence. In fact, she understood quite well what was transpiring, and why. Italy's irredentist ambitions clashed directly with Wilsonian self-determination. On April 27 she alluded to the dispute over Fiume and put the blame for the furor squarely on Orlando and Sonnino, whom she described as "selfish dangerous persons" ready to deceive the Italian people. "It is a cruel shame to mislead public opinion and to bring perhaps future discredit upon them, all for a foolish idea, and for a small spot on the map which was unknown by name to the masses but a short time ago," she declared.[54]

The morning newspapers of April 29, 1919, were worse than ever, Florence lamented. The press was doing its utmost "to stir up trouble with America, with Japan and Belgium and to affirm positively that England and France are absolutely opposed to the President's action." She intimated that she knew "some important things to disprove this entirely," an apparent reference to information communicated to her by Ambassador Page that neither Britain nor France was willing to challenge Wilson on an issue which could bring no benefit to them; she expected the dispute to be resolved by mid-June, "for good or ill."[55]

Although she felt no personal danger to herself or to the ambassador during this period of turmoil, the isolation and estrangement from the country of which she had grown so fond weighed heavily upon her. "At present I haven't a single feeling of being in the Rome where we have thought to have so many good friendly acquaintances," she wrote to Florence; "as I look out the windows nothing is changed, but my heart feels bruised, and I am lonelier than I have ever been, but for the few dear American friends who are nicer to us than ever." Despite anger and depression Florence remained discreetly silent throughout the ordeal. Inwardly, she boiled at the insults heaped upon the president, but she also confessed to her sister-in-law Helen that she was "profoundly saddened by events."

As the dispute worsened Florence's thoughts turned to home and to her family. She longed for "the quiet of domestic firesides, and to letting each nation paddle its own canoe." She acknowledged for the first time a growing anger and disappointment with the president for not having included her husband in the negotiations over Italian aspirations. Had Wilson done so, she believed the dispute might have been avoided. "But oh! I am so heartsick for dear Father, whose loyalty remains true to all sides, but who has certainly been neglected by his own official people, just when his advice would have been the most valuable, and had it been followed, conditions would be quite different," she wrote to her daughter Florence. She was referring to State Department bureaucrats whom Florence believed had blocked her husband's access to the president and rendered it impossible for him to explain the Italian position so that Wilson would have understood the legitimacy of Italy's claims. Florence, of course, could not have known that the Wilson administration for some time considered Ambassador Page to have contracted an acute case of "clientitis," an excessive tendency to defend and promote the irredentist claims of Italy, the country to which he had been posted.

Page seemingly had lost sight of the foreign policy objectives of the American government. His inability to assess the Italian situation in the context of American national interests meant that advice emanating from the Palazzo del Drago to the State Department or to President Wilson and his expert advisers was held at a discount.

And with good reason! Whereas Ambassador Page had endorsed the general contours of Wilson's program, he did not support his decision on Fiume. Italy had fought for liberty and self-determination, the two Wilsonian principles that Page argued the president's expert advisers had ignored in making their territorial recommendations. Denying Fiume to Italy risked throwing the country into political chaos. Page had cautioned the State Department that the domestic political situation was so tense that the country might fall victim to bolshevism or regress to absolutism, either of which threatened the Wilsonian peace. Florence believed that her husband's warnings finally had sensitized Wilson and the State Department to the seriousness of the Italian crisis, for she wrote to Florence on May 7, 1919, "I am willing to wager that it was his telegrams and letters that started the people at the Conference to think to a different tune regarding Italy's claims." But such proved not to be the case, and Page remained frozen out of the talks when issues affecting Italy were being discussed.[56]

Rather than give public expression to his disenchantment, Ambassador Page decided he could be more effective speaking directly with the president. On May 12, 1919 Florence informed her younger daughter that "things looked so black that finally Father decided to go onto Paris himself, and try what he could do to clear away the doubtful clouds." He had written and telegraphed the American peace delegation daily, "but to no avail apparently; so a personal statement was his last card." Though she longed to return to America after five years abroad, she did not wish to add to her husband's stress by bringing up the subject now, especially if he could help to break the diplomatic impasse between the United States and Italy. Alone and isolated in Rome, she wrote: "I am terribly torn by conflicting emotions, between the dread now of Father's being over persuaded and his pledging himself to remain at this post until *all* is quiet again? and the feeling that I must not plead for myself if his presence here can be for the general good."[57]

As her disenchantment with both her husband's official position and her personal situation intensified, Florence blamed Wilson personally for the deterioration of Italo-American relations. "I am persuaded that there is no ill will towards America nor us personally; all directed against one man," she wrote. "Why, oh! why did he ever leave our shores! I knew from the first moment that it was reported that he was coming over, that something fatal would happen." She was not with the president "in this matter in any way," and in one of her few overtly political references, she told Florence, "I would be only too glad to tell him so, if I had the chance." Americans were generally ignorant of Italy's security and territorial needs, she observed, but her heart was "set on Father's making some headway, and perhaps he may even accomplish something essential."

Meanwhile, Ambassador Page and French ambassador Camille Barré, who sympathized with Page's position, together left Rome for Paris on May 8, 1919. When the train pulled into Modena, Barré found instructions awaiting him from Premier Clemenceau to return to Rome immediately, a clear indication that France would not support Italy's claim to Fiume. Continuing the journey alone, Page arrived in Paris the following morning, assuming that Wilson would want to see him as soon as possible. He sent the president a note informing him of his availability but received no reply. Two days later, Colonel House warned Wilson that Page might resign immediately; Wilson replied it made little difference whether Page resigned then or later. When no answer to the first note came, Page sent a longer letter urgently explaining his beliefs in detail. Wilson finally agreed to meet with the ambassador. But on May 12 the ambassador sent Florence a letter by courier indicating that his mission was not going well. She wrote to her daughter in America, "I can see he is having to use his every energy mental and physical to combat obstinate objections on all sides." She hoped, nonetheless, that "his quiet calm but insistent arguments will carry some weight and that he may get certain concessions and help to restore good feelings."

Page's audience with the President failed to persuade Wilson of the legitimacy and the political necessity of Italy's claims to Fiume. Though Page voiced public optimism when he left Paris, privately he was bitterly disappointed. His failure to advance Fiume Italiana paradoxically won Page the friendship of the Italian people and government, who were cognizant of and appreciated his efforts on their behalf. Writing on May 18–19 Florence noted that "he has done all in his power for the good of Italy, and *now* the people realize it, and expressions of affection and gratitude are often told us." This did not alter Florence's plans, however. She had decided to leave Rome toward the end of the month for England to visit Minna and Henry Field before her return to the United States. Florence hoped that Tom would accompany her, for his mission was completed and "he can't help anyone by remaining for he has been to Paris . . . and saw *everyone* of any real moment, and has made a plea for Italy from a most intelligent standpoint." All he could do now was to repeat the same arguments, "and he is tired, and someone else can take his job, who is fresh and will have a different task to accomplish." That statement was as much a reflection of Florence's own feelings as it was an observation on her husband's future effectiveness should he decide to remain at his diplomatic post.[58]

With the war over and Page's mission in disarray, Florence longed to return to the United States to resume a normal life. This sentiment had appeared sporadically in her correspondence at least since 1916, but now it arose with greater frequency. Like many others, she had expected at first that Tom's ambassadorship would be largely ceremonial, lasting at most two years. With the outbreak of war and America's entry into the conflict, she believed the administration would replace him with a more experienced diplomat, but that had not occurred. For reasons not altogether clear, the president continued Page's appointment through the war years, and their two years in Rome had quickly stretched into five. The conclusion of the war followed by the internecine bickering at the peace conference only intensified Florence's desire to go back home.

Other considerations also came into play. Age and minor infirmities had taken their toll on Florence's health and emotional energies. She was nearly sixty-one now and suffering from arthritis and other minor ailments; her husband was sixty-six years of age, although basically in good health. Bryan Lathrop had died in 1916, and her family and friends were scattered over distant parts: Minna in Leicestershire; Florence in Southboro; Page family relatives in Washington, D.C., and at Oakland in Virginia; sister-in-law Helen was alone in Chicago; and then there were the friends in York Harbor, her beloved summer retreat, whom Florence had not seen in nearly five years. The moment seemed appropriate to pack up and leave.

On May 21, 1919, Florence departed alone from Rome for the short visit with Minna and her family at Baggrave Hall, leaving her husband behind to attend to embassy business. During her stopover at Claridge's in London, she received word of the latest diplomatic contretemps between Italy and the United States. The Big Three had decided in the absence of the Italian delegates to parcel out the former German colonies. As punishment for Italy's defection from the conference, they disregarded even its modest claims to enemy colonies, such as Togoland, an action which precipitated yet another crisis in Italy as the government seemed to be losing the diplomatic fruits of its military victory. On June 7 a member of the embassy staff wired Florence, asking her to persuade Ambassador Page to remain at his post because of the growing parliamentary crisis in Rome. While he might not be able to ward off a confrontation between the two governments, his staff thought that he could "soothe feelings, and can always do good for both sides."[59]

The president's actions by now had so thoroughly disillusioned Florence that she ignored the entreaty and left the decision of whether to remain at his post or to resign solely to Tom. Two weeks later, as a result of his failure to achieve more at Paris, Orlando's cabinet fell. On June 28, 1919 the peacemakers, despite their differences, signed the Treaty of Versailles, an event which inspired no celebration in Italy. It gave birth instead to the myth of the mutilated victory that Mussolini would seize upon in his rise to power.

The peace treaty that was signed by the new government allowed Italy not only Trentino and the city of Trieste but also the Alto Adige, with its strong German minority, and Istria, with its strong Slav minority. The question of Dalmatia, which the Treaty of London had assigned to Italy, remained to be settled with the new Yugoslav state, as did that of Fiume, which, according to Wilson's and the Allies' interpretation of the treaty, was to be left a free city. Despite Mussolini's later criticisms, Versailles was not a diplomatic Caporetto, even if the peace treaty probably would have been more favorable to Italy had the Italian government displayed less ambition.[60]

With his diplomatic mission in disarray, Page announced his resignation in mid-July and submitted a formal letter to Wilson shortly thereafter. Wilson's decision to accept the resignation allegedly was facilitated by Florence's indiscreet remarks in Paris in December while her husband had been arguing the Italian case before the president. According to Brand Whitlock, who eventually succeeded Page as ambassador to Italy, Wilson told him that Florence particularly had espoused the Italian cause and had made many remarks in Paris so "indiscreet that Harry White, one of the American Peace Commissioners, had told her that she was making a fool of herself." Wilson denied this, but the feeling prevailed that Page was relieved of his ambassadorship because of his wife's indiscretions.[61] It is difficult to determine conclusively the accuracy of Whitlock's account. There is little doubt that Florence had lobbied during the war on behalf of military aid to Italy whenever the opportunity presented itself and that both Pages identified too closely with Italy's irredentist claims and were out of step with administration thinking, but this was well-known to Washington policy makers long before the peace conference convened. Yet the administration continued Page at his post, notwithstanding his loss of objectivity. Wilson most likely concluded that Page had now become an embarrassment to his administration and seized upon Florence's alleged indiscretions to ease Page out.

Whatever the truth of the matter, the Pages' departure from Rome was bittersweet. In a poignant farewell audience with the king and queen, the Pages were given official photographs of the royal family. Queen Elena, in a personal gesture of appreciation for all the Pages had done for Italy, then presented them with a leather-framed photograph of herself signed, "Yours very affectionately Elena." To Florence she gave a diamond, ruby, and emerald ring with an inscription inside signed "Elena" and the date. The precious stones represented the Italian colors. On the eve of their departure for America, Florence wrote to her younger daughter that Gabriele d'Annunzio, the poet-revolutionary, had delivered a speech attacking Clemenceau and France but had said "nothing this time against Wilson and America." Recalling the criticism of Wilson's policy toward Italy and the Italians' ostracism of her husband, the ambassador, she added, "Perhaps it makes our going easier than if it had all been smooth sailing."[62]

When the Pages left Rome, they brought back with them to the United States not only five years of memories but also many valuable material possessions that Florence had accumulated along the way: antique rugs, Jesurum lace, Murano glass, china, and antiques. Florence supervised the packing of these treasures for shipment in an Italian freighter departing from Naples for New York. In a further cruel twist of fate, the majority of the items never arrived; en route across the Atlantic, each of the containers was broken into and its contents stolen. Only the shattered empty carton remained, a poignant reminder of the unfulfilled aspiration the Pages had had for Italo-American friendship.

Upon arriving in America, Thomas Nelson Page was offered the freedom of the Port of New York, a courtesy often given to a returning ambassador, especially from a wartime assignment. Ambassador Page refused the honor, saying that he believed half of the full customs duties should be paid.

After a brief layover in the city, the Pages once again took up residence at 1759 R and New Hampshire, their Washington mansion. Private citizens for the first time in nearly five years, they arrived home to witness the fight to ratify the peace treaty, including the League of Nations. President Wilson had called upon the Senate on July 10, 1919, to "accept this great duty." The force of Wilson's idealism had struck a deep vein of popular support; fully a third of the state legislatures endorsed the league, as did thirty-three of the forty-eight governors. But Henry Cabot Lodge, the Republican chairman of the Senate Foreign Relations Committee, who nourished an intense dislike for Wilson and the idea of collective security, resorted to delaying tactics and amendments to derail the league.[63]

By September 1919, with the momentum for the treaty slackening, Wilson decided to go to the people for support. He embarked upon a strenuous campaign to whip up popular enthusiasm for the treaty with the League of Nations. After a speech at Pueblo, Colorado, on September 25, the signs of exhaustion were so clear that the president's physician canceled the speaking tour and rushed Wilson back to Washington. When news of the president's illness reached York Harbor, Maine, where the Pages were residing for the remainder of the summer season, Florence was profoundly distressed. She still thought Wilson had treated her husband and Italy badly, but she respected his idealism and vision of a secure postwar world. The president's physical collapse was not only a personal tragedy but a calamity for the nation, which was facing a momentous crisis in foreign policy. "We are disturbed by the news of the President's illness," she wrote to Minna; "for him to die now would be to his eternal glory; but for our country it would be an incalculable misfortune; indeed a tragedy." He had done more for humanity and had fewer friends than any other person she knew, and his good reputation would live long after his detractors were silenced. If he were to resume his speaking tour, Florence believed that he would win support for the treaty and the league. But she was "doubtful of his recovery for more than a temporary flash."[64]

One week later, on October 2, 1919, Wilson suffered a severe stroke and paralysis on his left side, leaving him helpless for weeks. Over the next seven months he did not meet with his cabinet, and a protective wife kept him isolated from all but the most essential business. Illness intensified his traits of stubbornness and hostility, and he refused to compromise on the league. On November 6, while Wilson was still bed-ridden, Lodge presented his amendments to the Senate. The Massa-chusetts Republican had the votes for them to be adopted but not the two-thirds needed to approve an amended treaty. Wilson instructed the Democratic leaders to reject the treaty as long as it was shackled by the Lodge amendments and to move that it be accepted on his terms alone. The Senate maneuverings outraged Florence, who like her hus-band shared the Wilsonian view that destiny had singled out the United States to defend and spread the democratic ideal. "I can't talk about the action of the Senate," she wrote to Minna from Washington; "it makes me blush and puts me in a rage too. God help us if the Treaty is not rat-ified."[65]

Following Wilson's orders, Senate Democrats voted on November 19 to reject the treaty with the Lodge amendments. Yet they, too, could not muster the two-thirds majority needed to enact the Wilson league. "We are so depressed by the rejection of the Treaty, and by the appalling position in which this places us, that this alone has made us low in our minds," Florence wrote to Minna on November 22. She felt humiliated that the world was watching the Senate's "selfish" action. Conceding that the president probably had erred in not taking that body into his confidence, she nonetheless attributed the difficulties to "Lodge's per-sonal spite." The reservationists' patriotic pleas for America and the na-tional interest were "only to cover up their determination to defeat the Treaty, and the League, to satisfy their hatred of Mr. Wilson." The people should be allowed to vote on the issue, she observed; "at least this would show definitely American sentiment, rather than political spite." Feelings were running high on all sides and would grow worse, Florence predicted, as the presidential campaign of 1920 got under way. "I dread the consequences," she wrote.[66]

The American public, however, would not permit the treaty to be laid aside because senators professing support could not reach agreement on a few amendments. Former Ambassador Page broke his silence to support the treaty and the league. In the face of public reaction both at home and abroad, the Senate voted to reconsider. But Wilson, writing to the Democratic leadership on January 8, 1920, remained adamant and would not permit any concessions. His obstinacy also angered Flor-ence, and her perspective of the president shifted from his being the

leading advocate to the main obstacle to world peace and liberal interna-
tionalism. She still admired his ideals, "absolute honesty of purpose,"
and his intellect, she wrote to Minna on January 13, "but his obstinacy,
his pertinacity, and his stand off aloofness have estranged everyone from
him, and he has been the direct cause of bringing our country into disre-
pute." Wilson might have retained public support and a majority of
the senators with tact and consideration; instead, "he has antagonized
practically all the thinking men over the country, and has placed us
where we are now." Nor did she readily forgive his peevish attitude,
which made a travesty of his noble effort to create a world safe for democracy. "Someday we shall recover the goodwill of mankind, but our
attitude to the world today is unworthy of our standards," Florence declared. "I feel it bitterly, and place the blame where, as I see it, it
rightly belongs."[67]

If the Senate's actions were demeaning and unworthy of a great nation, so, too, was Wilson's stubbornness. Lodge and the isolationists had
much to answer for, Florence wrote, "but this does not excuse the President in his obstinate attitude and uncompromising one." Wilson was
badly splintering the Democratic party, she wrote, an assessment which
was wholly accurate. On March 19, 1920, the day of the final vote on
the treaty, twenty-one Democrats deserted the president and joined the
reservationists. The treaty fell short of the two-thirds majority for adoption by a vote of 49 to 35. The real winners in the fight for ratification
were the smallest of the three groups in the Senate, neither the Wilsoni-
ans nor the reservationists but the irreconcilables.[68]

If there was any doubt about the public's support both for the treaty
and the league, Wilson had told the Democratic leadership in early January, the issue could be resolved at the next election, which he hoped
would be "a great and solemn referendum" on the League of Nations.
This was the observation of a deluded man, for presidential elections
turned on many issues, not just one. There would be no "solemn referendum" in November 1920. The Democratic presidential candidate,
James M. Cox, supported the league, but not enthusiastically. The Republican candidate, Warren G. Harding, though he enjoyed the full
support of Republican internationalists as well as Republican isolationists, considered his smashing victory a repudiation of the treaty and the
League of Nations.[69]

8

Epilogue

As was their custom before the Great War, the Pages passed the winter of 1920–21 on the French Riviera, stopping in November 1920 at Baggrave Hall to comfort Minna who was recovering from a severe illness. They returned to the United States in May 1921, in preparation for the journey to York Harbor where they would spend the summer. On June 6, 1921, while she was visiting her younger daughter in Southboro, Massachusetts, Florence Lathrop Page died unexpectedly of a hemorrhage following a minor throat operation. She was sixty-two years of age at the time.

Thinking to spare him anxiety, Florence had not told her husband in advance about the surgery, and he was away on business when the tragedy occurred. Following a private funeral, she was interred in Rock Creek Cemetery in Washington, D.C. A very plain gravestone in keeping with her perception of her life—a simple pedestal topped with carved swirls on which were chiseled the two vital statistics of birth and death and the inscription, "In Loving Memory of Florence Lathrop Page Wife of Thomas Nelson Page"—marked her place of rest. At the base of the pedestal Thomas Nelson Page had inscribed the beatitude, "Blessed Are the Pure in Heart," which perhaps best defined the femininity of Florence Lathrop Page in her husband's eyes.[1] The values of True Womanhood embraced her in death even as she had embraced them in life.

Thomas Page never recovered from the loss of his beloved wife. On All Saints' Day, 1922, while planting a shrub in the bright sunshine of Oakland plantation, he quietly died. The lead article in the *Richmond*

Times-Dispatch of November 2 noted that he had just said to his valet and companion of many years, "Here Alfred, take this spade and do a little digging," when he fell. It described him as "one of the best known and best loved of latter-day Virginians" and noted that he had been married to "a woman of refinement, intelligence, and culture."[2]

This delineation of Florence Lathrop Page was accurate, but it failed to communicate to the reader any real understanding of the woman and the complex society in which she had lived. The obituary had been written for Thomas Nelson Page, of course, but had the *Times-Dispatch* writer probed more deeply into Florence's background, he would have noted that her life was in many respects a microcosm of the larger questions of gender, class, and family in the social history of the United States. She was a figure emblematic of a class and gender in transition from the Victorian to the modern era. A rich woman of little public note herself, Florence's very lack of distinction made her life story important. It offered insights into the paradoxical nature of women's lives, culture, and possibilities in the late nineteenth and early twentieth centuries. More so than she had intended or would have desired, Florence Page's life not only spoke to contemporaries but raised issues of class and gender that are relevant to the modern reader.

Florence Lathrop Page was born, reared, and spent the greater part of her adult life in a milieu which to the casual observer conformed to the received categories scholars employ in their quest to interpret women's history and social history. Patriarchy, separate spheres, the public/private distinction, True Womanhood, and sexual reticence seem on first reading to have been the dominant themes of her life, making her not unlike many women of her time and place. Closer examination of her life through her correspondence suggests that she was a more complex personality, one who embodied women's diversity as well as women's shared sphere. She accepted many of the traditional values and customs that defined gender relationships in the nineteenth century while embracing in her own life and actions some of the more modern ideas that defined a woman's role in society. The public and private worlds of Florence Lathrop Page, therefore, were inseparably connected. The mixture of the traditional and the modern in her thinking, attitudes, and actions reflected the gradual displacement of the prevailing Victorian gender ideology and the articulation of modern ideas that would come into their own by the 1920s.

Patriarchy was, as scholars have noted, the context within which nineteenth-century industrial society functioned. Its values assumed that biological sex differences implied a God-given or at least a natural separation of human activities by sex, and the further assumption that this led to a natural dominance of male over female.[3] Men defined not only the legal status of women and their place in the new industrial capitalism but also the ideologies of "True Womanhood" and "guardian of the hearth" that elevated and at the same time isolated white upper- and middle-class women from the world taking shape around them. Men excluded women from the public sphere, the aggressive world of business and power-seeking, and confined them to the home, a separate private sphere in which the defining experiences of their lives were motherhood and nurturance.[4]

Perceived in the context of a political relationship—of power and governance—women's sphere was subordinate to the masculine/public sphere. It was the location, the environment, in which women's culture took shape, but its parameters were drawn by a dominant male interest within the full society. The perimeters of the female sphere were policed by male institutions and legal codes, whereas its economic and ideological systems were interpreted, manipulated, and dominated by men.[5]

If patriarchy, with its gender-defined roles, was the organizational and ideological underpinning of nineteenth-century society, class and class consciousness were, if not the engine that pulled society, at least omnipresent facets of daily life. To the rich, the wellborn, and the powerful, upper-class status rested upon a configuration of money, occupation, power, and education which was manifested in one's lifestyle. The Lathrops, the Fields, and the Pages had access to each of these in varying degrees of abundance. They possessed great affluence by the standards of the day, although, with the exception of Marshall Field, the totality of their wealth remained considerably less than that of their more famous or infamous contemporaries: Rockefeller, Morgan, Carnegie, and Pullman. Their acquisition of wealth bore upon their rank within the hierarchy of elites. They were close to the top of the social and economic heap, but they were not, again with the exception of Marshall Field, at its very pinnacle.

As the biography of Florence Lathrop Page reveals, gender, age, education, occupation, political loyalty, and geographical mobility were the important components that defined her class and status within her locality and the larger community that composed America's national ruling class. The Bryan, Lathrop, and Field families exemplified the long-distance geographical mobility of Chicago's business elites in the last two quarters of the nineteenth century. The males of these families, whose antecedents were in the older established states of the Atlantic seaboard, rooted in rural and small-town New England and in Virginia, were relatively young men in their twenties when they arrived in the city to seek their fortunes. They came from old English stock and, in the case of the Bryans and the Lathrops, were quite well educated for the time. They identified with mainstream Protestantism, of the Episcopalian and Presbyterian varieties, and despite the Bryans' southern ties, they supported the Union cause in the Civil War.

The timing of their arrival in Chicago was significant, occurring as it did when the city was being transformed from a small quiet village into the dominant metropolis of the West. Chicago's emergence as a thriving commercial entrepôt and later a great manufacturing center had rested on its geographical location as the maritime portage between the Great Lakes and the Mississippi River valley. Its strategic site gave it early access to the natural resources of the Midwest, and by 1880 Chicago was the fastest growing city in the world. Urban growth meant economic opportunity in fields such as timber, banking, business, real estate, retail merchandising, agriculture, and meatpacking; economic opportunity attracted some of the most innovative and energetic entrepreneurs of the day to the Windy City, including Thomas Barbour Bryan, Jedediah H. Lathrop, Marshall Field, Cyrus McCormick, Potter Palmer, and the electric utility magnate Samuel Insull. These men were products of the expanding, dynamic economy of nineteenth-century America, which continually heaved up new moneyed elites through the rise of young cities, the advance of new technologies, and other shifts in economic activities.

Within this milieu a woman's class and social status derived from her male acquaintances: father, husband, or, in the case of an unmarried adult female, brother. Florence Lathrop's upper-class status derived initially from this familial connection, from the Bryan and Lathrop families whose male breadwinners had made their fortunes in timber, business, banking, law, and real estate. Like many wealthy businessmen, Thomas Barbour Bryan and Jedediah Lathrop migrated from the crowded, noisy center of Chicago to its periphery, to Elmhurst, Illinois, even as they maintained ties to the central business district of the Windy City. Florence's status as a member of the elite was solidified through her marriage to Henry Field, the younger brother of Marshall Field.

Epilogue

Intermarriage among the rich, the wellborn, and the powerful of Chicago was the ultimate associational tie that transformed an economic elite into a social class. Economic considerations probably were no less important than emotional ones in determining a suitable spouse for a woman of Florence's background and refinement. While we know little of the details of Florence's courtship and subsequent marriage to Henry Field, a junior partner in the retail merchandising empire of Marshall Field & Co., there is no doubt that the union solidified and perpetuated Florence's standing within Chicago's upper class. The same was true of the marriage of Helen Aldis to Florence's brother Bryan Lathrop. Helen's family had made its fortune in real estate and the law; her brother, Owen Aldis, participated in many of the associational activities that had engaged Henry Field and Bryan Lathrop.

Marriage, then, constructed a class network and defined rank within the local upper class. When the widowed Florence married Thomas Nelson Page in 1893 and took up residence in Washington, D.C., her class and status transferred with her. Her identification with upper-class elites was further enhanced from local (Chicago) to national (cosmopolitan) associations because of Page's links to the Virginia gentry and his national literary reputation. The Pages' Washington mansion, built entirely with the wealth Florence had inherited upon the death of Henry Field, became a salon for well-connected and powerful men: academics, literary figures, and politicians, including presidents Roosevelt, Taft, and Wilson. Summer residence in York Harbor, Maine, and winter sojourns to Jekyll Island, Georgia, and to Santa Barbara, California, brought Florence and Thomas Nelson Page into contact with the local elites of America's major urban centers. Hailing from Boston, New York, Philadelphia, Washington, D.C., and Chicago, they constituted a national elite.

Florence's marriage to Thomas Nelson Page suggested, too, that the concept of marriage among the elite was in transition between the nineteenth and twentieth centuries. The utilization of marriage as an economic liaison, wherein the female partner was virtually a passive actor in determining the choice of a spouse, was giving way to the companionate marriage. Widowhood had conferred economic independence upon Florence. As a wealthy widow unencumbered by economic constraints, she was empowered to decide whether to wed a second time, and also whom to wed. She exercised this power, following an appropriate period of mourning for Henry Field, without seeking prior approval from male

[*245*]

kin, such as her older brother Bryan Lathrop or her brother-in-law Marshall Field. Not surprisingly, Florence chose a man of similar social, albeit not economic, background.

Personal preference outweighed economic factors in the selection of Florence's new mate. Thomas Nelson Page was a literary figure of national stature whose ancestors traced back to the founding fathers of Virginia and the early Republic. The Pages of Virginia, however, were land rich and money poor in the aftermath of the Civil War and Reconstruction. Thomas Nelson Page's economic fortune, as adduced from his royalties as a writer and erstwhile career as a lawyer, was considerably less than his future wife's wealth. This suggests that her marriage to Page was a bargain in which Florence chose companionship over passion. Not sexuality but friendship, conversation, and paying attention to each other in public were the ultimate secret of Florence's happy marriage to Thomas Nelson Page. His well-documented insecurity and thirsting after social acceptance indicate that he may have married Florence, following the death of his beloved Anne Seddon, because of economic and status considerations as much as affection.

Whether Florence's marriages within the context of patriarchy constituted a gain of status over the course of her lifetime is an intriguing question. The evidence that marriage per se increased a woman's status is neither patently obvious nor unequivocal, because it is difficult to generalize or isolate marriage from the economic, legal, and public considerations that contributed to a woman's status. With respect to Florence's first marriage, it is likely that she did attain initial recognition and a secure place in Chicago society by virtue of being the wife of an influential businessman and philanthropist. But marriage also entailed a social cost, exchanging the freedom of a single woman for consignment to the private sphere of the home, where Florence assumed the traditional role of "keeper of the hearth." On balance, Florence's marriage to Henry Field did not result in gender equity. No matter how loving their union, the marriage was asymmetrical because he wielded so much economic, legal, and social power and she, as a woman, had correspondingly little. Love, except in the arena of sexuality where the evidence implicitly suggests that the Fields, like many upper-class couples, engaged in family planning, did not necessarily equate with a sharing of power. On the other hand, the sexual equality that Florence had achieved within her first marriage was a power she retained following her marriage to Thomas Nelson Page.

Epilogue

When Florence chose to wed a second time, her economic, social, and legal position was considerably different from that of the young woman of twenty-one who had married Henry Field. The second marriage provides further evidence that the prevailing Victorian gender ideology was on the wane and that newer ideas were being articulated which would come into their own by the time of her death. As a widow Florence inherited considerable wealth in the form of realty and securities and was by all accounts wealthier than her second husband. Widowhood was tragic, but it also conferred economic independence that led to empowerment. True, she became known as the wife of a famous literary figure rather than as a personage in her own right, but to a considerable degree Florence encouraged that perception by studiously avoiding the limelight and publicly deferring to her husband. This was a function of her personality as much as anything else. Of equal importance, she did not overtly challenge the separate spheres to which patriarchy had consigned women but probed their edges to blur the boundaries. It was she who decided to enlist her wealth for travel so that Page might participate in international café society and fulfill his thirst for recognition and it was her wealth that made feasible Page's career as an ambassador.

Economic considerations and their relationship to social status, while not unimportant, mattered even less by the time Florence's daughters married. We know little about the Fields' younger daughter, Florence, and her courtship and marriage to Thomas Lindsay, other than that he was a college graduate (Harvard) who embarked initially on a profession which was neither of high status nor financially lucrative. Lindsay was teaching at a private school while courting Florence's daughter, yet the mother did not object to their courtship and subsequent marriage, which indicates that emotion was beginning to displace or play a shared role with economics in the choice of a spouse. Florence's initial judgment that this was a good match was eventually confirmed, for Thomas Lindsay went on to become a successful Boston lawyer and decorated officer in World War I.

The same good judgment might, in a perverse way, be said of her opinion of Minna Field's marriage to Preston Gibson. Their precipitate elopement shortly before Florence had intended to present her eldest daughter to Washington society sent the mother's plans crashing. Even though Gibson came from a social and economic background as impeccable as Minna's, the circumstances of their union made it impossible for Florence to accept him as an appropriate son-in-law. Nonetheless, the loving albeit disappointed parent tolerated her daughter's folly; she never attempted to annul the marriage, which, given her economic resources, influence, and Minna's age, she no doubt could have. Florence likewise overcame her qualms about Minna's second marriage; it was not his being divorced that disturbed Florence but that Minna's fiancé was remarrying while his former spouse was still alive. Algernon Burnaby, a man of wealth, position, and power, was considerably older than Minna and not even an American citizen; these two factors also weighed heavily in Florence's calculations; but her daughter's happiness led her to suppress these reservations and hope, correctly as it turned out, that Burnaby would become the stabilizing force in Minna's life.

Minna's marital escapades illustrated a shift in society's norms and values. Parental control over children, especially adult children, was becoming more tenuous by the twentieth century. A young woman was freer to choose her own marriage partner despite a parent's reservations, and this new freedom defined a new understanding of marriage. Emotion, companionship, and egalitarianism were becoming dominant motives, whereas economic considerations, while not unimportant, were beginning to play a distinctly subordinate role even within the upper class. If marriage itself was in flux, so, too, was the nineteenth-century ideal of "True Womanhood." Minna never completely accepted the role that patriarchy had assigned to women, much as Florence herself had not; but whereas Florence did not overtly challenge that ideal, choosing to work around its perimeter to soften it, Minna unequivocally confronted it, unlike her sister, Florence Field Lindsay. This may explain why, of her two daughters, Florence had the more comfortable, less tense relationship with her younger daughter. Perhaps she saw something of herself in Minna's stubbornness and determination.

Florence's marital life with Henry Field and Thomas Nelson Page and her daughters exemplified to a considerable degree the privatization of the family. Within the patriarchal stratified society of late nineteenth-century America, there had emerged a cult of motherhood around a biological function to which Florence subscribed.[6] She, like other parents of her class and generation, felt considerable affection toward her children and grandchildren, often referring to the latter as "my babes." She was not the sort who invested little emotional energy in her daughters, but as her response to Minna's faux pas with the Yalie Preston Gibson indicated, neither was she the kind who insisted upon their unquestioned acceptance of discipline, self-control, and obedience to her authority. Florence's approach to childrearing suggests that Victorian family values, like other aspects of society, were in transition. She tolerated, albeit sometimes reluctantly, her daughters' independence of thought, always exhibiting tenderness and affection toward them even when she disagreed with their actions or decisions. She was bound to Minna and Florence emotionally, despite the often great geographical distances separating her from them. Her frequent correspondence, motherly advice, regular visits, summer reunions, and profuse expressions of affection were the mortar that fostered family cohesion.

Beyond the nuclear family Florence's affection extended to relatives male and female alike. She maintained a lifelong and loving relationship with her brother Bryan, and his wife, Helen Aldis Lathrop; her brother Barbour Lathrop was somewhat unconventional, but this did not trouble Florence and they remained close despite the barrier of distance. He was very much in evidence when Florence's grandson Henry Field decided to become an anthropologist. By contrast, she had little continuous contact with Marshall Field following the death of her husband, although he was nominally a cotrustee of Henry Field's estate. Of the many Pages, Florence was closest probably to Rosewell and Ruth, her brother- and sister-in-law, but theirs was a geographically distant friendship.

Her relationship with Elizabeth Burwell Page is less clear. Florence wrote extensively to her mother-in-law, who was elderly and fragile, whenever she and Thomas Page journeyed abroad, and she invariably closed her letters with terms like "affectionately" or "Your loving daughter." But she also signed them "Florence Lathrop Page" rather than the more familiar "Florry." Further contributing to the puzzle of their relationship is that despite the proximity of the Pages' mansion in Washington, D.C., to Oakland plantation in Virginia, approximately a two- to three-hour train ride away, Florence seems not to have made more than an occasional, obligatory visit. Indeed, she frequently wrote to her mother-in-law explaining her absences on various grounds: that she had to visit her daughters; they were coming to Washington to visit with her; or she would be in Maine from May through September. Thomas Nelson Page, in contrast, visited his mother whenever he returned home from abroad or a business trip took him to Richmond. The excessive formality that belied the chatty nature of Florence's correspondence, coupled with her failure to visit her mother-in-law with any semblance of regularity, leads one to speculate that Florence may have viewed Elizabeth Burwell Page as a rival. This may have been her way of asserting and maintaining her own independence as wife and householder.

Besides relatives acquired through marriage, Florence developed over her career an extensive network of friends and acquaintances who, in varying degrees, were close to her: Owen and Leila Aldis (Helen's brother and his wife), the Rozier Dulanys, the Russell Trains, Belle Hagues, Mrs. Charles M. Bruce, Nancy Langhorne Astor, the Herbert Wards, and numerous summer acquaintances from York Harbor. When Florence died in 1921, her will revealed that as her peers often did, she had arranged bequests to include kin and friends besides the immediate family. Even household staff like Alfred, the Pages' manservant, and Florence's personal maid were left modest sums. Friendship and loyalty did not go unrecognized and unrewarded within the upper class.

Finally, Florence's life illustrates two tendencies that were developing in marriage and gender relations at this time. The first relates to marriage and the family. Florence and Thomas Nelson Page were still within childbearing age, although their union produced no issue. This is a matter of some import given Page's distinguished lineage. It may indicate infertility on his part or a mutual decision not to have children of their own. In the absence of irrefutable evidence, a childless marriage—even a second marriage—at the least suggests that prudence, reason, and sexual equality held sway among urban, industrial America's upper class. In matters familial, couples no longer were passively accepting the arbitrary decree that they had to have large numbers of children. Florence and Henry Field had limited their family to a desired goal of three children. The sexual equality she attained in her first marriage continued into her second.

The second and perhaps more significant tendency relates to the composition of the family. Florence's marriage to Page witnessed manifestations of a matrifocal household, a phenomenon which was not very common in nineteenth-century society outside the black community. Minna and Florence were minors—eleven and ten years old, respectively—at the time of Florence's remarriage, and although he was very fond of them, Page never legally adopted the girls and they never assumed the Page surname. Despite nineteenth-century concepts of patriarchy that identified Thomas Nelson Page as the head of the household, Florence made the truly significant decisions affecting her daughters' lives. This flowed from her economic independence following Henry

Field's death. Even after the girls had attained their majority and left home, Page continued to defer to his wife in family matters.

Money and power, the two fundamental sources of upper-class status, enabled Chicago's elite to exert a dominant role in such secondary spheres of community life as philanthropy and culture. Once they accrued surplus wealth, Chicago's elite emulated eastern upper-class standards by busily establishing a host of cultural and educational institutions and by forming their own exclusive social clubs. Thomas Barbour Bryan, Marshall and Henry Field, and Bryan Lathrop actively founded or promoted the Art Institute, the Newberry Library, the Orchestra Association, the Chicago Symphony, and the Literary Club. Henry Field served not only on the boards of several of the cultural institutions, including the Literary Club, but he also was president of the Home of the Friendless and a director of the Chicago Relief and Aid Society.

This cultural and philanthropic trophyhunting was not simply an act of altruism, as other scholars have noted. In exhibiting a firm sense of public duty, Chicago's upper-class families were utilizing the integral relationship between economics and culture to legitimize their leadership claims. Here, too, the ideology of gender dictated roles assigned to men and women. It was the men who ultimately knit the city's sprawling array of charities and cultural organizations into a coherent, comprehensive system. They operated through a network of private clubs, overlapping directorates, and the prestigious Chicago Relief and Aid Society. Cultural institutions, such as the Orchestra Association, served mainly the elite who could afford them. As humanitarian endeavors became more bureaucratized and impersonal, upper-class males drew further apart from direct communication and contact with those less fortunate than they.

Women were rigorously excluded from the decision-making process whereby the city's rich and powerful males established the policies of these institutions, in much the same way that women were excluded from the wave of political democracy that had swept through the nation giving suffrage rights to adult white males regardless of class. They remained at the periphery, confined by the idiom of gender and sphere. To the extent that women of every class, but especially elite upper-class women, acquiesced in this separation, their silence spoke eloquently about the meaning and uses of power in a patriarchal society.[7]

Gender-determined economic relationships provide a clue to understanding why and how women were largely excluded from the decision-making process and hence from the power that might have accompanied their upper-class identification. A man's wealth in the late Victorian era was a measure not only of his own abilities but of his abilities relative to other men. Obsession with the "self-made man" was not simply the approval of one who had advanced himself without the help of an inheritance; it also implied that all men were to some extent self-made. This philosophy gained preeminence as Social Darwinism. In the eyes of society, wealth was the sign of individual success and poverty that of failure in the masculine competition. Within the household, a man's position became that of breadwinner, while the female's became "the guardian of the hearth."[8]

As a businessman Henry Field championed the liberal ideals of individualism, laissez-faire, competition, and reward according to merit. He was, by all the usual criteria, enormously successful in doing so: his accumulated wealth enabled him to retire early from the competitive world of business in order to pursue his literary and artistic interests; his wife, Florence, did not have to engage in commodity production either in or outside of the home, nor did she have to seek a "gainful occupation" (i.e., work for income) to help her husband provide the family with food, clothing, or shelter. Field's wealth enabled her to purchase all of the family's necessities rather than to make them herself. Florence availed herself of the latest technological innovations for the home and exploited the toil of others by hiring domestics and laborers to do the routine chores.[9] The presence of valets, servants, and groundskeepers was an important marker of the class boundary between the well-to-do and the rest of the population.

Henry Field had more than provided for his wife's and family's needs both during and after his lifetime. Following his death Florence's inherited fortune did not grow nearly so rapidly or so large as earned wealth, but she was still able to live a life of luxury and material comfort, to entertain often, travel abroad frequently, and in numerous other ways enhance her economic choices. She sent her daughters to exclusive eastern private schools; built substantial mansions in Washington, D.C., and York Harbor, Maine; contributed financially to numerous charities; and drew upon her late husband's estate to supplement the lifestyle and the ambassadorial career to which Thomas Nelson Page aspired.

As a married woman Florence was not unique in forgoing employment outside the home. Married white homemakers of the nineteenth and early twentieth centuries, regardless of class, income, or native or foreign birth, did not customarily participate in the labor force. They remained in the domestic sphere. In 1890, for instance, only 4.5 percent of all married women engaged in "gainful occupations," a percentage which increased to 5.6 percent in 1900 but still did not exceed 9 percent by 1920.[10] What was unusual was not that Florence had never been gainfully employed, but the degree to which she had the financial resources to exercise a wide range of economic choices.

This is not to suggest that a woman, even one of upper-class status such as Florence Lathrop Field, did not have economic or other significance within marriage. She did occupy a lofty sphere which was complementary to but separate in significant ways from the world of men. Within the Field household the family division of labor attributed value to Florence's domestic role implied in the ideal of True Womanhood.[11] As wife and mother, she complemented her husband's efforts as breadwinner by playing a social, entertaining, and decorative role. She supervised the household staff, made the necessary purchases for the family, and reared the children. That she identified positively with these roles is manifested in her reluctance to enter the public sphere of men, the world of politics. Her fleeting private criticism of William Jennings Bryan in the 1896 election was more the reflection of the conservative, hard money views of the wealthy males in her life than the product of a carefully conceived political and economic position.

It may also have been due in part to the psychological and material investment that she, like other women and men of her class, had in the status quo. Florence may have been manipulating the metaphor of the sphere to protect her interests in a time of change.[12] Enjoying the privileges that accrued with class and money, she had little incentive to challenge overtly the stratification of society or to render asunder all of the conventional expectations for womanly conduct. The reason, conceivably, that she did not march with the suffragists was because the franchise would not have materially altered her position in society. Perhaps, too, she did not denounce the trusts or widespread poverty because her class was the beneficiary of the large corporations and she would have been profoundly inconvenienced by changes in the status of the laboring class. There is reason to believe that the last was true. Florence perceived from the beginning that World War I was going to have a profound economic and social impact upon her and her family's life. This was the leitmotiv of her references to the servant and labor questions following the war and to the need for the Pages, the Burnabys, and the Lindsays to retrench their style of living.

From this perspective Florence may be more representative of the majority of women of her class, social position, and wealth than contemporary feminists might care to admit. She did not seek refuge from domesticity; instead, she carved out a life and culture of her own within it which were both satisfying and satisfactory. She accepted her roles as social leader, supportive wife, and mentor and confidante of her children. She shrank from the political, economic, and social activism that contravened the precepts of True Womanhood, and so she did not petition, lobby, or speak out on the great reform issues of Progressivism, unlike other, especially professional, middle-class women of this era. She was no Jane Addams, nor was she like the upper-class social feminist and education reformer Lucy Sprague Mitchell; her agenda was private, personal, and family-oriented. Whatever the reason, her silence on public policy issues also spoke eloquently about the meaning and uses of power in a patriarchal society.

These attributes of domesticity were the same qualities that Thomas Nelson Page, the Virginia gentleman, most admired and emphasized in the unpublished biographical sketch of his wife he wrote shortly after her death. He perceived her as the ideal Victorian woman, dutifully observing the constraints of gender and class imposed by a male-dominant society. Florence is portrayed as lacking in a feminist consciousness; she never questions gender-based power relationships; she is passive, a "nonactor" in an era of great economic, social, and political turmoil.[13]

The reader who probes more deeply and transcends the boundaries of gender, class, and time in which Thomas Nelson Page's sketch froze his wife may be able to discern cracks in this women's culture that was flattened by Page's categories of patriarchy, separate spheres, and True Womanhood, the same received categories that modern scholars often invoke to interpret women's history. Florence in certain ways did draw comfort from the constraints placed upon her gender, but in other ways she found them restrictive and subtly worked to soften the boundaries of the sphere to create her own space. A closer scrutiny of Florence's words and actions reveals fractures in Page's portrait that subvert his gender-defined categories in a manner which forces us to rethink them and to admit the possibility that Florence could and did function on different planes simultaneously; that she performed quite capably in the masculine/public sphere; and that she exerted greater public authority than Page and feminist scholars might care to admit. She did so without sacrificing or demeaning her essential femininity.

From this other perspective, Florence's feminism represented women's diversity, which, as Nancy Cott's pathbreaking work *The Grounding of Modern Feminism* demonstrates, was not limited to the narrowly political context of women's suffrage, important as that was. Her life was proof that a woman could navigate over and around gender barriers and that women and men did interact together both in play and in work as often as they functioned separately in different spaces. Also, in establishing her own identity, Florence demonstrated that being a feminist did not necessarily mean a woman had to destroy gender assignment, family unity, kinship bonds, social cohesion, and human happiness. Her feminism encompassed women's differences from men even as she sought equality of individual advancement within diversity.

Florence's economic independence and class identification helped to created this variety of feminism (just as they also made her unlikely to understand the position of ordinary women), but it was her personality that nurtured it. She was an extremely private individual, not normally given to making the personal aspects of her life public and only rarely assuming a public posture. She was intuitive, nurturing, and family-centered, and her agenda was a personal one. She did not publicly challenge traditionally male prerogatives but worked quietly to attain equality within marriage and the family. It was the confidence gained from victory in the private sphere that enabled her to create a public female sphere in World War I through the organization of a workshop to aid Italian military casualties.

Florence's personality, then, was more complex than the appearance she projected to contemporaries. Moreover, despite advantages of wealth and class, she did not have the perfect life. Her family life was beset by tragedy, including the premature deaths of a husband and infant daughter and then the deaths of both parents, all within a relatively short period of time. Tensions arising from her children's and grandchildren's actions and health disrupted the equilibrium of daily life. Minna's ill-considered elopement and her financial profligacy were continual sources of turmoil and anxiety to Florence. She worried whether her grandson Henry Field would grow into manhood with the appropriate male role models; whether he would abandon his American citizenship for a British passport and become a marginal man, suspended between two peoples and cultures without belonging wholly to either; whether his education would prepare him for a financially secure career. The influenza epidemic of 1916–18 was a particular source of anxiety. Would it claim her granddaughters, far away in Southboro? Would her sons-in-law survive the war, especially Algie who was at the front in Gallipoli and Egypt? It took a strong, confident, and self-willed woman to weather these anxieties, to assert her opinions in the hope of affecting behavioral changes, and to tolerate situations she did not particularly condone.

Florence's responses to these challenges suggest that the ideologies of gender and class were in transition. Women were challenging the older nineteenth-century traditions of patriarchy, but they still were groping to define modern ideas of gender and class. Her behavior called into question the clarity of the separate sphere phenomenon. On the one hand, the metaphor of the sphere, used simply as a descriptor, did delineate the physical space to which patriarchy had assigned Florence and in which she lived. On the other hand, even this physical space was more complexly structured. Unlike some women, Florence never perceived the home as a sphere of confinement and stultification. The death of Henry Field elevated her status to that of "surrogate patriarch" within her family, a role which she continued to fill even after she married Page. Florence made all of the important decisions regarding her daughters' upbringing; she exerted informal political influence even in the traditionally masculine sphere. While publicly deferring to Page and allowing the spotlight of public acclaim to focus upon him as a national literary figure, she managed him probably more than he would have admitted. Page was a man who needed to feel superior but who actually was bound to Florence by dependent emotional, psychological, and financial needs.

True, Page belonged to gender-specific social, cultural, and political clubs in New York, Washington, and York Harbor, and this physical separation implied the social subordination of women, but other realities came into play. Page's membership in many of these organizations was facilitated by Florence's wealth. She also organized the salons and important literary and political gatherings in their home over which her husband presided. She financed construction of the mansion in Washington, D.C., as well as their summer retreat. Her money assisted in the founding of the reading room and the country club as well as the historic preservation of York Harbor for which Page received the credit. Florence also comforted and resuscitated him during his bouts of nervous exhaustion by arranging and financing trips to Jekyll Island, Santa Barbara, and Cuba for recuperation. She underwrote their frequent trips to Europe and North Africa. Florence's managerial talents acquired in the domestic sphere were sophisticated and transferred readily outside the home, and her husband benefited from them.

Florence's management of Henry Field's estate provides further evidence that she was able to manipulate the perimeters of the sphere to assert her own will. The Illinois Married Woman's Property Act of the mid-nineteenth century established Florence's legal identity, which made possible inheritance, ownership, and control of property in her own right. The "widow's dower" provision conferred upon her one-third of her husband's estate; the law also permitted Henry Field to name her, along with two male executors, a cotrustee of his estate.

Florence eventually allowed the decision-making process to devolve upon one male executor, Bryan Lathrop, but she never surrendered her role as cotrustee. This was not the action of a weak woman but one of shrewd intellect who understood that women of her generation did not customarily participate in the world of finance and business. Delegating authority to Bryan Lathrop to manage property on her behalf conformed outwardly to the masculine sphere, except that Florence always insisted upon being apprised of his actions and retained the final decision to accept or reject his advice. A woman of lesser intellect and conviction might easily have lost complete control over her financial affairs.

Clearly Florence did not always seek safety and closure in the ideal of female destiny, nor was she as passive as she appears on first observation. At several critical junctures in her life, Florence took risks, some greater and some lesser, in order to carve out for herself a new model of individualism to legitimate her role as an equal. Any young woman eager to travel to Paris to study was engaging in an act of empowerment, for travel abroad, whether chaperoned or not, entailed risk; the decision to marry Henry Field was a risk. The remarriage of a widow of substantial means was a risk, given the laws governing property and the possibility that an unscrupulous suitor might marry her for her money. Travel abroad to exotic places, such as Egypt, exposed her to health risks. The organization of relief efforts in Italy both during the earthquake and the war years posed hazards for a woman who also was the wife of the representative of the government of the United States. And, of course, Florence's criticisms of America's neglect of Italy during the war years and her outspoken support of her husband's diplomatic activities on behalf of Italy's claims to Trieste during the Paris Peace Conference had to be considered risks.

Florence's understanding of power within the context of male dominance and of her willingness to manipulate its symbols to achieve her own goals was demonstrated in her memorial gift to the Art Institute of Chicago. She exhibited very definite ideas about the kind of memorial she wished to establish in memory of Henry Field, and she knew how to leverage her personal connections and financial resources to force the Art Institute's trustees to conform to her will. Rather than challenge directly and overtly the male trustees' authority and risk their rejecting her demands, Florence cloaked her determination in male garb. She utilized her brother Bryan Lathrop, a member of the board of trustees, as the instrument to effect her will.

Similarly, in deciding how to dispose of her wealth; which religious, cultural, and eleemosynary causes to support financially and which not; which heirs, relatives, and friends should benefit from her estate and to what extent; Florence was making a political statement. She was empowering herself to take control over her wealth by making choices that satisfied her alone. Religion was another sphere in which she displayed the empowerment that women were striving toward by the end of the Victorian era. The Episcopal church was dominated by a male hierarchy, and while Florence remained faithful to it, she was not especially religious or dogmatic in her practices and beliefs. She eschewed the democratizing influence of religion, and rather than work in the ghetto parishes among the urban underclass as Social Gospelers advocated, she wrote checks. She did support charitable works, but just as often she contributed to the restoration and reconstruction of Episcopal edifices. Whatever one thinks about her priorities or the choice of programs she supported financially, the willingness to make her own decisions was a manifestation of her empowerment.

Perhaps the most demonstrative examples of Florence's empowerment, of her capacity to act decisively and freely, occurred during the war years. In both the organization of the relief program for the earthquake victims of Avezzano and the establishment of the *ouvroir* to manufacture surgical dressings for Italy's military casualties, she found her cause. Her response to these crises, like her anger toward Germany for forcefully separating her from her family, was an attempt to regain and exercise control over her life and physical space and, as such, embodied woman's capability, not her fragility. Florence effectively utilized a personal, nonbureaucratic style and her upper-class background to realize her objectives. She demonstrated that she was an able organizer and fund-raiser, a persuasive communicator, and an expert executive who controlled her own agenda, raised and allocated her own funds, managed and disciplined her workers, and kept her own records. She obtained contributions of money, food, cotton cloth, and other supplies from a network of well-to-do and socially elite friends and acquaintances in the United States in part because she was one of them. Like her organization of earthquake relief, the *ouvroir* enabled her to acquire practical experience, to bridge the male/public-female/private hierarchy and to create a public female sphere.

Florence's accomplishments in this sphere unhappily went unnoticed and unadvertised in the male-dominant societies of Italy and the United States, where the traditionally ornamental role of the ambassador's wife presiding over the interminable round of luncheons, teas, and dinner parties without ever having or uttering a serious or independent thought about the war prevailed. Like the quake relief program, the *ouvroir* became subsumed into a large, impersonal, and male-dominated bureaucratic institution, the American Red Cross, while she and the other female volunteers of the American colony in Rome, along with their achievements, disappeared from the historical record and popular memory.

Why did Florence's humanitarian endeavors over a three-and-one-half-year period go unrecognized? The answer may be that Florence's work, like that of so many female volunteers before her, was on the whole neither controversial nor threatening to the patriarchal societies that typified both the United States and Italy. It also was "women's work," falling within the general parameters of woman's role as nurturer. People who had no firsthand exposure to disaster relief of any kind tended to think of the work that she, her women volunteers, and her few salaried workers were doing was nice but unimportant. When she and her female colleagues behaved in a decidedly unfrivolous way by going to the earthquake zone in and around Avezzano, or when they manufactured surgical dressings for a military hospital, those facts did not register with the patriarchal governments of either country, or even with a male-dominated organization like the Red Cross.

One of the intriguing questions left to ponder is whether Florence Page would have been at ease in the new American nation that came into

being in the aftermath of World War I. If one were to define Florence in
class terms, the answer would be a qualified yes. As historian Ellis W.
Hawley has pointed out, despite presidential candidate Herbert Hoo-
ver's claim that New Era America had no place for "privileged classes
or castes or groups who would hold opportunity as their prerogative,"
America in the 1920s remained in many ways a class-bound society.[14]
Florence's wartime concern about the labor and servant questions after
the conflict were always couched in terms of how they would impact
upon her and her family's lifestyles, not in terms of how to improve the
material condition or position of the working class. Gender identification in her particular case never cut across class lines; hence there is little
reason to believe that Florence would have been any more sympathetic
to ordinary working women or to prominent women's political issues
such as pacifism, prohibition, and wages and working conditions than
she had been to the suffrage question in the prewar period. However,
since wealth was one of several components of elite status and her own
family had entrepreneurial origins, Florence probably would have allowed the able and ambitious to move through the doors of opportunity
that were partially opened by wealth-based privilege.

Even if one were to define Florence solely in gender terms, she would
still have found her niche in 1920s society, especially if one accepts
Nancy Cott's broad definition of feminism to encompass the paradoxical
demand for the pursuit of sexual equality while maintaining recognition
of and protection for gender differences. The flapper would not have
pleased her nor would women who imbibed alcohol regularly and publicly or who flaunted their sexuality openly. These were matters of propriety to Florence and bore upon her perception of appropriate female
behavior, but they were not the redefinition of gender roles that she
would have been interested in. She had pursued and achieved sexual
equality during her lifetime but within marriage. She also had met
most, if not all, of the criteria of the "New Woman": she was not only a
wife-companion, childbearer, knowledgeable consumer, and homemaker; she also was, in her own quiet and understated way, conscious of
her personhood and her sexuality. Economic independence had conferred
upon her great freedom of choice, and throughout her lifetime she exercised her choices. Even as she achieved sexual equality within marriage,
she also had accepted the concept of separate spheres, not rigidly or exclusively defined but allowing for interaction at the perimeters. For she
recognized the importance for women, as well as for men, to have the

opportunity to develop and flourish within physical and cultural spaces of their own. Accommodation and flexibility rather than separate and unequal spheres were the legacy Florence would have wanted for her own daughters and granddaughters.

Notes

Bibliography

Index

Notes

Abbreviations

Box and folder numbers or letters are cited as: 74:1910.

CHS	Chicago Historical Society
EBP	Elizabeth Burwell Page
EHM	Elmhurst (Illinois) Historical Museum
FLP	Florence Lathrop Page
FRUS	*Foreign Relations of the United States*
OYHS	Old York Historical Society
TBBP	Thomas Barbour Bryan Papers
TNP	Thomas Nelson Page
TNPP (DUL)	Thomas Nelson Page Papers (Duke University Library)
TNPP (UVA)	Thomas Nelson Page Papers (University of Virginia)
TNPP (W&M)	Thomas Nelson Page Papers (College of William and Mary)

Introduction

1. TNP to John Fox, Jr., May 6, 1893, in Holman, *John Fox and Tom Page,* 16.

2. As quoted in Laurel Thatcher Ulrich, "The Hand That Rocked the Cradle Built the Library," review of Anne F. Scott's *Natural Allies: Women's Associations in American History* in *New York Times Book Review,* May 17, 1992, 11.

3. TNP, *Novels, Stories, Sketches, and Poems* 12:185–86.

4. See Fox-Genovese, *Within the Plantation Household,* and Clinton, *The Plantation Mistress.*

5. FLP, note, written probably in 1918, TNPP (W&M), 8:1913.

6. TNP to Minna Burnaby, Apr. 14, 1908, ibid., 1:1.

7. Stansky, "The Crumbling Frontiers of History."

8. Heilbrun, *Writing a Woman's Life.*

9. For useful methodologies that provide an understanding of women's lives

and culture, see Ulrich, *A Midwife's Tale*, esp. 27, 32–33; Hampsten, *Read This Only to Yourself*, 1–28; Hoffman and Cully, *Women's Personal Narratives;* Lystra, *Searching the Heart.* By utilizing hitherto neglected sources and shifting the focus somewhat, David F. Allmendinger, Jr.'s biography *Ruffin* demonstrates how we may better explain and understand men's lives, in this instance how Edmund Ruffin's concern for providing for his children influenced his thoughts and actions.

10. Fox-Genovese has made a persuasive argument that what evolved in the United States was not patriarchy in its original meaning but a mutation. She used the term *paternalism,* which, perhaps, more nearly describes the condition of nineteenth-century women. (*Within the Plantation Household,* 63–64, 101–2, 132, 201, 286, 290–91, 307, 324, 370). However, since *patriarchy* is commonly used in the literature, I have chosen to use that term.

11. I have relied heavily on Carol Ruth Berkin's excellent survey of the literature of women's history, "Clio in Search of Her Daughters/Women in Search of Their Past." See also Linda Gordon, "What's New in Women's History"; Ann D. Gordon et al., "The Problem of Women's History"; and Cott and Pleck, *A Heritage of Her Own.*

12. Lerner, "Placing Women in History," 1–2. Lerner was herself instrumental in the development of "compensatory history" with the 1971 publication of *The Woman in American History,* biographical sketches of notable women incorporated into a loosely chronological framework of United States history.

13. Berkin, "Clio in Search of Her Daughters/Women in Search of Their Past," 11.

14. Welter, "The Cult of True Womanhood," 152.

15. Lasch, *Haven in a Heartless World.*

16. Lerner, "The Lady and the Mill Girl."

17. Smith-Rosenberg, "The Female World of Love and Ritual."

18. Degler, *At Odds.*

19. Berkin, "Clio in Search of Her Daughters/Women in Search of Their Past," 11–12.

20. See Kerber, "Separate Spheres, Female Worlds, Woman's Place."

21. For a review of the literature on elites, see Doyle, "History from the Top Down."

22. The full title of Jaher's book is *The Urban Establishment: Upper Strata in Boston, New York, Charleston, Chicago, and Los Angeles.*

23. See Baltzell, *Puritan Boston and Quaker Philadelphia;* Pessen, *Riches, Class, and Power before the Civil War;* Story, *The Forging of an Aristocracy;* Ingham, *The Iron Barons.*

24. Lerner has called attention to this point in "Placing Women in History," 5–6.

25. See Antler, *Lucy Sprague Mitchell.*

Chapter 1

1. See Jaher, *The Rich, the Well Born, and the Powerful,* 258–84.

2. Saveth, *American History and the Social Sciences,* 204.

3. Pierce, *Field Genealogy* 2:706.

4. W. E. Hagans to Mrs. Thomas, Nov. 25, 1937, EHM.

5. *National Cyclopaedia of American Biography* 5:82; *Biographical History with Portraits of Prominent Men of the Great West,* 27.

6. Wade, *The Urban Frontier.*

7. Miller, "The Hogs Came with the Butcher."

8. For this paragraph and the next, see Cronon, *Nature's Metropolis.*

9. *National Cyclopaedia of American Biography* 3:170.

10. For this paragraph and the next, see *Biographical History with Portraits of Prominent Men of the Great West,* 28.

11. Creese, *Crowning of the American Landscape,* 206.

12. Lanctot, *A Walk through Graceland Cemetery,* 1–2.

13. For this paragraph and the next, see Simonds, *Landscape Gardening,* esp. app., 323.

14. Creese, *Crowning of the American Landscape,* 206.

15. For this paragraph and the next, see CHS, *Annual Report: 1916,* 173–75.

16. For this paragraph and the next, see Drury, *Old Chicago Houses,* 146–49.

17. "Large and Varied Gifts to Chicago," *Survey* 36(1916): 518.

18. "Bryan Lathrop," *Who Was Who* 1:707.

19. For the diplomatic passport and the 1877 photograph, see TNPP (UVA), 75:1916, and Neg. 137-6, EHM.

20. TNP, "Biographical Sketch of Florence Lathrop Page," n.d., TNPP (UVA), 34:1921.

21. See Anne F. Scott, *The Southern Lady.*

22. Chudacoff, *Evolution of American Urban Society,* 76–84; for Chicago specifically, see Hoyt, *Land Values in Chicago.*

23. Thompson et al., *DuPage Roots,* 151.

24. Ibid., 152.

25. The spaciousness of the proposed new Bryan Lathrop house of the 1870s is suggested in Bryan Lathrop's letters of July 7 and 26, 1875 to his Aunt Carry in TBBP, CHS, 64:449. Bryan proposed that Helen Lathrop furnish it with mirrors, furniture, and pictures, "some of which she might pick up abroad."

26. Berens, *Elmhurst,* 106–7.

27. Ibid., 110–11.

28. See Griswold and Weller, *Golden Age of American Gardens.*

29. Ibid., 152–53.

30. Ibid., 154.

31. See Barnes and Fairbank, *Julia Newberry's Diary,* vi–vii.

32. Thompson et al., *DuPage Roots,* 153.

33. See Ruth Strand's brief biographical sketch, "Florence Lathrop", (c. 1970), EHM.

34. For this paragraph and the next, see Twyman, *Marshall Field & Co.,* chaps. 2–5.

35. Pierce, *Field Genealogy* 2:707.

36. Berens, *Elmhurst,* 105.

37. For the economic significance of marriage, see Basch, *In the Eyes of the Law;* Lerner, *The Majority Finds Its Past;* Pessen, "The Marital Theory and Practice of the Antebellum Urban Elite."

38. Pierce, *Field Genealogy* 2:706

39. Galassi, *Corot in Italy;* Dulles, *Americans Abroad,* 140, 177.

40. *Richmond Times-Dispatch,* June 7, 1893.

41. Membership in the Chicago Historical Society, as in the clubs, was a means of fostering upper-class cohesion and influence over the city's cultural, economic and political life. See Arthur B. Jones to Albert D. Hager, Nov. 24, 1882, accepting membership in the society on behalf of Henry Field, CHS, Autograph Letters Collection, 129:194.

42. Pierce, *Field Genealogy* 2:707.

43. Quoted in Kerber, "Separate Spheres, Female Worlds, Woman's Place," 10.

44. Norton, *Liberty's Daughters,* 298.

45. Tocqueville, *Democracy in America,* ed. Heffner, 235.

46. Houghton, *Victorian Frame of Mind,* 343. Basch, *In the Eyes of the Law,* 40, also has noted that by the nineteenth century American women were, as a part of the cult of domesticity, coming to occupy a lofty sphere which was complementary to, but clearly separate from, the world of men.

47. The economic role of the wealth upper-class woman and its relationship to the cult of domesticity is discussed in Matthaei, *Economic History of Women in America,* 31.

48. Kessler-Harris, *Out to Work;* Ryan, *Cradle of the Middle Class,* esp. 56, 185. See also Blewett, "The Sexual Division of Labor and the Artisan Tradition in Early Industrial Capitalism."

49. Pierce, *Field Genealogy* 2:707.

50. *Chicago Daily News,* Dec. 24, 1890.

51. Copy of the inventory of Henry Field Memorial Collection, John W. Smith, archivist, Art Institute of Chicago, to author, May 22, 1990.

52. "Field Collection: Recorder's Office no. 1881157, June 6, 1893," Archives of the Art Institute of Chicago, copy in possession of the author.

53. Pierce, *Field Genealogy* 2:708.

54. The letter is in Clarke, "The Art Institute's Guardian Lions," 53–54.

Notes

55. Strand, "Florence Lathrop," 1–2, EHM.

56. The financial and social importance of inheritance in American and European society is discussed in Saveth, *American History and the Social Sciences,* 208–9, and Lerner, *The Majority Finds Its Past,* 133–34.

57. Tyler, *Men of Mark in Virginia* 5:333.

58. Biographical information on TNP is culled from Rosewell Page, *Thomas Nelson Page;* Holman, "Thomas Nelson Page"; Tyler, *Men of Mark in Virginia* 5:333–36. The loss of his wife was traumatic for TNP and in his extreme melancholy he turned to Catholicism, attracted by the absolute quality of church dogma; but he never converted and slowly his grief abated (Gross, *Thomas Nelson Page,* 40).

59. Strand, "Florence Lathrop," 1–2, EHM.

60. Florence's daughters retained the Field name (and share of their father's estate) until they themselves wed. The engagement ring story is told in Henry Field, *A Memoir of Thomas Nelson Page,* 14.

61. *Richmond Times-Dispatch,* June 7, 1893.

62. Companionate marriage is discussed in Lebsock, *The Free Women of Petersburg,* 17–18, and Houghton, *Victorian Frame of Mind,* 381.

63. FLP to TNP, Sept. 28, 1907, TNPP (UVA), acc. no. 8641-a, CF:1900–1921.

64. For Page's personality and dwindling fortunes before his marriage to Florence L. Field, see Holman, *Literary Career of Thomas Nelson Page,* esp. 33–40, 179.

65. TNP to Mrs. Charles M. Bruce, Apr. 21, 1893, TNPP (Duke), 3:1893.

66. Ibid. The last clause is a very curious statement which seems to imply that there were factors other than love or affection that led Page to propose marriage. One cannot conclusively rule out true affection, but neither can one discount material factors.

67. Florence Lathrop Field to Mrs. Charles M. Bruce, [?], 1893, ibid. Florence's overture elicited a favorable reaction, for Mrs. Bruce accepted her, attended the Pages' wedding, and visited them after they took up residence in Washington, D.C. See FLP to Mrs. Charles M. Bruce, May 7, 1897, ibid., 4:1897.

68. For a discussion of how this concept evolved to give the aura of stability in a society where values changed frequently, where fortunes rose and fell with frightening rapidity, where social and economic mobility provided instability as well as hope, see Welter, *Dimity Convictions,* esp. chap. 2.

69. TNP, "Florence Lathrop Page," n.d., TNPP (UVA), acc. no. 8641, 34: "Biographical Sketch."

70. See Welter, "The Cult of True Womanhood"; Kraditor, *Up from the Pedestal,* 9–10, 14; Lasch, *Haven in a Heartless World.*

Notes

71. See Joyce Antler, *Lucy Sprague Mitchell.*

72. Rosewell Page, *Thomas Nelson Page,* 118; Strand, "Florence Lathrop," 1–2, EHM.

73. See, for example, Florence's letter of Oct. 1, 1907, TNPP (UVA), acc. no. 8641-a, CF:1920–21.

Chapter 2

1. Tyler, *Men of Mark in Virginia* 5:335.

2. Quoted in Holman, *Literary Career of Thomas Nelson Page,* 37.

3. FLP to EBP, Jan. 12, 1910, TNPP (UVA), acc. no. 8641, 74:1910.

4. Wasserman, *Bula Matari,* 257, 260; Stanley, *Autobiography of Sir Henry Morton Stanley,* 354.

5. FLP to EBP, Jan. 12, 1910, TNPP (UVA), acc. no. 8641, 74:1910.

6. Unlike FLP, who thoroughly enjoyed "The Season" in 1911, TNP found it "monotonous" and "time killing" (TNP to Minna Burnaby, Feb. 21, 1911, TNPP [W&M], 1:4.

7. Receipts for contributions scattered throughout the various collections of Page manuscripts, Page's biographical sketch, "Florence Lathrop Page"; Strand, "Florence Lathrop," EHS.

8. See, for example, McCarthy, *Noblesse Oblige.*

9. The importance of female servants in upper-class Victorian households is discussed in Lerner, *The Majority Finds Its Past,* 133–35.

10. For this paragraph and the next, see FLP to TNP, Oct. 2, 1907, TNPP (UVA), acc. no. 8641-a, CF:1900–1921; FLP to Florence Lindsay, Mar. 26, 1919, to Minna Burnaby, Feb. 5–7, 1919, TNPP (W&M), 8:1919, ibid., 5:3.

11. *Chicago Tribune,* Aug. 18, 1974; W. E. Hagans to Mrs. —— Thomas, Nov. 25, 1937, EHS.

12. FLP to Rosewell and Ruth Page, Oct. 5, 1912, TNPP (DUL), 16:1912; FLP to Helen Lathrop, May 13, 1917, TNPP (W&M), 2:4.

13. FLP to Rosewell Page, Apr. 18, 1918, TNPP (DUL), 24:1918.

14. FLP to Helen Lathrop, Jan. 9, 1917, May 13, to Florence Lindsay, Oct. 14, 1916, TNPP (W&M), 2:4; 8:1916.

15. Nineteenth-century attitudes toward children are analyzed in Wishey, *The Child and the Republic,* and Cott, *The Bonds of Womanhood,* 46.

16. FLP to Florence Lindsay, Mar. 26, 1919, TNPP (W&M), 8:1919.

17. Ibid., Nov. 20, 1913, 8:1913.

18. Ibid., Jan. 22, 1919, 8:1919.

19. Ibid., Aug. 15, 1916, 8:1916.

20. FLP to EBP, June 4, 1910, TNPP (UVA), acc. no. 8641, 74:1910.

21. Ibid., Nov. 25, 1900, 72:1900. See also the letters of Dec. 9 and 30, 1900, ibid.

22. Ibid., May 24, 1910, 74:1910.

23. FLP to Florence Lindsay, Aug. 11, 1915, TNPP (W&M), 8:1915.

24. Ibid., Nov. 25, 1914, Dec. 7, 1915, 8:1914, 1915.

25. Ibid., Feb. 21, 1916, 8:1916.

26. Ibid., Feb. 3, 1916.

27. Ibid., Feb. 21, 1916.

28. Ibid., Jan. 4–5, 1918, 3:1.

29. For Minna's social life, see FLP to EBP, Nov. 25, 1902, TNPP (UVA), acc. no. 8641, 72:1902. There was only the briefest announcement of the wedding (*New York Times,* Jan. 29, 1900).

30. Bryan Lathrop to FLP, June 7, 1900, ibid., 72:1900.

31. FLP to TNP, Oct. 11, 1907, ibid., acc. no. 8641-a, CF:1900–1921. Preston Gibson subsequently cut a wide swath in society, marrying and divorcing three more socially prominent and affluent young ladies and earning the Croix de Guerre in World War I for his work in an ambulance corps in France. He died in a veteran's hospital in New York in 1937 (*New York Times,* Feb. 16, 1937).

32. FLP to Minna Burnaby, Oct. 6–7, 1918, TNPP (W&M), 4:3.

33. *Burke's Landed Gentry,* 288; *New York Times,* Nov. 14, 1938.

34. FLP to EBP, July 6, 1908, TNPP (UVA), acc. no. 8641, 17:1908.

35. FLP to Florence Lindsay, Nov. 30, 1915, TNPP (W&M), 8:1915.

36. Ibid., Nov. 25, 1914, 8:1914. On this occasion, FLP was asking her daughter's opinion of an acquaintance's fiancée, a Miss Evelyn Marshall of New York and Paris, who was twenty-five, handsome, clever, worldly and affected, "and with plenty of money of her own," liabilities in FLP's estimation, for she declared, "What a pity for that dear boy, only just 21, to tie himself down to a girl older, and probably more than she admits, and with a love of the 'smart' and 'affected.'"

37. FLP to EBP, Oct. 3, 1901, TNPP (UVA), acc. no. 8641 72:1901.

38. Burnaby's first wife, Lady Cholmondeley, passed away in 1911 (*Burke's Landed Gentry,* 288).

39. TNP to Algernon Burnaby, May 18, 1908, TNPP (W&M), 1:3.

40. FLP to Algernon Burnaby, July 19, 1908, ibid., 1:1.

41. FLP to Minna Burnaby, July 19, Sept. 7, 1908, ibid.

42. FLP to Minna Burnaby, July 19, 1908, to Algernon Burnaby, Sept. 7, 1908, ibid.

43. For this paragraph and the next, see FLP to EBP, July 10, 1908, TNPP (UVA), acc. no. 8641, 74:1908. When FLP visited Baggrave in 1909, she described it as "a noble old place, without any pretense and full of rare old historical objects." Life there was as quiet as at Oakland plantation, "except for the

hunting season, when everything that can ride goes to the meet" (ibid., Mar. 12, 1909, 74:1909). See also Henry Field, *The Track of Man*, 14–15, in which he recalls life at Baggrave during the hunting season.

44. In 1915 Minna raised the question with her uncle Bryan Lathrop of Henry legally dropping Gibson as his surname. Preston had contested the divorce and evidently was given a settlement to drop his opposition, but he never ceased trying to gain custody of his son. When FLP was told of Minna's proposal, she consulted her son-in-law lawyer Tom Lindsay, whose advice was "to let sleeping dogs alone." Another consideration entered in FLP's thinking: to change Henry's surname would have alienated the Gibson family, which had been supportive of Minna in her marital difficulties. As FLP wrote, "Change of name is always serious, and would probably antagonize all P.s family who are devoted to Minna." Minna evidently decided not to take legal action at this time, but Henry continued to use Field as his surname (FLP to Helen Lathrop, June 15, 1915, TNPP [W&M], 2:1).

45. FLP to Florence Lindsay, Dec. 7, 1915, ibid., 8:1915. FLP noted, as have other Americans in Europe, that children there often were clothed as miniature adults. Henry Field was dressed in tweeds and flannel shirt, prompting FLP to observe: "The boys all wear tweeds here and are men while they still are babies" (FLP to EBP, Mar. 12, 1909, TNPP (UVA), acc. no. 8641, 74:1909).

46. FLP to Florence Lindsay, Feb. 24–25, 1918, TNPP (W&M), 3:1.

47. Ibid., Apr. 22, 1919, Feb. 3, 1916, TNPP (W&M), 8:1919, 1916. To Rosewell Page, FLP wrote of Henry: "he is no scholar, but has a very good clear mind, and best of all a lovely nature" (FLP to Rosewell Page, Apr. 21, 1918, TNPP [DUL], 24:Apr.–Dec. 1918).

48. FLP to Florence Lindsay, Dec. 26, 1915, TNPP (W&M), 8:1915.

49. Ibid., Feb. 3, 1916, 8:1916.

50. TNP to Preston Gibson, July 25, 1911, ibid., 1:4.

51. TNP to Minna Burnaby, Feb. 22, 1912, ibid.

52. Field, *The Track of Man*, 18–19, 23–25.

53. FLP to Florence Lindsay, Dec. 7, 1915, TNPP (W&M), 8:1915.

54. TNP to Preston Gibson, July 25, 1911, FLP to Florence Lindsay, Sept. 19, 1916, ibid., 1:4, 8:1916. Algy was invalided out with the rank of major.

55. FLP to Florence Lindsay, Jan. 16, 1919, ibid., 5:3, containing a copy of Preston's letter.

56. Ibid.; ibid., Nov. 11, 1916, 8:1916.

57. For this paragraph and the next, see ibid., Nov. 11, 1916.

58. Ibid., Apr. 15, 1919, 8:1919.

59. Ibid. Field served for a time as curator of the Chicago Natural History Museum (which his uncle Marshall Field had founded) and research fellow at Harvard and was a member of anthropological societies in the United States and Great Britain. His published scholarship focused on the Middle East (Iraq)

and Southwest Asia (Moritz, *Current Biography 1955,* 207–9, and Field's obituary, *New York Times,* Jan 7, 1986).

60. "Deed of Trust," July 17, 1908, TNPP (UVA), acc. no. 8641, 74:1908.

61. TNP to Minna Burnaby, Feb. 21, Mar. 23, 1911, TNPP (W&M), 1:4.

62. For this paragraph and the next, see FLP to Bryan Lathrop, May 27–28, 1915, ibid., 2:1.

63. Ibid., Oct. 3, 1915, 2:2.

64. John P. Wilson, Jr., to FLP, Oct. 29, 1917, TNPP (UVA), acc. no. 8641, 75:1917.

65. For this paragraph and the next four, see FLP to Minna Burnaby, Feb. 5, 7, 1919, TNPP (W&M), 5:3.

66. For this paragraph and the next two, see TNP to Minna Burnaby, Feb. 10, 1919, ibid., 5:3.

Chapter 3

1. For this paragraph and the next, see Bryan Lathrop to Andrew Wylie, Apr. 24, 1869, TBBP (CHS), 69:65.

2. The tally is from the supplement to the *New York Tribune,* June 1892, reprinted in Ratner, *Great American Fortunes,* 12–15.

3. Hoyt, *Land Values in Chicago,* esp. chaps. 4–5.

4. Jaher, *The Urban Establishment,* 475.

5. FLP to TNP, Sept. 28, 1907, TNPP (UVA), acc. no. 8641-a, CF: 1900–21.

6. For this paragraph and the next, see Twyman, *Marshall Field & Co.,* esp. 62–64, 177 (table 15).

7. A copy of Henry Field's will dated July 30, 1888, is in TNPP (UVA), acc. no. 8641, 72:1891.

8. The complete list of millionaires and their occupations by state and city is in Ratner, *Great American Fortunes,* 1–93.

9. On the social and economic implications of nineteenth-century wills, see Lebsock, *The Free Women of Petersburg.*

10. Account of Edmund Wilson, Administrator of the Estate of William A. Bryan, Deceased, n.d. [1906?], TNPP (DUL) 56:Legal Documents; Helen Lathrop to FLP, TNPP (UVA), acc. no. 8641, 75:1916.

11. Holman, *Literary Career of Thomas Nelson Page,* app. B, 234–42.

12. In 1914, for example, Florence wrote to Ruth Page commenting on the expense of running the embassy and also of entertaining public figures who passed through Rome. She attributed their ability to cover the expense to her brother Bryan's cleverness in enhancing her income (FLP to Ruth Page, Apr. 2, 1914, TNPP [DUL], 20:1914).

13. I. S. Schlegelmilch to FLP, May 2, 1916, TNPP (UVA), acc. no. 8641, 75:1916.

14. Bryan Lathrop to FLP, Dec. 10, 1894, TNPP (DUL), 3:1894 Letters.

15. For this paragraph and the next, see Bryan Lathrop to FLP, June 7, 1900, TNPP (UVA), acc. no. 8641, 72:1900.

16. Following the death of Marshall Field in 1905, Henry Field's estate devolved into a mutual trust with Florence and Bryan the sole trustees. They decided not to name a third trustee, an option allowed by the terms of the will. On Nov. 30, 1908, the trusteeship legally ended, after eighteen years. Florence credited Bryan for the considerable wealth he had amassed for her in that time (FLP to EBP, Nov. 30, 1908, ibid., 74:1908).

17. "Expense Account of Mrs. Thomas Nelson Page for 1911," ibid., 74:1911.

18. FLP to Bryan Lathrop, Aug. 23, 1915, TNPP (W&M), 2:2.

19. John P. Wilson, Jr., to FLP, May 11, 1916, TNPP (UVA), acc. no. 8641, 75:1916.

20. FLP to Florence Lindsay, Nov. 26, 1916, TNPP (W&M), 8:1916.

21. Ibid., Aug. 3, 1916.

22. Estate Balance Sheet of Henry Field, 31, Dec. 1917, TNPP (UVA), acc. no. 8641, 72:1891.

23. FLP to TNP, Nov. 7, 1919, ibid., acc. no. 8641-a, CF:1900–21.

24. FLP to Ruth Page, Oct. 5, 1912, TNPP (DUL), 16:1912.

25. Receipt dated Feb. 6, 1902, TNPP (UVA), acc. no. 8641, 73:1902; receipt dated Nov. 26, 1906, TNPP (DUL), 30:1906.

26. John P. Wilson, Jr., to FLP, Oct. 29, 1917, TNPP (UVA), acc. no. 8641, 75:1917; Field, *A Memoir of Thomas Nelson Page,* 19.

27. The figures on the envelope may be found in TNPP (UVA), acc. no. 8641, 72:1897.

28. Ibid., 72:1900, 73:1902.

29. Both the estimates of the cost of travel to Europe and a description of the cottage, which truly was a mansion, are given in subsequent chapters.

30. For data regarding the Washington mansion see Bryan Lathrop to FLP, Feb. 13–14, 1896, ibid., 72:1896, and the photograph in ibid., 73:1907. The building contract of June 4, 1896, is in TNPP (DUL) in box 30.

31. Among the underwriters insuring the property were North British, Caledonian, Niagara, German American, New York Underwriters, the Insurance Company of America, and the Granite State. See the undated "Register of Insurance Policies on Property at York Harbor, Maine, in name of Trustees under the Will of Henry Field," TNPP (DUL), 30:Insurance.

32. John P. Wilson, Jr., to FLP, Oct. 29, 1917, TNPP (UVA), acc. no. 8641, 75:1917.

33. Ledger accounts marked "June Bills" [1899], "December Bills" [1899],

and the receipt dated Nov. 18, 1899, ibid., 72:1899; miscellaneous 1900 receipts, ibid., 72:1900; "Expense Account of Mrs. Thomas Nelson Page for 1911," ibid., 74:1911; and FLP to TNP, Oct. 5, 1907, ibid., acc. no. 8641-a, CF: 1900–1921.

34. For the importance of consumption expenditures for the affluent, see Matthaei, *Economic History of Women in America,* 243–44.

35. For this paragraph and the next three, see note 33 above.

36. TNPP, "Florence Lathrop Page," n.d., TNPP (UVA), acc. no. 8641, 34:"Biographical Sketch."

37. Williamson and Lindert, *American Inequality,* 47. Even the pioneering study of Wesley C. Mitchell and his associates for the National Bureau of Economic Research, *Income in the United States* is sketchy before 1910. King's *Wealth and Income of the People of the United States,* which attempts to delve into the nineteenth century, is idiosyncratic and not considered reliable by modern economists.

38. Spahr, *Essay on the Present Distribution of Wealth,* Preface and pt. 2:129; Holmes, "The Concentration of Wealth," 591–92.

39. Unlike Spahr, the modern economist Stanley Lebergott uses the higher figure (*The American Economy,* 45, 48).

40. The data are extracted from U.S. Bureau of the Census, *Statistical History of the United States.*

41. FLP to TNP, Nov. 7, 1919, TNPP (UVA), acc. no. 8641-a, CF:1900–21.

42. See Ratner, *Great American Fortunes,* and Lebergott, *The American Economy,* 169–73 and tables 5–6.

43. Hofstadter's *Social Darwinism in American Thought* remains the best exposition of these ideas.

44. Bryan Lathrop to TNP, Aug. 9, 1896, TNPP (DUL), 3:1896 Letters.

45. FLP to EBP, May 12, 1912, TNPP (UVA), acc. no. 8641, 74:1912.

46. For Clark's reputation, see Stockbridge, "Champ Clark, of Pike County."

47. "Last Will and Testament of Florence Lathrop Page," July 6, 1920, York Harbor, Maine, TNPP (UVA), acc. no. 8641, 75:1920.

48. Lebsock, *The Free Women of Petersburg,* xix.

49. Estate Inventory of Florence Lathrop Page, Dec. 28, 1921, TNPP (UVA), acc. no. 8641, 28:1921 Legal Documents.

Chapter 4

1. Drake, *The Pine Tree Coast,* 59.
2. Ernst, *New England Miniature,* 95–96; Fein, *Olmsted and the American Envi-*

ronmental Tradition, chaps. 1–3; White, *The Eastern Establishment and the Western Experience,* 79–93; James, *Charles W. Eliot* 1:319–24.

3. Baltzell, *The Protestant Establishment,* 116–21.

4. Of the two, TNP was more openly active in promoting the elite upper-class lifestyle at York Harbor, but he clearly had the support, both personal and financial, of his wife. She, too, actively lived the life of an upper-class woman at her summer cottage, but, as in other aspects of their relationship, FLP tended to defer to her husband.

5. Emery, *Ancient City of Gorgeana and Modern Town of York (Maine),* viii, 237–49.

6. Moody, ed., *The Letters of Thomas Gorges,* 34, 45, 53, 59, 88–9, 114–15; Banks, *History of York, Maine* 1:chs. 3–5, 11, 14–17; Repplier, "Where All Roads Lead," 509; Mitchell, *Along the Maine Coast,* 7. When the Massachusetts Bay Company took over the Gorges property in 1652, it revoked the charter, reduced Gorgeana to the status of a town, and changed its name to York.

7. Clark, *Maine,* 152ff.

8. Ernst, *New England Miniature,* 96; Evans, *York and Ogunquit,* unpaged (see section entitled "Town of York"); Rolde, *York Is Living History,* 58.

9. Drake, *The Pine Tree Coast,* 47; Rolde, *York Is Living History,* 60–61.

10. "Architectural Survey, York, Deed Research Sheet," map 52, lot 52, OYHS. A plan of the property, recorded on Aug. 30, 1906 in the names of Florence L. Page and Bryan Lathrop, as trustees under the will of Henry Field, may be found on page 4, Plan Book 6, ibid.

11. Amory, *The Last Resorts,* 11.

12. That the Pages had a color postcard of Rock Ledge printed may be interpreted as an affirmation of their position and prominence in society. The postcard suggests that they believed that other people, possibly friends and acquaintances, might desire an image of their home as a testament to having visited the cottage.

13. The data on the Page cottage are deposited in OYHS.

14. See, for example, Wright, *The Slums of Baltimore, Chicago, New York, and Philadelphia;* Jane Addams, *Twenty Years at Hull House;* Bessie Pierce, *A History of Chicago* 3:54; Mayer and Wade, *Chicago: Growth of a Metropolis,* 102–5, 116–18; Philpott, *The Slum and the Ghetto,* esp. pt 1.

15. Scully, *The Shingle Style;* Whiffen, *American Architecture since 1870,* 127–32; FLP to EBP, June 4, 1910, TNPP (UVA), acc. no. 8641, 74:1910; FLP to Florence Lindsay, Oct. 25, 1916, TNPP (W&M), 8:1916.

16. The basis for this conclusion is largely visual evidence: some photographs of Rock Ledge as well as pictures and the floor plan of the Aldis cottage in the collection of OYHS.

17. See the probate court's inventory, "Estate of Florence Lathrop Page," Dec. 28, 1921, TNPP (UVA), acc. no. 8641, 20:1921 Legal Documents.

18. The Pages had an automobile as early as 1907, when there were only 140,300 automobiles in the country (FLP to TNP, Oct. 2, 1907, ibid., acc. no. 8641-a, CF:1900–1921; Field, *A Memoir of Thomas Nelson Page,* 1, 18, and *Historical Statistics of the United States,* 783).

19. As quoted in Bartlett, *Familiar Quotations,* ed. Beck, 618; Morris, *Encyclopedia of American History,* 432.

20. The information in this and the following paragraphs on the cottage's furnishings is from the probate court's inventory cited in note 17 above.

21. The appearance of Charles Locke Eastlake's *Hints on Household Taste* in 1868 and Bruce J. Talbert's *Gothic Forms* (U.S. ed., 1873) in England (Birmingham, 1867) formed the basis of the American Eastlake style.

22. See Seale, *The Tasteful Interlude,* 64; Davidson, *American Heritage History of Antiques,* 387ff.

23. Mixing materials and mass was a common practice in Victorian homes and cottages. See Bishop and Coblentz, *The World of Antiques, Art, and Architecture in Victorian America,* 136–237, 317.

24. FLP to EBP, Apr. 17, 1910, TNPP (UVA), acc. no. 8641, 74:1910. See also Holman, *Literary Career of Thomas Nelson Page,* 41–42.

25. *Who's Who at Bar Harbor . . . York Harbor,* 1.

26. Ibid.; *Who Was Who,* 1:181, 265, 349, 486, 555, 604, 745, 1168.

27. Sources other than the cottage lists indicate that from the late nineteenth century on other distinguished visitors came to York Harbor for the summer. Besides President Eliot of Harvard, these included from time to time the young John Jacob Astor; General Charles Devens; Maine senator and presidential candidate James G. Blaine, Ole Bull, the Norwegian violinist; and Alice Longfellow, daughter of the poet. See Rolde, *York Is Living History,* 61.

28. The criterion for entry into *Notable American Women* was "distinction in their own right of more than local significance"; specifically excluded was distinction in purely domestic roles (James, *Notable American Women* 1:11. Two earlier works, Leonard's *Woman's Who's Who of America* (1914–15) and Cameron's *Biographical Cyclopedia of American Women* (1924–28), also contained no entries for these women.

29. TNP, "Florence Lathrop Page," n.d., TNPP (UVA), acc. no. 8641, 34:"Biographical Sketch."

30. FLP to EBP, July 14, Aug. 25, 1912, ibid., 74:1912; FLP to Florence Lindsay, Apr. 15, 1919, TNPP (W&M), 8:1919.

31. FLP to TNP, Oct. 2, 1907, TNPP (UVA), acc. no. 8641, 3:1907.

32. The trust, which was connected with but not a part of the hospital, had an annual interest value of $800 and was administered by TNP, Bryan Lathrop, and Arthur T. Aldis (Moody, *Handbook History of the Town of York,* 34).

33. For this phenomenon, see Baltzell, *The Protestant Establishment,* 140.

34. Amory, *The Last Resorts,* 52.

35. Virginia S. Spiller to author, May 19, 1990.
36. Quoted in Baltzell, *The Protestant Establishment,* 18.
37. Moody, *Handbook History of the Town of York,* 250–51.
38. Bardwell, *A History of the Country Club at York, Maine,* 1–4.
39. Ibid., 31.
40. Ibid., 5, 15, 17, 25.
41. Ibid., 23.
42. Banks, *History of York, Maine* 2:176–77; Moody, *Handbook History of the Town of York,* 236–37.
43. FLP to EBP, various letters, TNPP (UVA), acc. no. 8641.
44. Moody, *Handbook History of the Town of York,* 236.
45. FLP to Bryan Lathrop, Aug. 24, 1908, to EBP, Aug. 25, 1912, Aug. 15, 1909, TNPP (UVA), acc. no. 8641, 74:1908, 1912, 1909; Henry Field to Marion Knoblauch Franc, Jan. 24, 1974, CHS.
46. For this paragraph and the next see Rolde, *York Is Living History,* 77.
47. Ibid.; Roberts, *Trending into Maine,* 345, 343–44.
48. Roberts, *Trending into Maine,* 346; Sherman, "A Midsummer Paradise." See *Libby v. Petitioners,* 125 Me., 144, and Banks, *History of York, Maine* 2:432–36, for the details of the zoning controversy.
49. This pertinent bit of information was supplied to me by Virginia Spiller, one of the longtime local residents of York Harbor whose husband had occasion to inspect the plumbing in some of the early cottages. It was his judgment that the sophisticated plumbing would not have been familiar to local plumbers of the turn of the century but would have been routine for plumbers in metropolitan centers.
50. For this paragraph and the next three, see Banks, *History of York, Maine* 2:344–45.
51. For this paragraph and the next, see Bardwell, *History of the Country Club at York, Maine,* 17, 29.
52. FLP to Helen Lathrop, June 15, 1915, TNPP (W&M), 2:1.
53. FLP to Florence Lindsay, Aug. 7, 1916, ibid., 8:1916.
54. Wade, *The Urban Frontier,* 209.

Chapter 5

1. See Clark, "Travel Literature."
2. Bartol, "Bartol's Pictures of Europe, Framed in Ideas," 33.
3. The phenomenon of rich American heiresses being married off to foreign nobility is graphically described in Wecter, *Saga of American Society,* 386–427.
4. American motivation for travel abroad may be gleaned from Washington Irving's three-volume *Notes and Journal of Travel in Europe, 1804–1805,* Intro.

William P. Trent; "Letters from Europe of William Henry Talbot, 1849–1850," transcribed letters in possession of Carol Talbot of Williamsburg, Va.; Levin, "Miss Knight Abroad"; Dulles, *Americans Abroad,* 1–4.

5. FLP to EBP, Mar. 12, 1909, TNPP (UVA), acc. no. 8641, 74:1909.

6. See Hibbert, *The Grand Tour;* Ousby, *The Englishman's England;* Trease, *The Grand Tour;* Black, *The British and the Grand Tour.* American interest in Africa is discussed in McCarthy, *Dark Continent.*

7. In October 1913 FLP wrote that she and TNP has passed twelve days in Paris, "where I ordered my winter's outfit," and had dined and lunched out "nearly every day" (FLP to Ruth Page, Oct. 7, 1913, TNPP [DUL], 19:1913).

8. Dulles, *Americans Abroad,* 105, 108.

9. Booking rates, accommodations, and a 1913 schematic diagram of the *Mauretania* are in TNPP (DUL), 56:Blueprints.

10. Maxtone-Graham, *The Only Way to Cross,* 32–36.

11. FLP to Mrs. Cabell Bruce, May 7, 1897, TNPP (DUL), 4:1897.

12. FLP to EBP, Nov. 25, 1900, TNPP (UVA), acc. no. 8641, 72:1900. Many of FLP's letters were begun on one date but not finished until another, giving the effect of a running commentary on her travels abroad.

13. Ibid., Apr. 10, 1909, 74:1909.

14. For this paragraph and the next two, see ibid., Dec. 30, 1900, 73:1900.

15. Fuller's involvement with Italy is discussed in Douglas, *The Feminization of American Culture,* 383–87.

16. FLP to EBP, Dec. 30, 1900, TNPP (UVA), acc. no. 8641, 73:1900. On American expatriates in Italy see Baker, *Fortunate Pilgrims.*

17. For this paragraph and the next two, see FLP to EBP, Dec. 9, 1900, TNPP (UVA), acc. no. 8641, 73:1900.

18. For this paragraph and the next two, see ibid., Dec. 30, 1900.

19. For this paragraph and the next two, see ibid., Dec. 9, 1900.

20. For this paragraph and the next two, see ibid., Jan. 25, 1901, 73:1901.

21. For this paragraph and the next, see ibid., Feb. 10, 1901.

22. Ibid., Dec. 30, 1900, 73:1900.

23. "Aldis, Owen," *Who Was Who* 1:12.

24. FLP to EBP, Nov. 26, 1905, TNPP (UVA), acc. no. 8641, 73:1905.

25. FLP declared the automobile, "a charming way of becoming familiar with countries, and certainly preferable to trains." Their chauffeur, she added, was "quite remarkable" in making his way about despite not being able to speak the local language (ibid., Apr. 10, 1909, 74:1909).

26. Ibid., Nov. 26, 1905, 73:1905; ibid., Dec. 10, 1905.

27. Ibid., Nov. 26, 1905.

28. For this paragraph and the next five, see ibid., Dec. 27, 1905.

29. For this paragraph and the next see ibid.; ibid., Jan. 26, 1906, 73:1906.

30. Ibid., Jan. 26, 1906. Regarding the acquisition and disposition of the villa in Sicily, whose upkeep was neglected during World War I by the caretaker to whom it was entrusted for an annual sum, see the statement in TNPP (DUL), 56:1919.

31. Baedeker, *Italy* (1909 ed.), 379–80.

32. FLP to EBP, Mar. 11, 1906, TNPP (UVA), acc. no. 8641, 73:1906.

33. For this paragraph and the next three, see ibid., Apr. 13, 1906.

34. Ibid., May 9, 1910, 74:1910.

35. Ibid. Nancy Langhorne Astor was the daughter of Colonel Chiswell Dabney Langhorne, a civil engineer who made a fortune in railway construction and kept open house with lavish hospitality at Mirador, Greenwood, Va. (See Wecter, *Saga of American Society,* 116).

36. For this paragraph and the next three, see FLP to EBP, May 24, 1910, TNPP (UVA), acc. no. 8641, 74:1910.

37. For this paragraph and the next, see ibid., Feb. 4, 1912, 74:1912.

38. For this paragraph and the next six, see ibid., Mar. 6, 14, 1912.

39. Ibid., Mar. 28, 1912.

40. Ibid., Apr. 24, 1912.

41. Ibid., May 12, 1912.

42. My thinking on this and subsequent points regarding Florence's attitudes toward the Muslim Arab world of North Africa has been influenced by Said's *Orientalism,* 1, 27, 166–200, 252, and Robinson et al., *Africa and the Victorians.*

43. For FLP's comments on the staffing of Baggrave Hall, see FLP to EBP, Mar. 12, 1909, TNPP (UVA), acc. no. 8641, 74:1909.

44. Ibid.; May 12, 1912, 74:1912.

Chapter 6

1. *New York Times,* June 18, 1913; *Cong. Rec.,* 63d Cong., 1st sess., 1913, 50, pt.3, 2047.

2. *New York Times,* Oct. 27, 1912; Kaufman, "Virginia Politics and the Wilson Movement"; Dauer, "Thomas Nelson Page, Diplomat," 21.

3. Gaines, "Political Reward and Recognition"; FLP to Ruth Page, Sept. 6, 1913, TNPP (DUL), 19:1913; see also Gould, "Italy and the United States"; Dauer, "Thomas Nelson Page, Diplomat."

4. FLP to Ruth Page, Sept. 6, 1913, TNPP (DUL), 19:1913; *New York Times,* July 27, 1913.

5. FLP to Florence Lindsay, Nov. 1, Dec. 18, 1913, TNPP (W&M), 8:1913; FLP to Ruth Page, Oct. 7, 1913, TNPP (DUL), 19:1913.

6. Ibid.; *New York Times,* July 27, 1913. Page, in fact, presented his credentials to the king, who was at San Rossore, his summer retreat, on Oct. 13, 1913. That Florence also shared the desire for social recognition is evident from her letters to her younger daughter. See TNP to Minna Burnaby, Nov. 30, 1913; FLP to Florence Lindsay, Oct. 13, Nov. 14, 26, 30, 1913, TNPP (W&M), 1:5, 8:1913.

7. Baker and Dodd, *Public Papers of Woodrow Wilson* 1:1–6.

8. FLP to Ruth Page, Apr. 2, May 14, July 15, 1914, TNPP (DUL), 20:1914; Field, *A Memoir of Thomas Nelson Page,* 2–3.

9. FLP to Ruth Page, Sept. 26, 1914, TNPP (DUL), 20:1914.

10. TNP to Florence Lindsay, Oct. 8, 1914, ibid.; FLP to Bryan Lathrop, Jan. 4, Feb. 20, 1915, ibid., 2:1.

11. FLP to Florence Lindsay, Aug. 25, 1915, TNPP (W&M), 8:1915.

12. Ibid., Dec. 19, 1915.

13. FLP to Helen Lathrop, Mar. 18, 1915, to Bryan Lathrop, Feb. 20–22, 1915, ibid., 2:1.

14. For this paragraph and the next, see FLP to Bryan Lathrop, Aug. 23, 1915, to Florence Lindsay, Jan. 22, 1916, ibid., 2:2, 8:1916. In her letter to her brother FLP also wrote: "The whole British Expeditionary Force is a mystery to me. From the beginning to the present, it has been a huge failure."

15. FLP to Florence Lindsay, July 9–10, 1915, ibid., 2:2. As late as February 1916, Florence complained of the Allies' defensive mentality vis à vis Germany, especially the British, for whom she reserved her choicest barbs. See also the letters of Jan. 22, Feb. 15, 26, 1916, ibid., 8:1916.

16. FLP to Helen Lathrop, Oct. 2, 1915, ibid., 2:2.

17. FLP to Florence Lindsay, Aug. 25, 1915, ibid., 8:1915.

18. See Coolidge, *Origins of the Triple Alliance;* Schmitt, *Triple Alliance and Triple Entente;* Albertini, *Origins of the War of 1914* 5:5, 255ff.; Salandra, *La neutralità italiana,* 75–86.

19. See Albertini, *Origins of the War of 1914* 3:345–48. The Tripolitan War of 1911–12 also had been a considerable drain on Italian financial and military resources (ibid., 1:340–57).

20. Mario Alberti et al., *Italy's Great War And Her National Aspirations,* 55–74; Renzi, "Italy's Neutrality and Entrance into the Great War," 1415–18; Sforza, "Sonnino and His Foreign Policy." Salandra's views are articulated in *La neutralità* and *L'intervento.*

21. TNP to Minna Burnaby, Sept. 27, 1914, TNPP (W&M), 1:5; FLP to Ruth Page, Oct. 23, 1914, TNPP (DUL), 20:1914.

22. FLP to Florence Lindsay, Dec. 4, 8, 12, 1914, to Bryan Lathrop, Jan. 4, 1915, TNPP (W&M), 8:1914; 2:1.

23. FLP to Bryan Lathrop, Jan. 4, 1915, to Florence Lindsay, Nov. 25, Dec.

7, 1915, ibid., 2:1, 8:1915. See also FLP to Ruth Page, Feb. 8, 1915, TNPP (DUL), 20:1915.

24. TNP, "Has Civilization Failed?" n.d., TNPP (DUL), 19:1914; FLP to Bryan Lathrop, Mar. 15, 1915, TNPP (W&M), 8:1915.

25. See Toscano, *Il patto di Londra* (2d ed., 1934); Carnovale, *Why Italy Entered into the Great War*, esp. pts. 3, 4.

26. For this paragraph and the next, see TNP, "The Earthquake in the Abruzzi."

27. TNP to Minna Burnaby, Jan. 14, 1915, to Helen Lathrop, Jan. 22, 1915, TNPP (W&M), 2:1.

28. TNP, "The Earthquake in the Abruzzi," 425, 430.

29. Ibid.; FLP to Helen Lathrop, Jan. 17, 1915, TNPP (W&M), 2:1.

30. For this paragraph and the next, see FLP to Helen Lathrop, Jan. 17, 22, 1915, TNPP (W&M), 2:1.

31. For this paragraph and the next, see FLP to Bryan Lathrop, Feb. 8, Feb. 27, Mar. 15, 1915, ibid.

32. Ibid., Feb. 27, 1915.

33. FLP to Helen Lathrop, Jan. 17, 1915, ibid.

34. FLP to Bryan Lathrop, Feb. 27, 1915, ibid.

35. FLP made an automobile tour of Avezzano and its surrounding envions in August 1916 and reported that evidences of the destruction were to be found everywhere (FLP to Florence Lindsay, Aug. 24, 1916, ibid., 8:1916).

36. Page, *Italy and the World War*, 206.

37. FLP to Bryan Lathrop, May 27–28, 1915, TNPP (W&M), 2:1.

38. For this paragraph and the next two, see ibid.

39. Schmitt and Vedeler, *The World in the Crucible*, 92–95.

40. FLP to Helen Lathrop, June 15, 1915, to Florence Lindsay, July 22, 1915, TNPP (UVA), 2:1, 8:1915.

41. FLP to Bryan Lathrop, Aug. 4, 1915, ibid., 2:2.

42. Field, *A Memoir of Thomas Nelson Page*, 4.

43. FLP to Helen Lathrop, Feb. 1916, to Minna Burnaby, July 31, 1918, TNPP (W&M), 2:3, 4:1.

44. FLP to Florence Lindsay, July 12, 1915, ibid., 8:1915.

45. Ibid., Oct. 8, 1918, 4:3.

46. Ibid.; see also FLP to Minna Burnaby, Oct. 6–7, 1918, ibid.

47. Link, *Papers of Woodrow Wilson* 30:393–94, 31:243, 525–30.

48. Ibid., 31:90–91, 104–5, 163–65, 176–77, 310, 426.

49. For this paragraph and the next, see FLP to Bryan Lathrop, Feb. 20–22, 1915, TNPP (W&M), 2:1.

50. Link, *Wilson: The Struggle for Neutrality*, 321–24.

51. FLP to Bryan Lathrop, Feb. 20–22, 1915, TNPP (W&M), 2:1.

52. Link, *Papers of Woodrow Wilson* 33:527–29, 537–38, 540, 544–45.

53. FLP to Bryan Lathrop, Aug. 23, 1915, to Florence Lindsay, Jan. 27, 1916, TNPP (W&M), 2:1, 2:2, 8:1916.

54. FLP to Florence Lindsay, July 7, 16, 22, 1915, ibid., 8:1915.

55. FLP to Minna Burnaby, June 16, 1915, ibid., 2:1.

56. FLP to Florence Lindsay, July 9–10, 1915, to Helen Lathrop, July 23, 1915, ibid., 2:2.

57. FLP to Bryan Lathrop, Aug. 4, 1915, ibid.

58. FLP to Helen Lathrop, July 23, 1915, ibid.

59. FLP to Bryan Lathrop, Aug. 4, 1915, ibid.

60. Ibid.; see also FLP to Florence Lindsay, Aug. 21, 1915, ibid., 8:1915.

61. *New York Times,* Aug. 20, Sept. 2, 1915.

62. Because of normal surface mail to and from America arrived irregularly, Florence often was subjected to incredible emotional strain, as when she learned that a grandchild had contracted the dreaded influenza but did not learn until a month or two later that the child had recovered. At her husband's suggestion she began to use the diplomatic pouch to send out her letters, but this necessitated completing them in time for the courieur to take the pouch to Naples to be put on a ship bound for the United States (see FLP to Florence Lindsay, Feb. 10, 1916, TNPP [W&M], 8:1916).

63. FLP to Helen Lathrop, Oct. 15, 1916, ibid., 2:4.

64. FLP to Minna Burnaby, Nov. 10, 1916, to Helen Lathrop, May 2, 1917, ibid.

65. FLP to Helen Lathrop, Feb. 11, 1917, ibid.

66. For this paragraph and the next, see FLP to Helen Lathrop, Feb. 28, 1917, ibid.

67. FLP to Ruth Page, May 10, 1915, TNPP (DUL), 21:1915.

68. Ibid., Mar. 20, 1917, 23:1917; Dauer, "Thomas Nelson Page, Diplomat," 57–59.

69. Quoted in De Conde, *Half Bitter, Half Sweet,* 146.

70. See the 1917 volume of U.S. Dept. of State, *FRUS, 1914–1917,* supp. 2, 1:123, and *FRUS: The Lansing Papers* 2:60, 154–55; Link, *Papers of Woodrow Wilson* 51:386–87. The difficulty stemmed in part from point 9 of Wilson's Fourteen Points, which conflicted with Italy's territorial ambitions under the Treaty of London.

71. De Conde, *Half Bitter, Half Sweet,* 143–44; Albrecht-Carrie, *Italy at the Peace Conference,* 42, 61–62, 80, 102–4.

72. Falls, *The Battle of Caporetto,* esp. chaps. 7, 11–12, 19.

73. Link, *Papers of Woodrow Wilson* 51:529–30; *New York Times,* Dec. 5, 1917.

74. TNP to Minna Burnaby, Dec. 5, 1917, TNPP (W&M), 2:4.

75. FLP to Florence Lindsay, Feb. 16–17, 1918, to Helen Aldis, May 2, 1917, ibid., 3:1.

76. FLP to Florence Lindsay, Mar. 31, 1918, ibid., 2:1.

77. Ibid., July, 20–23, 1918, 4:1. See also FLP to Ruth Page, July 11, 1918, TNPP (DUL), 20B:1918.

78. FLP to Florence Lindsay, July 20–23, Aug. 25, Oct. 12–14, 1918, TNPP (W&M), 4:1, 4:3.

79. Ibid., July 20–23, 1918, 4:1.

Chapter 7

1. FLP to Bryan Lathrop, May 27–28, 1915, TNPP (W&M), 2:1.

2. See Douglas, *The Feminization of American Culture,* 283–87.

3. See, for example, FLP to Florence Lindsay, Nov. 21, 1916, TNPP (W&M), 8:1916.

4. See Anne F. Scott, *Natural Allies: Women's Associations in American History.*

5. FLP to Bryan Lathrop, May 27–28, 1915, TNPP (W&M), 2:1.

6. For this paragraph and the next two see, Procacci, *A History of the Italian People,* 404; Page, *Italy and the World War,* vii; FLP to Helen Lathrop, June 15, 1915, to Florence Lindsay, Oct. 9, 1915, ibid., 2:1, 8:1915. See also FLP to Ruth Page, Aug. 9, Sept. 27, 1915, TNPP (DUL), 21:1915.

7. FLP to Helen Lathrop, July 23, 1915, TNPP (W&M), 2:1.

8. FLP to Bryan Lathrop, July 23, Aug. 4, 1915, to Florence Lindsay, Feb. 3, 1916, ibid., 2:2, 8:1916.

9. FLP to Florence Lindsay, Nov. 1, 9, 21, 1916, ibid., 8:1916.

10. Ibid., Feb. 10, 1916.

11. FLP to Bryan Lathrop, Aug. 4, 1915, ibid.

12. FLP to Helen Lathrop, May 2, 1917, ibid., 2:4.

13. Ibid., Dec. 17, 1917.

14. TNP to H. Rozier Dulany, Feb. 17, 1917, TNPP (DUL), 23:1917.

15. FLP to Helen Lathrop, Feb. 4, 1918, ibid.

16. FLP to Florence Lindsay, Jan. 30, 1918, TNPP (W&M), 3:1.

17. Ibid., July 20, 1918, 4:1.

18. FLP to Helen Lathrop, Aug. 14, 1918, ibid.

19. For this paragraph and the next see FLP to Helen Lathrop, Mar. 19, 1918, ibid.

20. FLP to Minna Burnaby, Dec. 16, 1918, ibid., 5:2.

21. Link, *Papers of Woodrow Wilson* 51:253; FLP to Florence Lindsay, Oct. 6, 1918, TNPP (W&M), 4:3.

22. Link, *Papers of Woodrow Wilson* 51:255–57, 263–65, 268–69; Schmitt and Vedeler, *The World in the Crucible,* 284–92; Albrecht-Carrie, *Italy at the Peace Conference,* 36–42, 289–93.

23. FLP to Helen Lathrop, Oct. 13–14, 1916, TNPP (W&M), 4:3.

24. For this paragraph and the next two, see U.S. Dept. of State, *FRUS, 1918,* supp. 1, *The World War* 1:404–5, FLP to Florence Lindsay, Nov. 1, 1918, TNPP (W&M), 5:1; Bevans, *Treaties of the U.S.A.* 2:1–8.

25. FLP to Florence Lindsay, Oct. 6, to Minna Burnaby, Oct. 8, 1918, TNPP (W&M), 4:3.

26. For this paragraph and the next two, see FLP to Minna Burnaby, Oct. 8, 1918, ibid.

27. FLP to Florence Lindsay, Oct. 12, 26, 1918, ibid.

28. FLP to Florence Lindsay, Nov. 8, 9, 1918, ibid., 5:1; *New York Times,* Nov. 9, 1918.

29. For this paragraph and the next, see FLP to Florence Lindsay, Nov. 11, 1918, to Minna Burnaby, Nov. 12, 1918, TNPP (W&M), 4:3.

30. FLP to Florence Lindsay, Nov. 8, 1918, ibid., 5:1. Thirty to forty million people worldwide died from influenza (Crosby, Jr., *Epidemic and Peace, 1918,* 203–7).

31. FLP to Minna Burnaby, Nov. 12, 1918, TNPP (W&M), 4:3.

32. Ibid., Nov. 23, 1918.

33. FLP to Florence Lindsay, Nov. 15, 1918, ibid.

34. For this paragraph and the next, see FLP to Minna Burnaby, Nov. 17, 1918, ibid.

35. For this paragraph and the next, see FLP to Florence Lindsay, Nov. 15, 18, 1918, ibid.

36. Point nine dealt specifically with Italy, saying that "a readjustment of the frontier of Italy should be effected along clearly recognizable lines of nationality." See U.S. Dept. of State, *FRUS: The Paris Peace Conference,* 1:359, 463; House, *The Intimate Papers of Colonel House* 4:173–74; Bonsal, *Suitors and Suppliants,* 102.

37. FLP to Florence Lindsay, Oct. 26–28, 1918, TNPP (W&M), 4:3.

38. For this paragraph and the next, see FLP to Florence Lindsay, Nov. 3, 1918, ibid., 5:1.

39. U.S. Dept. of State, *FRUS: The Paris Peace Conference* 1:413; Gould, "Italy and the United States," 177–81; Snell, "Wilson on Germany and the Fourteen Points," 367; Dauer, "Thomas Nelson Page, Diplomat," 87–89.

40. FLP to Florence Lindsay, Nov. 14, 1918, TNPP (W&M), 5:1. For Wilsonian diplomacy and public opinion, see Arno J. Mayer, *Politics and Diplomacy of Peacemaking.*

41. Speranza, *Diary of Gino Speranza* 2:226; Link, *Papers of Woodrow Wilson* 53:496–97, 637–44.

42. For this paragraph and the next, see FLP to Florence Lindsay, Dec. 13, 1918, TNPP (W&M), 5:1.

43. For this paragraph and the next, see FLP to Minna Burnaby, Dec. 16, 20, 1918, ibid., 5:2.

44. FLP to Florence Lindsay, Dec. 30, 1918, ibid.; Link, *Papers of Woodrow Wilson* 53:613–24; De Conde, *Half Bitter, Half Sweet,* 150–51.

45. Edith Bolling Wilson, *My Memoir,* 211–21; Link, *Papers of Woodrow Wilson* 53: 696–97; Field, *A Memoir of Thomas Nelson Page,* 13.

46. Walworth, *America's Moment: 1918,* 168–71; De Conde, *Half Bitter, Half Sweet,* 151.

47. See Albrecht-Carrie, *Italy at the Peace Conference,* doc. 17:370–87; Gelfand, *The Inquiry;* Naval Attaché to Force Commander, Nov. 25, 1918, TNPP (UVA), acc. no. 8641, 75:1918.

48. *New York Times,* Mar. 5, 1919; Garraty, *Henry Cabot Lodge,* 353–56; Bailey, *Wilson and the Great Betrayal,* 3, 5, 10–11.

49. FLP to Florence Lindsay, Mar. 10, 1919, TNPP (W&M), 5:3.

50. Ibid., Mar. 26, 1919; De Conde, *Half Bitter, Half Sweet,* 157.

51. Link, *Papers of Woodrow Wilson* 57:60–70, 90, 343–45, 513, 527, 576; Albrecht-Carrie, *Italy at the Peace Conference,* 126–49; Page, *Italy and the World War,* 399–401.

52. FLP to Florence Lindsay, Apr. 27, 1919, TNPP (W&M), 5:4.

53. For this paragraph and the next, see ibid., Apr. 28, 1919; to Ruth Page, May 10, 1919, TNPP (DUL), 26:1919.

54. FLP to Florence Lindsay, Apr. 27, 1919, TNPP (W&M), 5:4.

55. For this paragraph and the next two, see, FLP to Florence Lindsay, Apr. 29, 1919, to Helen Lathrop, May 6, 1919, ibid.

56. FLP to Minna Burnaby, Dec. 5–6, 1918, Feb. 5, 7, 1919; to Florence Lindsay, May 7, 1919, ibid., 5:2,3; Newton D. Baker, *Why We Went to War,* 146. See also Thomas Nelson Page to Col. Edward M. House, Mar. 15, 17, 1919, to Robert Lansing, Apr. 22, 23, 1919, TNPP (DUL), 26:1919.

57. For this paragraph and the next two, see FLP to Florence Lindsay, May 12, 1919, TNPP (W&M), 5:4; TNP, "Certain Reflection on a Report Containing a Formula for Adriatic Settlement from Chief of Division of Boundary Geography, Paris, May 8, 1919," TNPP (UVA), acc. no. 8641, 35:1919.

58. TNP, "Report to the American Commission to Negotiate 'Peace,'" Paris, June 24, 1919, TNPP (UVA), acc. no. 8641, 35:1919; FLP to Florence Lindsay, May 18–19, 1919, TNPP (W&M), 5:4.

59. FLP to Florence Lindsay, June 7, 1919, TNPP (W&M), 6:1; Albrecht-Carrie, *Italy at the Peace Conference,* 226.

60. TNP, "Report to the American Commission to Negotiate 'Peace,'" Paris, June 24, 1919, TNPP (UVA), acc. no. 8641, 35:1919; Procacci, *A History of the Italian People,* 408, 413.

61. Entry of June 20, 1919, Nevins, *Letters and Journal of Brand Whitlock* 2:570–71.

62. Field, *A Memoir of Thomas Nelson Page,* 17; FLP to Florence Lindsay, July 24, 1919, TNPP (W&M), 5:4.

63. Field, *A Memoir of Thomas Nelson Page,* 18. For Lodge's opposition to the treaty, see *New York Times,* Aug. 13, 16, Sept. 9, 11, 1920; Garraty, *Henry Cabot Lodge,* chap. 20; Link, *Wilson the Diplomatist,* 150–54.

64. *New York Times,* Sept. 26, 27,1919; FLP to Minna Burnaby, Sept. 27, 1919, TNPP (W&M), 6:1.

65. FLP to Minna Burnaby, Nov. 18, 1919, TNPP (W&M), 6:2; Bailey, *Wilson and the Great Betrayal,* chaps. 10–19.

66. FLP to Minna Burnaby, Nov. 22, 1919, TNPP (W&M), 6:2.

67. Bailey, *Wilson and the Great Betrayal,* ch. 19; FLP to Minna Burnaby, Jan. 13, 1920, TNPP (W&M), 6:3.

68. FLP to Minna Burnaby, Jan. 13, 1920, TNPP (W&M), 6:3; *New York Times,* Mar. 20, 1919. See also Stone, *The Irreconcilables.*

69. Bagby, "Woodrow Wilson, a Third Term, and the Solemn Referendum"; Garraty, *Henry Cabot Lodge,* 390–91.

Epilogue

1. A photograph of the gravestone marker with the inscription is contained in TNPP (DUL), 56.

2. Field, *A Memoir of Thomas Nelson Page,* 19; *Richmond Times-Dispatch,* Nov. 2, 1922.

3. Lerner, *The Majority Finds Its Past,* 169; Joan W. Scott, *Gender and the Politics of History,* 18–19.

4. Berkin, "Clio in Search of Her Daughters/Women in Search of Their Past," 11.

5. Ibid., 14.

6. Ibid., 15.

7. McCarthy, *Noblesse Oblige,* 49–50. Florence Field's name does not appear in the club lists of prominent women, which further underscores the fact that she remained out of the limelight of publicity as well as the decision-making process.

8. Matthaei, *Economic History of Women in America,* 105.

9. John Mack Faragher has written that "the regulation of the sexual division of labor was achieved through the perpetuation of a hierarchy and male-dominant family structure, linked to a public world from which women were excluded" ("History from the Inside-Out," 550).

10. Matthaei, *Economic History of Women in America,* 105, 120–21.

11. Kerber's argument in "Separate Spheres, Female Worlds, Woman's Place" does not so much rebut the notion of separate spheres for men and women as it shows that our understanding of it over time has revealed it to be a more complex phenomenon than we have generally appreciated.

12. Lerner noted this phenomenon in *The Creation of Patriarchy*.

13. Joan W. Scott, *Gender and the Politics of History*, 23–24.

14. Hawley, *The Great War and the Search for a Modern Order*, 128–29. Unlike other scholars who see either the war years or the 1920s as marking a sharp break with prewar America, Hawley has emphasized the continuities between Progressivism, the war period, and the twenties.

Bibliography

Primary Sources

MANUSCRIPTS

The Thomas Nelson Page Collection (acc. nos. 8641 and 7581) in the Clifton Waller Barrett Library Manuscripts Division, Special Collections Department of the University of Virginia Library in Charlottesville is the largest collection of Thomas Nelson Page material, over 40,000 items. Included within it is limited material of Florence Lathrop Page, Henry Field, and Bryan Lathrop. The 1902–19 correspondence (acc. nos. 8641 and 8641-a) was of especial value in illuminating Florence's attitudes toward her husband and family and the lifestyle of the upper class. Within this grouping are the letters from Florence to her mother-in-law Elizabeth Burwell Page, which describe in rich detail the Pages' travels abroad and Florence's encounters with different cultures, religions, and peoples. Her letters reveal more about the attitudes and values of wealthy, white Protestant, upper-class women of the turn of the century than Florence ever intended.

The next largest collection of Page material is deposited in the Earl Gregg Swem Library of the College of William and Mary in Williamsburg, Virginia. Consisting of about 300 items, it covers the period from about 1913 to 1920 when Thomas Nelson Page was serving as the United States ambassador to Italy. Approximately 150 of the letters were written by Florence Lathrop Page to her children, Minna Field Burnaby in England and Florence Field Lindsay in Southboro, Massachusetts, and to Bryan and Helen Aldis, her brother and sister-in-law. The correspondence records Florence's observations and activities in Italy during the period from American neutrality to entry into World War I and the Paris Peace Conference. These letters constitute the single most important source of information about her life and times.

The Special Collections Library of Duke University also has a large Thomas Nelson Page collection. There are approximately thirty letters of Florence Lathrop Page and miscellaneous items illustrating various aspects of the Pages' wealth, lifestyle, and relationship to various acquaintances.

Bibliography

There are a number of minor collections that cast light on Florence's life in Illinois both as a young woman and the wife of Henry Field. None of the personal or business papers of Henry Field, her first husband, has survived. But Henry Field's will is recorded in the Probate Division of the Circuit Court of Cook County, Illinois, as no.15183, document 21, page 178. It constitutes the most important source of information regarding Florence's wealth, status, and personal relationships in the years before she married Thomas Nelson Page. The Final Report and Account of the Estate of Thomas Barbour Bryan, which is recorded as docket 87, file 20, page 196, in the same court, provides similar information. The Elmhurst, Illinois, Historical Museum contains miscellaneous information and photographs about the Barbour-Lathrop families, from which it is possible to reconstruct the milieu in which the young Florence Lathrop was reared before her marriage to Henry Field. The Chicago Historical Society contains only a few items about the Bryan and Lathrop families, but they establish the occupations and sources of wealth of the first generation in Chicago.

The Old York Historical Society in York Harbor, Maine, contains building plans, photographs, postcards, books, and other material which made it possible to reconstruct the Pages' cottage and the lifestyle of the upper class residents of that affluent summer resort community.

Finally, the "Letters from Europe of William Henry Talbot, 1849–1850," a collection of transcribed letters privately held by Carol Talbot of Williamsburg, Virginia, provided useful information about the motives, finances, modes of travel, accommodations, and lifestyle of nineteenth-century affluent Americans who took the Grand Tour. Besides London, Paris, and Basel, Talbot visited Genoa, Florence, Civitavecchia, and Rome, and his observations document Americans' interest in antiquity, the same interest the Pages exhibited in their travels abroad.

PUBLISHED WORKS

Adams, Jane. *Twenty Years at Hull-House.* New York, 1939.

Baker, Newton D. *Why We Went to War.* New York, 1936.

Baker, Ray Stannard, and William E. Dodd, eds. *The Public Papers of Woodrow Wilson.* 6 vols. New York, 1925–27.

Barnes, Margaret A., and Janet A. Fairbank, eds. *Julia Newberry's Diary.* New York, 1933.

Bartlett, John. *Familiar Quotations.* Ed. Emily Morison Beck. Boston, 1980.

Bevans, Charles I, comp. *Treaties and Other International Agreements of the United States of America, 1776–1949.* 13 vols. Washington, D.C., 1968–76.

Bibliography

Chicago Historical Society. *Annual Report for the Year Ending October 31, 1916*. Chicago, 1916.

Field, Henry. *A Memoir of Thomas Nelson Page*. Miami, Fla., 1978.

——. *The Track of Man*. London, 1955.

Holman, Harriet R., ed. *John Fox and Tom Page As They Were: Letters, an Address, and an Essay*. Miami, Fla., 1970.

House, Edward M. *The Intimate Papers of Colonel House*. Arranged by Charles Seymour. 4 vols. Boston, 1926–28.

Irving, Washington. *Notes and Journal of Travel in Europe, 1804–1805*. Intro. William P. Trent. 3 vols. New York, 1921.

Link, Arthur S. et al., eds. *The Papers of Woodrow Wilson*. 68 vols. Princeton, N.J., 1956–93.

Moody, Robert E., ed. *The Letters of Thomas Gorges*. 2 vols. Boston, 1931–35.

Nevins, Allan. ed. *The Letters and Journal of Brand Whitlock*. 2 vols. New York. 1936.

Page, Thomas Nelson. "The Bigot." *Scribner's Magazine* 48 (Nov. 1910): 533–547.

——. "The Earthquake in the Abruzzi." *Scribner's Magazine* 57 (Jan.–June 1915): 419–30.

——. *Italy and the World War*. London, 1921.

——. "Leander's Light." *Century* 52 (June 1907): 376–85.

——. "Miss Godwin's Inheritance." *Scribner's Magazine* 36 (Aug. 1904): 171–81.

——. "My Friend the Doctor." *Scribner's Magazine* 42 (Nov. 1907): 539–50.

——. "The New Agent at Lebanon Station." *Ladies Home Journal* 22 (Apr. 1905): 7–8.

——. *The Novels, Stories, Sketches, and Poems of Thomas Nelson Page*. The Plantation Edition. 18 vols. Washington, D.C., 1906–12.

Pierce, Frederick C. *Field Genealogy*. 2 vols. Chicago, 1901.

Salandra, Antonio. *La neutralità italiana*. Milan, 1928.

——. *L'intervento*. Milan, 1931.

Simonds, Ossian C. *Landscape Gardening*. New York, 1920.

Speranza, Florence Colgate, ed. *The Diary of Gino Speranza*. 2 vols. New York, 1941.

Stanley, Henry M. *The Autobiography of Sir Henry Morton Stanley*. Boston, 1890.

Tocqueville, Alexis de. *Democracy in America*. Ed. Richard D. Heffner. New York, 1956.

Ulrich, Laurel Thatcher, ed. *A Midwife's Tale: The Life of Martha Ballard*. New York, 1990.

U.S. Bureau of the Census. *Historical Statistics of the United States: Colonial Times to 1970*. Washington, D.C., 1975.

U.S. Congress. *Congressional Record*. 1913. Washington, D.C., 1913.

Bibliography

U.S. Department of State. *Papers Relating to the Foreign Relations of the United States, 1914–1917.* 6 vols. Washington, D.C., 1928–29, 1931–32.

———. *Papers Relating to the Foreign Relations of the United States: The Lansing Papers, 1914–1920.* 2 vols. Washington, D.C., 1939–40.

———. *Papers Relating to the Foreign Relations of the United States, 1918.* 2 vols. Washington, D.C., 1933.

———. *The Paris Peace Conference, 1919.* 13 vols. Washington, D.C., 1942–47.

Who Was Who In America. Chicago, 1943.

Who's Who at Bar Harbor . . . York Harbor. Salem, Mass., 1919.

Wilson, Edith Bolling. *My Memoir.* Indianapolis, 1938.

Wright, Carroll D. *The Slums of Baltimore, Chicago, New York, and Philadelphia.* U.S. Commissioner of Labor. Special Report. No. 7. Washington, D.C., 1894.

NEWSPAPERS

Chicago Daily News. 1890.

Chicago Tribune. 1974.

New York Times. 1900, 1912, 1913, 1915–19, 1937, 1938, 1986.

Richmond Times-Dispatch. 1893, 1922.

Secondary Works

BOOKS

Alberti, Mario, et al. *Italy's Great War and Her National Aspirations.* Milan, 1917.

Albertini, Luigi. *The Origins of the War of 1914.* 5 vols. London, 1952–57.

Albrecht-Carrie, Rene. *Italy at the Peace Conference.* New York, 1938.

Allmendinger, David F., Jr. *Ruffin: Family and Reform in the Old South.* New York, 1990.

Amory, Cleveland. *The Last Resorts.* New York, 1948.

Antler, Joyce. *Lucy Sprague Mitchell: The Making of a Modern Woman.* New Haven, Conn., 1987.

Baedeker, Karl. *Italy: From the Alps to Naples.* Leipzig, 1909.

Bailey, Thomas A. *Woodrow Wilson and the Great Betrayal.* New York, 1945.

———. *Woodrow Wilson and the Lost Peace.* New York, 1944.

Baker, Paul. *Fortunate Pilgrims: Americans in Italy, 1800–1860.* Cambridge, Mass., 1964.

Bibliography

Baltzell, E. Digby. *The Protestant Establishment: Aristocracy and Class in America.* New York, 1964.

——. *Puritan Boston and Quaker Philadelphia: Two Protestant Ethics and the Spirit of Class Authority and Leadership.* New York, 1979.

Banks, George. *History of York, Maine, Successively Known as Bristol, Agamenticus, Georgeana, and York.* 2 vols. Boston, 1931.

Bardwell, John D. *A History of the Country Club at York, Maine.* Portsmouth, N.H., 1988.

Basch, Norma. *In the Eyes of the Law: Women, Marriage, and Property in Nineteenth Century New York.* Ithaca, N.Y., 1982.

Berens, Helmut A. *Elmhurst: Prairie to Tree Town.* Elmhurst, Ill., 1968.

Biographical History with Portraits of Prominent Men of the Great West. Chicago, 1894.

Bishop, Robert, and Patricia Coblentz. *The World of Antiques, Art, and Architecture in Victorian America.* New York, 1979.

Black, Jeremy. *The British and the Grand Tour.* London. 1985.

Blumin, Stuart M. *The Emergence of the Middle Class: Social Experience in the American City, 1760–1900.* Cambridge, Mass., 1989.

Bonsal, Stephen. *Suitors and Suppliants.* New York, 1946.

Brown, Dorothy M. *Setting a Course: American Women in the 1920s.* Boston, 1987.

Burke, Bernard. *Burke's Landed Gentry.* Ed. H. Pirie-Gordon. 15th ed. London, 1937.

Cameron, Mabel Ward. *Biographical Cyclopedia of American Women.* 3 vols. New York, 1924–28.

Campbell, Helen. *Women Wage-Earners: Their Past, Their Present, and Their Future.* New York, 1893. Rept. 1972.

Carnovale, Luigi. *Why Italy Entered into the Great War.* Chicago, 1917.

Carter, Paul A. *The Twenties in America.* Arlington Heights, Ill., 1973.

Chudacoff, Howard P. *The Evolution of American Urban Society.* Englewood Cliffs, N.J., 1975.

Clark, Charles E. *Maine: A Bicentennial History.* New York, 1977.

Clinton, Catherine. *The Plantation Mistress: Women's World in the Old South.* New York, 1982.

Coolidge, Archibald C. *Origins of the Triple Alliance.* New York, 1917.

Cott, Nancy F. *The Bonds of Womanhood.* New Haven, Conn., 1977.

——. *The Grounding of Modern Feminism.* New Haven, Conn., 1987.

——, and Elizabeth H. Pleck. *A Heritage of Her Own.* New York, 1979.

Creese, Walter L. *The Crowning of the American Landscape.* Princeton, N.J., 1985.

Cronon, William. *Nature's Metropolis: Chicago and the Great West.* New York, 1990.

Crosby, Alfred W., Jr. *Epidemic and Peace, 1918.* Westport, Conn., 1976.

Davidson, Marshall B., ed. *The American Heritage History of Antiques from the Civil War to World War I.* New York, 1969.

De Conde, Alexander. *Half Bitter, Half Sweet: An Excursion into Italian-American History.* New York, 1971.

Degler, Carl. *At Odds: Women and the Family in America from the Revolution to the Present.* New York, 1980.

Douglas, Ann. *The Feminization of American Culture.* New York, 1977.

Drake, Samuel Adams. *The Pine Tree Coast.* Boston, 1891.

Drury, John. *Old Chicago Houses.* Chicago, 1941.

Dulles, Foster R. *Americans Abroad.* Ann Arbor, Mich., 1964.

Emery, George Alex. *Ancient City of Gorgeana and Modern Town of York (Maine) from Its Earliest Settlement. Also its Beaches and Summer Resorts.* York Corner, Maine, 1894.

Ernst, George E. *New England Miniature: A History of York, Maine.* Freeport, Maine, 1961.

Evans, H. E. *York and Ogunquit, Maine, as a Summer Residence.* York, Maine, 1896.

Evans, Sara M. *Born for Liberty: A History of Women in America.* New York, 1969.

Falls, Cyril. *The Battle of Caporetto.* Philadelphia, 1966.

Fein, Albert. *Frederick Law Olmsted and the American Environmental Tradition.* New York, 1972.

Fox-Genovese, Elizabeth. *Within the Plantation Household: Black and White Women of the Old South.* Chapel Hill, N.C., 1988.

Galassi, Peter. *Corot in Italy: Open-Air Painting and the Classical Landscape Tradition.* New Haven, Conn., 1992.

Garraty, John A. *Henry Cabot Lodge: A Biography.* New York, 1953.

Gelfand, Lawrence E. *The Inquiry: American Preparations for Peace, 1917–1919.* New Haven, Conn., 1963.

Gilbert, Paul T., and Charles Lee Bryson. *Chicago and Its Makers.* Chicago, 1929.

Griswold, Mac, and Eleanor Weller. *The Golden Age of American Gardens: Proud Owners, Private Estates, 1890–1940.* New York, 1992.

Gross, Theodore L. *Thomas Nelson Page.* New York, 1967.

Hampsten, Elizabeth. *Read This Only to Yourself: The Private Writings of Midwestern Women, 1880–1910.* Bloomington, Ind., 1982.

Hawley, Ellis. *The Great War and the Search for a Modern Order.* New York, 1979.

Heilbrun, Carolyn G. *Writing a Woman's Life.* New York, 1988.

Hibbert, Christopher. *The Grand Tour.* New York, 1969.

Hoffman, Leonore and Margo Cully. *Women's Personal Narratives* New York, 1985.

Hofstadter, Richard. *Social Darwinism in American Thought.* New York, 1944.

Bibliography

Holman, Harriet. *The Literary Career of Thomas Nelson Page, 1884–1910.* Miami, Fla., 1978.

Houghton, Walter. *The Victorian Frame of Mind, 1830–1870.* New Haven, Conn., 1957.

Hoyt, Homer K. *One Hundred Years of Land Values in Chicago.* Chicago, 1933.

Ingham, John N. *The Iron Barons: A Social Analysis of an American Urban Elite, 1874–1965.* Westport, Conn., 1978.

Jaher, Frederic C., ed. *The Rich, the Well Born, and the Powerful.* Urbana, Ill., 1973.

———. *The Urban Establishment: Upper Strata in Boston, New York, Charleston, Chicago, and Los Angeles.* Chicago, 1982.

James, Edward T., ed. *Notable American Women, 1607–1950.* 3 vols. Cambridge, Mass., 1971.

James, Henry. *Charles W. Eliot.* 2 vols. Boston, 1930.

Jones, Jacqueline. *Labor of Love, Labor of Sorrow: Black Women, Work, and the Family from Slavery to the Present.* New York, 1985.

Kessler-Harris, Alice. *Out to Work: A History of Wage-Earning Women in the United States.* New York, 1982.

King, W. I. *Wealth and Income of the People of the United States.* New York, 1915.

Kraditor, Aileen. *Up from the Pedestal: Selected Writings in the History of American Feminism.* Chicago, 1968.

Lanctot, Barbara. *A Walk Through Graceland Cemetery.* Chicago, 1977.

Lasch, Christopher. *Haven in a Heartless World: The Family Besieged.* New York, 1977.

Lebergott, Stanley. *The American Economy: Income, Wealth, and Want.* Princeton, N.J., 1976.

Lebsock, Suzanne. *The Free Women of Petersburg.* New York, 1984.

Leonard, John W. *Woman's Who's Who of America.* New York, 1914.

Lerner, Gerda. *The Creation of Patriarchy.* New York, 1986.

———. *The Majority Finds Its Past: Placing Women in History.* New York, 1979.

———. *The Woman in American History.* Reading, Mass., 1971.

Link, Arthur S. *Wilson: The Struggle for Neutrality 1914–1915.* Princeton, N.J., 1960.

———. *Wilson the Diplomatist.* Chicago, 1957.

Lystra, Karen. *Searching the Heart: Women, Men, and Romantic Love in Nineteenth Century America.* New York, 1989.

McCarthy, Kathleen D. *Noblesse Oblige: Charity and Cultural Philanthropy in Chicago, 1849–1929.* Chicago, 1982.

McCarthy, Michael. *Dark Continent: Africa as Seen by Americans.* Westport, Conn., 1983.

Matthaei, Julie A. *An Economic History of Women in America.* New York, 1982.

Bibliography

Maxtone-Graham, John. *The Only Way to Cross.* New York, 1972.

Mayer, Arno J. *Politics and Diplomacy of Peacemaking.* New York, 1967.

Mayer, Harold M., and Richard C. Wade. *Chicago: Growth of a Metropolis.* Chicago, 1969.

Mitchell, Dorothy. *Along the Maine Coast.* New York, 1947.

Mitchell, Wesley C. *Income in United States, 1909–1919.* 2 vols. New York, 1921–22.

Moody, Edward C. *Handbook History of the Town of York.* Augusta, Maine, 1914.

Moritz, Charles, ed. *Current Biography, 1955.* New York, 1986.

Morris, Richard B. *Encyclopedia of American History.* New York, 1953.

The National Cyclopaedia of American Biography. 63 vols. New York, 1893–1984.

Norton, Mary Beth. *Liberty's Daughters: The Revolutionary Experience of American Women, 1750–1800.* Boston, 1980.

———, ed. *Major Problems in American Women's History.* Lexington, Mass., 1989.

Ousby, Ian. *The Englishman's England: Taste, Travel, and the Rise of Tourism.* Cambridge, Eng., 1990.

Page, Rosewell. *Thomas Nelson Page: A Memoir of a Virginia Gentleman.* New York, 1923.

Pessen, Edward. *Riches, Class, and Power before the Civil War.* Lexington, Ky., 1973.

Philpott, Thomas Lee. *The Slum and the Ghetto: Immigrants, Blacks, and Reformers in Chicago, 1880–1930.* New York, 1978.

Pierce, Bessie L. *A History of Chicago.* 3 vols. Chicago, 1937, 1940, 1957.

Procacci, Giuliano. *A History of the Italian People.* London, 1968.

Ratner, Sidney, ed. *New Light on the History of the Great American Fortunes: American Millionaires of 1892 and 1902.* New York, 1953.

Roberts, Kenneth. *Trending into Maine.* Boston, 1938.

Robinson, Ronald, et al. *Africa and the Victorians.* New York, 1961.

Rolde, Neil. *York Is Living History.* Brunswick, Maine, 1975.

Ryan, Mary P. *Cradle of the Middle Class: The Family in Oneida County, New York, 1790–1865.* Cambridge, Mass., 1978.

Said, Edward. *Orientalism.* New York, 1978.

Saveth, Edward N. *American History and the Social Sciences.* New York, 1964.

Schmitt, Bernadotte E. *Triple Alliance and Triple Entente.* New York, 1934.

———, and Harold C. Vedeler. *The World in the Crucible, 1914–1919.* New York, 1984.

Scott, Anne F. *Natural Allies: Women's Associations in American History.* Urbanna, Ill., 1992.

———. *The Southern Lady: From Pedestal to Politics, 1880–1930.* Chicago, 1970.

Scott, Joan W. *Gender and the Politics of History.* New York, 1988.

Scully, Vincent. *The Shingle Style.* New Haven, Conn., 1955.

Bibliography

Seale, William. *The Tasteful Interlude: American Interiors through the Camera's Eye, 1860–1917.* Nashville, Tenn., 1981.

Spahr, Charles B. *An Essay on the Present Distribution of Wealth in the United States.* Boston, 1896. Rpt. 1970.

The Statistical History of the United States from Colonial Times to the Present. Stamford, Conn., 1965.

Stone, Ralph A. *The Irreconcilables: The Fight against the League of Nations.* Lexington, Ky., 1970.

Story, Ronald. *The Forging of an Aristocracy: Harvard and the Boston Upper Class, 1800–1870.* Middletown, Conn., 1980.

Thompson, Richard A., et al. *Du Page Roots.* Du Page, Ill., 1985.

Toscano, Mario. *Il patto di Londra.* Bologna, 1934.

Trease, Geoffrey. *The Grand Tour.* New York, 1967.

Twyman, Robert W. *History of Marshall Field & Co., 1852–1906.* Philadelphia, 1954.

Tyler, Lyon G. *Men of Mark in Virginia.* 5 vols. Washington, D.C., 1906–9.

Wade, Richard C. *The Urban Frontier: The Rise of Western Cities, 1790–1830.* Cambridge, Mass., 1959.

Walworth, Arthur. *America's Moment: 1918.* New York, 1977.

Wasserman, Jacob. *Bula Matari.* New York, 1937.

Wecter, Dixon. *The Saga of American Society.* New York, 1937.

Welter, Barbara. *Dimity Convictions: The American Woman in the Nineteenth Century.* Athena, Ohio, 1976.

Whiffen, Marcus. *American Architecture since 1870.* Cambridge, Mass., 1969.

White, G. Edward. *The Eastern Establishment and the Western Experience: The West of Frederic Remington, Theodore Roosevelt, and Owen Wister.* New Haven, Conn. 1968.

Williamson, Jeffrey G., and Peter H. Lindert. *American Inequality.* New York, 1980.

Wishey, Bernard. *The Child and the Republic: The Dawn of Modern American Child Nurture.* Philadelphia, 1968.

ARTICLES

Bagby, Wesley M. "Woodrow Wilson, a Third Term, and the Solemn Referendum." *American Historical Review* 60 (1955): 567–75.

Bartol, Cyrus A. "Bartol's Pictures of Europe, Framed in Ideas." *North American Review* 82 (1856): 33–78.

Berkin, Carol R. "Clio in Search of Her Daughters/Women in Search of Their

Past." In *Major Problems in American Women's History,* ed. Mary Beth Norton, 10–16. Lexington, Mass., 1989.

Blewett, Mary H. "The Sexual Division of Labor and the Artisan Tradition in Early Industrial Capitalism: The Case of New England Shoemaking, 1780–1860." In *To Toil the Livelong Day: America's Women at Work, 1780–1980,* ed. Carol Groneman and Mary Beth Norton, 35–46. Ithaca, N.Y., 1987.

Clark, Thomas D. "Travel Literature." In *Research Opportunities in American Cultural History,* ed. John F. McDermott, 46–65. Lexington, Ky., 1961.

Clarke, Jane H. "The Art Institute's Guardian Lions." *Museum Studies* 14 (1988): 47–55.

Doyle, Don H. "History from the Top Down." *Journal of Urban History* 10 (1983): 103–14.

Faragher, John Mack. "History from the Inside-Out: Writing the History of Women in Rural America." *American Quarterly* 33 (1981): 537–57.

Fraundorf, Martha. "The Labor Force Participation of Turn-of-the-Century Married Women." *Journal of Economic History* 39 (1979): 401–18.

Freedman, Estelle B. "The New Woman: Changing Views of Women in the 1920s." *Journal of American History* 61 (1974): 372–93.

Gaines, Anne-Rosewell J. "Political Reward and Recognition: Woodrow Wilson Appoints Thomas Nelson Page Ambassador to Italy." *Virginia Magazine of History and Biography* 89 (1981): 328–40.

Goldin, Claudia. "The Work and Wages of Single Women, 1820–1920." *Journal of Economic History* 40 (1980): 81–8.

Gordon, Ann D., et al. "The Problem of Women's History." In *Liberating Women's History,* ed. Berenice Carroll, 75–92. Urbanna, Ill., 1976.

Gordon, Linda. "What's New in Women's History." In *A Reader in Feminist Knowledge,* ed. Sneja Gunew, 73–82. London and New York, 1991.

Holman, Harriet. "Thomas Nelson Page." In *Southern Writers: A Biographical Dictionary,* ed. Robert Bain, et al., 336–38. Baton Rouge, La., 1979.

Holmes, George K. "The Concentration of Wealth." *Political Science Quarterly* 8 (1893): 589–600.

Kaufman, Burton I. "Virginia Politics and the Wilson Movement, 1910–1914." *Virginia Magazine of History and Biography* 77 (1969): 8–19.

Kerber, Linda. "Separate Spheres, Female Worlds, Woman's Place: The Rhetoric of Women's History." *Journal of American History* 75 (1988): 9–39.

"Large and Varied Gifts to Chicago." *Survey* 36 (Aug. 19, 1916): 518.

Lerner, Gerda. "The Lady and the Mill Girl: Changes in the Status of Women in the Age of Jackson." *Midcontinent American Studies Journal* 10 (1969): 5–15.

———. "Placing Women in History: Definitions and Challenges." *Feminist Studies* 3 (1975): 5–14.

Levin, Alexandria Lee. "Miss Knight Abroad." *American Heritage* 11 (1960): 14–29.

Bibliography

Miller, Donald L. "The Hogs Came with the Butcher." *New York Times Book Review,* Apr. 28, 1913, 12–13.

Pessen, Edward. "The Marital Theory and Practice of the Antebellum Urban Elite." *New York History* 53 (1972): 389–410.

Renzi, William A. "Italy's Neutrality and Entrance into the Great War: A Re-examination." *American Historical Review* 73 (1968): 1415–32.

Repplier, Agnes. "Where All Roads Lead." *Harper's Magazine* 145 (Sept. 1922): 509–11.

Sforza, Carlo. "Sonnino and His Foreign Policy." *Contemporary Review* 136 (1929): 721–32.

Sherman, Arthur J. "A Midsummer Paradise." *New England Magazine* 40 (Mar.–Aug. 1909): 490.

Smith-Rosenberg, Carroll. "The Female World of Love and Ritual: Relations between Women in Nineteenth Century America." *Signs* 1 (1975): 1–29.

Snell, John E., ed. "Wilson on Germany and the Fourteen Points." *Journal of Modern History* 26 (1954): 364–39.

Stansky, Peter. "The Crumbling Frontiers of History or History and Biography: Some Personal Remarks." *Pacific Historical Review* 59 (1990): 1–14.

Stockbridge, Frank P. "Champ Clark, of Pike County." *World's Work* 24 (May 1912): 27–36.

Welter, Barbara. "The Cult of True Womanhood: 1820–1860." *American Quarterly* 18 (1964): 151–74.

UNPUBLISHED THESES AND DISSERTATIONS

Dauer, Richard P. "Thomas Nelson Page, Diplomat." M.A. thesis. College of William and Mary, Williamsburg, Va., 1972.

Gould, John Wells. "Italy and the United States, 1914–1918: Background to Confrontation." Ph.D. diss. Yale University, 1969.

Index